Finding God in All the Black Places

Finding God in All the Black Places

Sacred Imaginings in
Black Popular Culture

BERETTA E. SMITH-SHOMADE

Rutgers University Press
New Brunswick, Camden, and Newark, New Jersey
London and Oxford

Rutgers University Press is a department of Rutgers, The State University of New Jersey, one of the leading public research universities in the nation. By publishing worldwide, it furthers the University's mission of dedication to excellence in teaching, scholarship, research, and clinical care.

Library of Congress Cataloging-in-Publication Data

Names: Smith-Shomade, Beretta E., 1965- author.
Title: Finding God in all the Black places : sacred imaginings in Black popular culture / Beretta E. Smith-Shomade.
Description: New Brunswick : Rutgers University Press, [2025] | Includes bibliographical references and index.
Identifiers: LCCN 2024003670 | ISBN 9781978839779 (paperback) | ISBN 9781978839786 (cloth) | ISBN 9781978839793 (epub) | ISBN 9781978839809 (pdf)
Subjects: LCSH: African Americans—Religious life. | African Americans—Religious aspects—Christianity. | African Americans—Social life and culture.
Classification: LCC BL625.2 .S64 2025 | DDC 200.89/96073—dc23/eng/20240509
LC record available at https://lccn.loc.gov/2024003670

A British Cataloging-in-Publication record for this book is available from the British Library.

References to internet websites (URLs) were accurate at the time of writing. Neither the author nor Rutgers University Press is responsible for URLs that may have expired or changed since the manuscript was prepared.

♾ The paper used in this publication meets the requirements of the American National Standard for Information Sciences—Permanence of Paper for Printed Library Materials, ANSI Z39.48-1992.

rutgersuniversitypress.org

Mommy and me. (Author's collection.)

PRELUDE
To my mother
Evelyn Inell Cain-Smith (1934–2003)

and all the other mothers who helped raise me and show me God
Helen Marie Davis Patterson (1932–2018)
Maxine Cobbs Lyons (b. 1939–)
Annie Clara Gardner Walker Fisher (1936–2018)
Sheila Walker Pierce (1940–2017)

Order of Service

Hammond B Playing Here

This project has been in the works for so long that acknowledgments span nearly twenty years. The foundation of scholarship often comes through good mentorship. I have had the very best, with John T. Caldwell, Herman Gray, Robin Means Coleman, Chon Noriega, the late, brilliant Teshome Gabriel, and the indomitable late Isabella T. Jenkins. Thank you. I keep stalwart and constant scholar-sistah-friends who provide intellectual, social, professional, spiritual, and mental health support, so I acknowledge them here: Miriam Petty, Kristen Warner, Bambi Haggins, Racquel Gates, Denise Davis-Maye, Tracii Patterson Hunter, Sheryl Kennedy-Haydel, Nsenga Burton (the best hype-woman ever!), Zabrina Furlow, Nghana Lewis, Mary V. Morales, Katie Acosta, Rebecca Chaisson, Charon Flowers Maple, Adria Nobles Kimbrough, Maritza Mora McCain, and Omeka Sanders. Valuable others provide me with positivity, possibilities, insights, and generous spirits that make me glad to do what I do, like Mark Cunningham, Andre Brock, Al Martin, Monica Ndounou, Ellen Scott, VaNatta Ford, TreaAndrea Russworm, Samantha Sheppard, and Brandy Monk-Payton. I thank and appreciate all of you.

Ministerial folks from all over the country talked Black church with me. I appreciate Pastor Olu Brown, the Rev. Drs. Anthony Bennett, Dominique A. Robinson, Khalia Williams, Daniel Black, and De'Edra Lewis-Johnson. My former pastor, Shawn Moses Anglim, encouraged and gave me grounding and permission to allow the love of God to flow through everything I do. Plus, my First Grace United Methodist Church family in New Orleans stood in the gap for me in so many ways that they would not be aware. I am thankful for each of you.

The value of institutional support cannot be minimized. I received a 2008 Fulbright Fellowship Award that allowed me to spend six months in Ile-Ife, Nigeria, at Obafemi Awolowo University. I thank Professors Beverly Seckinger, John Downing, and John T. Caldwell, who supported my Fulbright proposal, as well as Tani Sanchez (now Dr. Sanchez), who served as my research assistant at Arizona. I appreciate the Nigerian embassy staff (homegirl Mary Lou Johnson-Pizarro and Chinenye Uwadileke) for their on-point efforts in facilitating my stay and making sure everything was kosher while there. I thank posthumously Foluke Ogunleye for hosting me so graciously, even if inadvertently stuck with me. I thank Funmi Togonu-Bickersteth (former DVC-Academic) and Yisa Yusuf, former dean of arts, for their support while there. I thank also the OAU Conference Center staff for their hospitality during the five-week stay at the beginning of our trip (and continued support throughout our tenure). I am especially indebted to former Vice Chancellor Olusola Akinrinade for his early support of my Fulbright candidacy and his encouragement while in Ife. Ese!

Tulane University colleague-friends Michael Cunningham, Robin Hayes, Carolyn Barber-Pierre, Mohan Ambikaipaker, Mauro Porto, Marva Lewis, the late Frank Ukadike, and of course the invincible Marie Davis (Ms. Davis) held me down through the thick and the thin of my time there. My Emory Film and Media colleagues offer an openness with, if nothing else, smiling eyes and my former chair Matthew Bernstein has provided continued support. Thank you all.

I am especially grateful for my Fox Humanities Center Fellowship year (2019–2020) and the cohort that made it so sweet (especially in spite of COVID-19 happening in the middle of it): Walter Melion, Elizabeth Pastan, Javier Villa-Flores, Erin Tarver, Tonio Andrade, Julie Miller, John Brooks, Michael Patrick Vaughn, Ryan Carr, Ryan Kendall, and, of course, the ones who really kept us altogether and loved on, Keith Anthony, Colette Barlow, and Amy Erbill.

I thank members of my Emory Academic Learning Community for their contributions to The Message. Their insights, candor, and thoughtfulness helped me think through the world of spirituality and sexuality and helped shape my assertions there. They include Katie Acosta, Willie Bannister, Nsenga Burton, María Mercedes Carrión, Diana (Rodriguez) Click, Ashley Coleman-Taylor, Marcelitte Failla, Tiara Jackson, Monique Moultrie, Edward Phillips, Nicole Symmonds, Donna Troka, and Shannon Vassell.

Sarah McKee encouraged and helped me win an Emory TOME grant so this work could reach more than just the people (or their institutions) who can afford it. But more than that, she visioned possibilities with me (along with her replacement Mae Velloso-Lyons). Thank you both. I thank Elizabeth Ault for identifying this work early on as something worthy of publication, anonymous reviewers who wrestled with different manifestations of this project, and my amazing Rutgers editor, Nicole Solano, who read the work and said let's get it! And people who stepped in and up when I had questions and needs, like Aaron McCain (aka Canon) for all things musical knowledge, Trissi Hardin and Tara Williams for images of our church past, and Topé Fádìran for her magnificent indexical skills and general insights. Thank you all so much.

Students, where would I be without them? They let me take them down twists and turns, connect routes and beaten paths, as well as drive clear off the road.

Specifically, I acknowledge and thank those who knew what I was working on and wrestled with and sent me ideas, images, and memes that caught their imaginations: Leila Yavari, Jorge Mendez-Magaña, Natalie Moronta, Isabelle Lesh, Samuel Tsega, Charles Zakkour, Samah Sadig, and Carmen Cunningham. Jayna Puckett rode with me all over New Orleans to take pictures of all kinds of things that I saw as holy. Thank you. I thank former research assistants Jumoke (Jumi) Ekunseitan and Caitlin Sweet for their research, transcribing, and intellectual support; my ridiculously smart (organized and resourceful) research assistant trio, Kennedy Baskin, Kheyal Roy-Meighoo, and Anna-Frida Herrera; and my talented, smart, and hard-working image guru Alejandra Perozo Borges. I truly appreciate you all.

And finally, I say thank you forever and always to my everythangs . . . my heart Salmon, my first born Salmoncain, my second born Zolacatherine, and my Maker.

**Finding God in All the
Black Places**

Call to Worship

The Lord is in his holy temple; let all the earth be silent before him.
—Habakkuk 2:20 (NIV)

"God Is" . . .

● ●

Understanding Spirituality and Black Church Religiosity as the Sine Qua Non of Black Popular Culture

The Bible's last book, Revelation, prophesizes killings, plagues, and nature unleashed in punishment and promise for disobedience and hedonism. Consequently, many visualize national conflicts like Israel–Palestine, Sudan, Charlottesville, Washington, DC, Russia–Ukraine, natural disasters (China, Haiti, Los Angeles, and Puerto Rico's earthquakes; Myanmar, New Orleans, Haiti, Puerto Rico, and the Bahamas' hurricanes; Iowa and California's flooding), pandemics (COVID-19 and SARS), and the rise and price of celebrity as twenty-first-century examples of these prophecies' manifestation. Regarding culture, we are witnessing a nation and a world where people are more economically unequal than ever before. Social media dominates young people's time and siloes their interests and communication. The entertainment news cycle rivals hard news with very little "mass" in our information as algorithms create, cultivate, and curate for specialized demographics and users. Within Black popular culture specifically, we live amid racial discord prompted by murders and state-justified homicides of Black and brown men and women. People know more, are more formally educated in general, yet value less human-based aspects of life, mesmerized by the swipe of wealth and fame. These different contemporary illustrations mete out Christian-esque, apocalyptic visioning. Yet their full implementation often gets proclaimed as something down the road, coming if you don't "get your life right." As well, these multidimensional and religious assertions as evidence, challenge historic and theoretical presuppositions about religion's reach.

Academic and other learned prognosticators have long predicted and decried the fallacy of religion as well as its demise. Presumed great white male minds such as Karl Marx called religion the "opium of the people";[1] Sigmund Freud believed religion is an "illusion" comparable to a "childhood neurosis" and "untenable";[2] H. L. Mencken suggested "religion belongs to a very early development . . . and its rapid decay in the world since Reformation is the evidence of genuine progress";[3] and Fredrich Nietzsche simply proclaimed in 1882, "God is dead."[4] Anthropologist Clifford Geertz thought religion should be read as a system of symbols that act together to "establish powerful, pervasive, and long-lasting moods and motivations in men." This happens, he claimed, by the formulation of general existence notions, "clothing these conceptions with such an aura of factuality that the moods and motivations seem uniquely realistic."[5] Concluding that religion is dying or already dead gets validated by Geertz's half-truths, the emergence and dominance of capitalism and technology, and transforming mediated, visualized, and actualized forms. However, in spirit and truth, people often operate in opposition. Christianity, Islam, and all manner of spirituality continue to grow—particularly in countries dominated by peoples of color, and the world continues to be, largely spiritual, religious-leaning, and racialized.

Audiences, viewers, and users recognize and engage these shifts via media. Within television, film, music, and digital media narratives, connections between spirituality, religiosity, and Black popular culture provide a right-now foundation and, often, logic of an operating and vibrant way of being. The confluence of media and religion has been both fortuitous and highly toxic from its earliest iterations: fortuitous since proselytizing becomes much easier and more productive through radio, music, film, television, cable, and now digital modes of entertainment and communication. Toxic in the fact that the media renderings and discourses on the meanings of Christianity and Islam tend to cement a caustic notion of who believing folks are, what role they can and should play, and their existential value to anything beyond their religious framework. This assessment fails to include even the disparaging discourses around nontraditional religious practices—these practices reminding us that while Judeo-Christian readings of pop culture stand powerfully, they are not omniscient.[6] As well, it ignores the ways in which many religious leaders use the new media-rich platforms for seemingly ungodly purposes. The nearly fifty-year rise, growth, and force of the "Religious Right" in the United States as evidenced by pop cultural forms such as televangelism, shifts and growth in generic formats like *Change Your Life TV* as offered by Oprah Winfrey during her talk show run; increases of godly cinematic tales, and even the evocation of God within hip-hop and Black urban radio, all point to the usefulness of thinking through the contemporary Black and mediated religious landscape.

Finding God in All the Black Places: Sacred Imaginings in Black Popular Culture begins to reconsider and reframe the ground these and many other narratives tread. I contend that knowledge of Black spirituality and Black church religiosity ground audience understanding, value, and cultural competence of Black popular culture. In other words, I argue Black spirituality and Black church religiosity are the sine qua non of Black popular culture. Cultural, community, and social support live within the Black church. The deep entwinement of culture, spirit, art, and progress make these elements unravelable without an undoing and misunderstanding of what lies before the un- or underinitiated. To support these assertions, I look at Black contemporary arts offered in television, film, music, and digital culture as proof of and permission to claim their heightened dominance and impact. This exploration should matter to those who live infatuated with and sold on Black entertainment while simultaneously watching the nation and world reimagine itself, regressing in its approach to change, culture, and coloreds.

This project serves multiple purposes: (1) It offers a mediated vision for and of Black folks on the continued significance, power, and need for spirituality—as the Bible says: "Where there is no vision, the people perish" (Proverbs 29:18). Witnessing continues as a needed aspect of undoing problematic systems and ways of being. Cultural theorist bell hooks talked about being angry with her brothers and sisters for not continuing to watch their father put their mother out of the home. While the others obeyed his command to go to bed, she sat on the steps thinking: "I've got to witness this."[7] (2) This work excavates both benefits and hypocrisies of religion, particularly Black Christianity, as demonstrated within larger Black popular culture.[8] (3) While traveling on that same road, this project looks at the ways in which Black women in the church get (or do not get) their due. While a much higher percentage of Black women attend church regularly, they fail to occupy commensurate positions of respect and power.[9] This work may help many to live the life they sing about. And (4) it demonstrates the connections in and across Black spiritual practices and beliefs as articulated within Black popular culture. I believe acknowledging and comprehending the undergirding and subterfuge of Black spirituality and Black church religiosity within Black popular culture can provide a way for viewers, listeners, and users not only to endure but also to revive.

What This Is and What It Ain't

Renowned cultural theorist Stuart Hall spent much of his career discerning the ways in which things come to mean. Whether through representation or analysis of events, he writes that as human beings and those caught in the dance of a hegemonic patriarchy, we consistently attempt to fix meaning—to essentialize for understanding, normativity, and capitalists' sake. However, he reminds us of the slippery and malleable slope in meaning(s), noting: "Words, and images carry connotations over which no one has complete control, and these marginal or submerged meanings come to the surface, allowing different meanings to be constructed, different things to be shown and said."[10]

I share Hall's outlook and believe one of the central pleasures, critical understandings, and perhaps conundrums to be found in this text, as theologian Howard Thurman writes, and I cosign, God *is*. Thurman intones: "this is not merely an inference, but it is also a disclosure. He who comes to God must believe that He is."[11] Debates on whether God exists and the viable scholarship that comes from those existential and ontological questions find themselves in a multiplicity of works—but not this one. A large percentage of academics claim "none" as their religious status. This translates into their presumed neutral positionality in their investigations (and yours). Often your objectivity becomes suspect or even denied when it fails to align with theirs. Yet, as should be very clear in present-day mediated culture, no knowledge inhabits moral neutrality.[12] Thus, in *Finding God in All the Black Places*, I write from the critical lens of a believer. This means I value belief in God while recognizing various ways of believing.

Connectedly, as philosopher Fred Moten reflects upon in filmmaker Arthur Jafa's *Dreams Are Colder Than Death* (2013), remaining in the hull of the ship brings us to a Blackness, a continued thinking, a longing, and desire, but also a tangible place to wish for, fight for, and pray for freedom. I think we obtain some of this freedom through definitions. For this project, my constructed Black church order of service, I define Black church religion as a structure of knowledge, tradition, belief system, and guide centering a supreme being or force and one's relationship with Him/Her. It looks like taking communion, learning your Easter speech, coming up front for altar call, and fanning the seasoned saint overcome with the spirit. This same spirit or spirituality reflects the activation and articulation of internal processes of feelings, thoughts, memories, and experiences—a spirituality that gets demonstrated through praise breaks, the "sang chile" hype woman from the pew, the quiet and tearful rocking mother, and raised hands in prayer. And finally, sacredness, as imbued with religious understandings, ideas, and ideals, suggests holiness for both animate and inanimate things. All these ideas and understandings manifest throughout this service. In addition, I find exploring differences between white and Black folks' engagement with spirituality and religion visually, orally, or within industrial processes not particularly compelling or productive.[13] Thus, I locate this study outside of racial comparison. Grappling with the confluence of Black spirituality, religiosity, media for and produced by Blacks, and Black beings of the diaspora is sufficient in and of itself.

I argue for and with Black cultural homegrown knowledge, and consequently this text privileges the culture(s) of "the Blacks." (Side note: I want to make my usage of "the Blacks" in this text clear. Despite the ridiculous and often-idiotic ways undiscerning people, including the forty-fifth president of the United States, deploy it, I use the turn of phrase as a way of describing and thinking about heterogeneous populations of Black folks globally but also with recognition of its problematic and meant negative essentialism. So much so, while I'd normally place this parenthetical within endnotes, I know readers often skip them, and I want it known that the term is employed tongue-in-cheek.) Additionally, many on-fire scholars stay interrogating racially and ethnically ambiguous representational and industrial strategies. Because media studies scholars such as Catherine Squires, Ralina Joseph, and Kristen Warner already convincingly debunk the pretend "post-race" moment, *Finding God in All the Black Places* need not retread that ground.[14] I believe we create, as journalist George M. Johnson tweets, "home where you are."[15] And while television scholar Bambi Haggins suggests the mythos of home can conflate with the American Dream in a way that problematically foregrounds and privileges the imagined (Black) middle class,[16] home serves also as a place of deep cultural resonance, of soul-stirring and searching ambiguity, and of ultimate comfort (or at least comfort with a known uncomfortableness) that allows for a certain Black cultural competence.[17] *Finding God in All the Black Places* situates Black church religiosity and Black spirituality within Black popular culture as home and central.

Laying Out the Black Mediated Spiritual

Before delving further, perhaps a bit more on the multiple and complex meanings of Blackness requires address. Ideas of what Blackness means fall into several different categories of understanding and discipline. Blackness is offered as: (1) a racial categorization rooted in science, the legal system, and capitalism;[18] (2) culture (with a small c—as in shared experiences and Black people's ways of being or doing for "da culture");[19] (3) skin color (again, science-genetics); (4) historical and transcendent (claims of Blackness by some who assert that their placement in a particular society makes them Black-like, sharing a similar culture of oppression, struggle, and powerlessness); (5) an adjective; (6) function, nothingness beyond pure existence as pondered by philosopher Calvin L. Warren. Drawing on others, Warren writes: "African existence is an identity, whereas Black being is a structural position or instrumentality."[20] (7) Culture (with a capital C—as in highbrow, formerly getting invited to Diddy's white party, Martha's Vineyard, mainstream jazz); and (8) peoples of the African diaspora with a connectedness worldwide. *Finding God in All the Black Places* employs many of these conceptions of Blackness throughout this service, recognizing both their usefulness and tensions. Moreover, connectivity, similarities, and collaboration of Blackness, as expressed in Black popular culture, ground many of the implementations made.

Yet, with the plethora of distinctions between Black peoples diasporically, lumping and examining their ways of expressing religious practices all together via pop culture may appear foolhardy at best and First-World arrogant at worst. However, when it comes to representation, U.S.-based Christian religious practices dominate, and most especially as practiced by Black Christians. Thus, the preponderance of my focus here resides with those cultural artifacts. Once again, while Christianity dominates, it is not monolithic in its self-articulation, coherence, or its own absolute religious integrity. Religion functions as a corporate and formal demonstration and structure of an internal relationship, while spirituality and sacredness are the internal processes. Black filmmakers, media makers, musicians, and all manner of artists believe, explore, combine, and utilize religious and spiritual impetuses using a variety of Black religious belief systems. Moreover, spirituality and religiosity wonderfully permeate Black popular culture through their fluidity and synergy of terms, experiences, performances, and creativity.

In almost every media story told, those outside the culture depict people of the African diaspora with religious resonances. The perceived religiosity of Black folks often gets positioned in opposition to rationality, intelligence, development, and chastity. These spiritual and religious representations run the gamut from playful, fictitious, embellished, false, and partially true to contested, ugly, blended, and/or negotiated. Sociologist Katie Acosta writes about "situational femininity" (especially in private spaces where we gain approval from our mother's reflection), that in part characterizes the performance of Black religion.[21] Religiosity gets expressed through internal and external means; we expect to hear something, see something, or feel something that distinguishes one text from another. When a confluence of events makes the demonstration of religion or spirituality viable, productive, or necessary, situational religiosity results. Thus, the hands and mechanisms producing the texts are always tempered by the veracity of what readers, audiences, and users see, hear, and experience. Remembering, as Stuart Hall reminds us, popular culture, all of it, is "profoundly mythic."

Various scholars and laypeople craft discourses around the confluence of spirituality, religiosity, Blackness, and media. Religion historian Judith Weisenfeld lays out the ways in which cinema helped shape Black religious ideologies in the mid-twentieth century in her book *Hollywood Be Thy Name: African American Religion in American Film, 1929–1949*. Focusing on work that proselytizes Christianity to and about Blacks early on, she offers readers an opportunity to understand the terms of engagement with cinema and Black church expectations through cinematic representations.

Sociologist Shayne Lee provides *T. D. Jakes: America's New Preacher*, wherein he valorizes minister T. D. Jakes. Characterizing Jakes's growth and rise as an American hero's story, he also claims a postmodernist mix of neo-Pentecostal gospel, capitalism, and media as the rationale for his success. Calling Jakes a "spiritual celebrity," this book ushers in scholarly engagement with then blossoming Black media megaministries—a focus that white televangelists already offered.[22]

Religion scholar and minister Jonathan L. Walton calls for taking Black televangelism seriously in *Watch This! The Ethics and Aesthetics of Black Televangelism*. In this text, he puts the dynamics and success of Black televangelists in conversation with Black Christian religious scholarship. Weighing the consequences of a divide fueled in some measure by fortune and media, Walton frames his argument for dialogue and understanding—challenging "the erudite but isolating tendencies of the religious academy as well as the insular and illusory world of the African American pulpit."[23]

Anthropologists Carolyn Moxley Rouse, John L. Jackson, and Marla F. Frederick offer a solid interpretation of mediated religious meaning through the lens of civil rights and cognition. In their book *Televised Redemption: Black Religious Media and Racial Empowerment*, they assert African-American religion plays a significant role in "humanizing the race by unabashedly claiming that Blacks are endowed by God with the same gifts of goodness and reason as whites."[24] They give credence to this assertion by tracing how language and practices used by Black Christians, Black Muslims, and Black Hebrew Israelites within newspapers, comics, pamphlets, radio, and Black televangelism forward Black racial empowerment. Separately, Frederick takes on Black communities of faith when she focuses on how African-American televangelists impact Jamaican audiences in *Colored Television: American Religion Gone Global*. Examining this phenomenon ethnographically by talking with audiences, producers, and distributors, she explores what Black American Christian ministries offer the world toward salvation and a "contemporary history that allows us to explore not only the relevance of religious broadcasting but also the hopes and intentions of its global theater."[25]

These texts (including many other book chapters and journal articles) provide a perspective on engagements with media, Blackness, and religion. However, they emerge from disciplinary homes outside of television, film, and digital media studies, primarily from religion. Thus, their framing addresses a particular audience interested in the religious aspect of media engagement. Moreover, almost all the book-length scholarship, except for Weisenfeld's text, focuses on media (television and online) designed to address an already-identified religious demographic and what that means for and about them—pop culture for the already religious.

Two separate anthologies interrogate the works of one figure whose Black Christian leanings inform all his plays, films, and television: writer/producer/actor/executive/studio owner Tyler Perry. Religion scholars LeRhonda S. Manigault-Bryant, Tamura A. Lomax, and Carol B. Duncan edit the first one, *Womanist and Black Feminist Responses to Tyler Perry's Productions*. They stake considerable ground in trying to trouble Black masculinist Christianity, rabid heteronormativity, and misogyny in Perry's works. Even as they emerge from their "very own pew in Perry's global congregation," the editors feel compelled to express "righteous discontentment from time to time" as Black feminist and womanist scholars in religion.[26] In the second work, *From Madea to Media Mogul: Theorizing Tyler Perry*, media scholars TreaAndrea M. Russworm, Samantha N. Sheppard, and Karen M. Bowdre position Perry from the interdisciplinary perspectives of media, cultural, and industry studies. In the essays, scholars address the need for these disciplines "to grapple with developing theories and methods on disreputable media that challenge value judgment criticism and offer new insight on the industrial and formal qualities of such work."[27] And while not solely focused on the religious aspect of Perry's work, the totality of this text incorporates his religious imperatives while discerning respectability, media industry, culture, and affect as part of his oeuvre. Even with the works cited, the actual number of texts engaging the confluence of spirituality, religion, Blackness, and media from a media studies perspective remains quite small. *Finding God in All the Black Places* serves as a critical intervention into this lack.

"Blak Iz Blak . . . Hell Yeah": Black Popular Culture

Black popular culture often constructs Black life as a form of worship in its foregrounding of Black ways of being. This means attributes and activities like hair, sports, food, and the market get worshipped within mediated Black popular culture. For example, religious narratives undergird Black women's sense of self, aesthetics, business, protection, and even trauma via their hair. The almost religious status Black hair care receives places it in contention with traditional religiosity, a U.S. industry valued at $2.9 billion in 2022.[28] Black women's hair receives examination within many scholars' works alongside Chris Rock's documentary *Good Hair* (2009), the fictional narrative *Nappily Ever After* (Netflix, 2018), and the OWN/Hulu docuseries *The Hair Tales* (2022). These mediated offerings reenact daily dramas and traumas of hair and hair care as a form of worship. While hair resonates biblically as valuable, it more covertly signifies beauty, worth, and restriction for women. Yet, as Africana studies and religion scholar Monica A. Coleman writes, the combination of caring for Black women's hair (and their hands) invokes the divine. It represents a "language, a nonverbal language, for talking about God and God's activity in the world."[29]

Biopsychologist Niles Barber suggests sports shares some of these same ascriptions while facilitating transformative experiences.[30] With a heightened elevation in Black communities, sports uniquely impact behavior, goals, belief, economic wherewithal, and certainly media commentary and concern. Media studies scholars such as Aaron Baker think about the religiosity of sports and race from media perspectives,[31] and cultural theology scholar Joseph L. Price writes about specific sports and religious parallels—highlighting the devotion, rituals, and myths of the two.[32] Media examples like the films *Remember the Titans* (2000), *Pride* (2007), *42* (2013) and *King Richard* (2021), documentaries *Hoop Dreams* (1994) and *Being Serena* (HBO, 2018), and sports blogs often construct sports as the American Dream exemplar for Black folks, with faith, often dramatically deployed in the success structure.

Another central pastime and aspect of Black popular culture, Black folks' culinary delights, also find global, worship-like following and fascination. Religion studies and African-American studies scholars Jualynne E. Dodson and Cheryl G. Townsend make a case for the historical and connected significance of food in Black churches as being derived from the African continent and thus integral to Black popular culture. They theorize: "African American church members in the United States feed one another's bodies as they feed their spirits or, more biblically, one another's 'temples of the Holy Spirit.' In the process, an ethic of love and an emphasis on hospitality emerge, especially in the sharing of food, which spill over into the larger culture."[33] Media offerings such as *Soul Food* (Tillman, 1997), *Soul Food* the series (Henderson, Showtime, 2000–2004), MC Hammer and then Sherri Shepherd hosting *Holy & Hungry* (Cooking Channel, 2014–2015), and even Ayesha Curry's *Ayesha's Home Kitchen* (Food Network, 2017) showcase food (and its religious connections) as a significant cultural talisman for Black popular culture. Plus, the engagement and consistency by which Blackness and food get discussed (in terms of entertainment, health, scarcity, and popularity) make it another area of religiosity.

And we must also consider how the economic market has turned into a form of worship in Black popular culture. Religion scholar Harvey Cox reflects on "market theology" as a way of understanding the new worship and ideation of capitalism as savior.[34] One part of this worship emerges in the discussion of prosperity and wealth acquisition, demonstrated in Black prosperity gospel. The preponderance of scholarship and journalism on prosperity gospel revolve around Jesus, profit, and production. However, in other areas of Black popular culture, in music most explicitly but also within film, television, and digital media entrepreneurship, the worship of wealth forms a palpable center of motivation and praise regardless of how the financial riches are obtained. Case in point: the almost miraculous Black middle-class recuperation of Tyler Perry can only be understood through a certain market theology. Cox writes that like God, the "Market is becoming more like the Yahweh of the Old Testament—not just one superior deity contending with others but the Supreme Deity, the only true God, whose reign must now be universally accepted and who allows for no rivals."[35]

Alongside these important external worship dalliances of hair, sports, food, and the market, explicit spiritual and religious references appear in Black popular culture as well. Often Black artists, creatives, and texts offer a hidden transcript of Black religious and spiritual resonance within Black pop cultures. For example, in her groundbreaking work *Black Noise: Rap Music and Black Culture in Contemporary America*, American studies scholar Tricia Rose theorizes that the Black American cultural forms of hip-hop and rap provide hidden transcripts of knowledge and power. She argues that through dance, language, and music, hip-hop produces "communal bases of knowledge about social conditions, communal interpretations of them and quite often serve as the cultural glue that fosters communal resistance."[36] Historian and anthropologist James C. Scott suggests hidden transcripts offer covert critiques of power from the powerless. In comparing hidden transcripts of the weak and the powerful to the public, he suggests official transcripts of power relations gain "a substantially new way of understanding resistance to domination."[37] Within Black popular culture, these hidden transcripts exist in references, Twitter posts, memes, lyrics, gifs, films, podcasts, and television narratives.

Black audiences, users, and listeners share familiarity with "I wanna thank God and my mama" shout-outs; the point up thank you to God, the crossing of the chest and crosses worn on chests. They witness this in the spiritual conscious-ness, the "second sight" of Mozelle Batiste-Delacroix in *Eve's Bayou* (Lemmons, 1997), the healing powers of Nova Bordelon in *Queen Sugar* (OWN, 2016–2022), Ruby's frequent calling on Black Jesus in *black-ish* (ABC, 2014–2022), Prince's religiosity at "The Cross" or his constant conflation of sexuality with spiritual-ity in songs such as "I Would Die for You." When someone in the crowd yells "Take your time,"[38] or comedians show Black religiosity as a sign of their cul-tural competence like Issa Rae's Sister Mary in *The Mis-Adventures of Awkward Black Girl*, #choirsbelike's remix of the *Dora the Explorer* theme song, or the gospel-inflected Hamiltones remixing everybody, a certain knowledge bridges audiences across time and space and allows for not only a deeper reading and understanding of mediated texts but also a fuller acknowledgment of Black com-munities' complexity and humanity.

What lay audiences (and scholars) also need to consider and process are the ways in which these outward (and sometimes brand-notioning) gestures can mean. Black religiosity plays itself out in real, tangible, and felt ways even for the nonreligious in African America and Black diasporic culture more broadly con-strued. Knowing artists embody (or inhabit) a spiritual grounding in their work, we (audiences, consumers, fans, listeners, watchers, users, and scholars) gain a greater and more useful understanding of their impact, significance, and struc-turing within Black popular culture. For example, beginning this section with "Blak Iz Blak" brings congregants to Spike Lee's *Bamboozled* (2000) as rapped by the fictional Black nationalistic crew, the Mau Mau. However, since Hard Blak (Craig "muMs" Grant) had yet to read Fanon's *Wretched*, and the crew occu-pies a pitiful facsimile of *The Spook Who Sat by the Door*'s training (1973),[39] they manifest Dr. Dre's 1992 release "Let Me Ride," wherein he intones "hell yeah" as part of the chorus of an old Negro spiritual—a spiritual once removed by Par-liament Funkadelic—pastiche gone way left.[40]

Moreover, the growth of campus religiosity escapes much of U.S. textual notice. In film and television texts such as *School Daze* (Lee, 1988), *Drumline* (Stone, 2002), and *The Quad* (Henderson-BET, 2017–2018), religion plays no role, although these worlds exist on Black college campuses where not only are cha-pel services held weekly but also Black churches send vans to transport students to services. Organizations such as InterVarsity Christian Fellowship (a group that began in the U.S. around 1941) attract large followings on Black college campuses.[41] However, a ramped-up religiosity is especially evident abroad. On Nigerian university campuses, student fellowship groups meet outside to praise

Christ aloud during the week in addition to their regular Sunday church attendance. Often, the organizers sell religious materials (books, CDs, and cassette
tapes by U.S. televangelists like Kenneth Hagin and Creflo and Taffy Dollar).
Nollywood narratives capture this development.

In *Finding God in All the Black Places*, I argue that not only is God back but
more—He/She never left. The twenty-first-century difference in religious and
spiritual reverence and relevance lies in the shift into prominence and later dominance of capitalized Black popular culture—music, dance, and all manner of
visual culture. Jazz and the blues, both Black American forms, begin this shifting of the ground. R&B (fighting payola and outright theft) break new ground,
but hip-hop turns the U.S. into a culturally Black nation—a fact I preach about
in The Message. And, as ministry leader Carmen Cunningham writes, "The same
liberationist faith that birthed the Black church of today, no matter how far off
we may veer, remains as the primary plot line without which few Black stories
can be told."[42] Moreover, because Black popular culture endures as completely
and historically infused with the ritual, rhythms, and spiritual practices of Black
church religiosity, it shapes and helps reintroduce religion and spirituality to the
larger country and world repeatedly.

This work speaks primarily to mainstream visualizing and industry mechan-
ics of Black artistic practice. Not everyone, not all Black people, can be included
in this swath; but all are nonetheless impacted and influenced by the practices,
representations, industrial strategies, and critical engagements of and through
media. I employ strategies developed within television, film, and digital media
studies; Africana studies; sociology and cultural studies as a sort of Afridad of
thought as opposed to fusion. Like the raging critique of Latinidad, fusion pre-
sumes not only joining but also erasure and loss because of that merger—which,
while it creates something new, the new thing also eliminates and misconstrues
a great deal as well. Afridad (taking some of the progressive intention of Latinidad but attempting to eradicate the substitutions, erasures, and flattening out
for capital's sake) relies on the rhythms, energies, physicality, and thoughts of
African-Americans to come together like, as filmmaker and scholar Marlon
Riggs so richly illustrates, gumbo. Performance studies scholar E. Patrick Johnson asserts that Riggs's *Black Is . . . Black Ain't* (1995) forces viewers to grapple
with both materiality and discourse—calling attention to the embodiment, lived
experience, and differences between Black folks.[43] Riggs's work moves beyond
just performance to capture variant aspects of people's lived experiences. This
viable understanding frames my articulation of Afridad and the flow of this
program.

Back in the Church Office

Unlike other work being done in this vein or even previous work I've done, I
offer this writing not as a singular (or multiply driven) theoretical treatise. Its

coherence lies in the trajectory of the sections, the larger subject, and the Black church ritualistic structure as articulated within its Sunday morning printed program. Portions of the service provide a taxonomy of Black religious representations on screen, while other parts offer case studies of how Black religion and spirituality shapes the production, circulation, and reception of Black mediated images. I envision this service as, first, a media studies project. Mediation is meant to be central, and I hope readers—lay and scholarly—take it up that way. When I argue religion and spirituality stand as the sine qua non of Black popular culture, I assert them as foundational to and influencing how practitioners, audiences, and users imagine and take up Black popular culture. The theoretical trajectory for this project links the demonstration of this always already spiritual and religious foundation in various texts with how the foundation's presence in the lives of Black folks shapes the production and circulation of said texts. Returning to the work of literary scholar Carole Boyce Davies gave me a path before I even named it. She theorizes: "Black women's writing... should be read as a series of boundary crossings and not as a fixed, geographical, ethically or nationally bound category of writing."[44] I present these informed musings, writings, and scholarly observations as a series of incursions into the academic and social media universe—a social media world often parading as thoughtful and scholarly discourse.[45]

Embracing religion all my life, I grew up in a Sunday church-going household and was raised by an on-her-knees praying mother.[46] I wrote about the "World of Islam" for my tenth-grade honors English final assignment. I comparatively wrote about Confucianism, Hinduism, and Buddhism in eleventh grade. I devoted a chapter of my first book *Shaded Lives: African-American Women and Television* to Oprah Winfrey as a religious icon (and revisit her as a Black savior in this one). I extensively explored Black television evangelism in *Pimpin' Ain't Easy: Selling Black Entertainment Television*, my second book. I presented papers on African-derived religions and representation at the Society for Cinema and Media Studies conference and other similar spaces like the American Studies Association (ASA) and National Communication Association (NCA) conferences since then. I received a Fulbright Award to conduct research and teach at Obafemi Awolowo University in Ile-Ife, Nigeria, for six months in 2008. Living with my immediate family in the ancestral home of the Yorubas gave me an opportunity to exchange ideas with Nigerian scholars and students and visit sacred groves while living in the place that birthed other religious and spiritual expressions (Vodou, Santería, Candomblé) and informed more mainstream ones, particularly Black Christianity and Islam. The long and short of this reverie acknowledges religion and spirituality's consistent grounding of both my personal life and professional work. Thus, it seems appropriate that I finally yield to this subject as a directed endeavor.

Finding God in All the Black Places: Sacred Imaginings in Black Popular Culture presents a combination of theoretical reflection, careful critical, analytic, and canonical textual analysis, judiciously culled industrial analysis, ethnographic interrogation, and embodied experiences of living while Black and religious, hetero- and queer-allied, highly educated, working, and professional class while guided by spirit. Interactions and conversations with many, both named and unnamed, people of color in particular inform the analysis here as well and my stake in the subject. I attempt to situate the best and most relevant television, film, music, and digital media scholarship available as well as conduct deep dives into applicable and viable religion, sociology, anthropology, cultural studies, and performance studies scholarship. While a great deal of Black popular culture receives examination over the course of the service, television probably receives a larger proportion due to it being my area of expertise as well as the location of a significant amount of confluence and influence. As well, while this project is not exclusively about Black women in religion and media, they occupy a large swath of the service—reflecting the real-lived roles they play in Black religious spaces. The spirit works through them all. The Order of Service proceeds as follows:

Call to Worship

The call to worship in the traditional Black church provides an opportunity for the spirit to be summoned from above and within the worshippers. Those present get directed to silence the noise (talking and phones), prepare for the spirit, and be available to the presence of God at the service. I've tried to offer this directive by way of introduction to *Finding God in All the Black Places*.

Invocation

Mediation, Blackness, and religion come into scholarly and popular discourse via narrative—film, television, music, and digital media. In "God Is Trying to Tell You Somethin': Calling Up the Mediated Black Past," I give a short historical account of some of the key texts outside of directed religious programming. These media allow for lay and unchurched people to connect to the places where Black spirituality and religiosity manifest overtly and sometimes covertly, offering a sort of Black cultural competence. Looking at specific narratives, industry practices and rationales, and decades of genres, the Invocation offers a way to contextualize and understand Black popular culture in the late twentieth and twenty-first centuries.

Processional

Minister Charles E. Lewis Sr. describes the church processional this way: "Their services start with a choir marching in sometimes robed, and at other times dressed color coordinated. After the choir reaches the choir loft and concludes the processional song, spontaneous praise breaks out."[47] The processional in *Finding God in All the Black Places* centers the ongoing and fraught debates about the presumed sacred and secular divide. Always framed in opposition, these terms take on different interpretations in twentieth- and twenty-first-century Black popular culture. In "Jesus and Hennessy Go Good Together: Sacralizing the Secular," I explore these debates by placing "certain" women of the Bible in conversation with Black pop cultural icons: biblical figures Mary and Martha of Bethany and Mary Magdalene alongside gospel duo Mary Mary and queen of hip-hop soul Mary J. Blige.

Prayer of Confession

Writer Donna Jones defines the prayer of confession as "the acknowledgment of our sin, or the affirmation of God's truth, or both."[48] In "As for Me and My House . . . Spike Lee's Negotiation with Christianity as a Sign of Blackness," this Prayer of Confession grapples with one of the most prolific directors ever—Spike Lee and his (dis)agreement with Black followers of Christ. Lee's body of work, extending from the mid-1980s, constantly suggests Black people who follow Jesus pose an antithetical threat to progressive Blackness—a progressiveness he often equates with not only Black financial wherewithal but also Black Christian disavowal.

Testimony

Testifying to spiritual negotiations in real-lived academic settings, I offer "I Got a Testimony: Sistah Blackacademics and God." This part of the service recognizes the testimonies of five Black women academics who must negotiate faith and public secularity as a sign of intelligence—even when their work treads spiritual ground. Scholars who study the already side-eyed film, television, digital media, and journalistic disciplines talk about what it means to be a Black woman of faith, a scholar, and to work in institutions that disdain them (for both reasons in many cases). Their testimonies allow readers to reconsider not only the labor Black women academics undertake on college campuses in general but also, more importantly, how that labor (through scholarship, racialized and gendered professional expectations, mentorship, and real-lived experiences) permeate and shape their work, their effectiveness, and their daily lives.

Praise and Worship

As is often the case, conversations between Black women of faith lead to praise. Coming from the Testimony part of the service, "Dance, Dance, Dance, Dance, Dance, Dance, Dance All Night!" examines Black women's Christian performance via contemporary television and online to gain insights into how screen audiences receive invitation and encouragement to experience the Holy Spirit. I argue in these moments, with Black women (and Black audience members) performing, praising, and testifying, the Holy Spirit moves not only through the recorded, in-studio audience but also within screen audiences—television viewers and online users alike.

Tithes & Offering

This brings us to the collection portion of the service that I'm calling "I'mma Be Stupid Rich! Millennials and the Holy Grail of Tech Salvation." As part of the Tithes & Offering, worshipping with cash, I explore the ways in which the contemporary Black church uses media and technology to attract and engage millennials within church worship. Seeking to stem declining U.S.-based attendance, ministers and ministries invest time and resources into constructing a different type of service—a technologically engaged, media savvy, and pop culture–leaning one, despite the potential to foster nomadism and disconnection from Christian dogma and disaffection from non-millennials. I think through how this path gets disrupted with the COVID-19 pandemic shutdown beginning in 2020 and how that pivot impacts how Black church is done for everyone since.

Passing of the Peace

After the offering, many churches engage in the Passing of the Peace, adhering to biblical scriptures. Initially mostly observed in Anglican or Catholic churches, this practice facilitates members' personal communication, sharing, and touch. It has filtered into Black Protestant congregations as well. Formal church decorum relaxes (a bit) and reflects the ways Black church folks recognize that God wants not only holiness but also joy. "Playing with God! Black Church and Humor" finds this joy through humor as demonstrated within television, digital, and film narratives.

Selection

The musical selection preceding the minister's message generally sets the tone for the sermon. In this service, the Selection explores the ways in which spirituality permeates Black religious practices beyond Christianity. In "Never Losing Its Power: (Re)Visioning the Roots and Routes of Black Spirituality," I examine how certain media content incorporates and expresses Black African traditional religious practices. Within this tune, I think through not only how Black media makers subvert pejorative characterizations of African traditional spiritual practices, but more, how Black women in particular lead the way through conjure and traditional religious practices as shown in the media narratives *Beloved* (1998), *Eve's Bayou* (1997), and *Queen Sugar* (DuVernay, OWN, 2016–2022).

Message

The delivery of The Word, the message or the sermon represents the headliner of Black church service. The word offered here argues for the union of sexuality and spirituality as an ideal and aspirational goal. In "Urgent Like a Mofo: The Sublime Synergy of Spirituality and Sexuality in Black Music Culture," I examine the musicality and visuality of several Black artists as quintessential examples of how to achieve this confluence, featuring D'Angelo, Erykah Badu, Meshell

Ndegeocello, and Prince. Through their creative works, musical artists embrace and demonstrate synergies between sexuality and spirituality as a model of God's love.

The Invitation

Christians recognize the invitation as one of the most important aspects of the church service. During this time, the minister may ask congregants to stop moving because non-Christians are presumably making decisions about giving their lives to Christ (or in the case of returning Christians or Christians without a church home, folks coming to join that particular church). One central claimed person of God, Oprah Winfrey, invites people to a similar salvational opportunity. "I Shall Wear a Crown: Black Oprah the Savificent" looks at the religious and spiritual roles and ways of Oprah Winfrey as an example of salvatory impulses outside of the church, particularly after her twenty-five-year television talk show run. Her new professional lives (her magazine, network ownership, philanthropy, speaking tours, continued acting, and political turns) fascinatingly merge selling, sacrifice, and soul saving, most particularly this time around, for Black women.

Benediction

Hopefully, the journey this service takes allows for a fuller thinking about the necessity, viability, pervasiveness, and intransigence of Black spirituality and religion within Black popular culture. "But God" briefly reflects on what the confluence of media, Black folks, spirituality, and religion mean in this moment and for the future.

Invocation

In many Black church services, after the Call to Worship, the presiding minister offers a prayer called the Invocation. An Invocation appeals to God for guidance and discernment in the service or meeting to come.

God Is Trying to Tell
You Somethin'

• •

Calling Up the Mediated
Black Past

On first notes, Black church folks know and can hear Andraé Crouch's song, "God Is Trying to Tell You Something." The lyrics announce a turning point in the lives of the mostly oppressed Black women in the 1985 film *The Color Purple*. Asking the Lord to speak calls for a response of yes, and while the scene fails to overturn the sexist, violent, and abusively Christian visual telling, the song enunciates several tensions of living while Black with hope in God. From narratives like these and others across media platforms, audiences, listeners, and users get to see faith in the constructed and fictive (and pseudo-fictive) lives of Black folks. This invocative prayer recalls the presence, operation, and trajectory of Black church religion and spirituality in U.S. mediated spaces. Tracing media legacies of religion and spirituality supports the contention that they function as the sine qua non of Black popular culture. Knowing where you come from helps in moving forward with clarity and purpose.

Contemporary scholarship on the confluence of religion and media operates mostly within three arenas: God and capitalism (megachurches, celebrity preachers, prosperity dogma, global television ministries); God and politics (religious right, nationhood and sovereignty, elections, public policy, marriage equality); and God and popular culture (repping Christ, millennials, religious reality and narrative TV, gospel vs. CCM, new nonbelievers, religious memes, dark web). In mainstream news, abundant derisive commentary reigns. Yet despite the deluge of coverage, many humanities-based media scholars enter unfamiliar territory within the realm of the Holy Spirit. Both a seeming commonsense understanding and a sense of cluelessness exist about what it means to address spirit and media, especially the spirit of Black people.

Discourses of mediated Black religiosity live (and for a long time) within every communication format: newspapers, advertisements, radio, film, music, television, online, and social media. Thinking first about cinema, in her book *Returning the Gaze: A Genealogy of Black Film Criticism 1909–1949*, film scholar Anna Everett writes about the ways in which cinema and Black journalism serve as acculturating tools for migrant Blacks moving into urban spaces. She suggests these new urbanites "rely on the well-entrenched Black religious and journalistic institutional networks for additional sociocultural uplift strategies."[1] Moreover, in *Hollywood Be Thy Name: African American Religion in American Film 1929–1949*, religion history scholar Judith Weisenfeld reminds us that the early film industry relished the idea and economic benefits of combining African-American bodies and religious fervor with the advent of film sound. She argues: "Hollywood and independent studios recognized the aesthetic power of African American religious expression, so often grounded in using the body's sound and motion as conduits to the divine."[2] One critic, known only as "the Investigator," compares lessons conveyed in church versus those in film. The Investigator writes: "It is generally conceded that the moving picture shows, through showing the evils of whisky, have done more to bring about prohibition than any other medium. . . . Don't such plays deter our young people from such evils as much as a long 'Holy Glory' sermon to which they do not listen?"[3] Despite early supportive connections between Black religiosity and media, the Black church responds unenthusiastically to cinema and its influence. It largely perceives film as providing negative depictions and disruption, especially as reviewed by the Black press—even though Black actors achieve a certain uplifted status by appearing in this forum—an uplift early (and current) Black churches desire.

Beyond general disdain, filmic Black spiritual bodies deployed to guide white sojourns in their quest for success, safety, and sanity illustrate one of the problematic representations often mentioned. These spirit guides maintain a historic connection to colonization and slavery through which film scholar Regina Longo suggests, whites "acknowledge a certain type of [B]lack power that is safe for the whites [but] still keep the [B]lacks as something other than wholly human even if they are divine."[4] This early representational impulse winds its way through visual time, as demonstrated by *Ghost* (Zucker, 1990, for which actress Whoopi Goldberg won an Oscar for her spirit role) and *The Matrix* series (Wachowski, 1999 and 2003) to *A Wrinkle in Time* (DuVernay, 2018).[5] Beyond these "magical Negro" ascriptions, Black popular culture bears witness to Black stories of religious and spiritual engagement, whole cloth and as handkerchief, while serving as a source for both Black entrepreneurship and job training.

How I Got Over

As part of Black social existence, preaching and other examples of Black religious life appear in every era of Black cinematic production. Filmmaker and novelist Oscar Micheaux offers a certain depiction of Black religious life (in this case, pejorative), with his silent second film, *Within Our Gates* (1920). He positions preacher Old Ned[6] and religion as mechanisms to keep Negroes in their place.[7] Historian Daniel Leab asserts that a part of Micheaux's disdain for preachers stemmed from his acrimonious understanding of his minister father-in-law's work and finances.[8] Nonetheless, having made more than forty films between 1918 and 1948, Micheaux remains credited as one of the first successful and most prolific Black filmmakers and producers.[9] He found a method of making films that presumably uplifts while serving to "entertain, to appeal to his concept of Black popular taste, and to make money."[10] Many of his narrative impulses impact future filmmakers.[11]

Wanting to make a film with an all-Black cast, white film director King Vidor reminisces in his autobiography, *A Tree Is a Tree*: "The sincerity and fervor of [the Negroes'] religious expression intrigued me, as did the honest simplicity of their sexual drives. In many instances the intermingling of these two activities seemed to offer strikingly dramatic content."[12] Although the studios repeatedly refused, the advent of sound provided an opportunity to bring his long-standing Black fantasies to fruition. Gambling with the salary of his MGM contract on the film's success, Vidor created and directed the film *Hallelujah* in 1929, the first to expand the scope of Black representation via studio distribution. While the white press praised it, the Black press denounced the film as inherently racist— suggested through, if nothing else, the dual initial Black and white film openings in New York City, and more critically as bearer of old stereotypic tropes.[13]

From the beginning of the film, Vidor conflates Black Christian praise with Black sexuality, the synergy of which is marked as deviance. Set in a post–Civil War, anywhere-south-of-the-Mason-Dixon-line location, Vidor's first sound film documents the life of a rural Black farming family. The dramatic conflict arises from the struggle of the eldest son Ezekiel ("Zeke," played by Daniel L. Haynes) to resist evil in the form of a woman. In the baptismal scene, for example, Chick (Nina Mae McKinney) literally (bodily) overflows with the Holy Ghost, forcing Zeke (a repentant preacher) to carry her back to the tent for some additional spiritual attention. This, however, turns into sexual healing. While laying her down on the bed, his "Negro sexual impulses" overwhelm him. He begins to fondle and kiss her until his mother blows up the spot. Sending away her shamed son, she admonishes Chick with: "You got more 'ligion than what's good for you. You ol' hypocrite!" This comment resonates because it carries two interpretations. Some recognize possible abuses of specific religious practitioners, whereas others make religion itself the problem.

Zeke, Chick, and Mammy in *Hallelujah* (Vidor, 1929). (Courtesy of Photofest.)

The use of high key lighting on Zeke furthers Vidor's seeming desire to prob-lematize the confluence of Black spirituality and sexuality. By illuminating Zeke's face, Vidor suggests Black ministers are, at heart, satyromaniacs. At the church, as Zeke delivers his sermon, Chick's entrance transfixes him. In the heat of the congregation's Holy Ghost praise, he follows her from the church and runs away with her. Weisenfeld argues that in most of the scenes where the two worship together, "Zeke and Chick commit themselves to resisting sexual temptation but find that religious experience leads them, inevitably, to sexual expression."[14] Yet Vidor's Christian narrative and racial logic illustrate this connection as child-like, sinful, destructive, and Black wrong.[15]

As a counterpoint to both Vidor's and Micheaux's perspectives on Blacks and religion, writer, actor, and filmmaker Spencer Williams's cinematic career grounds itself in evangelizing Christ, especially in his films *The Blood of Jesus* (1941) and *Go Down Death* (1944). Mentored by actor Bert Williams (no rela-tion), Spencer Williams began his career as a writer for Hollywood productions after his service in the military. He traversed mainstream theater, Hollywood, and later television, starring as Andy in the short-lived *Amos 'n' Andy* television series (CBS, 1951–1953). Film critic Armond White characterizes both *The Blood of Jesus* and *Go Down Death* as "among the most spiritually adventurous movies ever made."[16] Scholars and media makers recognize Williams for forwarding

Blacks in front of and behind the screen, though not to the same degree as Micheaux, and not unproblematically.[17]

By way of religious background, African-Americans are depicted almost exclusively as Christian, specifically Baptist or Pentecostal, despite the nonmonolithic character of Christianity. Black Catholics, Methodists, Lutherans, Presbyterians, as well as Muslims and Buddhists, find limited screen time within all areas of representation. Even in film remakes such as *The Preacher's Wife* (1996, a remake of the 1947 *The Bishop's Wife*), a part of the title change comes from the perceived need to change denominations of the husband for it to be legible. Typically, Black Catholics appear only with the invocation of Vodou, Santería, or Candomblé (where religion becomes perverted), or through works outside of the U.S. context.

Only a handful of 1950s films center religion, the exceptions being epic studio productions such as *Quo Vadis* (LeRoy, 1951), *The Ten Commandments*[18] (DeMille, 1956), and *Ben-Hur* (Wyler, 1959). Financially successful and award worthy,[19] yet they target white audiences (mainstream cinema) and engage Black religiosity and spirituality only cursorily. It seems big Hollywood films, even ones foregrounding Black narrative strands, play down or eliminate Black life, religious or otherwise. In the 1959 version of *Imitation of Life*, the film ends with a grand-style Black church funeral and procession for nanny/housekeeper Annie (Juanita Moore). While the climax of the film centers gospel great Mahalia Jackson singing at the funeral and Annie's light-skinned daughter Sarah Jane (Susan Kohner) asking her dead mother for forgiveness, the more interesting aspect, at least for this purpose, is the nature of surprise that Lora (Lana Turner) expresses about the number of Black people attending the funeral service.[20]

Cinema begins to fight for its economic life with the emergence of television. By the 1960s, says writer Livia Gershon, "the FCC free[s] radio and television stations from a requirement that it give away air time as a public service, ramping up the media's commercialization, religious broadcasting [becomes] dominated by evangelicals."[21] This upgraded opportunity allows for a look into religious communities not universally known, even though nearly 94 percent of U.S. Americans claimed some form of Christianity in the 1960s.[22] United Artists released *Lilies of the Field* (Nelson, 1963) as a prize-wining vehicle for actor Sidney Poitier. It came as the NAACP continued to push for African-American representation on film and television. With a certain amount of Black backlash, Poitier won the Oscar for best actor in this film about German-immigrated nuns and the Black man "God sends" to help them. Poitier became the first African-American to win an Oscar for best actor.[23] He won not so much for the film per se as for the excellent way in which the film, according to film scholar Thomas Cripps, embodies a hero who "should not be too [B]lack, too much the loner, and should be, if done well, a Black figure set down in a microcosmic company of whites (who [are] the better for his having passed their way)."[24] The blending of cultures, language, and a little bit of Christianity offers a way forward together against the strife of the period. Otherwise, cinema (and early television) relegate religion primarily to an occasional narrative of church attendance by an older relative à la Aunt Bee. This dearth means in large measure that mainstream culture knows very little about the lives Blacks lived during this time. Transforming technology helps to shift this lack.

The confluence of citizen unrest and recognition of technology's power and position helps introduce empowerment possibilities through developments such as cable public access, which begin in the late 1960s. Created by the Federal Communications Commission, public access television gave ordinary community members the ability and means to create, express, and vision their concerns, beliefs, and ideas. As well, writes media studies scholar Michele Hilmes, it allowed citizens to access a wider public audience and add a "rich layer of local culture to television offerings, enriching the democratic public sphere."[25] For example, in Tucson, Arizona, even with a rather small Black population (less than 5 percent), Access Tucson hosted the series *Black Man Know Thyself* for several years in the early 2000s, providing a direct avenue for Blacks, and Black and religious groups, to find expression in the cable television realm. Yet before religion and Black folks became fully prime time on TV, both were segregated to televised Sunday morning church services and public affairs programming. The works of media scholar Devorah Heitner and English and American studies scholar Gayle Wald examine Black public affairs television programming that emerged on network (and off-network) stations in the 1960s and 1970s. These series appear particularly after the 1968 Kerner Commission report visualized enraged and rioting Black communities from Bed-Stuy to Jackson, Boston to Omaha as deviant and distressed, expressed through white men's eyes, perspectives, and media.[26] Others such as film scholar Ellen C. Scott and media scholar Steve Classen remind us of the difficulties of representing Blackness in any visual capacity at any time.[27] Often what these public programs broadcast is a combination of Black respectability, righteousness, and religiosity.

Chorus of Colored Angels

Filmmaker Melvin Van Peebles ushered in a period of Black-themed fictional narratives with his 1971 *Sweet Sweetback's Baadasssss Song*. While, according to film historian Gerald Butters, the film *Cotton Comes to Harlem* (Davis, 1970) proved the profitability of Black-cast films for the studios,[28] the financial success of *Sweetback* (made for $500,000 but grossing over $14 million over time), significantly impacted the film industry in two ways: (1) it helped galvanize and salvage the depressed Hollywood film industry—a depression caused by its competition with television and its extended commitment to big-budget films; and (2) It initiated replicas. This film, though inundated with explicit sexual scenes, provides one of the few cinematic times that Blacks fight against "the man" and live to tell about it. Hence the ending's visual statement: "A

Baadasssss nigger is coming back to collect some dues." Van Peebles even scripts the voices and music of the Black community in the film as the chorus of "Colored Angels."[29] Political activist Huey Newton reviews the film in *The Black Panther*, explaining: "[Sweetback] is only dealing with sexual symbols, the real meaning is far away from anything sexual, and so deep that you have to call it religious."[30] Clapping back on Newton's praise, journalist and social historian Lerone Bennett calls the film "neither revolutionary nor Black.... Now, with all due respects to the license of art, it is necessary to say frankly that nobody ever f***ed his way to freedom. And it is mischievous and reactionary finally for anyone to suggest to Blacks in 1971 that they are going to be able to sc**w their way across the Red Sea. F***ing will not set you free. If f***ing freed, Black people would have celebrated the millennium 400 years ago."[31] Yet from 1972 to 1976, around 200 films were produced. The president of the Beverly Hills-Hollywood branch of the NAACP, Junius Griffin, characterized these films as blaxploitation.[32] The term conflates two words: Blacks and exploitation, the confluence of which still sustains debate. While white men wrote, directed, and produced most of these films and offered often banal and problematic themes, this Blackified film industry also provided employment opportunities for many African-American actors and crew—opportunities that remain limited in the twenty-first century.

Several of these Black-cast films with Black directors include extended and notable Black religious and spiritual content. The Reverend (Flip Wilson) preaches about loose lips and no joy juice at the church picnic in *Uptown Saturday Night* (Poitier, 1974); Ossie Davis righteously governs his lodge as Elder Johnson of the Brothers and Sisters of Shaka in *Let's Do It Again* (Poitier, 1975); and *Car Wash* (Schultz, 1976) features preacher-pimp Daddy Rich (Richard Pryor) hustling money from blue-collar workers.[33] Black screenwriter and playwright Richard Wesley penned both *Uptown Saturday Night* and *Let's Do It Again*, while Sidney Poitier directed them. With *Uptown* in particular, certain long scenes of church service (the gospel choir singing the entirety of "How I Got Over," the man of God preaching for a good while, and the joy of fellowship illustrated by touch in both comedies) allow for ten-plus minutes of Black religious demonstration and understanding not found in most white-created spaces visualizing Black religiosity. Even in the most far-fetched Black cultural spaces, Black and white generated, religiosity and spirituality find expression as the sine qua non of Black popular culture.

The 1980s brought a completely new dynamic to the film and television industries. Cable television, though introduced in the 1950s to achieve better reception, blossomed with the initiation of CNN in 1980 and MTV in 1981. These networks shifted the industry mechanisms of production, marketing, advertising, and direction. Concretely, Music Television (MTV) targets a specific demographic (twelve to twenty-four, rock-loving white boys) rather than a broad one; it ditches concerns about where footage comes from—stock, live, or graphic;

Uptown Saturday Night (Poitier, 1974).

shows no concern for the material format (35 mm, 16 mm, or Super 8), or whether the material appears in black and white or color. CNN offers news in a radically different way, employing multiple electronic feeds, variant image-text combinations, video graphics, studios with banks of monitors that look like video installations, and twenty-four hours of content. In addition, advertisements (and their corporations) begin to push the boundaries of form and narrative to sell products, services, and ideas. Moreover, the reinstituted paucity of Black representation (post-1970s crush) finds a savior in filmmaker Spike Lee.

Lee's work reintroduces audiences to Black expressivity and certain Black life, although his primer includes deriding religious Black folks (Jehovah's Witnesses especially) and Black women. His *She's Gotta Have It* (1986), followed by John Landis's religious aspersions in *Coming to America* (1988) and later, F. Gary Gray's taunts in *Friday* (1995), critique Black religion for mass public consumption. Other work, such as Spielberg's *The Color Purple* mentioned at the beginning, positions religion and spirituality as long-standing, often problematic aspects of Black life. While television series such as the comedy *Amen* (NBC, 1986–1991) situate the Black church as a backdrop to Deacon Frye's antics (Sherman Helmsley), others such as the drama *In the Heat of the Night* (NBC/CBS, 1988–1995),[34] offer in small-town Sparta, Mississippi, characters who attend church routinely and ground religiosity as a significant plot device alongside the difficulties of race, culture, and change. The 1980s also began (or initiated) the narrative of young people (Black and white) moving away from the church.

The 1990s rise and growth of hip-hop helped host a new commodified, Black urban aesthetic where Black popular culture begins to forgo Christian reverence in exchange for questions, comedy, and a broadening Black spiritual articulation. Music leads the way in this regard as Black-mediated religiosity animates in music. Meaning that people of the African diaspora explore and express spirituality through and within music. Generically, this expression comes through gospel, R&B, and hip-hop artists (and has always been in play with blues and jazz). While religiosity was incorporated into the popular with artists such as Aretha Franklin, Al Green, and even Sister Rosetta Tharpe, gospel innovator Kirk Franklin transformed gospel music (and R&B) by combining them with the sound and dynamics of hip-hop (musically and physically). Earning Stellar and Dove Awards for his 1993 debut album *Kirk Franklin & the Family*, his 1997 monster hit "Stomp" was nominated for an R&B Grammy, playing on urban radio and in clubs. Like critiques leveled before him at gospel innovators such as James Cleveland and Andraé Crouch from the 1960s and the Clark Sisters from the 1970s, some in the Black church originally criticized and condemned Franklin for bringing hip-hop into the church house.

Yet music for God seems to find its way into every genre and flavor of Black music. For example, as alluded to in the Call to Worship, the hook of Dr. Dre's 1993 "Let Me Ride" uses the chorus (remixed) of the mid-1800s "Negro spiritual" "Swing Low, Sweet Chariot," first recorded in 1909 by the historically Black college choir the Fisk Jubilee Singers.[35] Dre's Grammy Award–winning rap fuses legacies from the first version in Black church to the second iteration in Parliament Funkadelic's 1975 "Mothership Connection" groove. The hit is problematic for sure, but also bumpin' as it addresses both societal conditions and Black faith.[36] In another example, when Beyoncé's now infamous 2016 visual album *Lemonade* streamed into consumers' lives, feminists took it up, queer communities shook it up, Black folks hooked it up, and of course, the Beyhive devoured it.[37] What has been lost (or certainly evaded) in the multiple translations of and scholarship around her work are the ways in which Beyoncé talks back to Black Christianity, honors traditional African religious practices, while still bathing in the blood of Jesus. Queen Bey is not alone musically and visually in this contemporary task of interrogating, clapping back at but still religiously negotiating Jesus the Christ, Islam's Allah, the Five-Percent Nation's ALLAH, and Yoruba religious practices, as will be shown throughout the service (even though traditions outside of Christianity appear very limitedly in Black popular culture).

Nineties cinema followed this Black religious trajectory as well. In the $47 million–grossing *New Jack City* (Mario Van Peebles, 1991), a minor story of Reverend Oates's (Nick Ashford) complicity in Nino Brown's (Wesley Snipes) drug operation settles there. The thriller *A Rage in Harlem* (Duke, 1991) makes Warner Sallman's 1940 white Jesus portrait a central punch line as the mocked image of its protagonist's mother. Filmmaker Julie Dash's lyrical and beautiful early 1900s tale of a family in transition foregrounds traditional African spirituality and Islam in *Daughters of the Dust* (1991).[38] And Lee's passion project about Nation of Islam leader *Malcolm X* (1992) hits in order to not only tell Malcolm's story but also to offer Islam in a progressive and viable light for Black people.[39] And unlike the unevenness of cinema, mainstream fictional religious television series appear quite resoundingly by the late twentieth and early twenty-first centuries across various broadcast and cable networks and streaming platforms. Black Entertainment Television's (BET) entire Sunday lineup features Black Christian programming.[40] Due to its immediacy, lowered costs, and responsive nature, television better demonstrates the temperature of U.S. audiences for exploring religious and spiritual life.[41]

Take It to Jesus

By the twenty-first century, due to shifts in production and exhibition again as well as another shift in technology (the internet and streaming), more consistent Black narratives center religion, religious settings, and/or spirituality in films such as *Kingdom Come* (McHenry, 2001), *The Gospel* (Hardy, 2005), *Diary of a Mad Black Woman* (Grant, 2005), and *First Sunday* (Talbert, 2008). This list fails to include Black film narratives with substantial religious subtexts such as *Deliver Us from Eva* (Hardwick, 2003) and *Pariah* (Rees, 2011), YouTube vignettes, web series, and the Black Christian direct-to-home DVD market where narratives such as the *Pastor Jones* series live at Walmart and Target or stream across Netflix, Hulu, and Amazon platforms. These film dramas, comedies, and documentaries all share a hidden (and not so hidden) transcript of Black spirituality and religiosity as culturally foundational.

A flood of mainstream television programs emerged in the twenty-first century,[42] offering an expressed (and problematized) religiosity before general and targeted television audiences. Even HBO's "quality" series *Six Feet Under* (2001–2005) incorporates scenes from an afterlife featuring the killed patriarch of the family and his drinking, smoking, and f-cking renegade of fellow spiritual wayfarers, life and death.[43] For target market Black television and digital media narratives such as *The Soul Man* (TVLand, 2012–2016), *The Choir* (YouTube, 2013–2015), *Black Jesus* (Adult Swim, 2014–2019), *Chewing Gum* (E4/Netflix, 2015–2017), *Greenleaf* (OWN, 2016–2020), *Saints & Sinners* (Bounce TV, 2016–2022), *Tyler Perry's Ruthless* (BET+, 2020–2024), and *Honk for Jesus. Save Your Soul.* (Ebo, 2022), all provide fictionalized Black negotiations with religiosity, both for laughs and drama.

Issa Rae's *Mis-Adventures of Awkward Black Girl* (YouTube, 2011–2013) puts born-again Christians on blast, and Ava DuVernay's *Queen Sugar* (OWN, 2016–2022) uses traditional African spirituality, conjure, and land to infuse and ground a central protagonist's power.[44] In fact, within scripted television, the religion episode or story arc often acts as a marker of quality or certainly seriousness for a series.[45] Episodic narratives (both online and televisual) may provide a space to examine religiosity in a fuller way.[46] For the culture, many of these series bring to the fore an embodied and lived Black faith and continue to demonstrate the grounded insistence of religiosity and spirituality in larger Black life.

Michaela Coel in *Chewing Gum* (E4/Netflix, 2015–2017).

Beyond the fictional realm, Black religious narratives abound within reality-like series including the music program *Bobby Jones Gospel* (BET, 1980–2016), gospel competition series *Sunday Best* (BET, 2007–2015, 2019–), reality series *Mary Mary* (WE tv, 2012–2017), *Preachers of L.A.* (Oxygen, 2013–2014), *The Sisterhood* (TLC, 2013), *The Sheards* (BET, 2013), *Preachers of Detroit* (Oxygen, 2015), *Preachers of Atlanta* (Oxygen, 2016), and *We're the Campbells* (TVOne, 2018). Media studies scholars Mark Andrejevic, Laurie Ouellette, and Susan Murray well document the efficacy and financial boon of reality series flourishing since the 1990s. Their low production costs, ease of syndication, and audience buy-in reach audiences already watching competition programs, talk shows, and the grandmothers to the current iteration of reality programming, *Candid Camera* (1948–2004) and MTV's *Real World* (1992–2017, 2019). Furthermore, another set of media studies scholars—Mara Einstein, Katherine Madden, and Diane Winston—suggest reality television and religious characters "reflect the same longings for identity, meaning and purpose—the building blocks of religion—as any other neoliberal citizen. Moreover, their 'lived religion,' daily rituals for meaning-making that point to ultimate values and concerns, raise up what is truly central in their lives."[47] The ministries of Black mega televangelists such as T. D. Jakes, Creflo Dollar, and David Oyedepo of Nigeria among many, many others work this ground well.[48] And, as Einstein and colleagues suggest: "Reality television turns intimate moments of prayer, confession, ecstasy and sin into spectacle."[49]

Fully entrenched and dominant hip-hop too allows for Black religiosity and spirituality to surface as a part of Black popular culture. Aesthetically, music director Hype Williams and cinematographer/director Malik Hasan Sayeed provide templates for artists such as rapper Kendrick Lamar to use music and musical visualization to comment on both codes of religiosity and media. For Lamar's 2017 music video "Humble," for example, veteran director Dave Meyers (alongside Lamar and Dave Free) construct a visual memory and connection of the lyrics to familiar, well-regarded film narratives including *Chinatown* (Polanski, 1974), *The Godfather* (Coppola, 1972), *New Jack City* (Van Peebles, 1992), *Clockers* (Lee, 1995), and a video of presumed killings in the Middle East. Meyers talks about his close connection with Lamar's work and his selection to direct "Humble" as spiritually led.[50] Many performers take up positions of integration and commentary about Black folks and religion and/or spirituality, including Christian rapper Lecrae, comedian/host/DJ/actor Rickey Smiley, gospel singing duo Mary Mary, singers/songwriters/actors Lauryn Hill, Erykah Badu, and Fantasia, and rap lyricists Jay-Z, Snoop, Kanye West, and Chance the Rapper, to name a few. Their riffs come via intracultural discourses of Black church, spiritualism, the Nation of Islam, traditional African and Caribbean spiritual practices, and invocation of the earth in day-to-day Black life. Scholars and audiences recognize and by/(buy) much of hip-hop's religious underpinnings. Embracing various spiritualities, this high-energy and contemporary Blackness works.

In addition to this deluge of twenty-first-century Black content, Black consumers/audiences/users/church members must navigate ministerial brand management (including public relations campaigns on billboards, buses, commercials), mega men's and women's Christian conferences, blog commentary, comedic offerings, Christian fiction writers (such as Kimberla Lawson Roby's Reverend Curtis Black series or the many works by Victoria Christopher Murray), app requests, and, certainly, Tyler Perry's dominant films, television, and live theatrical performances. In essence, a surfeit of entertainment and testament commodifying products sell Black religiosity and spirituality while still failing to undermine my assertion of their quintessence for Black popular culture. Creative content captures and expresses Black religiosity and spirituality, community and discord, bodies and faith, visuality and absence as part of a Black discourse of knowing. Disparate media recognize religion and spirituality as critical to understanding Black identity formation and ground Black popular culture. In this Invocation prayer, I believe tracing these old and new examples gives credence to where religion and spirituality have served as the sine qua non of Black popular culture already. In the rest of the service, we will begin to examine how. Everyone please stand for the processional.

Processional

The traditional Black church processional ushers in the intention of God's people through song and movement. Choir members march into the church, down the aisle(s), and into the choir stand. Literary scholar Adrienne Lanier Seward describes the processional as a "powerful and recurring performance element in Black folk drama and regular church services . . . [one] often carried over into other areas of Afro-American life."[1] While other Christian processions introduce service officiants or the ceremonial and/or consecrated elements to be included in the service, the Black church choir, coming this far by faith, organized through coordinated steps, sway, swag, and song, bring Black religious tradition, spirituality, and culture to attend to the souls of Black folk.

Joyful Sounds of Clair UMC. (Author's collection.)

Jesus and Hennessy
Go Good Together

• •

Sacralizing the Secular

Erica Campbell ✓
@ImEricaCampbell

My day has started out so Great! My cousin just gave his heart completely to God! And I had a great mani and Pedi #spiritual #carnal😂😂🙏🙏

11:36 AM · Apr 13, 2016   ⓘ

♡ 103   💬 5   ⬆ Share this Tweet

Tweet your reply

Twitter post by Erica Campbell of Mary Mary, 13 April 2016.

"When all (when all) of God's children (God's children) get together, oh what a time (what a time) [repeat three times)] . . . we gonna have." When the Joyful Sounds choir of my home church begins marching into the sanctuary singing this song, members stand and know it's time for "chuch." Led by the indomitable Carolyn Duncan, the singing saints of Clair Memorial UMC in Omaha, Nebraska, shift our unrighteousness and pedestrian concerns. As the choir prepares us for reflection and praise, we know our perhaps ratchet lives and behavior face scrutiny, but also understand grace comes along with it. The articulation of sacred and secular aspects of individual lives resonates within the souls of Black folks and identifies the humanity of God's people. So the elated tweet from Erica Campbell of the gospel duo Mary Mary pairing her cousin's salvation with her beautiful nails tracks for many Black Christians. Her simple exclamation demonstrates the paradox of faith found in these times.

In Black communities, people contend with duality as a part of life. Understanding W.E.B. Du Bois's double consciousness and the two sides of the human soul (sinner and saint), Black people grasp the socialized and/or inherent nature of humanity. And while it may not be respectable, the sinner rides as an accepted (and expected) part of humanity. In the practical parlance of the Christian church, the sinner must be present. If not, what is the point? And much to the chagrin of conservative and evangelical Christians, many Muslims, and atheists, the distance between the sacred and the secular continues to decrease. Sacredness and spirituality traditionally signify veneration of God. It includes acknowledgment and an understanding of grace but also traffics in fuller and sometimes different explorations of what should be considered holy and righteous. Secularity, on the other hand, retains its worldly pleasures, performances, and products but also now includes religious, spiritual, and sacred artifacts for public consumption and display. In other words, a certain kind of sacredness and spirituality increasingly encroaches on secular grounds and through the very means by which secularity operates.

In popular culture the bodies and lives of Black women exist as living sacrifice for the commodification of spiritual matters. Whether frenzied and left limp in *Angel Heart* (Parker, 1987), dissed and left to wither in *Amen* (NBC, 1986–1991) and *The Brothers* (Hardwick, 2001), abused, as are almost all the women in *for colored girls* (Perry, 2010), illustrated as Christian hypocrite with Sister Mary in *The Mis-Adventures of Awkward Black Girl* (YouTube, 2011–2013) and Jessie in *The Choir* (YouTube, 2013–2015), molested by family without conviction in *Greenleaf* (OWN, 2016–2020), or ratchetfied before redemption as found in Tyler Perry's many film, television, and theatrical narratives, Black women serve as playground for the entanglements of the secular and sacred. Yet these illustrations belie the inherent sacredness of Black women's bodies and beings.

The sacred spiritual of Black women in the church receives acknowledgment from most corners. Appearance (even when regulated), song, and the Holy Spirit merge strategically and naturally through the bodies of Black women in religious spaces. Black women usher in and embody the spirit of God, acting as "spiritual gatekeepers." For example, writing about the role and work of Black women in the Church of Our Lord Jesus Christ of the Apostolic Faith, Africana studies scholar Judith Casselberry maintains: "Holy Ghost anointing, singing, shouting, crying, speaking in tongues, and running collaborate, making women's bodies and the sounds they create definitive markers of community aesthetics, that which is deemed correct and valuable. The church relies on women's spiritual powers, exhibited in particular agreed-on ways, to set the church on fire and display the beauty of holiness."[2]

Writer Alice Walker also lays out the shape and scope of Black women's sacredness. Within her coined womanism, she calls not only for Black women's empowerment but also for their "autonomy in the spiritual, sexual, political, and artistic realms. Calling on Black women to 'Love [themselves]. Regardless.'"[3] As women's spirituality scholar Arisika Razak maintains: "Womanism asserts the body, psyche, spiritualities and sexualities of Black women [are] as important as the material conditions under which they struggle."[4] How Black women move, work, love, learn, dance, and talk mesmerizes, fortifies, strengthens, and holds communities together. Even though women, and Black women in particular, see few "embodied, female images of Spirit (God),"[5] they claim a space of sacredness that, while sometimes hidden (and often maligned), exists and reverberates through their presences in Black popular culture. Connecting this to Erica and Tina Campbell's gospel duo Mary Mary, many Black women embody this paradox of the sacred and secular.

In fact, the name Mary owns a prominent space in Christianity. In biblical narratives, the Virgin Mary, Mary Magdalene, and Mary of Bethany, sister of Martha and Lazarus, follow Jesus, and two of them witness his murder. As disciples, they watch over the crucifixion, burial, and resurrection of Jesus the Christ. Mary Magdalene sees him resurrected first. Their significance as some of the few women noted in the Bible makes the name itself exceptional and central to the foundation of the faith. Contemporarily, several other Marys, who claim Jesus as well, signify in Black popular culture (though in very different contexts). Remarkable and viable in their own right, they open a space to think more about the right-now sacralizing of the secular. Erica and Tina Campbell as Mary Mary and hip-hop and R&B recording artist Mary J. Blige each exemplify the landscape of a sacralized secular.

Though the biblical and contemporary Marys share the same name (a name meaning wished-for child, bitter, and rebelliousness), each woman comes to sit at the foot of Jesus the Christ via a different route. These new Marys win awards (including gospel ones), perform before thousands (and potentially millions when televised or accessed digitally), act, write, produce, and push the boundaries of what religion and sacredness mean in this century in general and for younger generations. While other singers such as Aretha Franklin and Fantasia well exemplify the paradox of the sacralized secular through their gospelized voices (and actual gospel recordings) and well-known complicated testimonies of lived lives, the Marys make themselves a unique part of both the sacred and secular historical record.

Twenty-first-century Marys' secular approaches clash frequently with traditional methods of evangelizing, worshipping, and being, especially as women—methods that require deference to men and conservatism in comportment. In their performances, productions, public personae, and profit making, these Marys fuse the long-held sacred and secular divide. While they embody the aesthetics and posture of the sacred (through their musical lyrics, their strategic imaging, and their rebirth), they simultaneously exemplify the secular and the so-called profane through their accumulation and pursuit of wealth, sexuality, and capitalization of sacred experiences. While some argue the binaries of the secular and sacred are already discredited, dismantled, and blended in the name of progress and modernity, many Black diasporic peoples continue to grapple with these tensions and view them as a point of critical contention. Moreover, larger mainstream discourses place these binaries in conversation through every facet of celebrity coverage.[6]

Selected for the Processional initially because of their name, both sets of Marys open a space for scholars and audiences to rethink their biblical and contemporary importance as well as to provide audiences, consumers, users, believers, and non-believers (especially young ones) opportunities to meet God in places where they daily live. Thus, I use the Marys to explore the sacralization of the secular and question what sacred truths and what pregnant possibilities remain for our increasingly secularized world. How do Black people reconcile the secular and the sacred in daily life and in visual presentation? I question what privileging women's faith narratives means in a hyper-visual pop culture. Does foregrounding the confluence of the sacred and profane (the secular shift) alter, transform, and/or impact Black women, Black women's culture work, and/or how we socialize Black girls to operate in this world religiously and/or spiritually? How can the sacralization of the secular be discussed in productive ways? This Processional opens up the work, relevance, and redemptive properties of the contemporary Marys as they resonate within discourses surrounding the sacred spiritual and profane, (mediated, digitized, and commodified).

Why You Talkin' 'Bout That Again . . . Aren't We Post?

As mentioned in the Call to Worship, some may question why I talk about a dichotomy already addressed and dismissed? Why even suggest a binary exists between the passé secular and sacred divide? Public wisdom suggests that in our post moment, *capital* structures our lives, so *that* particular separation no longer exists. I respond by observing that first, the U.S. operates not very much post anything, on any level, under any rubric. Surviving in the post-slavery but plantation-stuck economy, politics, and way of being that describes New Orleans where I've lived (and certainly, other less obvious places), post discussions remain void. Beyond this place, the (re)remembered, racialized, and ongoing murders and racist actions in Emanuel AME, Florida, Ferguson, New York City, Atlanta, Chicago, Baton Rouge, Brunswick, Minneapolis, Uvalde, and the greatness insurrection push for America, force recognition of post as present for all the

"Others" of U.S. society.[7] And let me include the sweeping COVID-19 pandemic of 2020 and 2021 that in the U.S. claimed the lives of a disproportionately large number of Black and brown peoples.

Second, many disciplines currently grapple with the ways in which religion and spirituality impact lives—both inside and outside academia. We see it in film, television, and digital productions, within the publishing industry, in megachurches, and in public policy. We find it within many nonprofits. For example, the Center for Healing in New Orleans holds an annual Sacred Music Festival, bringing together people of many different religious practices in conversation and communion through music.[8] The binaries matter because of their existence within the realm of the religious and their seepage into and grounding of secular popular culture.

Beyond the post rhetoric, many recognize and privilege the primacy of vision and visualization as never before. Media scholar John Hartley talks about textual sovereignty providing meaning for democracy, subjectivity, ideology, and even fantasy. Not to denigrate or demote the aural or the writerly, he suggests a "philosophical warrant for taking textual evidence seriously not just as 'representing' the human condition but getting about as close to reality as can be got. And contemporary life is promiscuously textual."[9] Or as photojournalist Jason Miccolo Johnson suggests in his book *Soul Sanctuary: Images of the African American Worship Experience*, "Church was and is a paradise of 'visualosity'— visual curiosity for the mind's eye."[10] These disparate indicators justify further exploration of the sacred and secular relationship.

Rock My Soul in the Bosom of Abraham

How the sacred impacts the secular realm sustains continued debate in various academic corners. While for the preponderance of Western history (some argue medieval), religion and belief exist as the de facto structuring life power, twentieth- and twenty-first-century understanding imagines the world as predominately secular. In a secularized society, "faith [often] lacks cultural authority, religious organizations have little social power, and public life proceeds without reference to the supernatural."[11] Despite this outlook, the sacred spiritual continues to the present day in Black popular culture. Sacredness and spirituality activate internal processes including thoughts, feelings, memories, and experiences. The physical manifestation comes through tears, hearts beating faster, and sound moving through the body. Some situate everyday life events as a site for the sacred. Religion scholar Conrad Ostwalt believes "mundane experience outstrips the imaginings of even the most creative visionaries. [They] can lead to wondrous occasions filled with transcendent possibilities. . . . Many individuals claim it happens outside the confines of sacred institutions or rituals. . . . In such a case, the secular become sacralized."[12] Everyday capitalized forms and forums of somewhat public address take up secular tools for presumably sacred purposes. Lamar billboards accost motorists with "We Need to Talk—God," lawn signs remind us "Thou Shalt Not Kill—God," Lil Wayne rocks cross necklaces, Rihanna's ribcage tattoo suggests in Arabic "Freedom is God," and T-shirts play on the International House of Pancakes logo with "I Hope."

Like Ostwalt, marketing scholars Russell Belk, Melanie Wallendorf, and John Sherry suggest the sacralizing of the secular occurs in all parts of our daily lives: political, scientific, and artistic. They believe consumption plays a significant role in this, arguing that while religious content overall has declined in music and art, both maintain a sacredness to many consumers. "Art, like science, is not only sacred, it sacralizes. . . . This leads us to consider evidence of the sacralization of the secular from the realm of consumption."[13] In other words, the commodification of the spirit for sale, purchase, and possession often re(dis)places the witnessing of the divine solely for the edification of the soul. How people come to know or envision God, Allah, Olorun, Yahweh, or Jehovah often falls in line with a sacralized media consumption experience.

The sacralization of the secular connotes a consistent global transformation of many aspects of living—globalization defined as the ideological, cultural, and technological encroachment and capitalization of another culture. Commodifying sacred works, both as a branding tool and as another way to stake a claim for you as a spiritual being, becomes described in increasingly secular terms. For example, scholars continue to theorize how hip-hop discerns and exposes spirituality. Communication scholar Timothy Huffman suggests: "Hip hop spirituality is the intersection of power and authenticity as many voices construct and reveal the self, the other, and the divine,"[14] while to that point, VaNatta Ford finds God in Lauryn Hill's song "Everything Is Everything."

One of the great privileges and wonders of teaching the perpetually young comes from their ability to keep cultural and historical debates, material, and evidence current. Born in the beginning year of Generation X, I know R&B, old-school rap, rappers, and hip-hop but am less conversant with the young ones much beyond edited radio airplay. In my Imagining the Sacred in Black Popular Culture course, students introduce and/or allow for collective grappling with the ways in which Kanye, Erykah, Kendrick, Tasha, Kirk, Chance, Tye, Mary Mary, Canon, Koryn, and PJ Morton move the needle of religiosity and spirituality within the secular realm. And quiet as it's kept, Black women play a key role in making this happen.

Often, centering the work of Jesus and "the faithful women around him bolsters churchwomen as they press through the challenges of life."[15] Black womenfolk, as sociologist Patricia Hill Collins argues in a slightly different context, continue to do the heavy lifting and domestic labor of bringing souls to Christ.[16] As womanist ethics scholar and minister Emille M. Townes reflects, Black women "need to know that we are not dipped, we are not sprinkled, we are not immersed—we are washed in the grace of God."[17] This invocation of the spirit spills over from the sacred to every aspect of the secular world for many believers. In the case of artist Mary J. Blige, her background, story, overcoming, and turn make her work in the world palpably spiritual. With the duo Mary Mary, they take on the world's conventions, invite the world in, and then say, "but God." To illustrate how sacralization of the secular shows itself, I turn to the presentation and performance of contemporary Marys (and a few other expected and unexpected artists) in Black popular culture.

Mary, Don't You Weep

The public dynamic between Erica and Tina Campbell resembles the biblical relationship of Martha and Mary of Bethany. The Bible's New Testament Luke, chapter 10,[18] centers the story of two sisters and their effort and equity of work for Jesus. According to the text (and interpretations), Jesus comes to visit their home and preparations commence to welcome him properly with a meal. Yet Martha is unhappy, pissed even, that her sister Mary hangs out and talks with Jesus while she slaves in the kitchen preparing food for him and his crew. Martha works while Mary appears to chill and do the unthinkable, sit at his feet and learn. Despite her lack of work contribution, the Luke text infers that Mary's choice to live her best life, to get the best part of Jesus's visit, endures as the better one, regardless of the gendered cultural context of the period. The scriptures highlight inequitable labor, the roles and restrictions of women, and a discernment and privileging of self for these sisters.

Erica (Atkins) Campbell and (Trecina) Tina (Atkins) Campbell grew up in Inglewood, California, with seven other siblings and very active church parents. Born in the 1970s but children of the 1980s and 1990s, the Black church cultivates the girls' singing talent, receiving recognition by gospel outlets such as *Bobby*

Mary Mary in their "God in Me" music video (2008).

Jones Gospel on BET. Before their entertainment industry big break, they performed with traveling gospel theater shows, sang backup for several R&B artists, and wrote songs for gospel star Yolanda Adams and others.

In 1998, they emerged as gospel recording sister duo Mary Mary, choosing their group's name from two of the Bible's women, Mary the mother of Jesus and Mary Magdalene. Though beginning their careers in R&B, the sisters became uncomfortable with that genre of music as it conflicted with their very religious upbringing. Said Tina Campbell in a 2010 interview: "I'm not against music that isn't Gospel. I listen to all kinds of music. All of it is a part of my life, but there are some things that are inappropriate. If you consider yourself to be a Christian, there are some areas that you should limit. There are types of music that we shouldn't be singing because it might affect our witness. . . . [Now, as Mary Mary] we are singing about Jesus."[19] Erica Campbell added: "You can't do everything, but everything that is not inside these church walls is not wrong. And the people that will not come in the church, how will you ever talk to them? How will you let them know about God? Not just who He is inside the church building, but let them know about who God is—His greatness and all that He can do for you—if you never go where they are?"[20] Thus, moving into gospel full-time, they bring with them an articulated Judeo-Christian–based love of God alongside a hip-hop and R&B energy.

Over their career, the Mary Mary duo has recorded six studio, one Christmas, and one compilation album. They have released ten music videos and won four Grammy and eighteen Stellar Awards.[21] Music historian Tammy Kernodle believes Mary Mary replicates the highly successful gospel-singing Clark Sisters' formula of "powerful vocals, stellar production, and glamorous stage presence," and thus find success with multiple audiences—traditional, contemporary, secular, and young.[22] From 2007 to 2019, they intermittently served as judges on BET's *Sunday Best* gospel singing competition series. In this role, audiences came to understand their personalities and different ways of seeing the world and work of God.[23] They starred in WE tv's reality series *Mary Mary* (2012–2017), appeared as the first gospel act on the main stage at the Essence Music Festival in 2012, and involved themselves in myriad other extracurricular professional activities that helped facilitate and expand the Mary Mary brand.[24] This brand requires that they operate in between reality and fiction, between the sacred and the secular.

Go Get It! Performing for the Lord

Mary Mary presents audiences with everyday entanglements of faith walks. In their musicality and in their public engagements (concerts, interviews, reality show), they perform the tension between holiness and the world. Achieving on this tightrope makes for a special kind of precarious sacralizing of the secular but also forces a grappling with tensions inherently manifest (if not always overtly) in the walks of people who rep God. Performance studies frameworks can help unpack how secular spaces get transformed and impacted by sacred presences.[25] For example, scholar Dwight Conquergood argues that the accomplishments of artistic performance and the remaking of culture and creativity should meld with scholars' analysis by knowing, understanding, and incorporating audience, form, and authorial presence.[26]

Mary Mary's "God in Me" music video provides one illustration of the tension between and confluence of the sacred and the secular. The song itself bumps hard on R&B and R&B oldies radio stations. Released in 2008 on their fifth CD, *The Sound*, the song peaked at number sixty-eight on the Billboard 100 chart. It won song of the year at the twenty-fifth annual Stellar Awards in 2010 and spent seventy-six weeks on the Billboard Hot R&B/Hip-Hop Songs chart, peaking at number five.[27] It charted number one for Hot Gospel Songs and Hot Dance Club Play lists simultaneously.

The hook of "God in Me" sells it. After they discuss fans' perceptions of how a person looks, what they own, where they've been that "gets a lot of shine," the duo sings about what they do at home once the doors are closed. Mary Mary reflect, "what they can't see is you're on your knees" praying. Thus, they claim that what admirers envision as success is really favor, the "God in me." While the lyrics are undeniably Christian, the beat and the look of the music video obfuscate what the duo promote—Jesus or just deserts.

The music video aesthetics of this monster hit replicates pop culture's best—using the latest techniques in music video production. Set on a 2009 New York fashion runway, the singers perform "God in Me" with Kierra "KiKi" Sheard (of the gospel-singing Clark Sisters family), attend, and model in the fashion show. Mostly Black and Latino hip-hop artists, moguls, models, and movie stars convene, presumably to look at the newest designer clothes, drink champagne, and live the life befitting those newly arrived and still reveling in their success and individuality. The flashy video frames the gospel of Jesus for millennials with rapid editing, a preponderance of recognizable hip-hop, R&B, and gospel performers, high fashion, and a bumping, synthesized bass beat and hook. "God in Me" pushes Jesus up front by bringing the message outside the church to places where people can hear it—inside the club, the barbershop, and urban radio—high secular places with low sacred intentions. But the presentation of this sacralized secular format allows questioning believers and nonbelievers to encounter the Christian God with limited effort and a cultivated feeling of commonality, without fear of recrimination. This approach captures young people who have been moving away from traditional Black church. Mary Mary helps usher in a sacralized secular performance style alongside hip-hop gospel pioneer Kirk Franklin and, later, rappers such as Kanye West, Lecrae, and Kendrick Lamar.

Beginning in March 2012, *Mary Mary* the reality series chronicled the respective homes, careers, and family lives of the Mary Mary singing sisters. The sisters exhibit a Martha and Mary confidence in mediating their lives through this WE

TV reality series. In the Bible, Martha works in the necessary ways women must to take care of business, while Mary of Bethany operates with not only conviction but also insight. Although aware of her prescribed role, this Mary knows what she wants and fears not seeking the word of God nor having a conversation with God's son. While she walks in the flesh, she possesses the potential to exist and live in the spirit. Mary and her sister Martha demonstrate faith, and their faith walk matches their actions. Because of the unique positioning of Erica and Tina as Mary Mary, their fame within this series resonates differently than other types of celebrities similarly situated.

Media scholar Peter Lunt characterizes the relationship of reality television and celebrity as banal or thin, without the structure and tensions of traditional stardom. He writes: "This lack of tension reduces the 'aura' around the celebrity and we are left with a simulation of celebrity or quasi-celebrity."[28] And when it comes to Black television reality fame, as film and media scholar Racquel Gates asserts, the fight against a perceived ratchetness borders audience expectation—a perception denying cast members' work, labor, and potential agency.[29] Yet from their gospel singing career, the Campbell women bring "legitimated" fame to their series, disrupting the typical reality "star" introduction to the public. They exemplify and demonstrate a call on their lives—a spiritual call that encourages them to sing, perform, and evangelize. And because Black audiences recognize and authorize their talent, they present a fascinating reality hybrid of celebrity and commonality—again, the betwixt and between.

Like all reality series, the program's editing heightens dramatic impact. Tina Campbell, the younger of the two sisters, wants her way and seems to get it often, behaving in almost complete oblivion to the needs of others. In a 2013 interview she remarks: "Though we would all like to pretend to be super-sanctified. . . . We're first natural, then spiritual. So, there's a lot of natural things that people have that don't have anything to do with promoting the message of God that we can all relate to, and we have to address that part of our lives."[30] For example, after discovering the multiple infidelities of her husband, Tina begins to incorporate her pain and confusion into the televised narrative—both as a flesh and spiritual battle and a financial move. Television and film scholar Kristen J. Warner believes Black women on reality television in general must continually "convince their producers that they have story lines and, to some degree, a measure of wealthy accoutrements that make them interesting enough to film."[31] When Tina appears on stage (in performance and on screen), she discusses her struggles. When she interviews on radio, she talks about it. And in season four, she puts on a one-woman show showcasing new music and a book written during this period about her overcoming the betrayal through forgiveness. By season five, she and Teddy, her husband, begin a tour together chronicling their suffering and redemption journey.

In *Mary Mary* the television series, audiences confront the grappling of both sides of Tina. She, like Mary of Bethany, exhibits seeming personal inconsistencies of walk, talk, and responsibility but still appears as one full of righteousness and grace. Townes defines grace as "the gift of unmerited favor from God and [suggests believers understand] how this gift provides guidelines for living in which we must open up our hearts and lives to others with charity and understanding."[32] In the case of Mary of Bethany, she listens to Jesus, offers him the best, and challenges but firmly believes. She is a woman confronted with the sexist and problematic norms of the day but willing to extend them to get what she needs—grace. In the narrativized case and lives of Tina and Erica Campbell, audiences witness similar trials and the grace that follows.

Not allowing for the denigration and acrimony most African-American television reality series encourage (e.g., *The Real Housewives of Atlanta*, *Love & Hip Hop*, *Basketball Wives*, *Sisters in Law*, *The Sisterhood*, *Love & Marriage*, etc.),[33] *Mary Mary* constructs a semisacred, separate reality universe. To be sure, the series adheres to reality show genre conventions, with cliffhangers, parallel dramas, and confessions. However, the confessions appear as always relational (meaning, not solely for the production, production teams, and larger audience). They handle cliffhangers with minimal televised drama and quickly. And the conflict typically revolves around work ethic, the balance of family and fame, and management conflict. No gendered or familial brawling allowed. The series mixes media and mediated platforms simultaneously: music, music video, live performance, recordings, book publication, video production, and the doubling down of reality watching reality on tape when the Campbell sisters watch the series alongside the at-home audience and critique it. They offer (and demonstrate) a particular kind of additional reading and understanding of their sacralizing brand.

Scott Collins, executive vice president of advertising sales for WE tv, describes series such as *Mary Mary* as "positive, uplifting, family image-themed shows that are a good environment for all brands."[34] On Thursday night, the night *Mary Mary* aired, WE tv hosts a female audience with a median age of 38.5. Adds Collins: "We over-index in households where women bring in the larger of the paycheck," married or not, and Thursday nights target African-American women he describes as an "underserved audience on television . . . [but one that is] very desirable for advertisers."[35] In its fifth season, advertisers (Pantene, T.J. Maxx, Quaker Oats, Skechers, Tracfone, KFC) clearly recognize the specific demographic who enjoy and watch the series. Each Campbell sister mediates the spirit of God and media—meaning, they illustrate a blended secular and sacredness through their appearance on reality television, their music, the extratextual materials that come from them, the branding of their series, and their name.

By the nature of what their careers suggest, repping God, discourses of authenticity dominate their imaging. Respectability politics play out here, even if not as much as in other Black women's narrative events. *Mary Mary* patterns its content to the expectations of what God presumably wants for their lived context.

Thus, the framing of the reality series is shifted due to its overtly religious foundation. After all, the sisters choose this path and walk a line not only fraught
with potential personal and career pitfalls, but also one that constantly challenges
their faith and honest reflection of their love of God as manifest in behavior,
actions, and embodied and mediated presences. When Tina loses almost all her
"celebrity religion"[36] in season four with her discovery of Teddy's actions, the network carefully walks audiences through her battle with anger, unforgiveness,
pain, and confusion alongside the reality show producer, camera operators, and
audio engineer, who are "conveniently" present to witness her collapse. Like Mary
of Bethany, whose emotional register runs both high and low as her described
different dealings with Jesus suggest, Tina Campbell allows the full weight of
her inner turmoil to be articulated for audiences (redacted by what the Campbells agree to show).

This Is Where I'm From

Unlike most reality series starring African-American women, *Mary Mary* taped
in Los Angeles as opposed to Atlanta. Los Angeles exists as a place of possibilities but one that squarely centers fame and fortune as the payoff. Los Angeles
visions secularity—open to all modes of expression—bodily, intimate, and
spiritual. Since the second wave of the Great Migration in the 1940s, African-
Americans have helped shape this city,[37] which now hosts several Black megachurches that appear to pray at the altar of Hollywood—merging sex, success,
and salvation as featured in series such as Oxygen's *Preachers of L.A.* This hometown of the Campbell women impacts how they understand the world and what
God's blessings look like. Audiences see these Los Angelinos in conversations
about remodeling the pool for $60,000, trips to various cities worldwide, with
costs often split between artists and venue, and birthday parties with recognizable and popular Black entertainers. Yet unlike other representations of
celebrities, *Mary Mary* gets taken up differently because of their self-proclaimed
commitment to God and His word in this sacralized secular milieu.

   While many write about Mary of Bethany, her sister Martha, on the other
hand, wrestles with the burden of unrecognized and seemingly unappreciated
responsibility, obligation, and potential frustration and anger. Like many women,
Black women who remain to pick up the pieces, support emotionally, financially,
and physically without ceasing (and often for children not their own), defer their
own plans, hopes, and potentialities, Martha gets cast as the one who doesn't
know better, who fails to make the best choice. Jesus assails her with "Martha,
Martha," a reprimand, after her requests to make Mary help. This part of the
Martha and Mary dynamic lives powerfully and proves instructive for the ideas
of the secular, the sacred, and Mary Mary as well.

   Within the public narrative, Erica Campbell functions very much as Martha—
equally talented, gifted, and hungry. Yet her shine, at least on its initial public

face, dims in comparison to her sister Tina. However, she appears steadfast in supporting, even as shown angry, feeling ignored and neglected, and continues to build. While the biblical account neglects to show the end of Mary and Martha's lives, audiences see what becomes of the Campbell sisters in *Mary Mary*. In 2019, Tina Campbell continued to produce music and write, while Erica Campbell hosted a nationally syndicated Urban One radio show, appeared on a reality series with her husband and family (2018), received a 2014 solo artist Grammy and a 2023 nomination, and published a book in 2019. Erica as Martha got busy earning her merited grace. And because the sisters together operate in suspension—as cushion, as prevention, and as musical discord—they demonstrate the fallacy of a sacred and secular divide. They anthropomorphize a yin and yang.

Invoking the tweet by Erica Campbell as the choir marched in, the Campbell women negotiate #spiritual, #carnal. Erica and Tina grew up in a ritual of Black church environment that still maintains a certain decorum and expectation of its members—a desire for things to happen "decently and in order." The respectability politics Black women and men contend with continue to exist as Mary Mary operate within its framework. And because they bring the sacred with them, they sacralize the secular, the public popular culture, and the places they go. They strive not for perfection but for grace. Their operation in multiple secular places provides one demonstration of the sacralization of the secular. Artist Mary J. Blige provides a different path toward the same phenomenon.

The Lie of Mary: Mary Magdalene and Mary J. Blige

Mary Magdalene[38] stands as one of the most recognized biblical Marys—not due to her virtue but because of her association with vice. According to scripture, she

Mary J. Blige in her "Just Fine" music video (2007).

comes to God through the mercy of Jesus himself. Luke 8:1–3 says Mary rides with a group of women healed by Jesus of various illnesses and demon possession. She becomes one of the women who follow and minister to Jesus and who, as Luke writes, help "to support [him and his crew] out of their own means."[39]

Several accounts of the role and work of Mary Magdalene endure in the Bible's New Testament—specifically in the gospels of Matthew, Mark, Luke, and John. Despite the never-ending assertion that Mary Magdalene works as a prostitute who anoints Jesus with oil, no biblical basis for this claim exists.[40] Many argue when reading her actions after the crucifixion, one may (re)think of her as not only a woman of character but also as a leader among women. Yet Magdalene's significance receives limited acknowledgment, her sacredness sidestepped or obliterated in favor of the narrative of her purported illegal and immoral sexuality.

Religion scholar and pastor Renita Weems characterizes Mary's life this way:

> Imagine: Here was an otherwise gifted, intelligent, bright, charismatic woman living in a society which had no place for gifted, intelligent, bright, charismatic women. Like many women today, Mary's emotional and physical infirmities were probably symptomatic of the stresses she was forced to live with on a daily basis. . . . When we live under circumstances and within relationships that are hostile to our talents, we find our contributions ignored, our possibilities limited, and our dreams under constant attack. . . . Indeed, the "demons" that claimed Mary are the same demons that prey on many of us: depression, fear, low self-esteem, doubts, procrastination, bitterness, and self-pity.[41]

The truth of Magdalene sits at the heart of the sacredness and profanity lie. Many already assert, as I have as well, that the juxtaposition of the two is a false dichotomy. In looking at the center of the Judeo-Christian tradition, where a woman bears a child (without a physical man) and with the Mother/Father God, she becomes not only the giver of life and the savior's light but also the direct path to salvation. As Sojourner Truth intoned in her famous speech: "Where did your Christ come from? From God and a woman! Man had nothing to do with him."[42] Brandishing women with a label of ill repute serves to suture men in, to make them relevant to the salvific process. Black popular culture wrestles with this concretized and ingrained framework especially in relation to Black women.

Mary Jane Blige entered mainstream consciousness under this Magdalene blight and developed into the hip-hop poster child for womanist survival. She becomes a part of U.S. consciousness through her pain and round-the-way girl approach to singing. Introduced by Sean Puffy (P-Diddy, Diddy) Combs, then Uptown Records President Andre Harrell dubbed her Queen of Hip-hop Soul for her raw singing style and her problems. Blige's blend of hip-hop and R&B recalls the blend of R&B and gospel—the soul-stirring and toe-tingling sound of which, in the beginning, caused considerable consternation (and undercover pleasure) to Black religious communities, as previously articulated through artists such as Sam Cooke, Aretha Franklin, Al Green, Marvin Gaye, and even Teddy Pendergrass.

Her 1992 debut album *What's the 4-1-1* peaked at number six on the Billboard 200 chart. It topped R&B charts, spawning six singles. Some fans recall her emergence as the "ghetto girl who [can] sing."[43] Her Yonkers, New York, upbringing included considerable church attendance. Moreover, like the characterization of Mary Magdalene, Blige came into public consciousness as seriously disconnected emotionally, physically, and spiritually. Yet her connection to Christianity seems always present, just below the unpolished and left of respectable exterior.

While others penned her initial album, Blige has written or co-written many of her lyrics since. Over her career, she has garnered over a hundred wins and two hundred music nominations, including her nine Grammy Awards, four American Music Awards, six Soul Train Music Awards, twelve Billboard Music Awards, six ASCAP Pop Music Awards, four ASCAP Rhythm & Soul Awards, six BET Awards, one MTV Video Music Award, and ten NAACP Image Awards. She became a two-time Oscar nominee for the 2017 film *Mudbound* (Rees) and earned a 2019 BET Lifetime Achievement Award. She commands center billing, as evidenced in her routinely closing the annual Essence Music Festival in New Orleans, one of the highest-grossing music festivals for that city.[44]

In 2013, Blige released her first Christmas CD, *A Mary Christmas*. In the liner notes, she begins with the requisite: "First I would like to thank God, my lord and savior Jesus Christ for the gifts and talents and opportunity to make my 1st ever Christmas album."[45] This recording became a part of a Christmas special shown Thanksgiving 2013 on the REVOLT TV music network owned formerly by Diddy and Harrell. Harrell reminisced on the development of Blige over her twenty-five-plus year career:

> What we were able to do was frame her honesty. She was feeling unloved and it was during the era of the crack generation. A lot of parents were not involved with their kids in a certain way, and daughters especially were growing up feeling unloved, and didn't really have a good relationship with men. So, we just framed that with the music of that time, and at that time R&B was dying out for young teenagers and New Jack Swing had [come]. So, we took from New Jack Swing, and Mary's voice was such a soulful voice that we knew we had to put soul into New Jack Swing, and it ended up graduating into Hip-Hip Soul. So, Mary J. Blige became the Queen of Hip-Hop Soul, and that was basically a whole generation's take on R&B. So, her graduating to singing a Christmas jazz album produced by David Foster is just a testament to the fact that she's such a great vocalist that she can move through time effortlessly.[46]

Beyond her vocal ability, it speaks also to her ability to sacralize the secular and make the need for the division disappear.

Ride or Die or Let Me Ride: Mary and Public Memory

A narrative of abuse (both drug and physical), dependence, and bad behavior undergirds the persistent public understanding of Mary J. Blige. Often labeled a "diva," but not so much for her phenomenal performance abilities as for her actions and choices, this construction frames how critics and audiences interpret her music and contributions to culture. In writing about Mary Magdalene, public memory, and the many erroneous and fictionalized historic accounts of her life with Jesus, rhetoric scholar Tammie Kennedy interprets how public memory functions to secure a consistent idea of Mary Magdalene as a whore against that of her as an apostle—in fact, one who serves as an apostle to the apostles. Kennedy argues: "While popular culture offers an arena for resisting the hegemony of remembering practices . . . the consequences of misremembering are especially salient for those figures marginalized by gender, class, and sexuality, as well as for those who seek a more expansive, nuanced representation in public memory."[47]

Like this remembering (or misremembering) of Mary Magdalene and the overwhelming desire to discredit her sacredness, Blige is positioned as a woman who will sacrifice herself for whomever. From her music, audiences understand that she is down for whatever man, come hell or high water. For example, women's studies scholar Treva Lindsey analyzes the lyrics in Blige's song "Love No Limit" through the framework of ride or die as a "distinct heteronormative politics that privileges male pleasure."[48] Not unlike similar secular narratives positioning women's need to tolerate almost anything, "No Limit" presents Blige as sex positive while also potentially reifying "the controlling image of the hypersexual [B]lack woman/Jezebel."[49] Both Lindsey and Kennedy critique the popular assessments of Marys new and old as delimiting their value to humanity. These Marys live in a suspension of disdain. Moreover, other scholars, such as cultural historian Saidiya Hartman and American studies scholar La Marr Jurelle Bruce, suggest that the replication and mass dissemination of Blige's suffering (along with other Black women artists like her) create a "spectacular character of Black suffering" that "coarsens audiences to the lived reality of such pain, romanticizes and aestheticizes that pain, invites audiences' narcissistic projections onto it, and fetishizes it for voyeuristic consumption."[50] These prevailing counternarratives complicate the ability to discuss how Mary J. Blige actually sacralizes the secular. Nevertheless, she absolutely finds ways to use her seeming secularized and disreputable self for sacred spiritual purposes.

Like a Bridge over Troubled Water

Working alongside men, Black women often receive scant recognition for their contributions. Yet within and outside of church, they physically and spiritually transform internal and external lives. Aligning biblical workers to

African-American women historically making a difference, Weems writes: "Like their sisters of antiquity—Mary Magdalene, Joanna, Susanna, and the others—[Black women such as Ida Barnett Wells and Nannie Helen Burroughs] contented themselves with living on the periphery of authorized ministry, despite the fact that their labors impacted the heart of the movement."[51] Although emerging on the scene over thirty years ago, Blige continues to supply a balm in Gilead, representing "the people." For example, her "Whole Damn Year" (2014) recording lyrically manifests the pain, duration, and consequences of domestic abuse of women and gay men. In stark black and white, the accompanying music video showcases women and men from various ethnic groups and ages who live this pain, their truth, and recovery. The testimony she makes constantly through song embodies her everywoman positioning. The same impetus returns with her 2023 Grammy-nominated *Good Morning Gorgeous* recording. Blige remains a round-the-way girl, the common chick with whom many continue to identify and use for edification and inspiration.

To be sure, Blige works in the realm of the secular. Her music foregrounds hetero (and sexist) tensions and drama women negotiate—women who frequently get the short end of the relationship stick. Yet, Lindsey believes, "Blige invites her audience into both her world and the narrative space of [B]lack women's interiority."[52] She suggests Blige offers spirituality "as a weapon against the obstacles African American women confront.... [She] rearticulates the necessity of freedom, peace, faith, and joy for African American women's survival. The sacred is privileged as a site of possibility and of unconditional love."[53] Her connection to the sacred, her interior monologue and external dialogue, presume a certain move of the spirit (if tilted toward classist and patriarchal manifestations). This evidence comes through her invocation of God and the ways in which, over time, audiences see her transform—not just in terms of maturity, but also with her outward God walk. These are expressed in her recordings and reach into other types of performance,[54] consistent changes (body strengthening,[55] abandonment of addictive substances and abusive men), and upper-class associations.[56] Some might argue she transforms toward Christ, others toward capitalism. Perhaps it reflects a bit of both. But with the sacralizing of the secular, the two go hand in hand.

This outward face shows in her performances as well. For example, African-American studies scholar Daphne Brooks places Blige in conversation with protest through her body, voice, and testimony. She uses Blige's performance with Bono at the 2005 *Shelter from the Storm* telethon for Hurricane Katrina relief as evidence of her significance in this regard. For Brooks, Blige stands in the gap for all Black women. She writes: "Offkey ... Blige's performance reminds us of the ways that the [B]lack singing voice is not confined to the ethereal netherworld.... Indeed, her rendition of this song ... [allows] her instead to enter in the flesh into the public conversation to which she has been denied access."[57] This assessment of Blige's powerful vocal presence rings true in her other duets with artists such as Andrea Bocelli singing "Bridge Over Troubled Water" (2009) or even with Lauryn Hill in "I Used to Love Him" (1998), where her gospel background, life travails, and public memory marshal together to elevate and sacralize the secular platforms in which these songs originate.

In 2015, Apple Music began running a series of commercials capitalizing on Blige's continuing narrative aura and featured Blige with actors Kerry Washington and Taraji P. Henson as girlfriends. In this commercial series, Apple Music (and director Ava DuVernay) asked these Black women to illustrate their lives—history, events, and ways of being—through song. Blige's selections included music from back in the day (Slick Rick) but also "heartbreak recovery" music. She says for real: "It takes a lot of courage to wish a man well. . . . This is when you're done," as she plays Adele's "Someone Like You." She achieves a heartbroken, just-need-Jesus girl glow-up with an all-white, immaculate, and beautiful home, celebrity friends, and a commercial plug. Blige's downtrodden and wronged positioning juxtaposed against her magnificent "now" self not only magnifies her connection to those in need, to those at the bottom rungs of America's racial-gendered-socioeconomic ladder, but also to those who connect directly with God (often one and the same people). God's grace and promise (alongside the capitalist narrative of uplift) find illustration in Blige's faithfulness and success. She embodies what poet Essex Hemphill suggests might be the standard for Blackness—the ghetto Black American Express card that gives you access to all inner-city things cool and hip and real coupled with an American, secular pull yourself up by the bootstraps mantra.[58] Despite this come-up, sociologists Vaughn Schmutz and Alison Faupel argue Blige sustains an inability to be musically consecrated in contemporary secular terms.

Cultural consecration venerates "a select few cultural creators or works that are worthy of particular admiration in contrast to the multitude that are not."[59] Meaning, even "when women [achieve] consecration in popular music, the ways in which their inclusion is legitimated draws on existing frameworks about gender that emphasize female dependency in contrast with male agency. In subtle ways, this gendered discourse limits the amount and types of critical legitimacy female artists can accrue."[60] Blige's anointing as Queen of Hip-Hop Soul fails to place her on par with her male contemporaries. The most profound narratives about her, including most of her lyrics, are dominated by women-identified concerns and shortcomings. In other words, Blige's status, her cred, emanates from and gets limited by gender. Nonetheless, this theory fails to undermine her ability to sacralize the secular and reflects a larger move in Black popular culture. Black woman's bodily sacredness makes for a transformative experience within the secular entertainment realm—for both the artist and the audience. Similar to the ways performance studies scholar E. Patrick Johnson suggests Black gay men "refuse to be held to the conventions of and limitations placed upon the [B]lack body in the [B]lack church," Blige and these men proclaim "'I'll shout right here,' in this space—this 'secular' space—that I call home."[61] Mary J. Blige stands and continues to, as Kirk Franklin would say, "shout right now!"

Take the Shackles Off My Feet . . .

In both her *A Mary Christmas* and 2015 *The London Sessions* releases, Blige reimagines common perceptions of herself, her talents, and her staying power by tapping into other aspects of her secular and sacred brand. One way she begins to do this is by explicitly expressing her sacred connections. Listening to her discography online as well as hearing it on radio, audiences chart her growth. She said in a November 2014 interview: "I am a soldier. . . . I come through it. I am a phoenix. I rise through the ashes and here I am. . . . I have been chosen to do this job. And now I serve people. I am nothing but a servant and they see that."[62] Blige changes the ways she presents herself publicly and the kind of music she performs. As well, her mediated personal drama receives less billing.[63] Her moves reflect similar ones made by other Black, existing-in-between artists as they embrace their sacralized secular.

For example, 1980s and 1990s hip-hop and pop artists such as the rap group Salt-N-Pepa, rapper Kurtis Blow, and even Prince use part of their public platforms to shout out God in the twenty-first century. In fact, they straddle a new fence—between secularity and religious evangelism. Evangelism's global resurgence across communities and mediums over the past fifty years champions repping God in all places, all the time. Many artists take the Psalmist's words, "I will bless the Lord at all times. His name will continually be in my mouth," quite literally into their performances.[64] In Salt-N-Pepa's first, brief VH-1 reality series (2007–2008) and on tour, (and prior to Salt's 2018 divorce), she talks about her relationship to God, refuses to perform certain songs from their catalog, and shouts praises to God during live performances. She incorporates acknowledgment of Him in song where it wasn't prior. In another case, rapper Snoop Dogg released his thirty-two-track *Snoop Dogg Presents Bible of Love* in 2018 (with Mary Mary as one of several gospel guest artists featured).[65] Rapper/minister Kurtis Blow (Walker) reflects: "The music biz is really a spiritual business, whether we know it or not."[66]

Beyond this evangelizing trend, musical artists sacralize formerly secular ground by spiritually narrating the human condition. In the past, songs such as Marvin Gaye's "What's Going On" (1971) made political critical commentary by way of God. As Gaye calls to mother and father, he returns to a mother-father God need for understanding. Erykah Badu's catalog incorporates reflections and adherence to a God presence and a need for renewal. In her 2000 first top-ten release "Bag Lady," for example, the music video moves in and out of an actual church with Black women colorfully attired, fanning, and angelically mouthing "oh" as Badu sings about the bags women carry (including serving as punching bags, alcoholism, body shaming, and drug abuse). D'Angelo, Kendrick Lamar, and Chance the Rapper use their musical genius within neo-soul, rap, and hip-hop to incorporate their faith understandings onto human rights violations, general Black suffering, and police brutality.[67] Every interstice of Beyoncé's visual album and film *Lemonade* (HBO, 2016) focuses on a connection and communion with God and Black women. The "illuminati mess" she and her husband Shawn Carter (Jay-Z) dismiss suggests to audiences and fans they should really know her heart and commitment to Christianity. In the "Formation" music video specifically, one location of the ladies' consciousness raising is a Black Pentecostal church. As a Black male preaches, the Black women of the church shout bodily to the bass beat of Beyoncé slaying.[68] And even Childish Gambino's (Donald Glover) "Black ass"[69] 2018 music video for "This Is America" connects atrocities of church shootings and random gun murders of students with the rhythms, dance, and religiosity of Africa and the Caribbean.[70] These musicians, marching into the listening pleasure and lives of primarily Black audiences (or certainly directed toward them), reify the Marys' demonstration of a normalized sacralized secular.

We Can Church Anything

Beyond the world of music, film, and television, digital technologies widen the door for a multiplicity of voices to enliven Black secular online and streaming spaces with a bit of sacredness. The subhead for this section comes from James Finley and his singing Chorale. Finley, a comedian and talented gospel musician, forges these disparate passions by remixing children's television theme songs with a gospel inflection, like the Nickelodeon series *Dora the Explorer* and PBS's *Reading Rainbow*. He uses these opportunities to entertain believers with what they are already familiar with and to evangelize about Jesus to those who are not. In one of the online versions of the Chorale's performance at an actual church, Finley analogizes *Dora*'s fox character Swiper as another name for the devil operating problematically in people's lives. The choir sings, "Swiper (Swiper won't), win this time (win this time)." The call and response and dance of the choir infuse Black church into an animated children's television theme song. With over 100,000 views on YouTube, perhaps more than the faithful engage this work.[71]

This sort of sacred incursion into the secular inserts itself into all sorts of digital configurations. For example, along with his soulful backup singers, old-school R&B crooner Charlie Wilson creates a *Tiny Desk Concert* church in his appearance on their online series. He sings/preaches about his fall and redemption when he taps into a higher power.[72] The Hamiltones, the background singers for R&B crooner Anthony Hamilton, routinely craft beautiful gospel harmonies from the most random, and dare say I profane, acts of popular culture. For example, an online favorite revisits rapper Birdman's clap back to the syndicated *Breakfast Club* radio hosts in 2016. Angry about the ways in which the radio DJs have, in his mind, disparaged his name, he curses them out and abruptly leaves the studio without being interviewed.[73] The Hamiltones took this incident, crafted a harmonized gospel rendition of it, and uploaded it to You-Tube three days later. The over one million viewers not only gave them mad props for the ditty but also recognized the sacralized secular. For example, Shawnee H. comments: "They make me want to go to church and dance at the hole in the wall all at the same time!"[74] Another tune they constructed, gospel rhythms and all, addresses former presidential candidate Donald Trump's taped recording suggesting men should aggressively grab women. With a rare disclaimer of their feelings about their work and encouraging citizens to vote for Hillary Clinton, the song's chorus admonishes to not vote for Donald Trump because he will grab your pussy.[75] In digital, streamed, and televisual spaces, male dancers praise God on the pole, memes and GIFs connect praise and Blackness, and audiences forever love Ruby (Jenifer Lewis) calling on "Black Jesus" in the television sitcom *black-ish* (ABC, 2014–2022). But despite this surge, many Christians and non-Christians alike mentally still separate church-house praise from the everyday, even as sacredness and spirituality mediate everywhere around their secular pop lives.

No More Drama

The pregnant possibilities of contemporary Marys and others like them reside in a recognized and celebrated humanity. An artist bringing the sacred into the secular realm broadens the road of compassion, demonstrates humility and fallibility, and recognizes stray paths. When these things happen, one can still fall before God and be forgiven. Grace. Bringing the sacred to the secular is not easy and is fraught with many pitfalls and potential side roads. The highest climbers have fallen the hardest.[76] Easter Sunday 2014, Pastor Shawn Anglim of First Grace United Methodist Church in New Orleans talked about Mary Magdalene as resurrected. Putting her in conversation with Janis Joplin, he suggested that as crazy as Mary is, having been possessed of seven demons, she is probably Jesus's best disciple. Like Mary Magdalene, hip-hop and R&B singer Mary J. Blige signifies many things simultaneously: disrespect and hurt alongside prestige and redemption. And according to both Marys' narratives, Jesus takes away that hurt. This enables the women to hear His message, heal their souls, and begin to spread the good news. The synergy of the considered sacred and profane produces not only profit but also a strategic entryway and platform for audiences to know Christ, Allah, Yahweh, and the Mother-Father-God of the ancients. It inserts women, not as an afterthought, acquiescence, or plus one, but as central to the creation and salvation story.

Already present before the pandemic, a need for connection, community, and grounding continues to grow among people. New and increased technology use make people simultaneously more linked and more siloed, allowing people to exist virtually everywhere but really exist (and by extension belong) nowhere. The problematic binaries of hopelessness and hope, sacred and secular, Jesus and Hennessy call people to rethink potential synergies, discrepancies, and meaning for their coexistence as well as a will to choose another path. Pastor Anglim believes power lies in people finding their voice. He suggests: "The further you get away from the Marys of the world, the more strange and distant her words sound in Luke."[77] When artists such as Mary Mary and Mary J. Blige offer their talents as God-given and represent God in their own unique ways, they allow for a larger swath of individuals to see, hear, and potentially take up a sacred spirituality. Because of their careers and their grace, they best operate in the space between the secular and the sacred. And when notions of sacredness universally expand, little comes from reiterating the distinctions between the secular and the sacred.[78]

This new normal offers an opportunity for young girls, Black girls, and others who watch and listen to them, to situate their stresses, successes, drama, and aspirations within the cut and know by example, grace can surely follow. Many scholar-sistahs argue, I am my sister's keeper. And as such, we recognize the importance of keeping "dialectical relationships with other sisters" in order to "dialogue, to affirm, to exhort, and to admonish each other verbally and non-verbally."[79] While the combination of Jesus and Hennessy, as found on Lecrae's track "Indwelling Sin," offers temptation and the potential for downfall, Marys of old and creative Marys of the new traverse this ground and demonstrate the possibility of another interpretation in between.

Prayer of Confession

I do believe; help me overcome
my unbelief.
—Mark 9:24

As for Me and My House . . .

. . . .

Spike Lee's Negotiation
with Christianity as a Sign
of Blackness

During a pivotal scene from the podium in Spike Lee's *Malcolm X* (1992), Malcolm (Denzel Washington) rebukes the gathered Harlem crowd: "Ya been had! Ya been took! Ya been hoodwinked! Bamboozled! Led astray! Run amok! This is what he does." The very next cut leads to the inside of a theater-like space where three banners hang proclaiming "There is No God but Allah," "Muhammad is His Apostle," and "We Must Create Our Own Empowerment." While Malcolm references the white man in his speech, his assertions address Christianity as well. In the fictional works of Spike Lee, the confluence of blackness, Christianity, and the home space tend to equal disruption, confusion, and sometimes death. I argue that Lee constructs "authentic" Blackness, in its most radical and sincere form, as antithetical to Christianity. Moreover, Christianity's presence, especially in the home, not only evokes violence but also psychologically destroys the race.

Lee's substantial filmography addresses many of his seeming preoccupations, with different themes capturing his imagination such as New York (the setting of most of his full-length narrative films), sports (*He Got Game*, *Jim Brown: All American*, *Spike Lee's Lil Joints*), the south and HBCU experiences (*School Daze* and *Crooklyn*), real-time living while Black (*4 Little Girls*, *When the Levees Broke: A Requiem in Four Acts*, *If God Is Willing and da Creek Don't Rise*, and

Get on the Bus), and male-conceived women's empowerment (*She's Gotta Have It, Girl 6, She Hate Me, Chi-Raq*, and *She's Gotta Have It* remixed on Netflix). Yet, as a teacher and scholar who for over twenty years has taught and written about the works of Spike Lee, I know his understated yet constant grappling with religion receives only limited attention. Lee's struggle with religion gets expressed in nearly all his work in some way—generally pejoratively. In his early films, *Jungle Fever, Malcolm X, Crooklyn, He Got Game*, and even *Joe's Bed-Stuy Barbershop: We Cut Heads* (his master's thesis film), this tension manifests. But before 2012, he failed to take up religion directly or in a sustained manner—that is, until *Red Hook Summer*.

Scholars and journalists write prolifically on Lee's filmic relationship to larger cultural preoccupations such as Blackness, patriarchy, and women. Lubiano (1991), hooks (1996), Massood (2003), Smith-Shomade (2008), Cobb and Jackson (2009), and Bowdre (2016)[1] all question the ways in which his films define and confine Black women as well as merge masculinist discourses with ideals of Blackness. Early on, literary scholar Wahneema Lubiano called into question the lauding of Lee in "comparison to what" and suggests that for a filmmaker who "claims the mantle of transgression, cultural opposition, political righteousness, and truth-telling,"[2] his films and their valuation are at best problematic. Or when cultural critic bell hooks asks, "Whose Pussy Is This?" readers understand Lee's positioning of "feminist" discourses in *She's Gotta Have It* indeed turn left.[3] Even with the many useful engagements of his media texts, I suggest Lee's films need careful reconsideration through the conjoined lenses of Christianity and Blackness, as the presence of these two themes underpins so much of his work simultaneously. Thus, this confessional prayer aims to think through Lee's many religious narrative tangents as a sign of Black retrograde and how his ideas reflect the growing transformations of religiosity in African-American lives.

"Must a Been a White Guy Started All That"

In the nomenclature of twentieth-century scholars and journalists, Spike Lee is a race man. Drawing on sociologists St. Clair Drake and Horace Cayton's 1945 *Black Metropolis*, African-American studies scholar Hazel Carby agrees with their definition of race men as those who understand their need to prove themselves as superior in a field of achievement. In their minds, these men's success becomes the success of all Black folks. However, she argues, while Black male intelligentsia seem to understand the complexity and social formation of Black masculinity, they fail to "challenge the hypocrisy of their own assumptions about [B]lack masculinity"[4] and believe a community in crisis may need "proper affirmation of [B]lack male authority."[5] Lee's posturing and filmic worldview embody this masculinist mindset and many tropes of Black nationalism. His very traditional view of Black masculinity stands as his calling card and centrifugal force.

Yet his *commitment* to Black cultural ways of being and Black communities rarely gets questioned—his cultural positioning reminiscent of BET's 2000 network tagline, "Now that's Black."

Lee's films offer historic knowledge, current news, and perceived correct Black perspectives on life in Black America. From "Tawana Told the Truth" spray-painted on the brick wall outside of Sal's Pizzeria in *Do the Right Thing* (1989) to the Charlottesville Black Lives Matter/white power protest in *BlacKkKlansman* (2018), he offers Black audiences a running commentary on what they should know or already be familiar.[6] Even when the setting is not a contemporary one, Lee finds a way to connect the film's narrative with present-day Black struggles. For example, in the biopic *Malcolm X*, even though set in the early to mid-twentieth century, Lee opens the film with a burning cross and the 1991 video footage of white Los Angeles police officers beating a Black man, Rodney King. In some ways, Lee's veracity of circumstance makes his assertions more palatable and truthful for Black (and white) audiences.[7] In fact, what appears then as a ridiculous ending to the internecine infighting between Black collegiates in *School Daze* (1988) has become a calling card for those down with the Black Lives Matter movement: "Wake up" is now "Stay woke."[8]

In this vein, Lee's soundtracks usually ally with the most significant songs in "woke" Black America. Audiences are energized by Public Enemy's "Fight the Power" in *Do the Right Thing*, recognize Curtis Mayfield's "Keep on Pushing" in *Get on the Bus*, and Sam Cooke's "A Change Is Gonna Come" in *Malcolm X*, to name a few.[9] These selections characterize a Black cultural aesthetic that leaves no room for fence sitting; in other words, the lyrics call for an understanding of and response to the acrimonious social conditions of Black life in various epochs of U.S. history. Lee asserts that for him, "[m]usic is . . . a great tool of a filmmaker, the same way cinematography, the acting, editing, post-production, the costumes are. You know, to help you tell a story."[10] Moreover, film scholar Ellen Scott believes that in Lee's works, "music exceeds the diegetic realm and is often used to point to a 'place' outside the diegesis. . . . [His] choice of popular music points, with utopian tonal and lyrical strains, toward an alternative iteration of [B]lack masculinity [and I add, Black life more generally] to that presented on the image track or within the narrative."[11]

Throughout his works, Lee successfully privileges the beauty, vitality (even when thwarted), and specificity of Black cultural communities. In his earliest works, such as *Joe's Bed-Stuy Barbershop: We Cut Heads* (1982), audiences are regaled with then Black-owned WBLS radio as part of the diegesis, copies of Black-owned *Essence* magazine lay about, debates about jheri curls take place in front of a framed, naked Black woman layered across velvet on the barbershop wall; and Black mafioso character Lovejoy (Tommy Hicks) lectures on economics and numbers running as the Black Wall Street. The constant presence of Deltas, Alphas, and Ques as extras convinces audiences about the proliferation and significance of Black Greek life on Black college campuses in *School Daze*.

With his visual and narrative insistence, Lee assures audiences that he knows and is down with "the people" through his infusion of cultural signifiers of Black life.

Yet when renowned cultural studies scholar Stuart Hall asks "What is this Black?" or when questions around post-Blackness emerge, Lee's name is not mentioned. I suggest this absence comes from Lee's positioning (and being stuck) in mainstream, Black middle-class, talented-tenth Blackness. Religion scholar Ron Neal argues Lee represents a "high-brow crisis"—existing as part of an "embattled minority of high-brow critics whose perspectives and voices have been eclipsed by a young generation of charismatic cultural producers, mainly, enterprising Black men."[12] He suggests Lee's disconnection from the larger, less talented-tenth Black audience informs his work. Moreover, Lee gets increasingly called into question on his Black political and cultural grounding. For example, writer Mychal Denzel Smith suggests Lee's *Chi-Raq* (2015) gets it wrong exactly because of its masculinized Blackness. He writes: "The times we live in, where young people are taking to the streets to declare that '[B]lack lives matter,' are not defined by the patriarchal impulse to save [B]lack men and therefore save the community. Our politics moved beyond that. Spike Lee didn't come with us."[13] And more germane to this prayer of confession, one of those new bloods, Tyler Perry, unabashedly wraps his work in the blood of Jesus. Says Neal, Perry's success lies in his ability to conjure "religious symbols and religious yearnings that tap into the conservative element in African American culture."[14] Based on Lee's film canon, it is Perry's Christian insistence that likely infuriates him the most.

Hell Naw

Returning to a discussion of Black public intellectualism in the early twentieth century, sociologist Patricia Hill Collins argues: "Racism had a profoundly gendered subtext that feminized blackness."[15] I suggest this decidedly belittling connection between Blackness and femininity mirrors a similar corollary Lee makes with Blackness and Christianity. "Real" Black men are strong and independent. Christianity makes them soft and ill thinking. Women are believers, and women bring men down.[16] In a sign system, Christianity can connote myriad things. When juxtaposed with Blackness, its framing takes on a more singular meaning, but only if texts get read in a certain way. Lee suggests Black Christians often invoke a loving, forgiving white Jesus—believing a better life comes after death while leaning on Jesus's everlasting arms. In other words, Lee's work infers Black folks suffer from a mode of religiosity that often fails to address the systematic racism endemic to the U.S. or to transform the conditions this racism produces.

Lee equates Christianity with the continued oppression of African-Americans. Their inability to move ahead economically and educationally, broadly construed, stems in part from their Christian beliefs. In support of this view, he often presents valid critiques of the church as a contemptible institution, the recognition of which brings pangs of familiarity to many Black viewers. For example, he dramatically demonstrates Christian hypocrisy in *Jungle Fever* when the Good Reverend Doctor Purify (Ossie Davis) murders his own son while quoting the Bible. The Reverend intones: "Father, I stretch my hand to thee, no other strength I know." BAM![17] Beyond drama, Lee also explores the tension of religion and Blackness through humor.

Even before Craig (Ice Cube) slams the door in the face of the Jehovah's Witness sisters in the F. Gary Gray comedy film *Friday* (1995), Lee cinematically expresses contempt for the ways of Christ humorously. For example, Ossie Davis as Coach Odom in *School Daze* invokes God's words to Jonah to motivate the perennially losing football team. Coach questions: "Do you like the devil?" The team yells "Hell no!" He responds: "Well, the devil is in the other locker room. . . . By the name of all that is holy, go out there and kick some butt!" The club bouncers (Steve White and Charlie Murphy) in *Mo' Better Blues* (1990) regale Giant (Lee) with the Nation of Gods and Earths understanding of the Black man as God—all the while sounding, at best, ill-informed. In *Joe's Bed-Stuy*, Lee nods toward his annoyance with Jehovah's Witnesses when they enter the barbershop to offer the *Watchtower* and proselytize. Barber Zechariah Homer (Monty Ross) ushers them out the door. But by the time of his film *Do the Right Thing*, Lee angrily illustrates his position.

As two Witnesses approach Mookie (Spike Lee) to share God's word in print, he doesn't even allow them to open their mouths before he shouts, "Hell no!" Lee's *Red Hook Summer* finds him reprising his role as Mookie, now Mr. Mookie, in a cameo, only to yell "Hell to the naw!" at a Witness again. This time the

Spike Lee as Mr. Mookie and Tracy Camilla Johns as Mother Darling in *Red Hook Summer* (2012).

Witness is Mother Darling (Tracy Camilla Johns), literally twenty-three years since her very non-Witness-like appearance in *She's Gotta Have It*.[18] In both films, Lee frames Mookie's exhortations as humorous and justified. Whether the humor stems from remembering Witnesses proselytizing door to door in Black communities on Saturday mornings or externalizing a frustration and/or pissivity at their evangelical insistence, Lee exhibits a narrative snarkiness and dismissiveness of their call and work.

I'm Building Me a Home

Lee opens his ode to the HBCU experience called *School Daze* with the singing of the Morehouse College Glee Club. Morehouse, founded in 1867, as an all-male, Black institution of higher learning, stands as a bastion of Black masculinity and pride in Atlanta and nationwide. King graduated from there. Benjamin Mays taught there. Maynard Jackson, Julian Bond, Herman Cain, Louis Sullivan, Samuel L. Jackson, Raphael Warnock, and, of course, Lee himself (and his daddy) graduated from this institution.[19] Taking audiences to a Black homecoming in *School Daze* allows for an understanding of the gravity and historical weight of HBCUs. But beyond that, Lee connects audiences to these schools' foundation— descendants of formerly enslaved Black men and women who cultivate crops for whites and make them wealthy. Thus, while *School Daze* audiences hear the choir sing "I'm Building Me a Home," they first see the drawing of the eighteenth-century *Brooks* slave ship with Black bodies crammed tight and situated for maximum cargo and economic efficiency.

Through *School Daze* and *Crooklyn*, Lee takes audiences to his family's home in the South. The South already exists in the national imaginary as strange, cruel, and backward. The U.S. slave South stands as the origin place for most African-Americans, beyond the continent of Africa. Virginia, Florida, Georgia, Mississippi, Alabama, Louisiana, Texas, Arkansas, Delaware, Maryland, Tennessee, Kentucky, Missouri, and South and North Carolina serve as literal and figurative ancestral homes for the preponderance of this country's 45 million African descendants. This South psychically and geographically allows for a connection to and perpetuation of culture. Metaphorically, the tree symbolizes African-Americans from the South—a deep rootedness (of time, people, place, and culture) and a limb (for maiming, burning, swinging, and remembering). And, as Billie Holiday and later Nina Simone sing about so painfully in "Strange Fruit," descendants of this tragic dichotomy take up its cultural complexity in sometimes schizophrenic ways.[20]

Disruptive Christian expressions at home emerge frequently throughout Lee's canon. Traditionally, in this ideal place (and inside space), Black folks learn about God and how God works. At home, everybody eats similar foods, listens to music, listens to music in a certain way and a certain type of music, watches TV and the same programs and laughs aloud because all know themselves as family, at home. Definitions of home often include the surrounding community. People often reference their church home, even in death on funeral programs, as part of understanding home and origin. Home can also harbor pain and regret, ostracization alongside expectation, angry voices, hurt feelings, sorrow, depression, and fear. In Lee's films, home emerges as disruptive, surreal, antiquated, and wrong with the practice of Christianity.

In *Crooklyn*, for example, his distrust of Christianity comes through the Carmichaels leaving his hometown of Brooklyn to visit family "down South." By taking the protagonist, nine-year-old Troy (Zelda Harris), from her beloved Brooklyn to visit relatives in Maryland, her parents offer her up as a living sacrifice to a people and a place positioned in direct opposition to her home—a home that makes Black cultural power paramount and keeps religion at bay, despite the occasional forced prayer before eating. In Aunt Song's (Francis Foster) home, Lee uses an anamorphic lens and lurid lighting to make the Southern and religious environment feel disconnected from the rest of the world. The "sanity" and urbanity of Brooklyn disappear. Lee says: "I really wanted to show how Troy was in a different world. It was almost like *Alice in Wonderland*."[21] Within this twenty-minute disturbed world space, Aunt Song's devotion to her dog Queenie, her aversion to Troy's braids, and a shown image of a white Jesus make her religiosity more than suspect. It makes her and the religion she believes in crazy and out of step with progressive Black America. Very much in the vein of *Red Hook Summer*'s Da Good Bishop Enoch in terms of white Jesus iconography and "praise continually being in your mouth," Aunt Song forces her adopted daughter Viola (Patriece Nelson) and Troy to watch a TV program featuring a white couple singing to an in-studio audience of white children.

1-2-3, The devil's after me.
4-5-6, He's always throwing sticks.
7-8-9, He misses every time.
Hallelujah, hallelujah, hallelujah! Amen.

As Viola sings along with the televisual hosts and encourages Troy to join in, Troy gives her a quizzical look of "what fresh hell is this?"[22]

While 1970s white television texts hold sway in the Carmichaels' Brooklyn home as well, fights of watching the Knicks versus *The Brady Bunch* and *The Partridge Family*, the Christian sing-along of the Southern program presents a different type of white acculturation and preeminence. In the Christian text, the program symbolizes a historic and cultural throwback—a time where whiteness reigns in totality—in suburban neighborhoods, in positions of power (government, education, and business), on television, and "down South." These systematic hierarchies exist under the watchful eye of God the Father, in slave states that sometimes seem to forget they lost the war. Cultural critic bell hooks[23] argues that Lee's attempt at comedy simply doesn't work in the South—in a film that

Zelda Harris as Troy in *Crooklyn* (1994). (Courtesy of Photofest.)

obfuscates Black death. I suggest, however, Lee's imagined Carmichael household of Brooklyn succeeds for him because Christianity stays parenthetical, and people of color dominate the landscape—even on TV with the Knicks.

"Everything about This Place Is Dead"

In a later work, *Red Hook Summer*, Lee links Christianity to child molestation in the church. The main protagonist, Da Good Bishop Enoch Rouse (Clarke Peters), mentioned prior, gets "released" by his Southern congregation to flee North because of his molestation of a young boy. Seeing the film's trailer, I think, "Finally, Spike's religion film." This focus, I assume, will provide audiences with a declaration of Lee's intention around Blackness and religiosity. On this conundrum, the film isn't a concrete assertion. However, more than any of his other films, *Red Hook Summer* exemplifies Lee's condemnation of and contempt for the ways in which Christianity seems to have a stranglehold on Black progressiveness and lies to its people.

Red Hook Summer loves on Brooklyn in the typical way Lee does in all his films. Vibrant colors, contrasts of concrete and foliage, bodies, and buildings with sweeping pans of an environment that to the U.S. suburban eye might look worthy of demolition. In the film, Da Good Bishop Enoch demonstrates a Black manhood Lee touts—looking out for those around him (even the gangbangers), trying to help raise his Black grandson as strong and proud and Christian; supporting the women and children of the community—all things central to civil rights and talented tenth uplift programs of leadership and pulling as we climb mantras. In his sermonizing (which he does a lot), Da Good Bishop talks about the evils of the world, including radio, television, and film that circumscribe who Black children think they are and can be—"the devil's words to fill an idle mind."[24] Audiences actually hear Lee's voice through Da Good Bishop's grandson Flik (Jules Brown).[25] From his first arrival in Red Hook, Flik chronicles the ways and downfall of his grandfather's Christianity with his iPad 2. Commenting on the contemporary media moment when Da Good Bishop asks him what happened to his Christian name Silas, he replies: "I rented it out on Facebook."

Lee renders Da Good Bishop's Christianity as contemptible throughout the film. He adorns Da Good Bishop's house (and the church) with images of a white Jesus—taking audiences through Da Good Bishop's bedrooms, kitchen, and front door littered with these images.

FLIK QUESTIONS Isn't Jesus Black?
DA GOOD BISHOP REPLIES We don't know what color Jesus was.
TO WHICH FLIK QUIPS Well, why is he white then?

This exchange, this questioning of the Black Christian enterprise with white iconography, elucidates Lee's side-eye to Christianity. Historians such as Edward Blum and Paul Harvey write about the many factors influencing portraits of Jesus as white in American culture from colonial times to the present. Jesus becomes white through colonialism and missionaries, expansions of slavery, the illustration of Jesus in human form, and the constituting of the U.S. as a Christian nation. White "Christ imagery has had the power to last and shape-shift even after massive assaults from civil rights crusades, scientific discoveries, and demographic transformations."[26] Thus, a white Jesus continues to adorn many Black churches and Black Christian homes—fictionally and real-lived.

When Da Good Bishop preaches outside the church, trying to recruit Black and poor and old people for Old Timers Sunday, Lee captures him as if from an old VHS camera with graininess and dropouts. This dour imagery appears adjacent to an area of Red Hook where gentrification has started (aka where white people now live). The Black characters call "this section" Paradise—different, better than the Red Hook housing projects and the Lil' Peace of Heaven Church limitedly filled with Black members. Showing Da Good Bishop and other images of the past gives weight to Deacon Zee's (Thomas Jefferson Byrd) comment: "Everything about this place is dead"—Christianity included.

Throughout the film, Lee shrouds Da Good Bishop in purple when preaching in the house of the Lord. While Lee employs vibrant colors liberally in most of his films, interestingly, he uses purple rarely. Traditionally, purple signifies royalty, wealth, and significance, as it has been an expensive color to produce. Thus, only those with means and status (royalty, the aristocracy, and clergy) adorn themselves with it historically.

Clarke Peters as Da Good Bishop Enoch in *Red Hook Summer* (2012).

However, in the Bible's New Testament, Roman soldiers clothe Jesus in purple before beating and crucifying him.[27] In this sense, they mock his supposed holiness and their designated status of him as king of the Jews. When parishioners learn Da Good Bishop is a child molester, he wears the most beautiful purple robe. Before a purple-shrouded altar and using a church tambourine, gang members, former members of a Lil' Peace of Heaven, beat him for his acts. In Lee's world, the majesty of purple becomes desecrated again when associated with Christ.

In trying to make sense of what in the world Lee could have been thinking in making the climax of *Red Hook Summer* about the discovery of child molestation (nearly three-quarters into the film) and then letting it fall out of the narrative, writer Andrew Lapin muses: "It should not be that anyone who would anoint themselves the gatekeeper between us and God would act out on such moral turpitude and then conceal the sin. Yet we know that what should not be *is*. And if we started doing a better job talking about these things, then maybe Lee could, too."[28] While Lee may have wanted to introduce the larger Catholic Church child molestation atrocities that were on full display during this time, he actually demonstrates an inability to handle child molestation by a man of God adequately, appropriately, or even skillfully. Moreover, his entire cinematic canon positions Christianity as a sort of raper, molester, and noose around a particular kind of male-centered Blackness. In Lee's world, indeed, Da Good Bishop's relationship to a feminine-allied Christ brings him to bad.

In the Shadow of the Cross

The year 2014 found Lee connecting Christian beliefs to Black people at a crossroads of right and wrong—in this case, equating vampirism with murdering for one's capitalist benefit. In *Da Sweet Blood of Jesus*, a reimagining of Bill Gunn's 1973 *Ganja and Hess*, Gunn's (and Lee's) central protagonist Hess Green (Duane Jones and Stephen Tyrone Williams, respectively) comes to the Black church for help. And in each film's conclusion, Jesus (and the Black church) sets him free to renounce his taste of blood and die by the shadow of the cross. Film scholars Manthia Diawara and Phyllis Klotman argue Gunn intended *Ganja and Hess* as a referendum on the capitalist construction of Black life and as an indictment of Euro-American Christianity for African-Americans. They write: "Green is often composed in the same frame as African artifacts and paintings of devils. . . . [He] attempts to build an earthly 'white' paradise and to live forever with servants around him to fulfill his every wish. . . . Unlike Green, who tries to revalorize the Africa which ignored Christ, the minister exhorts his parishioners to turn back on Africa's dark moment and to trace history from the time Christ arrived. It is in this sense that we see Christ as the hero of the minister's narrative, and the Africans—and Green, when he was following their example—as the villains."[29]

Whereas the African artifacts in *Ganja and Hess* are problematized by their connection to colonialism, paganism, and anti-Christianity with Hess trying to valorize them, the African artifacts in *Da Sweet Blood of Jesus* seem mere accoutrements—ones accepted as any other art form in progressive Black America. In fact, I argue, the art, in some way, makes Dr. Hess's belief in Christianity much richer and more potentially palatable as it seems to merge an understanding and appreciation of both.

In *Ganja and Hess*, Gunn equates capitalist accumulation with white colonialist conquest of Africa—artifacts offered against "authentic Black" ways of being imagined through African-garbed women. Diawara and Klotman's analysis assumes the African presence as anti-Christ. Perhaps lover-turned-wife Ganja Meda's (Marlene Clark and Zaraah Abrahams, respectively) survival in the end (and her smile in *Ganja and Hess* only) signifies a renunciation of Christ and African things as she embraces the trappings of materialist (white) success at any cost. The experimental nature of Gunn's entire film, however, leaves this position unclear. Lee's *Da Sweet Blood of Jesus* fails to clarify this point as well and possesses ambiguity of another type.

While retelling Gunn's narrative, Lee's film title references Spencer Williams's 1941 *The Blood of Jesus*. In so doing, Lee makes his version particularly about Black folks and Christianity. As director and actor, as discussed in the Invocation, Williams's early film serves as a moralistic and evangelical tool to help support African-American audiences in their Christian walk, although, according to film scholar Ellen Scott, white censors often call into question the morality of Black people.[30] Religion scholar Judith Weisenfeld believes films like *The Blood of Jesus* help cultivate "Christian character and . . . illuminate some of the ways film helped propagate [B]lack religious thought and shape [B]lack church cultures."[31] Williams's work serves as a corollary to the more famous and prolific filmmaker Oscar Micheaux and his work's noted disdain of Christianity. And in the tradition of Micheaux, Lee's film complicates the Christian path. In fact, some argue Lee follows a legacy of several Black male cultural producers who have long decried the relationship between progressive blackness and Christianity.[32]

The church in *Da Sweet Blood of Jesus* (the same Lil' Peace of Heaven Baptist Church shown in *Red Hook Summer*) establishes Bishop Zee (the same character and actor screened as Deacon Zee in *Red Hook Summer*) as the new pastor of a Lil' Peace of Heaven. Like many Black churches in the past and contemporarily, Bishop Zee receives respect and privilege as the leader of the church on Sundays but also works a second job—in this case, as Hess's city driver during the week. Connecting his own *Red Hook Summer* to *Da Sweet Blood of Jesus*, Lee installs Deacon Zee as a replacement for Da Good Bishop Enoch when Enoch's past "indiscretions" are discovered. Bishop Zee's opening prayer references the death of Da Good Bishop, his assumed purple robe, and the shift in racial appearance of Jesus in the front and back of the church. This allows audiences to understand some things have changed at Lil' Peace of Heaven. If nothing else, Lee replaces the prominent white images of Jesus with Black ones. Yet remembering Deacon Zee as a lazy alcoholic in *Red Hook Summer*, Lee's minister choice, even in this Gunn remake, forces audiences to question the Black Christian enterprise since forgiveness and belief themselves both seem to belie the preceding Lee joint.

In both *Ganja and Hess* and *Da Sweet Blood of Jesus*, Hess grows weary of his fictionalized Myrthian of Nigeria and Ashanti of Ghana-gained blood life and lifestyle. He returns to the church for redemption and to renounce his sin. With Lee's cinematic flourish, Hess dollies his way toward the altar for a Holy Ghost filling and forgiveness. Afterward, he eases out of the church to return home and die in the shadow of the cross. Yet something about the blood permeating Lee's Black Christian–focused version of this narrative confounds. In *Da Sweet Blood of Jesus*, blood red colors every scene: Ganja's sultry red fingernail polish and red lipstick, blood puddled in the bathroom seduction and strangulation scene of Tangier (Naté Bova), and blood red firelight in the discussion between Ganja and Hess as he talks tiredly of his current life. The red-gel-lit bedroom where the cross hangs point to the blood as an inescapable part of a larger engagement with Christianity.[33]

Yet, despite his painting scenes this way, Lee eschews gospel music filled with blood—songs such as William Cowper's "There Is a Fountain Filled with Blood," Tennessee Ernie Ford's "Just as I Am," and "The Blood of the Thing" that all appear on the soundtrack of *Ganja and Hess*. He even ignores traditional Black gospel music oozing with tales of blood and the cross such as the venerable Andraé Crouch's "The Blood Will Never Lose Its Power." This last song would intimately connect Lee's notion of paradoxical Christianity and progressive Blackness together. In fact, Lee uses no known gospel lyric in his version of the film. For this soundtrack, he conducted an open call for musical artists to submit songs.[34]

Music, as has been discussed, breathes power into Lee's filmmaking. Not using any of these songs suggests his antipathy to Christianity may be more complicated than initially and visually imagined. Thus, perhaps his visioning tilts toward a more contemporary understanding of Christianity than the gospel of yesteryear.

As Hess sits in a coffin-like wooden room under the shadow of a cross, he asks Ganja to move into the shadow with him so he won't die alone. They talk:

> GANJA The shadow of the cross against our hearts will destroy us.
>
> HESS The cross is only an implement of torture. The shadow is the darkness it casts. . . . We've taken God's gift of death.

Ganja and Hess (Bill Gunn, 1973) and *Da Sweet Blood of Jesus* (Spike Lee, 2014).

Da Sweet Blood of Jesus forsakes saving or condemning. It leaves its characters in a state of the in-between, living and living well but also quite vacuously, devoid of meaningful life. In the end, the cross resonates for Hess, death means living again. He must die to have eternal life. Ganja, a nonbeliever, stands at the precipice of the earth alive and well but also dead and enslaved to the liquid that brings her there. Lee leaves audiences to ponder life and death with Jesus.[35]

Despite his mostly critical frame, Lee's films sometimes offer an uneasy recognition and reverence for the impact and practice of Christianity in Black life. He seems to acknowledge how Black Christians worship and put into practice a wrathful and powerful God. Naming in Lee's films frequently leads back to the Bible. Zechariah, Ruth, Thaddeus (Teapot), Jeremiah, Enoch, Silas, Martha, Jacob (Jake), Jesus, and Mary serve as protagonists in several of his narratives.[36] Lee knows Black Christians take up the God found in biblical scriptures such as Amos 5:24[37] and apply that God belief in the fight for civil rights, as demonstrated in his documentary *4 Little Girls* (1997), in the grit of those unwilling to drown or keep quiet in *When the Levees Broke* (2006) and *If God Is Willing and da Creek Don't Rise* (2010), and even in the monologues delivered by Ossie Davis as Coach Odom in *School Daze*, as the Good Reverend Doctor Purify in *Jungle Fever*, and as Jeremiah in *Get on the Bus*.

In fact, regardless of actor Ossie Davis's personal religiosity, Lee casts him continuously as the quintessential example of solid, Black Christian manhood. As Coach Odom, da Mayor, the Good Reverend Doctor Purify, and Jeremiah, each character references and reveres the Bible as the word of God—both directly and indirectly. Each character receives an empowered framing and space to offer soliloquies in the form of encouragement, quotations, admonition, and prayers.

Ossie Davis, Ruby Dee, and Samuel L. Jackson in *Jungle Fever* (1991).

This respect of Davis and Christianity extends to Lee's documentary work in *4 Little Girls* and in *When the Levees Broke*. Perhaps Davis's eulogy of Malcolm X in 1965 cements his downness for Lee.[38] As Davis says there: "Malcolm had stopped being a 'Negro' years ago."[39] And after his enjoyment and pride of being on the set of *School Daze*, Davis remarks: "knowing deep in my heart that whatever the case, win, lose, or draw, this was a Spike Lee Production. . . . And most important, he will have done it blackly . . . to remind me just a little— one more time—of Malcolm X."[40] Significantly, Davis's characterization of Malcolm X and the words he speaks during his lifetime become conduits by which Lee's seeming alternative to Black Christian possibilities manifests.

Bamboozled

Beginning with the production of *Do the Right Thing*, Lee hires the Fruit of Islam as film set security. The Fruit of Islam serve as the security force for the Nation of Islam. Efficient, well-dressed, polite, and controlled, the Fruit command respect in Black communities where they exist. Lee illustrates their presence distinctively in *Malcolm X*. The mise-en-scène and structured dialogue by a white police officer who remarks, "That's too much power for one man," accord Malcolm X a respect beyond Black communities. The Nation of Islam, under the leadership of Minister Louis Farrakhan since 1975, exists as both a religious organization and a Black empowerment group. The organization numbers between twenty and fifty thousand members and demonstrates its commitment to religious obligations by virtue of dress, prayer requirements, food intake, and courting rituals. It also holds a particular Black nationalist directive governing its actions in Black communities, and action *is* the operative word. Over the years, the Nation of Islam has built community centers, created meal programs for children, and offered economic plans to stimulate growth and independence in urban Black locales. Its larger enterprise, according to its leaders, has always been to praise Allah and build Black communities.

Perhaps Lee's privileging of this religious group, both narratively and pragmatically, or maybe excusing its religious part, happens because of the Nation's demonstrated commitment to changing the lives of Black people. The Nation fears not white men and seemingly equates meaningful, unapologetic Blackness with maleness. With the Nation of Islam, religion doesn't get in the way of nation building. In fact, the articulation of Islam with Black maleness defines nation building. In *Malcolm X* and *Get on the Bus*, aesthetically and narratively, the films' themes center Black male uplift of the race. *Get on the Bus*, beyond Black male bonding, articulates what Black men can do for a nation brought together by Islam and its messenger Minister Louis Farrakhan. While presumably recognizing the contributions of African-American women, it "rightfully," according to its own narrative, places value on Black men to move Black America forward.

And Lee's visualization of Malcolm X, El Hajj Malik El-Shabazz, always comes through powerful, upward tilted angles. Even with his signature dolly shot as Malcolm moves toward his death, audiences see him as unafraid, strong, smart, and complicated. Lee presents Malcolm X as thoughtful about his choices and his passion for African-Americans. In *Bamboozled*, Lee even inserts the clip of Denzel Washington as Malcolm X speaking to Black folks on how they have been "bamboozled" by their affiliation with Christianity—the first time, shown in the context of Black national development and the second, in the context of visual representation. Lee frames Malcolm X as unbowed, uncompromising, and as the embodiment of what Blackness should be and do. Lee's directorial relationship to Islam suggests he believes progressive states of Black being are possible in relation to religion—that is, if the religion values Black male leadership and underplays whiteness. This last aspect may be at least part of the problem Lee maintained with fellow media maker Tyler Perry.

Hallelujer!

Perhaps some of Lee's antipathy toward Tyler Perry and his work, beyond just a little hateration, lies with Perry consistently making Christianity and home right and okay, central and necessary, Black and female-dominated. Both Lee and Perry create insider work—work that targets a collective Black audience conscious of history, current circumstance, and the Black church. Neither Lee's nor Perry's notion of home exists in an origin type way. Neither advocates a return to Africa; they are not Garveyites. Both men support capitalist endeavors and firm roots in the U.S.—grounded in a way that says, "Yes, this is the home my family built." So audiences never get a sort of displacement or longing narrative for another place to be in their works. Lee's visioning seems to come from a desire for Black people to be better, to want more, to recognize their inalienable rights to be here and to do something about those who impede your way.

Perry, on the other hand, makes films to entertain the other 90 percent of African-Americans. Connecting Black progress to tradition, Christianity, and woman-centered (yet male-led) normalcy characterizes his narratives' larger intent.[41] In the constantly evolving media landscape, scholars continue to be confounded by the ways Black audiences take up and run with Perry's narratives, especially ones implicitly or explicitly grounded in Christian authority. All of Perry's work, minister T. D. Jakes's narratives, and even white-directed and -produced films like *The War Room*[42] (2015) feature and target African-American Christian audiences, especially Black Christian women. Journalists and scholars write repeatedly about how well Perry knows his audience. This lauding places longtime Black soothsayer Lee in a pinch. For Lee, who I imagine still thinks of himself as understanding and speaking for all Black America, Perry's Black audiences exist outside of his mediated purview.[43]

At the 2016 American Studies Association conference, the post-panel discussion began with the prologue query: "when we were Black."[44] While failing to quite capture the representational and entertainment industries' quandary that African-Americans face in this moment, the prompt destabilizes Lee's Christianity against Black progressiveness stance. In the face of refined, mediated but ideologically similar past circumstances, I wonder: Do audiences "feel" and support Tyler Perry's work because they ally with his positions regarding Blackness and Christianity? And by the same token, are Lee's longtime rantings of pro-Black and anti- (or ambiguous) Christ elements what audiences reject? Is it both or neither?

. . . We're Going to Praise the Lord

At a twenty-first-century protest about the umpteenth Black boy/man/woman shot down by police, several protesters hold the sign "We are not full of rage but full of righteousness."[45] The young Black protestors sing the gospel of Jesus Christ as part of their response. In Black Christianity, adherents know and understand the alpha and omega of this Prayer of Confession's beginning revelry for Lee's notion of Christianity: "As for me and my house, we're going to praise the Lord." For Lee, the Jesus of M. L. King Jr. may be righteous but impotent. His mostly pejorative depictions of Christianity reign when positioned against his masculine Blackness. While his dismissal of Christianity could almost be considered a formalist flourish, Lee often finds a way to characterize the religiosity of African-Americans as problematic.

Yet the longest scene of his 2015 *Chi-Raq* features a white male priest telling his Black congregants to just praise God and fight. In *Chi-Raq*, where "pussy power" is supposed to save the world, Lee crafts real-lived priest Michael Pfleger as a fictional savior for Black communities. Played by John Cusack, the character stays in line with offering up the reality of the actual Chicago priest to infuse this narrative with veracity. But in the case of *Chi-Raq*, a film already living in a fantastical Greek narrative space, adding this characterization and according to the character as much screen time as it does forces audiences to reconsider Lee's ultimate perspective. In an interview with writer Jen Yamato, she questions Lee about his faith. He replies: "Do you believe in God? I believe in God. I don't go to church, though."[46] Yet he attended Father Pfleger's Easter Sunday mass at St. Sabina Catholic Church in 2017.[47]

Moreover, in Lee's reimagining of his own *She's Gotta Have It* as a series for Netflix in 2017, he liberally makes Christianity a significant and complicated aspect of several characters. An early scene of men verbally hailing women features one who tells Nola (DeWanda Wise) her mother's placenta is filled with holy water: "God blessing you, girl. Hmm. Good God!" Another says she looks so good, "Jesus on the cross must be doing your taxes." And one of the main characters of Nola's male trilogy (the simultaneous good one and rapist in the 1986 version), Jamie Overstreet (now played by Lyriq Bent), introduces himself to audiences by including his thoughts: "You know God is a trickster. In life God doesn't give you the people you want, instead he gives you the people you need. Nola Darling is my need."[48]

Regardless of Black audiences' feelings about Lee's narrative facilitation, manipulation of the form, didactic constructions, or mountaintop proclamations, his sincerity and righteousness of Black visioning rarely come into question. And perhaps, as happens with many, the wisdom, reflection, and realities of age and shifting times give Lee a greater and deeper perspective on the ways of Christ in Black life. Within the fourth episode of season one of Netflix's *She's Gotta Have It*, audiences hear the voice-over of Nola in prayer with Father God, Mother God, and a communion of prayers to the Orishas. With soft diegetic jazz playing, Nola paints and introspects in prayer as success awaits her in the form of a second-round selection for an artists' competition. Through this progressive, liberated, and pseudo-woke Nola, perhaps Lee demonstrates a recalibration of progressive Blackness with an inclusive spirituality that incorporates Christianity and Black women.[49] Similar to the powerful exorcism conducted by a bevy of praising and praying Black women in *Beloved* (Demme, 1998), Lee may also now recognize the power Black women derive from belief in God and Black Christianity. As part of his latest films, a title card presents the work as being made in the year of our Lord. Conceivably, Lee no longer visions Christianity and progressive Blackness as incompatible. Perhaps his own negotiations have helped him overcome his unbelief. Amen.

Testimony

Testimony helps believers purge, receive redemption, and witness to God's goodness.

Black women supporting at Dallas City Temple SDA Church in 2014. Creative Commons.

I Got a Testimony

• •

Sistah Blackacademics
and God

I got a tes-ti-mo-ny 🎼♩♫

These four words as sung in Clay Evans's monster hit resonate within the souls of Black church folks. Testimony demonstrates faith but also exposes failings. And religion talk can be hard, even at church. So when it comes to the workplace, it is even more challenging. While politics brings forth uncomfortable and problematic working relations too, religion potentially damages more due to its head, heart, and spirit connections and implications. For academics, the prospect becomes even more precarious. Scholars position themselves and are positioned as experts—knowledgeable, thoughtful, objective, and atheist. Research suggests that in elite institutions, belief in God, belief in a higher power, and agnosticism/atheism are almost equal, with atheism/agnosticism leading the way. In other types of institutions (community colleges, four-year bachelor's degree and nonelite doctoral granting institutions), belief in God overwhelmingly predominates, with another 15–30 percent believing in some type of higher power to nonbelief.[1] Yet because many academics claim nonbeliever as their moniker and badge of honor, especially in elite (read ultra-white and media-loved) institutions and disciplines, those who embrace spirituality and/or religiosity face a conundrum of disclosure—fear of response as limited to disdain to outright condemnation.

Moreover, the notion of atheism in the academy exists as a popular perception throughout U.S. culture. It is exacerbated by the religious right consistently decrying a "liberal" academy—equating the two. In her Grammy-winning 1997 song "On and On," artist Erykah Badu remarks matter-of-factly: "Most intellects do not believe in God but they fear us just the same"—an assessment capturing a widespread sentiment held by people of color about the white professorate.[2] Yet with academics of color, Black women in particular, they are perceived as both the intellect and the feared, proving not only problematic to their being and ways of being but also particularly counterproductive for their life-work synthesis.

Filmmaker Roxana Walker-Canton's documentary *Living Thinkers: An Autobiography of Black Women in the Ivory Tower* (2013) beautifully and thoughtfully walks audiences through the ways in which Black women professors (and graduate students) negotiate the academy—through family background and expectation, relationships with colleagues, classmates, and friends, research visions, opportunities, and threats, and in the end suggests how to not only survive but also thrive. The film gives audiences a glimpse into the many unique challenges Black women face working in the academy. It leaves mostly unsaid, however, the ways in which spirituality and religiosity impact and shape the work, the engagements, and the lives of scholars, especially those dealing with popular culture. Believing Black women academics face an arduous daily task of acknowledged authority and respect alongside the potential silences of their spiritual selves—despite the ontological nature of their work and real-lived processes.

To fill this unsaid, I offer redacted conversations—testimonies—with five Black women scholars who daily negotiate their own spiritual and religious journeys with popular culture and the academy. This dialogue provides insights into the complexity, negotiations, and humanity work engaged in these spaces. Hearing (reading) the voices of people's faith walks, especially for those who do critical popular culture work, provides an understanding of the tension, misperceptions, and seemingly antithetical nature of both arenas. Conversations with these believers allow for a unique look into the tightrope and ways in which those on it somehow "get over."

Can't Nobody Tell It Like Me . . . Cause It's My Testimony

Everyone offers a different testimony; their trials and ways of making it through life circumstances diverge. Yet testimony allows stories to blend. Education scholars Kirsten T. Edwards and Denise Taliaferro Baszile suggest: "Testimony . . . is not simply a story about what happened but also a story about how faith carried you through the storm. The emphasis centers how faith helps believers imagine and thus move beyond rational evidence to embody dialectical tensions."[3] Publicly narrativizing faith walks allows testimony to become a part of supporting the larger body. Moreover, adds communication scholar Steven Halliday, the "traditional Pentecostal practice of encouraging public prophecies by laymen—based on 1 Corinthians 14:26–29 . . . [gives] a Bakhtinian polyphonic voice to 'ordinary members' of the church and by a Foucaultian redistribution of power from the paid clergy to the rank and file, resulting in a greater sense of God's presence."[4] Even an artist like D'Angelo calls testimony his "aha" moment when talking about his *Black Messiah* release.[5] In other words, the rank and file get to have a say about their salvation during testimony.

Testimony works in a multiplicity of ways. Ideally, the grace of God/Allah/ Yahweh centers experiences, of all manners and places, allowing for a powerful and productive sharing. For the purposes here, I provide three different functions of testimony: as disruption, as witness, and as connection as they emerge for media scholars and the scholarship they produce. First, testimony can be read as disruption or divine intervention, underscoring and valuing a certain truthfulness to the narrative being told.[6] Film scholar Miriam Petty talks about how in filmmaker Tyler Perry's media works, he uses testimony to disrupt relationships. A secret revealed or a trauma addressed comes as testimony in many of his narratives.

Edwards and Baszile believe testimony acts as "the practice of bearing witness to trauma that results from academia's continued reproduction of racist/sexist/ classist/homophobic ideology and practice, which works against empowered writing, reading, and community-building."[7] Many online groups facilitated by Facebook, for example, function as a therapeutic and valuable space for witnessing the sometimes unbearable whiteness academia (re)produces, as well as to living while Black and academic.

Third, like the disintegrating sacred-secular split interrogated during the Processional, testimony demonstrates the need for women to connect, support, and recognize not only the differences within and between each of us but also the ways those differences combine to make us whole. And as mentioned there, Black women need dialectical relationships with other women in order "to dialogue, to affirm, to exhort, and to admonish each other verbally and nonverbally."[8] We must be our sisters' keepers.

The dynamic and bombastic nature of popular culture facilitates many crises and adds to debates about what religious faith means in this moment.[9] As the Invocation suggests, televisual, filmic, digital, and musical narratives often prove tricky and ripe for contest in relation to faith. Scholars of popular culture engage this conundrum readily and constantly because they know where and how to look but also because their job demands attending to these incidents, snippets, programs, memes, clips, films, news stories, videos, industry hires, tweets, and larger cultural signs that impact, nourish, and distract from and feed audiences' information and entertainment needs alongside their faith walks. Thus, the study of popular culture, especially Black popular culture, requires a constant (re)grounding in the importance of a spiritual self. Studying Black popular culture as a believer makes you particularly attuned to (and often algorithmically fed by) content like KevOnStage's dissection of a Black woman's interrupted church testimony online,[10] BET's feature of R&B singer Fantasia on *Bobby*

Jones Gospel,[11] and the continued visualization of Judas Iscariot as a Black man in both the cinema version of *Jesus Christ Superstar* (Carl Anderson) (Jewison, 1973) and the same narrative reimagined forty-five years later on NBC live with Brandon Victor Dixon in 2018.

I asked Black women scholars to talk about themselves as religious and/or spiritual beings, and to reflect on how their belief impacts and guides the work they do, the workplace, how they do that work, and what they want it to do. These media scholars come from all over the U.S. and work all over the U.S. They emerge from film studies, television studies, journalism, and media and cultural studies programs; their training, research, and teaching have prepared them to examine the most prescient elements of today's mediated life. They work in big state public institutions with thousands of students and hundreds of majors, in historically Black colleges and universities (HBCUs), in medium-sized elite universities, and as adjuncts or with no university affiliation at all. They profess Protestant Christianity (Baptist, Methodist, and Bapticostal), Catholicism, and sometimes a blend of these denominations while incorporating African-centered traditional beliefs as well. The English they speak varies across conversations—from the King's English to a Black Southern-inspired vernacular of plain and praise speak. All of which, as cultural studies scholar bell hooks writes, undermines the presumption and hierarchy of certain speech and recognizes, "we do not necessarily need to hear and know what is stated in its entirety . . . we do not need to 'master' or conquer the narrative as a whole . . . we may know [only] in fragments."[12]

I have changed the names of the participants, except mine, not to protect the innocent but to respect the ways in which faith, even when talking about it for public consumption, remains not only extremely private but also potentially deleterious professionally. I include the work of other scholars' writing as part of the discussion and frame and set those ideas off in italics—both outside the conversations and sometimes within them. In addition, I interrupt or add to the testifying moments to broaden out, contextualize, or sometimes even include how popular religious-spiritual cultural frames are imagined outside of the discussion.

They Don't Know . . . Who We Be

Lynn opens by talking about herself, what appears in Black mediated culture religiously, and scholars who interpret it with her.

LYNN I grew up Catholic. I didn't grow up in a Black church. So I feel like I learn shit. [Laughter] I didn't know what a praise [dance] was . . . there are lots of things I didn't know. And . . . I feel like there's a certain weird way in which knowing these things . . . gives my Blackness more legitimacy. It's interesting, Larry Wilmore was talking about certain things that he does and doesn't do in his comedy, and even in the comedy he's written. And he said he was raised Catholic too. The Black church isn't a part of his upbringing.

BERETTA So, the Black Protestant church? Because there [are] lots of Black Catholics. And in New Orleans, some of the Black Catholics get it crunk. So Black Catholic in a certain context, not as a Black space.

LYNN Yeah . . . it just feels good to me . . . like nobody is going to say, "You don't know what that is?" Or they may say that. [Laughter] But it's not in a judgmental way. And in terms of spirituality . . . I think spirituality is something very personal, and not necessarily something that I would or could share with other colleagues. And I, being a person recovering for twenty-two years, I know it's by the grace of God that that's so. And I know that. It's not open for debate on some level. And so it's nice to be able to have these spaces where I can say something like that and not have people roll their eyes. I know I'm not religious, but I am spiritual. . . . I think there are ways that we process these belief systems into our scholarship [and] into our life. . . . In order to stay sober, a huge part of it is being of service. We can't keep it lest you give it away. And I think there are ways in which the same thing operates with scholarship. [Jo: Absolutely.] It's about teaching; it's about sharing; but it's ultimately about being of service.

MICHELLE My faith is very important to me, especially, I think, in going through the experience that I went through at my former institution. Because in putting it in context, one of the things I'm realizing in my real life and then how it impacts my faith is the extent to which I can be a perfectionist and how that type of performance-oriented thinking impacts my relationship with God, because He's not a performance-oriented God. But that's the environment that I was raised in, and so really grasping ahold of the fact that I am loved regardless of how many times I screw up is sometimes challenging for me as a concept. So working through and putting what I can view as a failure in a more healthy context, and trying to get God's perspective on it has been really, it's been challenging. But it's been a good process to go through. Because if nothing, I can help other people.

You know, when I hear someone tell me a story about their department and some of the things going on in their department, I'll be like, "Yeah, no, you can't. This is what you're gonna have to do, and you need to find allies. And if you don't find allies, you need to at least document the fact that these things are happening." So yeah, I think that's been really important. . . . One thing that was always interesting to me, I think definitely in grad school to a lot of my friends, not surprisingly are people of color, was just always how it's kind of accepted, especially as you're getting a doctorate. . . . "Well, you Black people, you know you do have God, but the rest of us are rank pagans." And it's like okay, that's fine. But you know my faith is important to me. And I'm not going to necessarily proselytize to you, but understand that that's important to me. . . . It's not an optional activity. It is what, especially during difficult times . . . gets me through. I don't understand what other people rely on. . . . But it is a really critical component of my faith, and it's not something that I'd say outside of [a] context like this. I would not. . . . Well, most people, because they don't believe in God, you're not gonna have that conversation with them. And so they're not going to talk about . . . the moral or ethic of me doing something like this. I mean they talk about morality or ethics, but I'm thinking about, "Okay, in my relationship with God . . . I believe that I'm somehow not being true to that. Am I violating that? . . . Because it's not so much about following rules as it's my relationship with Him. So, are we good?" And those conversations, unless the person identifies as a Christian . . . [don't] happen most of the time in the academy, especially with my white colleagues.

JAMAYA I have been in church all my life, all of it. Black Baptist churches . . . it was just something you just did. You get baptized you do all of that. . . . My mother is my best friend, so she in many ways treated me like a peer. So when she was trying to figure out what church to go to and trying to figure out how to hear God, I was also trying to mimic that. And so, my walk has always been sort of tied with hers. . . . [I] visited several churches, learned a bunch of stuff, did a lot of service, did a lot of leadership, and in the process of doing that, I sort of met the white Christians, the nondenominational charismatic ones. And they have a whole different approach to everything. So it was going to meet with the white Christians, the nondenominational ones, that I started to sort of think about God differently than how I had thought of Him and been raised to think of Him. And I started to learn other things about who God could be and what God could do. And so, [I was on a] long path toward realizing who I could be and what gifts God could give.

So I remember when I was seventeen, and I sang my first solo . . . something switched over and before I knew anything, words were coming out of my mouth that I didn't say. And it was English, but it was not my own thoughts about what was happening or what I was saying. And so that switched to this other thing, this other gift thing. And you know at seventeen, I don't know what's happening. It's like this flood that happens. It would just flip on. I'd be doing something, and it'd flip on, flip off, flip on, flip off. So . . . you learn to control it. And I had some interesting experiences with churches who didn't really know what to do with prophetic gifting, so you know, you get some injuries. . . .

But one of the things that happened with that was, I just felt really inspired, really led to find all these promises in the Bible, like all these scriptures. And so I just went on this long journey of underlining. And then I typed them up and printed them out . . . put them on like some construction paper and then labeled them all over my wall; so something that I would always just look at. And somehow, [I considered] the focus of that, what that meant, and thinking about what that would be for me long term. And I think that was the beginning of laying out what was coming. . . . I didn't know that that's what I was doing. To this day, my mother made me frame them, and so they're all over my house, and they've moved with me. So there's broken glass in one of them. But she will not let me take these damn things down. So when you walk along my hallway, you'll see these scriptures from seventeen. But that's sort of the beginning and . . . how I started with graduate school. And I was so fervent in my faith. . . . It looked very different than what I am now. . . .

Graduate school does something to you. You learn stuff that feels contrary to what you hear, what you know, what you hear in church, and what you believe. . . . The challenge was to always figure out how to still be real and also learn the stuff. But it can't help but sort of mix with you. . . . And also, when you discover that most folks that are around you, don't nobody believe. You can't talk about church. The first thing I did when I moved to [the West] was to try and find a church. And I hooked up with the Chi Alphas, which were a Christian org. They didn't really fit me, but I was just like, I needed something. And I trekked and traveled, trying to find a place that matched what I was into, and what I felt was so crucial. But I was doing this on my own. What my classmates saw Monday through Saturday was one thing. What I was trying to do on Sunday was a whole other thing. And so, it's like, I can't speak to this part of my life with this, and I don't know how to make these two things talk to one another. I don't know how to make that work.

And so, pushing that all the way to my doctoral program, I found a church and had a whole situation, was in the choir. But as I'm doing my research . . . and I'm in this multiracial church with a predominately Black choir, a Black music director, and with a 80 percent white congregation, you cannot help but notice things. And I would start to sit and watch the white pastor in our introductory meetings talk about doing things that were weird and how we can't do weird things. And I remember raising my hand. . . . "Well, what's weird?" And he was like, "You know, being loud or overly expressing." And this is a nondenominational. This is supposedly where you can be free. And so, what I noticed was a lot of the Black folks, and they were mostly college students or post-college, a lot of them in the choir. They would be coming from COGIC. They would be coming from Black Baptist.

So there would be these moments where . . . our music director, he would play contemporary Christian. But he would play it with this spin. So it would be gospel chords. And so we know four-part harmony, like everybody, it was an amazing moment. . . . The Spirit would be high, but nobody could move. So you'd be watching these Black people roll or shake in their seat, because you couldn't express anything, because they're gonna get you. [Jo: They're gonna feel some type of way.] . . . We could never express what was there.

And you could never be from where you were. You could never be COGIC there. And so it was a question of, what does it mean to be Black in this church? And what I heard was it's not supposed to matter, and your Blackness does not count; and your Black experience in church doesn't count. 'Cause if you wanted that, you would go there, and you wouldn't be here. [Jo: And it makes white people uncomfortable.] Right. Always, as if they don't have Pentecostals and as if they're not helicoptering all over the church. But they can't also be who they might want to be. . . .

Spirituality and religiosity often emerge in this way for believers working in popular culture—even when examining texts from this realm. The lack of acknowledgment feels exhausting and often overwhelms. Filmmaker and scholar Trinh T. Minh-ha writes about a "realm of emotion" as a place where "we are not willing to acknowledge, especially in intellectual and academic milieus. How a film affects your body, how a work affects your senses and yourself is something that I rarely encounter in analyses of my work. The only critics who dare to do that are apparently those who are themselves dealing with many levels of emotion in their own works."[13]

JAMAYA Everybody says you need to have this and that, and I just have to trust that whatever it is that got me here is what's going to continue. Because I didn't put myself here. So this has to keep pushing, and that makes no sense. There is no reason to it. There is no logic to it, but I just have to keep doing that. And I think over time that persists even to now. But you know, there are losses.

My mother often talks about how . . . I don't look, I don't act like the Christian I was when I started. . . . She thinks in many ways that I lost something because I got more educated or because the education somehow . . . I couldn't somehow find a way for Jesus. And I get it, I get what she means. I understand what it is she's looking for, but . . . you cannot not be influenced by what you know. And I . . . have to believe that God is smarter than me. So, if I'm thinking too hard about it, then He might very well be able to meet me there and still be that person He was to me when I was seventeen, still be what He is now. And so that's been the difficulty. It's always having to be able to both understand this fundamental impossibility of God, the impossibility of who He is and what He can do. And how I have unnatural favor and not in a braggart way. . . . He just meets me. He's there before I get there; He does it before I do it. Yet it's still hard, that and the fact that I'm in this system that is fundamentally dependent upon so-called meritocracy and so-called smarts and intelligence and skill set and networking. That's the path having to sort of figure out these two competing forces.

JO It's so funny to hear all of these stories . . . 'cause I feel like I can identify with something from all of them, each of them. And at the same time, each of our journeys is so individual. . . . The thing I probably identify with from you, Lynn, is as a child growing up, I was raised in a Black Presbyterian church.

And it was a Black Presbyterian church—me and Beretta were talking about this earlier—where if the preacher said something and somebody in the back row said "Amen," you'd be like: "Are you getting loud?" . . . "You kinda, c'mon now, don't show out." That was the equivalent of getting happy. That was the extent to which that happened in the church I grew up in. . . . I think my spiritual road is also complicated by the fact that my parents were both always unconventional Christians in certain kind of ways, or certainly unconventional Black Christians, certainly from the perspective of mainstream thought about what Black Christianity is or can look like.

My dad was a preacher's kid, and he was a preacher's kid of a preacher who was a Baptist preacher in [the South]. But just that animatedness of that kind of preaching style, alternately sort of amused and terrified my dad as a child. . . . He used to tell these stories about this one woman who would run every Sunday, and she would literally run down the backs of all the pews, all the way to the back of the church and all the way back to the front. He tells that story like "that is what happened, don't look at me like I'm crazy, 'cause that's what happened."

In thinking about the visualization of the Holy Ghost run and religious meaning, film scholar Miriam Petty argues that within Tyler Perry's works—his films and plays—he carries "the kind of structural unpredictability and mutability predicated by the sensibility of testifying. . . . At the plays themselves, spontaneous applause and affirmation from the audience are entirely routine, mirroring Black church and cultural practices of call-and-response and reflecting the ways in which Perry's plays revolve around particular moments of testificatory power."[14] This same sort of impetus resounds strongly during the Praise and Worship section of the service here, the stage performance of Van Peebles's New Jack City Live *by Je'Caryous Johnson (2022), and what happens frequently when Black women identify with one another's stressors.*

JO My mom was raised in a very middle-class family that looked down on all that my mother used to call hoopin' and hollerin'. If you're just doing too much, it's too loud, [she'd wonder] "Why you got to do all that?" So my mother would play something like "Great Is Thy Faithfulness" on the piano, and if you divulged or moved from a note, tried to put a little too much blues on it, she'd [be] like: "Why are you shaking your voice?" "Why you doing all that?" . . . So my mother could turn any gospel song into a John Phillips Sousa march. [Laughter] We would just have some little dum-di-dum-di-dum, and I'd be like "Oh my God, that's [not how] it's supposed to sound!" . . . My mother had a lot of formal music training. . . . I mean to this day, one of the things I listen to all the time that helps me in my spirit is Mendelssohn's *Elijah*. That is spirit work for me when I listen to that.

Because part of it is my connection with my mother . . . that is what she raised me listening to. So I just get to think about her and talk to her sometimes when I listen to that. So they had us in this Presbyterian church that was very kind of staid. At one point the young people took over the choir and we sang "Oh Happy Day," and everybody was like "Look at the young people!" You know, we had people clapping and stuff. It was like oh my goodness; you know that was a big deal.

So I had a funny kind of rebellion in my teenage years partially because of the impact of the children's choir I grew up in. I grew up in a children's choir, and we sang all kinds of music. We had a conductor who had us singing gospel music, and once we started doing that, we started going and doing concerts at Baptist churches. Now, this was a really integrated children's choir, lots of Black kids, lots of white kids, rich kids, poor kids, it was incredibly diverse. And so there were kids in the choir who were a part of that Baptist and Pentecostal background also. So when we would go to these churches and their children's choir would get up and sing "My Liberty" or something . . . inevitably some child in our choir would get the Holy Ghost. . . . We'd be sitting out in the audience singing, listening, and we had these twins in the choir who we called the "Holy Ghost paramedics," because they would come and take care of whoever, get them and say, "That's alright, baby." So, it was funny 'cause it was sort of anthropological for my sister and me. We didn't grow up in that context, but we knew from Black people and Black religion. We were not totally [clueless though], it was [a] little touristy for us. We were kind of like "wow." But the white kids would be like: "Oh my God, what is happening?!" They'd be completely confused. [Laughter] But I think it was partially because of those experiences that I started going to this little storefront church when I was about sixteen or seventeen years old. I got saved. I accepted Jesus Christ as my personal savior. They fixed me a little certificate that I took home to my stunned and vexed parents [Laughter], who were just like "What is happening?" [Laughter] I was like I want to be a Christian in my heart, and they were like "gotcha." [Laughter] They were just baffled by the entire thing. But I think I was always seeking in a certain kind of way. And the other thing that I felt really with you, Lynn, was there were all of these ways in which our Blackness was never quite homogenous with a kind of Blackness that we were surrounded by.

We were middle-class, but not middle-class enough to be doing cotillions or Jack and Jill, or any of that kind of stuff. . . . We weren't doing that stuff. And my parents were not big dressers, and as a result they were not outfitting us in every Guess and all that stuff. And we spoke the King's English in a way that made our Blackness suspect. So it's like "You're talking like a white girl, whatchu doing?" So we weren't working-class enough to be working-class, and we weren't middle-class enough to be actually bougie. So there was something about that church experience that felt like authenticating Blackness to me on some level. But there was also a part of it that really spoke to my heart. . . . I have never had the Holy Ghost in my life. I have never run. I have never actually shouted, and I'm careful to make that distinction. I play a little but even when we were kids, my mother was like "Don't you play with God." . . . Mom didn't do all that running and shoutin' stuff, but she's not going to have you joke or mocking it. You not going to do all that. So I remember feeling very moved. And so I think that, in some ways, most of my spirituality has almost always come through music.

And that's a really good thing, I think, in part because when I was here in Atlanta in . . . school, I think I may have said this to each and every one of you at a certain point, there's a level of diversity in Black church experience that you can have here. You can go to a Black church of any flavor. You can find a Black church that has a great choir, that is queer-friendly, that is Afrocentric, that believes in Sun-Ra. You can find a Black church of almost any variety that you want here. And that was something that was so wonderful to me in school. There was a point in school where every weekend, before I had a car, I would get on the bus and get on the train and go to a different church every Sunday until I found some place. . . . And I have not found that kind of diversity anyplace else that I've lived. So when I moved to [the Northeast], just conservative. The man is the head of the household, woman be silent, blah blah blah. Ain't nobody got time for that.

When I got to [the Midwest], it's the same thing. It's just so conservative. And . . . I'm real out there. My Christianity . . . I think a lot of people who are Christian would say I'm not Christian, right. It makes me cringe to hear people call God "He," and I struggle with that. When we pray in my house, we say Mother Father God. I'm trying to change up the Bible and be like "she," or "them," or "they," you know what I mean? So, in some ways, having left here and [gone to] some other places, I've been able to re-create a certain kind of spirituality for myself just by listening to music. Because I can't go to church and have people saying crazy stuff, I just can't. That's the opposite of what I need church to do, and I think it's also complicated by the fact that I was very spoiled here as well, because I was a part of an African rites-of-passage community that was very much spiritual and ethical and progressive in ways that just fed my spirit. There was ritual and ceremony and community, and it's a really beautiful community of people. And so, once you've had that kind of spiritual experience, it's hard to go to some old humdrum, people trying to tell you to put on your lap skirt or whatever. I'm just like nah, dude, I can't do it. I can't do that.

Her feelings reflect many contemporary believers' sentiments. Christian rapper Lecrae's lyrics get at it best: "If God gon take me as I am, I guess I already got on my church clothes."[15]

JO So I think for me, my spirituality as a scholar, it's true, there's a way that I feel doubly silenced in terms of talking about it. Because not only is it Black, but it's ooga booga African, and it's Jesus. Don't none of my colleagues want to hear anything about any of that, at all. And so there are very few people that I share that with. I share it with my family. I share it with close friends, and it feeds me. It's refreshing and it's nourishing to even be in community in a way where it's not the thing that dare not speak its name.

MICHELLE Can I add something? Thinking about your faith in the context . . . we were basically in white communities. So when I think of my faith in that context as well, because we would go to predominately white churches, but during the summers when we'd visit our extended family, that's when we'd go and see a Black church. So I do remember having those moments too, where I would wonder about my Blackness. And I remember being so excited once, hearing one of these comedians on *ComicView* talk about "you know you're really Black when." "You know . . . how you go and visit your grandparents and they have a big dog and it's a German shepherd, and his name is either King or Rex, and it's either Kang or Rex?" And I was like "Yes, that was us!" [Laughter] Okay, okay, I might be Black. [Laughter] And also, just within the context of churches, because my father was probably, like yours, probably traumatized because he was a preacher's kid in the Church of Christ. And then my mother, she was Baptist, but when we were living in California, she got affiliated with the Jesus movement. So she would and could, I won't even say be "out there," but she would definitely speak in tongues. So it was hilarious because I just remember especially during my teen years when we had finally moved to [the East Coast], and we went to what's a secessionist church. So they believed that none of the gifts of the Spirit are active. That was for the first-century church and then no more. And I remember always being like, "nah, my mom speaks tongues." [Laughter]

LYNN . . . I need the smells and bells sometimes. I need the smells and bells . . . there used to be our choir director . . . for like forty years, and he has this incredible operatic voice. And he was really less interested in the choir singing than in him singing. [Laughter] . . . But that voice and the incense, and all of that come together to be comforting. But I do have that experience that you were sharing about, Jo, that I go into a church and I'm saying yeah, I'm going back to Mass for a while. And then they're going to say something that's a hot mess, and I'm done. I'm done for a while. You know, I can't do it. . . . It's just sometimes I feel like, "Did you like read anything that Jesus said?" Seriously. Because, you know . . . I believe in Jesus. I know I believe in God, the Trinity.

JO God made all them feelings, and not a thing wrong with that. That's the gospel according to Shug Avery. [Laughter] You wanna be mad at Shug, go on and be mad at Shug.

In examining the ways Judeo-Christianity influences Black women faculty's pedagogy, Edwards suggests womanist theology and the Black church "emphasize the potency of human interaction and community investment as a sacred endeavor."[16] *Monique agrees, saying . . .*

MONIQUE: I think for me, [religiosity] manifests just in my treatment, meaning of others, of students and colleagues. I find myself going the extra mile when I know I don't have to. Not because I just feel spiritually it is the right thing for me to do, I need to always be doing the right thing. So, when I was at [one HBCU], spirituality . . . it was okay for me to do that. [At another HBCU,] much the same. . . . Since I've been at these smaller, private religiously affiliated institutions, I've been able to talk about. . . .

BERETTA And Black folks.

MONIQUE: And Black folks, so it has been freeing to talk about [spiritual matters]. And I have had a lot of students who don't identify religiously and who are clear about that. But I think they respect the fact that they have chosen to be in a place that is proudly whatever it is, Methodist, Catholic, and they just kind of go along with it.

BERETTA . . . Like many of you, or some of you have been raised in the church, raised like "We go [every] Sunday." . . . My mother was raised Baptist. She raised me in the United Methodist church in Omaha. There were Baptist churches too, but she always said she liked the minister [at Clair Methodist] and what he had to say. Jo and I were talking about this earlier. It's not hallelujah, in fact you'd be like "What? Whatchu doing?" But we also, especially the youth choir, we did a lot of . . . "We've Come This Far by Faith."

JO We sang that too! Yes, we did!

BERETTA . . . We about sang every Andraé Crouch song because my choir director loved him, and our pianist loved him. So we sang all of those songs. So it was that kind of blend. So when I went to Clark, going to an HBCU, you can be openly religious, and it's fine. You can also not be. You can't be atheist, not really. I don't know if anybody would say that, espouse that. But, whatever your religiosity or spirituality, it's fine. And I was sharing with Jo earlier today because whenever I'm in Atlanta . . . you think about these things and the relationship[s]. [I had] . . . a whole group of friends who were really religious; "You can't do this, can't do [that]." So I was always the friend that [thought], "I guess I'm going to hell [Laughter] 'cause I'm doing all that. I'm gonna be in the club." But I'll still go to church. But I was also very comfortable with them and what they were talking about. But as you get older, you get closer or farther away. When you get a certain age, you start getting closer because you're closer to death. You see people getting more religious as they get older. But I've always been.

I've never been in a space where I didn't feel comfortable believing what I believed or espousing it in a certain way. I didn't have to do it a lot, but . . .

I'm going to church. I'm going to find a church. I'm going to sing in the
gospel choir, which is what I did at Clark, go to chapel, whatever. And I've
been that way. . . . So, when I went to Brooklyn in New York, I had a church
that was way far, but I liked this church. . . . It was a Baptist church, but I had
some friends who were in theology school who were going to this church,
Saint Paul. And that church was really, really very progressive. [Well,] not all
the way progressive, but progressive in Blackness. . . . My parents were kind
of civic activists, so I was kind of raised in that [progressiveness]. . . . They
started [MAAFA] at this church in Brooklyn. The MAAFA is commemorat-
ing the passage of the slaves over to the New World. And in New Orleans, it's
kind of articulated as kind of African-centered, Yoruba; it's a whole combination of things . . . you're wearing white; it's a very different kind of thing. But
it's the whole idea of celebrating or putting your Blackness in play with your
religiosity, and I like that. . . . That was my New York time. And so, when I
moved to Los Angeles to go to school, and it was crazy-ass from the very get
up. . . . Some of it had to do with UCLA and what they were talking about,
how I got there and what I was going to have to do. But I had a friend [and]
we went to Faithful Central, in Los Angeles. Faithful Central is huge, it was
big when we joined. . . . There were probably 2,000 members there then. . . .
Now it's probably about 17,000 members. . . .

Schooling never changed my path, but it makes you real heady. And we all
know, those of us who went to school in California . . . you can see the
possibilities of whatever it is you're talking about. If you're talking about
Baudrillard and simulacra, you can talk about it in a way, in California, that
makes sense. And some of it's just about the iconography. It's something
about the demographics. It's something about the way that it's articulated
there, that makes any kind of theoretical framework possible.

Embodied Knowledge

*"[A] knowing in your body before it reaches your conscious mind . . . entering the
academy, where the cardinal rule is you do not know until you read, until you
research—until you find your thoughts held hostage by Rationality and its demands
for linearity, control, evidence ensconced in whiteness, and writing for/as
commodification."*[17]

BERETTA But what always disturbed me and worked my spirit, being a Black person
on UCLA's campus, where people felt like they couldn't connect because you're
trying to negotiate California in a certain kind of way, where the numbers are
small. . . . People examine a brick wall, or bore a hole in [the sidewalk], trying to
avoid speaking to you, trying to avoid looking at you. Because they don't want
to be identified in that way. And I was like what the hell is this? What are y'all
doing? What is this about? And then all the propositions were coming on when

I was in school. And [it] was like "We are the world," "Can't we all just get along?" Let me pass this proposition. Let's do all this crazy shit, and [I] was just like, oh I can't. You know it's one [thing] to live where somebody's going to call you a nigger, and you're going to be clear. It's another thing when they're like "Oh I love [you]—let me kill you now." And that dichotomy was very difficult. So Faithful Central to me was absolutely where I needed to be built up and affirmed. And then to be tied to the other kind of normative bullshit you do in grad school, when you're about to finish and then it's "I'm concerned about your writing." "I'm concerned about this," and [I'm] like what? I called my mother collect one time, this was pre–cell phone, after [an encounter with one of my professors]. I'm about to defend, and she's like "I'm concerned about your writing." I was so upset. This is middle of the day, and I called my mama. She said, "Can you write? What's she talking about? Why are you pressed?" I said, "You right, okay, alright, let me go to church, pray about this." But you know that kind of constant challenging of your ideas and your perspective and your ability, it's like, what Lord is this? This is why I went to Texas to write, because I said "No, I've got to get up out of here."

LYNN   You know, that goes along with a lot of the stuff, in presuming competence about the ways that you're always interrogated in ways that you don't expect. And I had a [professor] moment too, when I was writing the prospectus, and she was like, "Lynn, you write so well!" [I thought] "I sho' is happy you likes it!" [Laughter]

JO   Yessum, we learn three times a day back at home! Like what? How do you even?

JAMAYA   You have this sort of frame . . . how you imagine yourself to be in relationship to your classmates and your colleagues. . . . I think the challenge for me, and what has always been sort of my fight internally, is I am not about to go crazy. It seems silly to say, but it's the truth. I'm not going to go crazy. In graduate school, I first started going to therapy, and that interest-ingly . . . I never felt any sort of confliction about it. And it turned out to be a wonderful God-given thing. Because I had this professor, who I was TA'ing for, who for some reason, either before or after, I TA'ed with him that one particular semester, he never was that cool. And there were three of us, three women, who TA'ed for him. And he treated us like bad daughters. And I didn't realize how all these things connected to my family and my own relationship with my father, and all those things. I had no idea.

So, sitting down and talking about that, going to therapy for that, ended up becoming a conversation that ended up helping me not go crazy for the years I was there. . . . It will mess with you. And it was uncanny how these little things, these little erosions of who you are can affect that very core. Like somebody saying, "You write so well" or somebody saying, "You can't write," or somebody saying, "You can't read my mind and figure out what movie I want you to pick." Or . . . "I just don't know how you're going to find a job when you don't have any articles published." "I don't know how you're going to—" You know, all those things start to mess with you. And so it is only at the most basic core, even when I couldn't get it together to pray, you just sort of have, okay, I'm not going crazy. God, you're going to have to keep this. You need to have people around . . . somebody who goin' pray. Somebody who's going to say, you don't have to believe this for yourself, I got it. I'll believe for you. . . .

And even through the process of being at [a PWI in the South], and all of the foolishness there. . . . There were these moments where I literally was like . . . this is a moment where I could just slip off and go completely off grid, and let all of the paranoia and the fear and all of that take over and become the shell. It was only through walking down my hallway and looking at those promises again—that thing I did when I was seventeen. It's only that, that is what keeps you. So okay, I'm going to make it one more day.

Emotional resilience becomes paramount in higher education. When presumed incompetent, as Black women often are, daily living can be grueling. The presumed incompetence of your theoretical grounding, questions about any media selected outside of Black narratives, and YOUR demand for everyone to contribute (aka, please do some service, white male colleagues), matches your presumed supreme ability to mentor any and all students of color, sit on every department committee about diversity and inclusion, and be the diversity two-fer for all other campus committees. Yet, as poet Ruth Forman writes and Black women must remember:

. . . I know that my face is authentic
my mind is authentic
my words are authentic
so I will speak genius to myself.[18]

JAMAYA And I remember . . . you get those moments of clarity when you're in the middle of all of that. I remember having this moment. . . . I saw *Selma*, I didn't like that movie . . . but that's another story. [Laughter] But I remember seeing in the one scene they were in the jail and King was talking to the other guy, and he quoted Matthew 6. And I remember watching that scene and sobbing. That's the only part I cried in but that scene. Because it was something like if He'll take care of the birds of the field, what won't He do for you? And I remember being like okay, so, if he'll do that for them that's right, that's right. So I took that, found that scripture, just like I did when I was seventeen and made six copies and put it everywhere I would be. Put it in my office, so when I looked down, it was there. Put it on my bathroom, on my mirror. Put it on my couch, on my refrigerator door because I just needed to see that everywhere I went so that contrary thing in me, that would be "It's not going to make it; you're not going to make it; it's not enough." . . . [It was] the only place that I found what I knew would come up. It doesn't have to be pretty, it's not pretty. But we're going to get through this somehow. And that was the thing that made the difference.

Because I don't have a church [where I live. The city is] hard . . . all-Black churches are very traditional, but all-white churches are traditional in their way. And the ones that are supposedly mixed, they're mixed in like the most basic definition of integration where you can sit together, and you can touch if you want to. So there's not anything there . . . cleaving onto stuff that I know and learned early, hoping that'll be enough to get you through to the next place. It's always so crucial. So I don't know how to not do it. . . . When I see people who I think are going through stuff, and I know you started off in the church or you had an experience in church, I want to say to them: "Okay, you're just going to have to cling to that thing that you had," and they let go. That part is . . . I don't really know what to tell you. So, do you have enough faith to sort of carry you to this next thing? And they're like, "I don't have, I don't know what faith is. I don't believe in God, or I can't do that anymore. That doesn't seem to be my story in the working." But the story is if He was there to get you here, then He's there to get you. If you don't have that, I don't know what to say. I don't really know what to tell you because I don't know how to help. There is nothing in this field, particularly for women, and women of color in particular, there's nothing but God to be quite honest. Because we're damned doomed. It's just that. I don't see it any other way. The way that this works in the secular, there is no logic to help you get to the next step. It has got to be something else, something spiritual, supernatural to get you . . . so I don't know what to say to people.

LYNN   And I think there are times in life where it's really that no human power can get you through things that you're facing. But that it has to be, there has to be something else. My youngest sister doesn't really have any faith anymore. And when she [was] going through all that hard time . . . it just broke my heart that I couldn't give her that comfort that comes from knowing there is a God. I'm not God. There's a freedom with that. . . . And . . . when you do the steps in the twelve-step program, one of the things you do is to talk about a God of your understanding. How do you conceptualize God? And my old sponsor, who I love . . . used to say when I was getting all up in my head . . . "You need a bigger God. If you had a bigger God, you'd know that He has this."

MICHELLE   . . . There're so many aspects of academia that I think, why do we do it this way? To me, the whole of how we critique people . . . I remember reading this study and thinking, this is why this is so messed up. Because basically, it was showing how most academics think the more harsh and bitter you are in criticism, that's more rigorous. . . . You've already set the frame, and the frame is completely left out there.

JO   Because it's like, why would that encourage anybody to share their gifts? Why would you then share your gifts into a context that's like immediately coming for your neck? That's what we're doing, we can embarrass you, get you, and come for your neck.

JAMAYA Yeah, because there's a place for suffering. . . . Easter, right? [Laughter] It's about suffering. It's about the suffering, but then there's something productive in it.

JO Yes, yes! Yes.

JAMAYA Should we always suffer? That's the minor chord. Should that be the focus? And I think for many, and parts of why I think people leave God, is because their church theology, their church dogma makes suffering the major chord. Life is suffering. This is what this is. There's no redemption; there's no resurrection; there is no productivity; there is no success. Or it comes in the after as opposed to in the now. And so, I can see why somebody would leave, if that's what you think. If He never rose, then what's the point? What's the benefit? So I think we often focus too hard on the suffering, or we don't realize that the suffering has . . . this component to get you to this next thing. So, would I ever choose to suffer? I hate pain. [Laughter] I like to be comfortable.

JO But the other thing is . . . there's also a way that we can avoid suffering but be glad somebody else is doing it. I feel like that is the way that most Christians treat Jesus, like, "Thank God Jesus did it, now I don't have to." And the whole point is, if we all just do that, then nobody will have to do it, basically. The idea is not for Jesus to be the standard that none of us can live up to. That's not really the idea. There's a kind of comfort that I think people can get used to.

MICHELLE Then there's the part of that theology that you were talking about. I think there's a certain sense that we know there's some suffering to go through, but we'd like to kind of put God on a timetable with regards to it.

JO Right. Make me good, but not right now—

MICHELLE Exactly, or this isn't going to be like this in a month or two. So, when it's going longer than we anticipated, it's just like. . . .

JAMAYA No, you're right. It's a thing. And with this process of academia, because I think what you're asking [with] these kinds of questions, what's this place of Christianity? What do we bring to it with what we do? You suffer a lot, in your head. You suffer a lot, the whole internal process of is this good enough? Is this ever going to be enough? Am I ever going to get to the next thing? What's the next thing? You know, all of that, you suffer. And it's hard, and people will think it'll be over with, and it's like "Well, you've got a job so it should be over with." Then you get a job and it's like "Oh no, this is worse. This is worser." [Laughter]

JO The amount of times that I have played "How I Got Over," thinking that I was done, and I had got over. And then it was something else to get over! [Laughter] I mean, I played that song . . . when I graduated, when I got my PhD, the way we were blasting that song on the day of my graduation. And Aretha Franklin is just singing the devil out of it. I mean, when I got a job, when I got my second job, when I got a postdoc. But it's like, your soul looks back and wonders, but your soul is looking ahead, like damn [Laughter] it just continues to be—

JAMAYA   Like you ready for this next piece? Because folks crazy and stay crazy. I think to do academia you sort of have to be a little bit off. I think in general . . . people can do it well because you have to have an obsessive nature. There's a degree to which you have to be willing to fixate on a thing long enough to see it through and—

JO   Unravel it and wrap it back up. Yes.

JAMAYA   So you sort of have to be a little bit off. Like, people who are regular, they don't stay long. Because they can't sit down and have a conversation about the same thing for fourteen minutes. You know? [Laughter]

JO   And not 200 times neither. [Laughter]

JAMAYA   You've got to sit and have these same conversations and be like, but you know what? Let me say this. And so, I think you've got to be a little bit off. And so I think that just makes you more vulnerable to all those other things.

JO   Right. Because that's the places where you can either have a preoccupation or an obsession, right? And the anxiety that can so easily creep into that. For me it really manifested around teaching. Right. When I first got my postdoc . . . I was so happy because I didn't have to teach. So happy. And in the second year of it, [a colleague] who is a dear friend of mine, she's like "I'm going to teach this class on Black popular culture, come teach this class with me." And I was like, "Oh hell nah." . . . My husband was like, "You better go teach that class!" I was like, "Don't nobody want to teach no class with her." He was like "Go teach that class!" [Laughter] So I ended up teaching the class with her. I was so anxious and terrified. I was so sure that these [elite school] students were smarter than me, undergraduates. I was so sure that I was going to come to class and have them not know what I was talking about. And the way I would just be in a flop sweat on the regular. . . . I was a hot mess for fourteen weeks straight. And . . . I just would be struggling. . . .

What was it you said? Polishing and polishing, Jesus, that's such the perfect. . . . Y'all remember in PCs, you would search for something, and they had that little dog that was doing that? That was my mind. Whenever I would have an exchange, that little dog [would appear]. What can we find that is terrible? That seemed like it was a good exchange, but here's some shit. That was bad right there what you said, go back and find the bad thing. . . . That anxiety, that depression, you're right. There's a way that it fits right in with the structure of what it is that we do. It fits right in. And it's not healthy at all. But it can seem healthy in the kind of culture that you're talking about where the whole thing is slash and burn all the time. So you're slashing and burning yourself, right? You're being rigorous, right?

JAMAYA And after a while . . . unbeknownst to you, that anxiety was spurring you along, but then it becomes harder to muster that up. It's like trying to jump over hurdles. . . . After a while, in order to jump it, you have to . . . okay, I'm going to get it. And then you just end up standing in front of it. That's where you get to "Oh I just can't."

JO . . . Part of it is the toll that it takes on you, leaves you less able to do what you need to do in the first place. Because you done beat yourself down so bad, that you get there "Well, you know." You're tired. You feel bad. It is the opposite of empowering.

JAMAYA . . . I defended my dissertation [in July]. I moved to [my institution] August 2nd, started the job August 19th. And in my mind, I was like this is going to be good. I'm going to roll right into. . . . But unbeknownst to me, I was in my last little group therapy sessions, and I was for some reason, "I just can't wait to get to October." And she [said], "What's going on?" And I said I can't wait to get to October, because I'll come back [here for the conference], and it's going to be fine. And I couldn't ever process why I was trying to get to October. I couldn't quite see it.

So I get to [my institution], and at the time I had a relaxer. My hair had grown out, it was nice. I was like okay, I'm ready. That was August. By September, my hair had fallen out. And I'm just doing what I'm doing. Nothing is happening. I'm not thinking anything is wrong. All of it fell out. I'm like, Jesus, what's going on? [Laughter] I get [back for the conference], go back and see my hairdresser, and she's like "Girl. . . . [Laughter] What happened to your hair? We're going to have to cut this off." So this is how I ended up with this. So somehow, I'm sitting outside myself, watching myself get this done. Because I'm like what the hell is this. Go to this conference and scheduled an appointment with my therapist. She didn't tell me then, but after when we started having calls, she [said,] "You walked in, and it was like this cloud walked in with you. I had never seen you so depressed." And I'm like, how am I depressed? I've got a job. It's alright [Laughter], it's alright. How you feel guilty telling folks that something about this just don't feel right. I get to October, my mother and my sister [say] "What's wrong with you? Why ain't you happy? You got a job, you're good." And I just feel hot on the inside. I felt like I've run out, like a sponge that has run dry. There is nothing on the inside to cool. So this hot light is just on. I can't turn it off. I started having all these thoughts and saying stuff to myself that was just not good. Like nothing is wrong. Nothing is happening. Nobody is pushing me. I can't decorate my office, so I'm sitting in this office . . . nothing here just sitting in the chair. I had no idea. . . .

It was like, everything was just dark. And everything was supposed to be good. But it's the mixture of the anxiety, a mixture of trying to do all of this stuff, and you've not had one minute to process, figure out what it means to be a professor. You've got to make sure everybody around you, all your classmates underneath you, they see you as this goal. And you've got to try and keep up face like, "Yeah, life is good over here."

JO Ooo! Child, you really gon' make me run. I said I've never done it, but I might right now. Chile.

JAMAYA It might take you two months to get your first paycheck, and you better make sure you've got a bank that's your bank in your town. . . . Because if you don't, what are you going to do? They didn't have my bank in the state. I ain't know. [Laughter] My little simple ass. [Laughter] . . . I done went through all this, written this damn dissertation. I don't even know what it's about anymore. [Laughter] I get home from school because I ain't got nothing to do, watching the news. [Laughter] That's why I ended up on Facebook. [Laughter]

BERETTA When you said it, I said, yeah, that's why. . . .

JAMAYA I hadn't made one friend, not one. Couldn't call nobody no friend. . . . That was the only people I could talk to, those people who knew me.

JO You're trying to get your community on somehow, some type of way. That thing is so real, my God.

JAMAYA . . . Nobody ever talks about how crazy your first six months are. Your first six months are ridiculous. You have no money. You have to figure out how to not live on loans because you're used to having a plush sense of cash. What is this little bit of money supposed to do? [Laughter] How are we supposed to keep this up?

JO You need to preach all of that. All.of.that!

MICHELLE And like you said, your networks, because you don't have [them] . . . you go from being a graduate student where you have some type of support network, to being an assistant professor—

JAMAYA By yourself. Sitting in an office that can be like a jail cell. . . .

JO Sat in that jail, sat in that jail, 'til I rot to death! [Laughter] It ain't worth it, Miss Celie! [Laughter]

JAMAYA Exactly. And you're supposed to have won! So it's like Lord, what are we supposed to do now?

JO Girl, that thing is so real.

JAMAYA I had no idea. And not nan Negro, or white person, told me. So it's like, well, Lord, maybe this me just sitting here struggling.

JO Nah, and then plus, the honeymoon is over. So all these people who done wooed you and courted you to come on down are acting just as simple as they can. [Laughter] Just acting a complete ass. Whoo, chile!

MICHELLE You'll ask them a question, and they'll be like "Well, you know, I hope things will work out." [Laughter] I remember telling my people after, "They're really hostile, the students, when I teach on race." And they're like, "I hope you'll keep on doing it." And I remember going to the seminar later, [thinking] ... "Hope is not a strategy. You need to give me a concrete strategy."

Honey, You Can Shout Right Now!

"[T]estimonies of Black women provide some of the most powerful work in regard to struggle, perseverance, and healing in negotiating academic life."[19]

JAMAYA I had to teach a grad class my first semester because the person who was supposed to teach it left to go to a different place. And I decided to teach a race class, just like what I was taught at [grad school in the West]. I took a class with [a well-regarded white professor of race], same way he trained us, same way I was trying to train them. Had these white kids shaking. [Laughter] One of them, child shook herself and me. [Laughter] ... I had no idea. It's like, what are you supposed to do in graduate school? She shook so hard. ... When we read bell hooks, this baby shook. She was like, "I just don't believe any of that is true. I lived in New York and I ain't never seen that. And I lived in England and I ain't never seen that." And I was like, well—

JO You was white in all them places. [Laughter] Were you Black in any of those places? No, ma'am, you were as white as could be.

JAMAYA To this day, that class, those seven children ... still brings my damn score down. It makes me mad because they all went into the class the next semester with a white man, who taught the exact same material I did, but they were like "Oh yeah!" So now I'm going to write an article called "Sometimes It Takes a White Man." And sincerely, sometimes it takes a white man.

The importance of Black women's support and voice in general, and in the disciplines of Black popular culture more specifically, cannot be understated. When writing about the survivors of Hurricane Katrina and Spike Lee's visualizing their humanity in When the Levees Broke, *film scholar and maker Prajna Parasher argues: "witnessing interrupts silence and allows for the enunciatory moment which brings trauma into language."*[20] *Said a different way, despite ridiculous academy encounters, Edwards and Baszile maintain that textual pedagogues, "by virtue of their truth-telling in writing, which is often an act of faith and spirit ... create the epistemic space where they can teach what is often silenced."*[21] *Dichotomies weave vast mazes in the mediated realm, and villages provide sustained insider knowledge, uplift, direction, and respite. Ultimately, the additional benefit (and sometimes burden) of belief shapes many Black academicians' ability to maintain, survive, and thrive. The witnessing voices here stand in for others living in private Facebook groups, text messages, group chats, and conference hallways.*

While testimony recognizes the speaker and affirms their hurts and pains, it also calls for collective truth telling and, most importantly, release. The testimonies given today disrupt, witness, and provide connection for those caught in the constructed false dichotomy of belief and brilliance. Religion scholar and bishop Thomas Hoyt believes: "The power of testimony is to give voice to the faith that lets people run on to see what the end's gonna be."[22] This Testimony service draws to a close to make room for Praise and Worship and the continued race running sistah Blackacademics must do with God.

Praise and Worship

I will bless the Lord at all times: his praise
shall continually be in my mouth.
—Psalms 34:1 (KJV)

Dance, Dance, Dance, Dance, Dance, Dance, Dance All Night!

• •

Mediated Audiences and
Black Women's Spirituality

After the Testimony service, the praise team leader may holler: "When I think about Jesus, what he's done for me. . . ." If you can finish this stanza, you'll be in good stead for what comes next. What accompanies this call—the organ, the drums, the tambourine, and the exhortation—might provoke you to shout and dance. Insert media and you may get a crunk religiosity, or performance of religion. For Black Christians, this performance of spirituality gets visualized and expressed through the preacher, the choir, the work of the ushers, the parishioners (who become the audience in a mediated context), and, critically, the viewers and users.

Believers see the Holy Ghost run as one of the most highly visible and visceral religious performances. In most Black Pentecostal and many Bapticostal churches, men and women run.[1] The biblical admonition/justification for running lies in many books—both in the Old and New Testaments.[2] But something about a woman's run, a woman's tears, a woman's shouting, a woman's jumping forges a connection, emotion, and a realization between the "what is" and the "what can be." In other words, women's visualized belief moves from acknowledgment to participation to performance and, in turn, transforms believers and audiences. Moreover, "catching" the Holy Ghost offers a freedom to which people of color, and women even more, get limited access. Psychologist

Louis Hoffman talks about U.S. notions of freedom and their erroneous connection to only political freedom and individualism. He argues: "Choosing to be a part of a collective can be a profound expression of freedom. Choosing to embrace one's culture, its norms, and its rituals can be one experience of freedom."[3] Being overcome with the Holy Spirit often provides that type of freedom.

The Holy Ghost represents one of the three foundations of Christianity—the father, the son, and the Holy Spirit. The manifestation of spirit comes as God and from God through people, unplanned, and certainly unmediated. Clergy and scholars characterize the Holy Ghost as "the Lord, the giver of life,"[4] "the divine presence in our lives,"[5] and as a "transformative power . . . felt both physically (the 'feeling' that penetrates from head to foot) and emotionally (the rapturous infusion of joy)."[6] This spiritual "gift" represents acceptance of Christian precepts and the activities thereof. It often also suggests a familiarity with particular Christian denominations that not only recognize but also subscribe to spiritual gifts such as these. Despite its non-media orientation, researcher Giuseppina Addo argues that the Holy Spirit can serve as an "embedded element" in the digital realm.[7] For example, one of my favorite praise breaks comes from the Pentecostals of Alexandria (Louisiana). This predominately white megachurch demonstrates its belief bodily and through shouting God's praises. I encountered them online when they hosted guest evangelist Wayne Francis leading them in praise and worship—this Black evangelist conjuring all manner of Black Southern affective spirituality, with which they seem familiar.[8] My getting to them, and their spirit, comes through media.

Mediation, in the context of this work, refers to the conduit, structuring, and transformation of what is televised, digitized, and streamed. Thus, to examine mediation of Black women's spirituality, I offer two examples of praise and worship—praise breaks (as bodily expressions of the Holy Spirit are so often characterized): a 2010 performance on the BET network's gospel competition program *Sunday Best* featuring winner Le'Andria Johnson, and a 2007 performance by R&B singer Kelly Price, aired on BET's annual *Celebration of Gospel* in tribute to the deceased singer Gerald Levert. These national cable programs offer central viewing opportunities for Black Christian communities. Performing in these spaces situates the performers in a particular arena of Black music and music traditions. I examine Black women's Christian performance via contemporary television and online to gain insights into how screen audiences are invited to experience the Holy Spirit. In other words, I argue that in these moments, with Black women (and Black audience members and judges) performing, praising, and testifying, the Holy Spirit moves not only through the recorded, in-studio audience but also within screen audiences—both television viewers and online users. And despite the justified rebuke of Black churches for their frequent dismissive dealings with women,[9] the manifestation of the Holy Spirit allows for an exaltation of women in the revelation of the spirit.

What's the Buzz? Tell Me What's Happening?

In looking for ways to enter a discussion about the visceral impact of Black tele-visual religiosity, I employ the theoretical framework of phenomenology in its address of structures of feelings, emotions, and bodily experiences related to external stimuli. I am especially interested in using a theory that allows for a consideration of mediation across and through embodied Black women. This type of theoretical framing is needed because something tactile can emerge for audiences when watching, for example, the clairvoyance and fortune-telling life work of Mozelle Batiste (Debbi Morgan) in *Eve's Bayou* (Lemmons, 1997), the past's traumas as shown in *Daughters of the Dust* (Dash, 1991), *Sankofa* (Gerima, 1993), *Beloved* (Demme, 1998), and *Underground* (WGN America, 2016–2017), and the soul-stirring notes of soloist Yolanda DeBerry captured on a YouTube-posted church funeral recording in 2019.[10] Beyond these mediated narratives and the tactility they engender, examining television and online texts particularly encourages a grappling with race, gendered bodies, and religious practices, as shown in examples such as Toni Child's (Jill Marie Jones) redemption from past friendship failings in season two of *Girlfriends* (UPN/CW, 2000–2008) or Mercedes (Brandee Evans) strip club dancing while paying a sin tax to her mother's church in *P-Valley* (Starz, 2020–). This encouragement comes, in some measure, from the immediacy and presumed connection of televisual narratives to our real-lived selves. Something in the confluence of the image and audio moves audiences, listeners, viewers, and users between active critical engagement and bodily response, as prescribed within film scholar Teshome Gabriel's theorization of memory, identity, gift, and culture.[11] Utilizing phenomenology as a methodological tool helps us instructively get at meanings and understandings of mediated raced and gendered bodies and their connection with the spirit.

Marrying phenomenology and religious practices requires understanding key aspects of the phenomenological enterprise. The phenomenology of philosopher Edmund Husserl has been modified and continually retooled for useful contributions to several disciplines, including media discourses. With both phenomenology and religious practices, visuality and the visceral connect—when you watch something and are moved by it, the phenomenon ties not only to a physiological response but also to a mind/body and, I argue, spirit connection. Hoffman suggests: "Phenomenology and qualitative methods tend to assume one can better understand the experience of individuals through utilizing multiple ways of knowing."[12] In other words, phenomenology takes up and focuses on subjective experiences—experiences informed by cultural and personal elements that help shape meaning. A phenomenological inquiry takes account of philosophical criticality encountered with a phenomenon (the mind) in relation to its bodily manifestation. However, knowing the trajectory of a phenomenon is not enough. Additional grappling with mediation and its operations is needed to understand how they work in relation.

In media scholarship, debates about the means, methods, and sometimes via-bility of phenomenological inquiry have continued since the late 1970s. For example, film scholar Vivian Sobchack writes in her 1992 *The Address of the Eye*: "The cinema uses *modes of embodied existence* (seeing, hearing, physical and reflec-tive movement) as the vehicle, the 'stuff,' the substance of its language. It also uses the *structures of direct experience* (the 'centering' and bodily situating of exis-tence in relation to the world of objects and others) as the basis for the struc-tures of language."[13] She directly compares the nature of film to human embodiment, arguing for their similar operation. Film scholar Harald Stadler in a *Quarterly Review of Film and Video* review contested many of her assertions (to which she responded in the following issue of that journal), yet their debates continue to be salient for twenty-first-century media discourses.

Film studies teaches that cinema (and its cousins television and digital media) do not exist simply as visual offerings. These media can produce in their audiences and users something tangibly felt. As cultural theorist Elizabeth Ste-phens argues: "Film is not simply a 'vision machine' . . . but a sensation machine, a technology for the stimulation and cultivation of all the senses."[14] To that end, media scholar Michele White amalgamates several women scholars' writ-ings on the body (the conduit of the spirit) and media to suggest: "bodies, other people, and technologies are mediated and mediators. Phenomenological accounts, including the concept of flesh of the world and connective tissue, do not distinguish between the body and representation. The 'medium that signi-fies the body, its *representation*' . . . is no longer distinct from the 'raw material' of the body."[15] Even in the contemporary valuation of Presbyterian minister Fred Rogers and his work on *Mr. Rogers' Neighborhood*, his notion of television as "holy ground" helped create "a liminal space between an on-screen performer and an audience member . . . [a space that becomes] a site for intimacy, reflec-tion, and growth."[16]

Ostensibly, embracing these theoretical understandings allows a consideration of viewers' ability to become a direct part of a spiritual and/or religious experi-ence through media. Mediation not only fails to hinder the relationship between text and audience, it can also help facilitate representation standing in for an actual being. As media apparatuses function in a similar way to human's embod-ied selves, they pose no impediment to accessibility. In the case of this analysis of mediated spirituality, flesh does not bind the Holy Spirit, and thus spirit becomes actualized in the flesh of and for mediated audiences who believe.

Viewers' experiences are shaped also by generic knowledge of media and some-times said viewers' responses to a certain genre. Audiences know television genre constructions, even those of religious programming. Be it a game show, a physical challenge, or a singing competition such as *Sunday Best*, the basic aes-thetics and production choices remain the same regardless of content. Music rises in climactic scenes, pauses for effect, close-ups, zooms, and other production and editing devices form the complete televisual experience, with online video and streaming employing these same techniques as well. While some scholars argue that spaces reserved for religious activity carry a "distinctive character," one that sets them apart from mere "profane" spaces,[17] I suggest audiences' familiarity with these types of programs, religious or otherwise, sets standard expectations despite any higher purpose—this is the "reality" of reality television.

Moreover, many African-American audiences bring their cultural relationships to bear on mediated forms. Black audiences can be as comfortable talking with one another in person, commenting online, or chatting through social media about a particular screening as they are to the nonresponsive screen itself. It stands to reason, then, that believing Black folks can access the spirit of God across platforms. In fact, argues sociologist Christian Smith: "In 'good worship,' Christians believe, the self opens up and mystically pours itself out to and unites with the transcendent source of all life, being, and truth.... Even rough approximations of such experiences can do things to people's bodies and spirits that are deeply emptying and fulfilling, challenging and affirming."[18]

The phenomenological approach forwarded by Stadler offers a way to deploy phenomenology for screens. Stadler argues for engaging a spectrum of experiences involving: "1) doing things as an active participant in events; 2) looking at events as a nonparticipant yet with an active evaluative attitude; 3) visualizing, in memory or imagination, things past or anticipated . . . ; 4) listening to representations . . . of actual events we missed seeing . . . ; and 5) listening to the telling of things that *might* happen."[19] Using this framework, I turn first to *Sunday Best* to explore deeper meanings and associations between the visual, the visceral, and the Spirit.

And the Word Became Flesh . . . *Sunday Best*

Beginning in the fall of 2007, BET's *Sunday Best* became one of the network's most successful programs.[20] With recognized and loved contemporary gospel artist/host Kirk Franklin, judges (including singers BeBe Winans, Donnie McClurkin, Yolanda Adams, CeCe Winans, and the sisters of Mary Mary[21]), quality competitors, and high production values, it created a recipe for televisual (and ratings) success. More importantly, the program encourages audiences to emote with it—to get up and clap, sing along, root for and empathize with the contestants. For twelve weeks, competitors perform always-evocative contemporary and traditional gospel musical selections. Coming from a network with a music video ethos, the program allows for audiences to really get to know the participants and to observe their holiness through outside-lives vignettes and voice-overs. In the example used here, competitor Le'Andria Johnson sings the song "I Love the Lord" as part of the finalists' round of season three in 2010.

The production practices employed for this series are commonplace for televised music competitions. A wide shot of the stage opens the performance and pushes in to the singer slowly. The audience follows her singing from a cut to a

Le'Andria Johnson performing "I Love the Lord."

close-up and then back out to a wide dolly shot. The sound mix includes audio inputs from Johnson's microphone, the audience, piano, and later, some of the organ, drums, and background singers. Shots cut between singer, audience, musicians, the judges, and specifically Johnson's family (her mother, father, and brother), sitting in the studio audience. While she performs the song powerfully and with in-studio audience support, what happens after the song provides the source of this phenomenological inquiry.

When Johnson finishes her song, she appears spent, exhausted.[22] Her eyes are closed, and her head is thrown back. She seems overcome. She places her hands on her knees and then raises both hands in a praise-like position. She has "kilt it." On stage she waits for the judges' comments but with eyes filled with tears. Franklin verbally celebrates how incredible she is and proceeds to ask the judges what they think of the performance. However, judge Yolanda Adams disrupts this routine continuance of the gospel competition proceedings and says to Franklin, "Kirk, let the child shout. Let her shout."

With this invitation and permission, Johnson's tears begin to fall, and she allows her belief in the manifestation of the Holy Ghost to flow through her body. Audiences hear and see this from the two chords of the Hammond B and beginning of her dance. The organ, drums, and guitar play in tandem, and the whole place erupts. Rhythmic edits match the bass line of the drums and the guitar. Media audiences see, can actually feel, the beat as Johnson begins her Holy Ghost dance. She backs up like a runner beginning a race and offers a combination of foot tapping and dance, arms akimbo and moving in time. Because of the palpable emotion of the performance and the in-studio response, willing at-home audiences can inhabit the rush of the ghost in their hearts and spirits.

On his blog *Uppity Negro Network*, cultural critic Joshua Lazard describes praise breaks as a feature of the modern church and "the influence of Gospel music as a genre through the ages. . . . The sound that is associated with the shout is all based on the music—namely the organ. And much like the ring shout, a *true* praise break or shout is spontaneous. That is to say, often times a praise break'll happen after a song that the choir sang really stirred up the emotions of the congregation and the praise break acts as the cathartic release."[23] Philosopher Gregory Currie maintains that in such cases, audiences play a dual role as "both spectators of, and actors in, the production. They play, if they are willing, characters participating in the action, and may come to make-believe that they are those characters, bearing relations to the characters on stage and to each other. They are also members of the audience, and observe themselves playing these roles."[24] When the music ends and Johnson stops to regain her breath, the judges talk with her about the blessing she's going to be around the world.

Watching Johnson's presumed connection to God through her dance, her tears, and the music of praise, audiences can forge their own personal connections. Starting with chest tightening and following with tears, a connection oftentimes provokes expressions of praise for television and/or online audiences. Unlike the notion that this enthusiastic praise originates from the unacknowledged and involuntary impulses of a thoughtless mind, "excited utterances" if you will, a certain distinction and blend exists between cognition (thinking) and the visceral expressions of emotion during Johnson's break. The thoughtful, considered, and joined exhibitions of a mind-body-spirit connection crystallize with the confluence of memory and recognition. Articulated throughout the season for audiences, the combination of Johnson's history of loss (her memory), stellar performance despite loss (recognition), and praise break (spirit) allow audiences to enter her head and heart space and potentially replace it with their own personal narratives of loss, recognition, and redemption. Thus, at-home audiences can take up her praise as part of and prescriptive for their own challenges with and through the support of technology.[25]

For This I Give You Praise

Unlike with Johnson's performance, screen audiences must get their praise on without the auditory support of the in-studio audience in the performance of R&B singer Kelly Price. The *Celebration of Gospel* audience is clearly moved, with Black women and some men crying, shouting, singing background, raising hands, rocking, and dancing. However, due to differences in which microphones are privileged for this performance, screen audiences are removed from the gravitas of the aural worship, only seeing the performance and hearing Price and the choir's microphones at its end.

Gospel singer and writer Kurt Carr penned the song Price sings, "For Every Mountain." Released on his 1997 album *No One Else*, the album and song achieved enormous success and became a staple for gospel choirs nationally.[26] Thus, the opening notes of this song alone produce an anticipated call of the spirit for those familiar with the world of gospel music. Her 2007 performance during BET's annual gospel celebration program pays special tribute to R&B singer Gerald Levert, who died suddenly in 2006. It holds the trappings of other similar tributes, including projected video of Levert singing with Price as well as renowned gospel singer Shirley Caesar on the same stage with him.

Before she sings, Price talks to the audience about being shocked by Levert's death, but sums up with the reflection: "The Bible does tell us, though, that there is a season for all things. There is a time to love; there's a time to laugh; there's a time to be born; and there's even a time to die. And even though we don't necessarily understand all the time, we know that God is sovereign, and we accept His will as being what it is. I would like to say that I count it a privilege and an honor, and I know that all of you do too, be you friend, family, or fan, to have been blessed with the life and the gifts of Gerald Levert. So, for this we give God praise."[27]

Her rendition of the selection begins like any other televised performance, beautiful singing from a clear and strong mezzo-soprano. Dissolves to audience members (celebrities[28] and others) show them sitting in repose and prepared to enjoy the performance of a cherished song in reflection of Levert. The early part of the song chronicles reasons why Price (and by extension all watching and listening) should be grateful to and praise God. Dissolves move between the audience, Price, and the choir (with smoke filtered below their silhouetted frames). "For Every Mountain," however, is not a song for stillness.

The lyrics, organ, and voices of the choir begin to visually transform the space. The song itself changes rhythm. It slows and encourages a very deliberate call and response but also crescendos. The simple chorus intones: "For every mountain, you brought me over. For every trial, you've seen me through. For every blessing, hallelujah! For this, I give you praise." By the second iteration of it, the onscreen audience members are clearly engaged with the singer, the song, the music, and their own personal narratives. Screening audiences see the cuts of Price singing and auditorium audiences shaking their heads, raising their hands, singing as backups, and beginning to stand.

By the third round of the chorus, the choir worships enthusiastically, and the studio audience has become much more involved. While the preponderance of shots focus on Price, the choice of edits speaks to the director's familiarity with the performance style of Black church, about the rhythm of expectation and the gravitas of the repeated verbalization of the words and meanings to audiences both live and at home. In what should have been the final iteration of the chorus, the impact of what she sings overcomes Price, so much so that she misses the arranged song out. And as the choir director and musicians reset the ending, she repeatedly asks the audience, "Has He ever brought you through anything?" For those who somehow missed the call of the spirit earlier, this

Kelly Price performing "For Every Mountain."

questioning invites audiences across platforms to make their own connections with God. Price asks audiences to remember and to suture themselves into the space. She appeals directly to them, unbounded and unfettered by tangible bodies.[29]

Although sanitized due to the aural exclusion of the in-studio audience, the familiarity and popularity of the song helps at-home audiences join viscerally to Price and the feeling of the moment. The way she sings and shouts "hallelujah" throughout the song and as she walks off the stage after the song encourages audiences to shout with her and to God. The word *hallelujah* means to praise God. And by the end, when the television director brings the house audio up for viewer consumption, the in-studio audience is engaged in its own praise party that continues into the commercial break.

The explicit connection to minds (memories, experiences), bodies (emotions), and spirit (God) make this song and its articulation a wonder. Tapping into many Christians' biblical interpretation of Jesus speaking in Matthew, saying where two or three are gathered in my name, so shall I be,[30] mediation makes a way for autonomous and singular viewers outside of the studio to tangibly join with other believers in praise and worship. Thus, the presence of God moves as easily in the live (recorded) body of worshippers as it does with those watching remotely. Moreover, as television tends to be a particularly audio-driven medium, not so much because of any acutely attuned attention to the sound but because so much of its articulation depends on dialogue, orality gets a further lift in this space—orality being central to Black diasporic cultural practices.

The two praise breaks and their impact on screen audiences differ for believers—one in response to a move of God as demonstrated by the singer, the other as a part of the singer's actual performance. In both cases, the spirit moves bodily across mediated spaces. The movement of the Holy Ghost in believing bodies makes visible what is ostensibly invisible. The combination of familiarity and knowledge, music, memory, sincerity, and spirit cut across space, time, and technology to touch believers where they are.

God Don't Need No Matches . . .

Black folks' Christianity often embodies performance. Notes anthropologist Glenn Hinson, as early as the 1790s, African-American Christians articulated their faith in the language of experience.[31] Various expressions, movements, and ways of being exude a mark of religiosity. Getting/catching the Holy Spirit, lifting a finger up to move through church, the "You know you're a Black Christian if . . ." meme, all mark a certain type of religious predisposition known to both participants and many outliers of the culture. With most churches' overpopulation of women, it seems almost commonsensical that the reflection of what "good church" looks like moves through their gendered presence. The *Sunday Best* judges affirm this transference through their praise of Le'Andria Johnson. Judge Tina Campbell of Mary Mary tells her: "The thing about you that gets me, you are honest. You are genuine. You are true. You are a real gospel singer because you have the heart of God. You ain't no fake. That stuff that be going on with you . . . that ain't for the stage, that ain't for the people, that ain't for entertainment. . . . I see it in your eyes. You so serious, so honest about it. Girl, you deserve to be here. God is all over you. You are anointed; you are real, and people are going to be blessed and they gon' come to God watching you."[32]

While Campbell's comments certainly resonate with my description and discussion (and her personality as described in the Processional), naysayers exist. Some argue the Holy Ghost and phenomenological example can be incompatible, suggesting that when spiritual "sensations are prized for these reasons—because of their phenomenological feel or as a way of underwriting one's sense of one's own importance—then they will be religiously defective . . . and they are likely to be epistemically defective, because of the suspicion that the believer, whether consciously or not, is engineering the production of such experiences for the advantages that they confer in these respects."[33] I assert, however, this rendering of the mind-body-spirit tie as "fake"—to make it plain—bears no weight on the audience and users who enjoy it. This interpretation becomes the burden of the person who disbelieves (either in the practice or the person)—not the one caught up. Moreover, as film scholar Carol Clover postulates in a different context, in the same way in which women are supposed to be more "open" to the image, they may be "more open to the supernatural—and perhaps, ultimately for the same reason."[34] This attuned state, this phenomenological enterprise, certainly forms a part of what screening audiences access and feel so concretely.

From a historical perspective, art historian Babatunde Lawal talks about ways in which the visual is used for communication in certain parts of continental Africa. Specifically, he outlines two types of visual metaphors: (1) the exoteric—where meanings are accessible to adults of a given culture who pass that knowledge to young ones, and (2) the esoteric—metaphors that require intimate knowledge considered not for public consumption.[35] Most visual metaphors code folklore for spiritual beliefs, political ideology, and proverbs. These ideas resonate here inasmuch as both exoteric and esoteric visual modes of communication play out with mediated offerings of the Holy Spirit. Like many people of color, Black folks frequently convey stories, histories, relationships, and spirit orally and visually. The body, the music, the voices, and the larger visual register foster a syncretic understanding—a code that, while public, is intimate; while accessible, can be highly unknown to nonbelievers.

While scholarship addressing the Holy Spirit consistently suggests the tangibility of it cannot be measured nor necessarily put into words, the very inexplicability of the spirit works for these praise break examples. As Hinson suggests, the "[e]ssential untellability of holy experience, combined with the experiential prerequisite of 'membership' in the fellowship of saints . . . have led many to dismiss sanctified experience as 'emotionalism' . . . the emotion in this equation is *reaction* rather than *cause*. When the Spirit truly touches, emotion is the artifact of experience rather than the other way around."[36] In thinking about the various elements of this performance, social work scholar Rebecca Chaisson remarks: "I find it empowering to think about women as subject of something that is liberating and that we can be liberated from our living rooms. Dancing and singing with abandon resemble a kind of freedom of expression that occurs nowhere else. . . . If this leads to some kind of restoration from daily Microaggressions related to race and gender then television is making a contribution in invaluable ways."[37]

Can I Get a Witness?

Phenomenology allows and calls for adherents to employ multiple aspects of culture and sensibilities to assess a phenomenon. In other words, the framework embraces the articulated feelings of others as part of the theorist's memory and own experience. For example, I participated in a Facebook discussion about Johnson's break with several sistah-scholars around the country in September 2012. The audience commentaries from the online iteration of the break, and a Facebook discussion, support the assertions made and felt here:

M that's one of my favorite praise breaks!! i just looked at it too!!
K Mine too. It actually gives me chills. And the fact that Donnie can't hold his
    peace cracks me up.
B I look at the praise break regularly. I often have to get up and join her!!
K I'm like that girl's mama making that rolling move with my arms!
B HALLELUJAH!!!
K I'm on my second run of the night.[38]

This closed dialogue flows between Black women who hold a collective relationship to and experience with this break and praise and worship in general. It operates with an understanding of what these breaks mean and their impact. The discussion takes place online and requires repeated viewing of the video by the participants to tap into the power of what it continually offers. This works for others engaging the performance.

YouTube comments primarily center the blessing of the performances. People continue to find these video clips, watch them, and post about them. Twenty-first-century digital media allows for a global, on-demand, and repeated experience of what appears on most platforms. Posters become, as Addo calls them, "digital spiritual hype people," with posts such as "SOMEBODY . . . BRING ME MY TAMBOURINE!!!! YESSSSS_ LORD" (Valinda Jarmon); "like my post if you_ shouted or cried!!!!" (Arnella Flowers); and "Makes me wanna get_ saved!" (Charles King). One comment especially captures the feelings expressed by the more than 705,229 views for Johnson and over 820,000 views for Kelly Price:[39] "Oh my my my my my. WOW WEEEEE!!! I felt that through my phone so much so that the Spirit of God surely descended down into my car. She got me speaking in tongues. Glory to God, Praise Him. They just had church and I wanted to be there. But instead God met me where I was, in my car parked outside of work getting to go to work. What a amazing way to begin the day after prayer. 10 Thumbs Up!!!" (JolynF).[40] And for Price: "Praise God! Six sessions of chemotherapy, bald, and still praising GOD! Kelly Price is a gift from God. I have listened to this version of For Every Mountain throughout my entire health challenge. Thank you Jesus, for every soul who has lifted my name up in prayer, thank you for covering me with your grace, strength, and endurance. Thank you for encouragement via the voice of Sister Kelly Price. Praise you Sister!" (Purple Green).[41]

Descriptors such as "anointed" and "blessed" reign—characterizing Price's singing, the song, and her ability to move people. People make comparisons to Whitney Houston's version of the song and even Richard Smallwood's singers, who originated the selection. Even as recently as January 2021, people have found it and commented—one saying: "Lord!!! As we end this awful year, 2020 . . . this song was in my spirit this morning!!! Kelly's version was the first one I came across and WOW!!!! I remember watching this and almost running out the house!!! SHE DID THAT!!! Happy New Year and Thank you LORD, keep moving those mountains!!!" (cake :3). In a personal conversation about this break, one nonbeliever (a lapsed Catholic) remarks that this performance "makes you want to believe."

Shabach!

Praise breaks craft one of the few anointed spaces where Black women "live and breathe, grieve and celebrate."[42] I employ phenomenology to capture the ways in which this believing group embodies, expresses, captures, and is then freed by the spirit within and outside of the screen. Some scholars, such as philosopher Erazim Kohák, argue, however, that when the divine presence functions in religiously resonant ways, "as to be rooted in certain experiences of the world," someone who lacks those experiences will not have the same idea of divine presence.[43] Or, as one anonymous reviewer of this work suggests, some may be "uncomfortable . . . with the positing of the Holy Spirit as a material reality . . . that can't be supported by analysis."[44] While possible, literary and Africana studies scholar Nghana Lewis disagrees, noting something in Johnson's eyes, in the sincerity of her song and in her praise performance moves even unbelievers. It allows them to dabble a bit.[45] Said another way, Tina Campbell ends her assessment of Johnson's performance with: "If I didn't know your God, I'd wanna know him." Plus, a great many things we cannot quantify or fully comprehend, nevertheless exist.

As Black women, and women in general, are situated as the keepers of culture in families, in communities, and in nations, so too do they valiantly illustrate the power of God. Spirituality is an important aspect of many African-American women's belief systems. While it remains a highly contested term, religion scholar and pastor Carlyle Fielding Stewart writes that spirituality represents the "full matrix of beliefs, power, values and behaviors that shape people's consciousness, understanding, and capacity of themselves in relation to divine reality. [It is also] a process by which people interpret, disclose, formulate, adapt and innovate reality and their understandings of God within a specific context or culture."[46] And while Black and gendered bodies endure continued denigration, Black Christianity, surprisingly (patriarchal and homophobic as it can be), allows small avenues for women's whole being to be valued and validated.[47] When the spirit manifests in praise, Black women receive the call most often to serve as the evidence. Mediation broadens this scope of being and perhaps helps forward progressive thought and action in larger sociocultural discourses surrounding the viability of visual media to impact lives, the visceral necessity of Black and female bodies, and the value of the Holy Ghost to believers and beyond. Hallelujah!

Tithes & Offering

Churches operate largely through the largesse and financial commitment of its members. Giving 10 percent of one's income to the church, the first fruits, puts faith into a demonstrable practice and obligation. Ministers often use the biblical scripture Malachi 3:10 as the basis for asking members to contribute. "Bring the whole tithe into the storehouse that there may be food in my house. Test me in this, says the Lord Almighty, and see if I will not throw open the floodgates of heaven and pour out so much blessing that there will not be room enough to store it" (NIV).

"I'mma Be Stupid Rich!"
••••••••••••••••••••••••

Millennials and the Holy Grail
of Tech Salvation

Click This

The Scene:
Youth service Sunday (Rock Nation), already crunk from an earlier period
of praise

William Murphy, III, Lead Pastor, dReam Center Church of Atlanta.

Bishop William Murphy concludes the reading of his scriptural text (Matthew 17:24–27, KJV), and from the pulpit instructs the media ministry on how to fix the font and projected page so the congregants/audience can read it better. He then says to the church: "Everybody turn around and tell somebody, 'I'mma be stupid rich.'" He bends his head as to consult his impending message on his iPad when we hear the swirl of a rising synthesizer pumping loud. The lyrics "I'mma be stupid rich" blare into the space with a booming bass beat. Murphy looks up, begins to dance, lets this play twice, and stops it. He laughs, "Yaw ain't ready. . . . Some of yaw'll ain't ready. . . . You so stuck up. . . . Is there anybody in this church who loves God and says God I want some more money too?" Whereby the music comes banging back with the hook, "I'mma be stupid rich." It was one of the best club environments and tracks I've encountered in a long time.[1]

Contemporary church worship often reflects the passages of the young—their style, their music, their dance, and their impatience with tradition. Bass beats and lighting schemas are designed to attract them. Crossless sanctuaries resemble stadiums, announcements are made on projected screens, and robed choirs have disappeared in favor of concert-like performances of a few Grammy seekers. Sounds pulse through bodies and get attendees to move. In many places, the frenetic beat and pace of contemporary Black church service (one hour and fifteen minutes W.P.T.[2]), signal not only the target demographic but also those excluded from it. It suggests this worship service no longer exists for the sickly, the poor, the dowdy, the insane, and the old. The Hammond B, traditionally serving as the heartbeat of the church, grounding people's connection with one sound and one way of being (one band, one sound) fades in favor of the four-piece band or alternatively, a prepared playlist. In trying to forge paths for new voices, feelings, and attendance in Black church, all things spiritual get situated before the mediated altar. Demonstrated in the Processional earlier and also shown through global megachurches, televangelists, and online church, this secularization of the sacred is not a new phenomenon. This shift examples, more intangibly, "successful" church 3.0 in the twenty-first century. All these things are done, presumably, to make the crowds go wild. In the midst of writing this Tithes and Offering, the COVID-19 pandemic shut churches down for almost all of 2020 and half of 2021, making tech the *only* way to do church.

Yet, contrary to what the pre-colon title suggests, this collection is not taken up as an attempt to critique prosperity gospel or megaministries (though they both undergird this mode of address in contemporary worship). I'm not denying media use value nor trying to address a theological sacred–secular divide. I've already done this. As I take up Tithes and Offering this morning, I insist on the importance of looking at how technology and popular culture get deployed to reach millennials within Black church worship. This particular attempt to stem the tide of departure from the church creates questions. Does this new audiovisual reach bring people closer to Jesus, and if so, how? Do these new approaches cultivate faith? Where and what are the roles of spirituality in contemporary

Black church worship? What does the concert-type singing do for the spirit? Does it usher worshippers before the Lord more effectively? Is the church's worship programming the reason for disaffection? Why announcement vignettes by millennials—job training or something cute to include? Does offering no printed programs serve a green initiative or another agenda? Philosophically, I question when Black churches seek to attract millennials using approaches popular within different cultural milieus and church traditions, and with technology and media, does an affine transformation actually result?[3] Meaning, while these changes are instituted to encourage both millennials and nonbelievers to come, worship, and believe, do they actually just preserve the status quo of parallel existence? And beyond this millennial focus, what happens (and has happened since COVID) with the seasoned saints? In other words, where does this millennial-driven tech focus leave non-millennials in Black church? These questions guide my thinking during this portion of the service.

A Smart Jesus Move: Framing the Conversation

In preaching about his church's "Meet Me at the Corner" outreach ministry event to the poor and Black community of Candler Road in Decatur, Georgia, Senior Pastor Marlin Harris of New Life Church talks about the community where the church stands. While the church had other options for where to locate, they select a place where they can help the neediest among us. In defending this position, Harris says: "It's not a smart business move; it's not a smart ministry move; it's not a smart church move; it's a smart Jesus move."[4] To think about the work of and worship in updated Black church spaces, I employ business marketing and religion studies scholarship. An unlikely pairing, the confluence of the two best situates the impact and effectiveness (or lack thereof) of what happens in new Black church worship.

As a practicing Christian with an opportunity to attend and participate in the life of Black churches all over the country, I recognize generational, gendered, regional, racialized, and classist disparities that surely color my engagement within these spaces. Quiet as it's kept, although not millennials, many late baby boomers and Generation Xers also share technology-use expectations for the twenty-first-century Black church.[5] If a church fails to provide some sort of online presence (website, Instagram, and/or at minimum, a Facebook page), it signals a lack of young people and young families attending, and quite possibly a lack of desire to attract and keep them. If the church refuses (or doesn't possess the womanpower) to keep events pages updated or Instagram and Twitter (X) feeds fed, this too signals nonengagement with certain technologies and, de facto, populations.

As people continue to move about the country and the world for opportunities, they can discern houses of worship through technology. Church websites, Facebook pages, Twitter (X) feeds, and Instagram posts allow potential parishioners to see into and understand a little bit about these spaces with limited effort. It allows interest to develop through observing the service, listening to the ministerial staff, understanding church mission and focus, and getting a sense of the "look" of the membership.[6] COVID-19 made this not only a necessity but also a valuable opportunity. Moreover, religion scholar and elder Erika D. Gault argues that a generation of "digital Black Christians" have moved from Black church to "more racially and religiously diverse spaces and alliances." This movement allows for a closeness needed by digital Black Christians "to form intimate connections with one another, and to develop feelings of closeness to media itself."[7] In the past, people stayed put in the spaces and places where they first encountered God, mostly via their families. If you don't move from your city of origin, it likely becomes your last church home. However, changed work prospects, societal patterns, and cultural inferences help shift this phenomenon. Additionally, technology makes choices (and differences between churches) more readily apparent and accessible.

In his essay (and later book) "Jihad vs. McWorld," political theorist Benjamin Barber parallels ideas of both jihad and McWorld as similar and equal eliminations of democracy. While both approach the world in a dogmatic way, neither forwards democracy or civility—a civility sometimes encouraged by religious and spiritual ways of being. Barber's notions of what McWorld promises for our future make his writing prescient here. McWorld looks seductive in comparison to the representation of jihad (jihad characterized as all things destructive, irrational, and chaotic). Yet McWorld's deliverance of "peace, prosperity, and relative unity" comes at the expense of "independence, community, and identity."[8] This illustration well describes the corporatization of Black church worship and its shifting worship aesthetic—a similar dispensation of sanitization and standardization in a quest for relevance and prominence.

The implementation of business ideologies in religion has reached new heights in the twenty-first century. In fact, various corporate products such as Godtube and the example it sets for Black church and Black Christian musical artists, Cokesbury as the retail and customer service arm of the United Methodist Publishing House, or even the Givelify app, a company "born out of a passion to make the world a better place . . . and the simple goal . . . [to] make it easier to give,"[9] all assume corporate, capitalist-driven business models for church.[10] Thus, examining business imperatives helps discern performance, aesthetics, and possible spiritual meanings for Black church worship services, helping to understand what the smart Jesus move looks like now.

"This Is My Bible. I Am What It Says . . ." Megachurches

Before the turn of the twentieth century, megachurches existed in the U.S. The Moody Church of Chicago, founded by white evangelist D. L. Moody, "bears the distinction of being the oldest to both break the 2,000 threshold in attendance and to also be over 2,000 in the current era."[11] Built in 1876, it held up to 10,000 people. As mentioned in the Call to Worship, extensive scholarship has examined the growth and work of megachurches worldwide. Since the 1980s, the world has witnessed Christianity explode. Evangelizers proclaim the Word via cassette/DVD/CD, radio, television, satellite, in stadiums, and online. In some capacity, to reach global numbers, megachurches *require* sophisticated media usage.

Many megachurches preach prosperity Christianity, or what some call "health and wealth" religion. Starting as a largely North American religious movement, it connects to Pentecostal Christianity and Word of Faith teachings and often ties to Oral Roberts and other evangelists who became well known in the 1980s and 1990s. In addition, prosperity Christianity relates historically to two other "spiritual" enterprises: faith healing and Christian free enterprise. In the early twentieth century, evangelicals, focusing on physical well-being as a therapeutic ethos of culture, became normative and popular, with activities such as the "mind cure," which stressed the power of positive thinking as a cure for disease. In the mid-twentieth century, Christian free enterprise and the relationship between professional business and theology took root, helping to expand the notion of what, where, and how Christianity looks.

Mega-media preachers and churches (Black and those with Black following) no longer claim the mantle of newness. Scholars Shayne Lee (2005), Jonathan Walton (2009), Sandra L. Barnes (2010) and (2013), Tamelyn N. Tucker-Worgs (2011), Kate Bowler (2013), and Ezra Chitando (2021) write extensively about mediated Black megachurches and Black purveyors of the gospel such as T. D. Jakes, the late Eddie Long, Noel Jones, Creflo Dollar, and Charles Blake. This list fails to include scholarship on Black media godfathers such as Rev. Ike (Frederick J. Eikerenrotter II), Carlton Pearson, Father Divine, and white forefathers/mothers and contemporaries such as Joel Osteen, Oral Roberts, Robert Schuller, Jim and Tammy Faye Bakker, Jerry Falwell, Charles and Andy Stanley, Joyce Meyer, Rick Warren, Benny Hinn, Kenneth Copeland, Paula White, Robert Tilton,[12] Bill Hybels, and Mark Driscoll.[13] These latter ones have extensive amounts of scholarship and journalism written on them as well.

In particular, ministers Joel Osteen, T. D. Jakes, Creflo Dollar, and David Oyedepo of Nigeria dominate the terrain of pastorpreneurs who reign over the mediated Christian world industry. As mentioned specifically in the Call to Worship and applied here as well, sociologist Shayne Lee writes about Black celebrity ministers in his book *T. D. Jakes: America's New Preacher*. He discusses the "new Black church," and the ways Black ministers of megachurches now claim a central space in mainstream acknowledgment of religion. Speaking of Jakes but applicable to many megaministers of the modern age, Lee suggests: "Jakes' commercialized spirituality celebrates the hyper-capitalist values of his age. He often defends his extraordinary wealth by reminding critics that he is both a businessman and a minister and that God has bountifully blessed both missions. . . . Jakes the preacher offers spiritual wisdom and insight while Jakes the businessman is an aggressive entrepreneur exploring the most effective ways to market his spiritual gifts."[14] His millennial daughter, Sarah Jakes Roberts, is following in his footsteps.[15]

Mentioned during the Invocation, the media and monetary moves of these ministers receive acknowledgment in the larger entertainment industries as well and for a long time, including Jakes's own film productions. For example, the Wilson sisters (the Pointer Sisters) castigated Duane-Abdullah (Bill Duke) for his politics and disdain of Christianity in the 1970s film *Car Wash* (Schultz, 1976). Their jazzified, gospel singing admonition accompanies an impromptu offering orchestrated by Daddy Rich (Richard Pryor), encouraging the car wash workers to "believe in something." From direct-to-DVD, low-budget film *Father of Lies* (Phenomenon, 2007) to reality series *Preachers of L.A.* (Oxygen, 2013–2014) to fictional narratives *Greenleaf* (OWN, 2016–2020) and *Saints and Sinners* (Bounce TV, 2016–2022), the business of God forms a central part of understanding Black church ministries in popular culture. So, while Pastor Harris suggests "faith works through love, not naming and claiming it,"[16] many nonfictional and fictional voices beg to differ or demonstrate otherwise.

You Got to Believe in Something, Why Not Believe in Me? Marketing Brands

The success of megachurches and their wannabes comes in part from marketing. Brand differentiation exists as a longtime part of the promotion aspect of a marketing mix (product, price, place, and promotion). However, with the beginning of the twenty-first century, branding became a central, distinguished, and usurped aspect for not only products and services but also for people. Following the success of worldwide megaministries, old-new churches and church plants aggressively incorporate business practices—learning and borrowing from one another. Increasingly, they introduce branding as a necessary tool for millennial outreach and continued existence. Writes media studies scholar Mara Einstein: "Churches have revised their 'product' (shorter, more entertaining services), provided a menu of services (12-step groups, networking classes), and employed focus groups and surveys to learn the needs of their congregants."[17] While this shift attempts to incorporate worshippers' ideas, it also encourages them to explore other churches and potentially switch. Einstein argues that in this moment, denominations have fostered brand disloyalty because they "no longer act as brands, something they once did. Instead, churches have increasingly become nondenominational."[18]

On the other hand, minister Sheron Patterson suggests effective evangelism comes through relationship innovation—meaning, changing how you relate to both those in your congregation but more importantly, to those who are not a part of it. Using a fishing analogy, she argues fishers need to know how to use bait—bait being the things that attract the unchurched or reclaim those who have left the church. She writes: "If we use bait and lures like great programming, professionally generated publicity, and God-fearing, smiling congregants, we will be successful."[19] The need to market and brand touches not only organizations but also individuals. As mentioned in the Call to Worship, theology scholar Harvey Cox talks about the commonalities of the market and religion—with individuals' ability to undergo a "dazzling display of reverse transubstantiation [making] the human body . . . the latest sacred vessel to be converted into a commodity."[20] He questions the value of human life in this market theology, harkening to discussions of needed humanity recognition, and this theology's play into media's commodification of everything.

As Black churches attempt to not only slow the bleed of young people from its pews, they also seek to emulate the platforms (and dollars) of white Christian ministries. Attending Abundant Life Cathedral in Houston, Texas, in 2001, for example, a certain kind of bait, commercialism in this case, ran rampant inside even this then-modest Black church. During service, a screen descended into the space with projected promotions for the church itself and advertisements of its products. The pastor hawked wares even before giving The Message. He recognized that his church services aired on various television platforms. And if it was unclear to audiences to what he refers, the pastor made sure to say where the church aired/emerged as he welcomed visitors.[21] In these new mediated worship services, conferences, workshops, and sermon series get neatly packaged and presented to attendees—in-house and online.

Even with widespread use, church marketing is certainly not without its detractors. Senior Pastor Carlyle Fielding Stewart suggests that despite the many manuals on how to grow churches abounding since the 1980s, understanding cultural context and the need for spiritual growth remain paramount. He does not see a problem with using marketing tools and strategies as well as elements from popular culture to attract people to the church. He suggests, however, these "strategies should not negate or obviate the importance of spirituality in creating a climate that will optimally enable people to grow spiritually. The more successful models of church growth stress the importance of developing a living, personal, spiritual relationship with Christ."[22] Connectedly, marketing scholar Bruce Wrenn believes theologians sometimes object to marketing in religion because it "mixes" the presumed profane and sacred. He writes:

> Marketing is anthropocentric, embodying the world . . . in the sense of the ways of fallen humanity, while religion is theocentric—life is to be understood from the perspective God himself has provided for its understanding. . . . God's supernatural nature—his transcendence—is lost when "theocentric faith (i.e., faith centered on God as an objective reality) becomes anthropocentric faith

(i.e., faith centered on the therapeutic interest in the self)." . . . Because marketing's focus on exchange is an appeal to self-perceived value, its use in trying to consummate religious "exchanges" limits God's ability to reveal himself to us in his own way.[23]

Yet, the reality is that you cannot get to theocentric truth if no one is present. By way of sociologists Roger Finke and Rodney Stark, writer Bolashade Hanson suggests religious economies produce religious pluralism—a pluralism catering to specific market segments—one of those being millennials.[24] Reminiscent of the television industry's shift from broadcasting to narrowcasting, a large part of this redirection happens when an infusion of technological and mediated resources transforms worship services.

Techno-Miracles

Anxieties around changing technologies continue to shape human experiences of them. Whether these include historical changes such as oral to written communication, development of the printing press or the telephone, to more contemporary ones such as global cable ministries, online worship, seven ways to give possibilities, Bible apps, or even Way of the Future AI church,[25] change can foster fear and intransigence. According to a reviewer of the 1993 science fiction novel *Parable of the Sower*, Octavia Butler presents "the future we will make if we continue to be distracted by the holy grail of techno-miracles."[26] Butler's apocalyptic premonition becomes increasingly more manifest with each new technological and mediated offering. Yet, as the Rev. Dr. HyeMin Na suggests, technology and its usage carry misconceptions, especially within the church. Many behave as if technology is: (1) ahistorical, (2) neutral, and (3) a miracle drug.[27]

While presumed with millennials because of their birth into a technology-rich environment, actual media literacy is not uniform within their ranks, for those producing the technology, or for those in church leadership (typically NOT millennials). Being media literate entails understanding that all media are constructions, messages are representations, messages have and serve economic purposes, individuals interpret messages differently, and media have unique characteristics. Churches use media and technology to proselytize, mobilize, and monetize—however, the clarity and consequences of their usage appears vague in contemporary church worship and marketing.

Specifically, expanded technology use in new church deploys a multiplicity of tools: elaborate and expensive lighting grids (and schemas), enhanced sound systems with sound boards, and huge LD and LCD screens projecting texts and creating a certain visual ambience with what has been marketed (and presumably tested) as soothing screensaver tools to serve as part of the worship experience. Font capabilities, streaming video, and even smoke machines (as in a rock concert) seek to also enhance church worship. Pastor Olu Brown and his team

Service at the Impact Church of Atlanta.

write in their book *Zero to 80: Innovative Ideas for Planting and Accelerating Church Growth*: "Our Creative Worship team seeks to create a worship experience where people can honor and adore God in new, different and unique ways.... During our worship experiences, we seek to maintain an atmosphere of surprise as we facilitate having an encounter with God."[28] In addition, many large (and increasingly small) churches use their ability to stream church services (live or recorded) to reach members and potential virtual ones. Before the pandemic, churches typically had about 15 percent of their members watching online while the other 85 percent came in person.[29] On average in 2023, churches are hosting around 85 percent of their pre-pandemic numbers, numbers that were already declining.[30] And according to a Pew Research survey, since the pandemic, only 37 percent of Black protestants attend church both in person and online, with another 20 percent who only attend virtually.[31]

Worldwide, it seems, Christians (Black and other people of color) embrace mediated religiosity. In Nigeria, for example, several church ministries fall within the top twenty in membership and growth worldwide. The South Africa–based One Gospel Network (1G) features continental and diasporic Black gospel performers beamed around the continent on DSTV Satellite. And in Seoul, South Korea, Yoido Full Gospel Church stands as the largest church in the world, with 580,000 members. Founded by Rev. Yong-gi Cho and now led by Rev. Lee Younghoon since Cho's death in 2021,[32] the church works in prosperity and social gospel.[33] Media use proves critical for them to praise God efficiently and on time, effectively move people in and out of the seven Sunday services, and collect tithes and offering.

Despite both the ways domestic and international churches use (or don't use) technology and media, the pandemic upended all church offerings globally. Planning to stay in business, houses of worship were forced to pivot toward sophisticated technology use. "Everyone was scrambling," says Rev. Dr. Anthony Bennett.[34] Many ministries turned to Facebook Live and Zoom as a way to facilitate some sort of service and connection. Bigger churches, which already used technology and media as part of their services, leaned in to create more robust ways of reaching their members. Yet the language around media use (pre-, during, and post-pandemic) comes mostly from its functionality, its nuts and bolts, rather than a critical understanding of what it does and more importantly, how it matters. And reflective of pre-pandemic operations, the faithful of this new worship world, the tithers, tend not to be the well-sought millennial demographic.

Climbing Jacob's Ladder

Understanding millennials, the group occupying press de jour coverage, becomes paramount when discussing how churches try to capture them. While the precision of their generation varies, widely held beliefs about millennials situate the generation as born between 1981 and 1996 (1995, 2000, or 2002, depending on the writer). More than 80 million of them exist, about one-third of the U.S. population.[35] Characterized in vastly oppositional ways (narcissistic and concerned, globally connected but infantile), a fairly agreed-upon description entails their comfort with technology, assumption of its usage, and general social acceptance of difference. This social acceptance of difference helps shape their beliefs. "[T]hey are not necessarily looking for absolutes and certainties in the ways their grandparents' generation did . . . many of the habits of today's younger Americans were inherited from the trends established by their parents in the 1990s."[36]

In fact, this group maintains a very different relationship to the church than their parents and grandparents. According to research fellow Daniel Cox, in 2016: "only 41 percent of Millennials attended religious services with their family at least once a week, compared with 55 percent of Baby Boomers. . . . Similarly, only 40 percent of Millennials attended Sunday school or some other religious education program weekly [compared with] . . . Baby Boomers (62 percent reported at least weekly participation)."[37] Moreover, in a 2019 Pew Research Center finding, only 49 percent of millennials identify as Christian (with another 9 percent as other religiously affiliated and 40 percent as unaffiliated).[38] By 2023, according to Barna Research, millennials now have moved up to 45 percent attending, with millennials of color producing the spike. Most scholarship and news stories report the lessening importance of religion to millennials. For example, in reports from CBN News, Pew Research Center, *Religion News*, and

PBS, the prophecy of the end of religion coming true, at least for this demographic, bears itself out.[39] And yet, while young people are leaving formal religion, they assume religiosity about other things, including work.[40]

And despite these statistics, African-Americans continue as some of the most committed and religious of all groups. Yet while Black millennials understand the church as a site *historically* committed to and leading fights for social justice issues, an area keenly important to them, it appears much less a concern for Black churches now. Black Lives Matter activist and culture and performance scholar Shamell Bell believes: "Jesus was in those streets and so should we [be]."[41] Adding to this sentiment regarding the Black church's limited engagement with Black Lives Matter concerns, writer Tyree Boyd-Pates laments: "I began to think that if the Black church couldn't take a basic stance on my life, maybe God was incapable of it, too."[42] Thus, some argue, the Black church's own shift of focus provides one reason for Black millennials' departure from the church.

In addition, scholars and church laity acknowledge that early church shifts to accommodate young people's differing ideas impact church attendance and growth as well. Even before BLM, the 1980s and 1990s explosion of hip-hop in popular culture forced churches to seriously reassess their approach (or lack thereof, as African-American studies scholar Emmett G. Price suggests[43]) to young people and their cultural proclivities. Steadily, over the last twenty-five years, an unaddressed generational divide has helped shutter many churches across racialized strata. Churches wanting to survive have needed to alter and shift what happens in worship. Writes Price: "the Black Church must reengage in the lives of the youth and young adults who compose the Hip Hop Generation. It is mandatory, it is necessary, and it is urgent!"[44]

In her thesis on branding and Christian ministries, Hanson says many millennials think of the contemporary church as "irrelevant, narrow-minded and divisive."[45] Millennials want to know the most efficient and effective ways to spend their time. They value belonging and relationships, interactive experiences, creativity, and recognition that their early exposure or immersion online and within social media structures (their communication style and preferences) matter. Says Hanson: "Millennials value story in brands, honesty, and want more transparency, clarity, [and] authenticity. . . . [They] also want the lights, the music, the experience, the technological integration, and the high production value, but they do not want those things to be so pronounced that they cannot discern what the organization is about."[46] Moreover, as many attest, they crave a certain type of authentic and intimate experience.

The difficulty for religious communities, according to minister and scholar Joy K. Challenger, "is to capture the imagination and allegiance of the next generation!"[47] To attract millennials, the service must reflect all things cool and current. Brand specialist Eric Thomas writes: "If you are going to market to millennials, remember you're going into an open forum. This is not a one-way conversation. This generation is especially brutal when it comes to being patronized or talked down to."[48] Theologian and scholar Leonard Sweet writes about capturing groups in these "postmodern" times with the acronym EPIC—experiential, participatory, image-driven, and connected. This type of impulse reflects the incredible success and prowess of Singapore's City Harvest Church, for example, as analyzed by marketing and management scholars Jeaney Yip and Susan Ainsworth. This church's ultramodern approach to "church production" includes a titanium-clad church building (modeled after the Guggenheim Museum in Bilbao, Spain), one of the world's largest musical water fountains, and lighting structures designed by the same consultants as the Sydney Opera House. Moreover, the worship service features popular music and state-of-the-art sound and lighting systems.[49]

Challenger believes the Black church "must be in active bi-lateral relationships with millennials in order to facilitate mutual respect that allows each group to hear the other."[50] Thinking about how to reach people over forty while trying to address people under that age, Rev. Dr. Anthony Bennett believes the sweet spot of membership is having an abundance of folks who are ten years younger and ten years older than the pastor. He suggests many millennials want the proficiency (and efficiency) of a large church and the intimacy of a small one.[51] For millennials, Challenger thinks worship needs to be intergenerational, "using pillars of hip hop culture [and] . . . E.P.I.C. . . . without compromising the faith of our mothers and fathers."[52] She says they need religious education, "which includes not only worship and education but also the full of religious practices and activities *intentionally* designed for spiritual formation and fostering maturity."[53] Thinking about all of these elements helps to discern what sort of conversations should exist around technology and media deployed in Black church worship in general as well as to attract millennials. And while contemporary Black church reaches millennials (and others) through diverse small groups, tweets, and Eventbrite activities, worship continues to be the focal point of connection. It is also the space of the most significant change currently. Thus, I turn to focus on what happens in Black church worship, pre- and post-COVID, for those who attend (or attend online in some measure).

Worship 3.0

Worship serves as the heart of engagement for followers of Christ. The apostle Matthew, speaking for God, writes, "for where two or three are gathered together in my name, there am I in the midst of them" (Matthew 18:20, KJV). Religion scholar Melva Wilson Costen believes "God's call . . . for corporate gatherings lends itself to a time when the community can claim and affirm kinship and mutual interdependence in a space where both social and spiritual hospitality are evident."[54] She notes the need and value of worship for Black people, specifically citing its traditional roots and meanings. She writes that people gather "to offer thanks and praise to God in and through Jesus the Christ, and to be spiritually fed by the Word of God!"[55] These "communities of faith" gather under the power of the Holy Spirit to learn about, relish, and continue forth with the good news provided by the continual presence of God. These through lines connect Black worship across denominations—not in a homogenizing way but one recognizing cultural resonances.

Anglican priest Nicholas Buxton distinguishes between a "'congregational domain' of traditional forms of religious life" and a "'holistic milieu' of new age alternative spirituality." Quoting Paul Heelas and Linda Woodhead: "To step into a worship service is to find one's attention being directed away from oneself towards something higher. By contrast . . . to enter into the holistic milieu is to find attention directed towards oneself and one's inner life."[56] Similarly, renowned religion scholar and theologian Howard Thurman believes religious experience includes prayer, connection (relationship and communication with God), meditation, suffering, and, as I discussed in the Call to Worship, the recognition that God is.[57] He teaches, "humans need to seek an inner spiritual happiness that would lead them to share their experience in community with others."[58] The worship experience carries a history of formality, familiarity, and sacredness. Granted, some of what occurs during worship happens because of tradition, the way it's always been done. Stripping that away, however, leaves the need for a certain spirituality, routine, and community to be invited, felt, embraced, and understood.

In this same vein, church physical plants have undergone significant changes since the middle of the twentieth century. Beyond the exorbitant costs associated with running major facilities (mortgage, insurance, utilities, maintenance, and staff), the understanding of design for worship and commerce has transformed spaces too.[59] Black megachurches (and wannabe megas) tend to favor the iconography of white megaminister Joel Osteen's Lakewood Church in Houston, Texas, where sophisticated lighting schemas, camera movement, sound system, gorgeous and talented performers (praise team and choir), and editing (for digital and television broadcast) rival any national performance arena. Asking about sanctuaries, altars, windows, and outside gardens, the evangelical-leaning Barna Research Group and Cornerstone Knowledge Network[60] conduct a multipart survey of millennials' preferences of Christian worship spaces. The survey finds while "no cookie-cutter, mass-production solution for welcoming Millennials to your space" exists, they do prefer a "community that calls them to a deeper meaning."[61]

The Impact Church of Atlanta, for example, markets to those who envision a certain God-ish, affluent-leaning lifestyle, aesthetic, and demographic. And, as successful branding plans call for, the church uses multiple strategies to deliver its worship service. For the 2017 service "experience" celebrating its tenth year of operation, and more importantly its recognition as the fifty-sixth fastest-growing church in the nation by *Outreach Magazine*, Impact demonstrated its unique form of church worship.[62] During the service, the pastor and thus the mood of the church were celebratory (congratulatory even) and worship involved dimming the lights, distribution and waving of glow sticks, and a musical beat and directive that encouraged members (I mean, Impactors) to jump up and down as in a rave. Similar to any good pop or rock concert, the scene visualized well. However, the scenario bordered on false flattery for young people's passions. Orchestrating spontaneity frequently falls flat, but particularly in a perceived congregational domain. Moreover, it virtually (and viscerally) excludes non-millennials while promoting an outside (white) cultural practice.

The "creative worship team" of Impact, in another example, provides a fusion of artistic forms to set the stage for a millennial-inflected worship. Imagine Theodore Witcher's 1997 *Love Jones* meets Tyler Perry's 2006 *Madea's Family Reunion*. In both films, club scenes of jazz music (featuring the bass), low lighting, and poetry coalesce to create a pallet for love and lovers (not to mention beautiful brown skin). As I'll reference in The Message on spirituality and sexuality, these cinematic scenes are constructed for lovemaking. Transport these scenarios to a church worship service. In talking with Pastor Olu Brown about this service, he noted the need for Impact to be on top of all things "latest and greatest" aesthetically, and also the collaborative nature of their worship service—that's their brand. Explaining more, he said: "So that was an experience to where we were trying things differently, trying to evolve it. And there are some cases where we look back and say okay, we never want to do that again. There are some cases when we do."[63] In all things, Brown states, his worship team tries to answer the larger question: "How do we engage people on a deeper level?"[64] The depth sought in these two examples leaves questions nonetheless. How are millennials transported from the haze of cool to the spirit of Jesus? How are God and Jesus glorified here? Furthermore, Atlantans (and their transplants) follow trends and can be transitory—making a deeper level difficult if members/Impactors/visitors stay on the move, always looking for the next best thing.

Worship leaders in many contemporary Black churches seem to recognize this migratory impulse of millennials and others[65] and design their worship services to always be on and poppin', to the possible detriment and elimination of the Holy Spirit and larger connections of people. Rev. Dr. Khalia Williams believes all churches, new and old, are considering different methods of worship. But she also suggests many churches are engineering backward. She says if the goal becomes "the experience" and we attempt to slap God on top of it, the work of the church isn't being done. Ultimately with this method, a better experience must be produced each time, continually moving further from spirituality. Williams observes: "If we say the heart of millennials is authentic[ity] and transpar[ency], why are we manufacturing experiences?"[66] Womanist and literary scholar Audre Lorde's revelatory insight, "[t]he master's tools will never dismantle the master's house,"[67] resonates during this collection. The inverse too may be true . . . that you cannot use the master's tools to build your own house—the master's tools in this case being white megaministry models.

Minister and scholar Jeremiah Wright believes the heart of church growth comes through worship. He argues excellent preaching (with preparation), Black music synthesis, and the Holy Spirit facilitate church growth.[68] Using the second chapter of Acts as his foundation, he writes: "Luke says that more than three thousand people joined the church on one day because of what happened in worship. The people *saw* something. The people *heard* something. The people *felt* something, and they were convinced in their heads about Christ. [Wright asserts] people joined the church in Luke's day because of worship, and joined Trinity United Church of Christ from 1972 [through his tenure and presumably join today] because of worship."[69]

Moreover, Challenger (and Williams) argue: "Congregations that are unwilling to consider contemporary styles of worship expression—Hip Hop, dance, spoken word, mime, drama, multi-media, and various music forms—often lose their ability to hear the message of the Church, not because of their objection to what is being said, but because of how it is being expressed. The medium may change, but in every generation, the church must be able to be in conversation with the culture, translate what is heard for the church, and find ways to influence with the power of Christ—evangelizing those outside of a covenant with God."[70] Even in this moment, two of the most significant aspects of Black church worship remain its music and preaching. Thus, I turn to each of these areas to discern more about this address of millennials in Black church worship.

Church Girl Don't Hurt Nobody

Black folks historically often find ways to merge Black popular cultural forms into the "what is" of church spiritual and worship engagement. As such, the articulation of Black gospel music perpetually morphs over time. Historian Jerma A. Jackson traces gospel music from its beginnings as a mode of worship to its expansion into commercialized culture. She notes even the term gospel, derived from the words "God-spell," suggests "good tidings" or good news as conveyed through performances within the Bible's New Testament. I think through an unacknowledged but felt recognition, most Black musical forms can be considered and operate as soul music—music necessary for the soul.[71] Jackson reminds us that composer and musician Thomas Dorsey "made the rhythmic dimension of the music synonymous with the older definition of 'gospel' and its religious significance."[72] And as is preached about more during The Message, each generation finds a new musical way to honor God.

Examples abound. The Clark Sisters' 1960s and 1970s bold singing shifted the gospel standards into four-part harmonies and "innovative instrumental vamps."[73] While they achieved success in religious circles by the late 1970s, their 1981 song "Is My Living in Vain?" moved them into national secular prominence. Their follow-up recording, "You Brought the Sunshine" (1981), became the first contemporary gospel song to be played on mainstream radio. Their trajectory was chronicled in the 2020 Lifetime biopic *The Clark Sisters: First Ladies of Gospel* (Swanson). In fictional narrative, *The Color Purple* (Spielberg, 1985) offers the sax wail and honky-tonk rhythmic piano juxtaposed against the voices and traditional gospel piano to make for a powerful redemption. The updated version takes that impulse further and fuses them better (Bazawule, 2023). Gospel innovator Kirk Franklin layered hip-hop and R&B into gospel in the 1990s (paving the way for Mary Mary, Tye Tribbett, and many others). Christian rap or gospel hip-hop developed into its own genre in the late twentieth and early twenty-first centuries with Grammy winner Lecrae as its poster child.[74]

When the pop beat becomes part of the church, when once more secular and commercialized aspects are adopted wholesale to reach a particular demographic, questions emerge around the efficacy or performativity of the Holy Spirit. Yet the music of new Black church attempts to alter the trajectory and legacy of Black music altogether. This shift comes in part with the incursion of white contemporary Christian music into Black church music repertoire. Sociologist Patricia Hill Collins's indictment of Black male intellectuals and their masculinist ties to successful public intellectualism mirrors the mostly men of God who run big (and small) churches. Collins remarks: "For artists and intellectuals [and ministers] alike, the real money lies not in [B]lack markets but in white ones. . . . [B]lack musicians and [B]lack public intellectuals alike cross over from the particularism of race into the allegedly universal (and white) space of the public, carrying with them race music and ideas that are valued in a society where colorblind racism rules."[75] Examples from predominantly white megachurches and white popular culture have become a part of the tool kit utilized by contemporary Black church.

Limited theological grounding, many argue, contributes to contemporary gospel and Christian music's vacuity. Music minister, literary scholar, and novelist Daniel Black considers the lyrics of contemporary gospel shallow because in his estimation, 95 percent of new songs are written by folks younger than twenty-five—many of whom have not grown up in or come out of the Black gospel tradition, or even necessarily the church. He suggests, literally, they create off the top of their heads.[76] The propensity to employ well-paid praise worship teams of five or six members while eliminating church choirs and hymns, to have songs (really sound bites of praise) with minimal words (and minimal allusion to scripture), to bounce/jump as if at a rock concert (along with synchronized lighting schemes and a focus on guitar strings), all originate from rock music and white church. CCM, the organizing body of the Christian music genre, retains a segregation of church worship styles. Overwhelmingly white, the chords, rhythms, and focus differ from traditional Black church gospel music, and very few Black artists participate in this realm.[77] In addition, as analyzed by communication scholars Omotayo O. Banjo and Kesha Morant Williams, CCM's themes center God as the subject with a goal of attaining the promises of a Christian walk, while Black gospel music focuses on struggles and opposition, with songs giving encouragement through hardship.[78] Both strive to worship God but demonstrate that the journey looks different. This worship music environment belies the historic innovation strategies of Black artists and dominates the entire Christian landscape.[79]

Beyond the music, many Black churches now purchase prepackaged intertexts of holiness or aesthetic appeals for their worship services. Sometimes small video vignettes, other times kids' church curriculum, are designed to offer a formal, professionally produced (and de facto uniform) worship experience. Often written, voiced, and visualized (otherwise acculturated) in whiteness, the narratives feature millennials and children primarily—with a smattering of colored folks for good visual measure.[80] This new Promised Land looks a lot like the old, where people of color and their culture are parenthetical to the main story—more *Star Trek* than *Matrix*. While I argue during Praise and Worship that mediation provides and allows for a move of the spirit, I believe too, this move requires a cultural knowledge of the worshippers at hand. Mapping white Christians' praise onto Black church acculturates rather than supplements faith. Ironically, listening to and watching online the largely white Pentecostals of Alexandria (Louisiana) that I reference during Praise and Worship, their style reflects twentieth-century, ecstatic Black church worship. As visiting Black evangelist Wayne Francis leads, the worship radiates through the screen using a particular Black body, Black cultural understanding, and musical knowledge to witness a powerful, soul-stirring worship service—demonstrating a style from which contemporary Black church worship seems to be distancing itself.[81]

Many believe this new white-ified worship reflects a reentrenchment of white domination—previously enacted through mental indoctrination within colonization and slavery. The notion of "if it's white, it's right" rematerializes. Despite Black people's time-tested and spirit-filled ability to worship, to walk upright with God, to praise and invoke His/Her presence musically, the ways of white church undergird much of new Black church worship services. While Black worship and Black belief systems have always expressed themselves vocally and physically, experientially and communally,[82] we see an old-is-new phenomenon operating through white "touching and agreeing," call and response, and calls for integration. The hokey pokey, turn yourself around of it all is that the sacrificed innovation of Black gospel music—its histories, knowledge, and experiences of Black folks—is being replaced in the name of progress and millennial recruitment. Yet we stay worried about the church girl Beyoncé elevates who actually comes from the will of God the Clark Sisters created.[83]

The Preaching Moment

Communication scholar Quentin Schultze suggests megachurches resemble televangelism incarnate. With "dynamic and entertaining" worship services, ministries often float by on the "charismatic power of one or more pastors."[84] In Black churches, the minister has always served as a central draw to the church. The ability to tell relational stories grounds their success. They come with a long history of dynamic and soul-stirring articulations of the gospel that rely on knowledge of biblical stories, admittance to interpersonal struggles and connection, and concern with the social-cultural-political happenings of the moment (and of the past). In other words, they present a word and world of experiential magnitude and evangelical zeal. This zeal, according to Rev. Dr. Dominique Robinson, fits well with new technology and media tools.

A millennial herself, Robinson argues that the use of technology and media sits as an essential part of her preaching moment. Using the school of thought she coins ihomiletics (a method of preaching to millennials that makes the word tweetable), she believes using social media and technology helps her "make God concise, sleek, user-friendly and accessible."[85] She argues, "if we develop our sermons the way Apple markets its products, then our young people will connect to the gospel. However, I also know adults want the message very clear and concise and user-friendly as well, and so I feel like the use of social media linguistics connects to the generation, but I feel like Black preaching has always used the language of the day."[86]

Both Challenger and Hanson argue for the need and reinscription of storytelling as part of reclaiming millennials. For example, the K–12 corporate ministry curriculum Orange sells includes a purposeful space for the speaker (youth pastor, worship leader) to insert her/his story into the message. As rich oral historians and conveyers of life, this prescription fits well into the always-already ways of Black being. Yet Challenger argues that in addition to what ministries produce now, worship needs "a rich biblical content that helps believers wrestle with the theological, ethical, moral, and ideological struggles they face day to day. The presentation indeed must be moving . . . layered . . . and multisensory. Worship is the launching pad for the transformation that is necessary for discipleship."[87] As mentioned, many millennials (both believers and unchurched) are not well versed in scripture. Thus, the word needs explication beyond a sound bite. Moreover, if the invocation and participation of the Holy Spirit are basic elements in creating a climate of spiritual growth, ensuring authenticity and long-term viability of the spiritual health of congregants,[88] it requires thinking through how the Holy Spirit gets loosed in right now Black church. The question remains whether the truth of God for today's millennials manifests with new preaching tools.

Returning to and using Bishop William Murphy from the beginning of this Tithes and Offering as an example, technology seems not to appreciably impact Black preaching style—yet. It adds, however, parameters and tools to presumably enhance the lesson. While Murphy (a well-known gospel artist) uses music quite well to illuminate his points, the PowerPoint demonstration of scripture remains quite basic. Yet, argues Williams, using technology and media such as PowerPoint, Facebook Live, or posting the preaching moment online can be seen as a blending of the old with the new. During her church's worship service, for example, they still print Sunday bulletins so the ninety-year-old member can both hear and write down the main points as written on the projected PowerPoint. Brown and colleagues suggest incorporating a tangible thing that visually demonstrates a point. Thus, Impact Church routinely employs props as part of the teaching moment. And, as rather an afterthought, they write: "All worship leaders understand that God is the ultimate designer and developer of every worship experience."[89] These technology-rich articulations of Black worship experiences call for business expectations of evidence—what do the data suggest, and more importantly, what is the impact?

At that same workshop on the church in the digital age mentioned earlier, participants grapple with understanding the development of technology and its use (and potential usefulness) in the contemporary Black church. When dealing with whether sacredness is possible or even desired in the contemporary moment, one participant cautions: "Sacredness is contextual. . . . We need to be careful not to confuse sacredness with tradition."[90] According to communication scholar Steven Halliday, megachurches produce "tightly controlled worship services designed to carefully script everything, from songs to speeches to banter. The resulting curtailment of spontaneity often prompts complaints of a decrease in organic community, as well as a lost feeling of divine immanence."[91] The television drama series *Greenleaf*, for example, captures the tension of corporatization, traditional Black church, and worship. When the fictional white Harmony and Hope (H&H) megachurch franchise becomes the parent company of Black Calvary Fellowship, scenes of standardized (and anglicized) catchsongs and recommended shortening of the preaching moment immediately ensue. Real-lived ministers in many Black churches have shifted to this shortened preaching moment—believing millennials would rather be at brunch than in church. However, that intent to abbreviate the message in many spaces may still be overridden if the Holy Spirit is allowed to take root. The need for online pre- and post-COVID church may place an unplanned permanence on the practice.

Ain't Nobody Praying for Me but Every Goodbye Ain't Gone

As has been suggested several times here, scholars and news outlets insist that millennials crave authenticity, relationship, and address of issues important to them in the church—not so much programs but opportunities to know God and His/Her people.[92] A particularly poignant and circulated demonstration of this need comes from blogger Kimberli Lira, who posted after her husband died of cancer in 2017, which seems particularly apropos as we emerge changed from the worst health pandemic in over a hundred years. She writes in part:

When church leaders sit around and discuss how they can reach people, I don't think they have the widow in mind. I don't think they have the cancer patient in mind. I don't think they have the children who are growing up without a parent in mind. I am not paying attention to the church décor when I walk through the doors. I don't want to smell fresh brewed coffee in the lobby. I don't want to see a trendy pastor on the platform. I don't care about the graphics or the props on the platform. I am hurting in a way that is almost indescribable. . . . There are people whose marriages are crumbling, people whose finances are deteriorating, people whose children are rebelling and people like me, whose husband has passed away after a brutal fight with cancer. And these people are not impressed with the stage lighting. They could care less about the coffee flavor. They don't need to be pumped or hyped. They need and are desperate for Jesus. And they may actually be turned off by all that they consider gimmicks to get people to go to church.[93]

With all this branding, shifting, and capitulating to millennials, I continue to wonder about the end game. Beyond the need due to COVID-19, what ultimately are Black churches trying to do with their heightened use of technology and media? Is the argument for millennials to replicate the high of a club experience? What happens to the social-political-cultural context of Black life in this new worship environment? Can the focus on and consequences of evangelism, reaching people through mass media, be considered a desertion of local neighborhoods? In search of sacralizing global places, I wonder, does it please God more to save souls in Haiti or Burma but not right on MLK, Auburn Avenue, or Jackson Street? What happens to the address of the poor or the invitation of the sick when the screens raise and the doors open automatically, literally, for you to exit? Moreover, as religion scholar Monique Moultrie argues, nontraditional church members often replicate what they grew up with in old Black church. For example, lap cloths still get distributed and expected, maintaining the damaging things that uphold patriarchy and sexism. In this, it seems women have only their "gift" of virginity to offer—the gift you can't take back with a receipt. Moultrie maintains you can't do anything new on an old foundation.[94] Further, I ponder what these new, technology-driven, and media-rich churches want from older generations beyond tithes. How do they think we feel, or do we even matter? Thus, the reliance on and turn to mediation and technology to make good church may ultimately move Christians further away from Christ. It may feel like, stream like, as Kendrick Lamar raps in "Feel," "ain't nobody praying for me."

Yet juvenescence, and our focus on it, plays an integral role in our humanity development. During this moment, many readily create, anticipate, crave, rebel, and dream without borders. Concurrently, the impulse to do church differently sweeps the U.S.—in part because of the young, but also because of what the young seem to suggest with their movement away from the church. Technology and media are being used to help recapture them. However, mixing theological ways of being with mediation is an endeavor needing critical thought if indeed salvation is the goal. While if nothing else, something actually sacred exists in *disconnecting* from technology and reconnecting with humanity and spirit, mediation can (and should, if being used for this purpose) help cultivate and forward the vision a church has for its members' lives on earth as well as in heaven.

Many certainly appreciate and seek technology and popular culture for religious purposes. Creating Black church media should facilitate and encourage a modicum of discernment, spirit leaning, and understanding of Christian precepts. Media deployment needs to be thought of with the same care with which music is prepared for services. For example, media usage can be used to research and honor a certain efficacy of God. Visualizing texts on the screen could promote critical understanding as opposed to just reiterating biblical scripture. Dramatization of the word can be shown through video with the goal of engagement as opposed to entertainment. Critical exegesis of biblical texts can be done with different versions—demonstrating how different writers interpret the scriptures via the culture of that day. Short narrative pieces, plays, poems, and other products of artistic life could not only encourage and make it interesting for the entire church body but also facilitate prayer, song, communion, and the word of God. Pastor Ricky Temple of Overcoming by Faith Ministries in Savannah, Georgia, says of church and tech in these times: "I think people define things differently now. We evolve and grow. Jesus said, 'Go out into the world.' Digital allows you to do that."[95] Informed media usage can help craft stories of Black cultural Christian walks, new and old.

From the small, Black Providence Missionary Baptist Church (Atlanta), member Ponce Turner comments as she watches service via YouTube: "Thank you lord for Social Media I cant begin to ThankYou enough I'm still able to be with my church family I am blessed."[96] Black folks, including Black millennials across class, continue to attend church, believe in God, and use mediated and technological resources in greater numbers than their racialized counterparts. This provides an opportunity for Black church ministries to evolve, integrate, and innovatively use media, technology, and Black popular culture to (re)capture minds, feed souls, and center the call of God. For different types of learners and feelers, providing a digital media component can not only help them with their journey of religious and spiritual understanding but also make them feel seen (and targeted) by their church.[97] Creating community for millennials (and others) comes through intention. Pastor Shawn Anglim of First Grace UMC in New Orleans believes the church and Jesus offer divine adventure. He asks people to consider: "So whatever . . . technology you use . . . does it take you there?"[98] Moreover, Rev. Julian DeShazier of the University Church Chicago eloquently questions in his sermon-talk online: "In these times, where all manner of calamity is happening, where 'capitalism without community' exists . . . are we builders or not?"[99] He asks the online congregants to think about and write in the comments what gifts they could share to help build beloved community. He says we are using this virtual forum to serve as a witness to someone who might not feel they have a place. Using very simple technological tools, direct address, and the word and heart of God, DeShazier demonstrates exciting possibilities of worship 3.0 for millennials, and maybe even Gen Z and Gen X will come too.

Passing of
the Peace

Our mouths were filled with laughter, our tongues with songs of joy. Then it was said among the nations, "The Lord has done great things for them."
—Psalms 126:2 (NIV)

Playing with God!

●●●●●●●●●●●●●●●●●●●●●●●

Black Church and Humor

After collecting the Tithes and Offering, many churches begin what might be seen as spontaneous community. Hugging necks, greeting one another, and catching up across the sanctuary constitute the Passing of the Peace. It is a joyous time, a playful time, a fun time. But speaking the terms Black church and play in the same sentence might be considered, for some, heresy. The admonition "Don't play with God" enjoins believers to understand that while you may have questions or even doubts (God forbid), you cannot poke fun or play in the house of the Lord. (Recall Jo's comments during the Testimony.) But Black folks do poke fun and play at church all the time. And beyond the human aspect of these actions, poking fun is as much a part of the Black church tradition as is understanding the community of saints, the forgiveness of sins, and life in Christian piety.

As we Pass the Peace, let's examine Black church through the framework of playful piety, its aesthetic forms and its expressive culture. Specifically, I look at how Issa Rae's *Mis-Adventures of Awkward Black Girl* YouTube series, entertainer Rickey Smiley's stand-up, and the *Preachers of L.A.* reality television series mix Black religiosity and humor. These pop cultural forms and forums offer an opportunity for Black folks to not only see themselves enacted religiously but also to enjoy the foibles, fallacies, contributions, and even grace of Black religious ways of being. Using scholarship from performance, media, communication, and religion studies, I discuss how humor in and about Black church functions to expose, engage, and display multiple ways of living while Black. In so doing, the confluence of play, fun, and Black church gets understood and taken up in not only completely different contexts but also in productive ways that help believers and nonbelievers rethink their understanding of religious criticality as well as express their humor in religious community.

Let Me Be Clear—Black Is . . . Black Ain't

As discussed in the Call to Worship, religion—Christianity specifically—and spirituality for Black folks in the United States operates neither homogeneously, evenly, nor innately. Meaning, who Black people are, the ways people practice, the denominations people participate in, and the capacity to believe vary from church to church, from community to community, and from state to state. Said another way, not every Black religious and/or spiritual person attends church/mosque/temple/synagogue or worships in the same way. The gumbo of Blackness, so thoroughly interrogated by filmmaker and scholar Marlon Riggs, demonstrates that essentialist claims should never serve as adjectives.[1]

Yet, as has been considered through this service, the Black church stands as a central and significant aspect of the African-American experience in the U.S. In various epochs, it endures as a location of strategic comeuppance, refuge, improvement society, and, as historian Evelyn Higginbotham argues, an "agency of social control, forum of decision and debate, promoter of education and economic cooperation, and arena for the development and assertion of leadership."[2] Its lessening role in the lives of African-Americans in no way undermines its historic significance or its impact on how African-Americans, directly or indirectly, come to understand religiosity and spirituality in relation to politics, education, achievement, and social engagement. To that end, the Black church serves as a barometer and taskmaster for African-American interaction and comportment within larger white society. Meaning, ideas of how to behave, how to appear, what should and shouldn't be said, and who matters foment historically through slave owners and within slave religion.

Yet theologian William B. McClain believes Black church worship "celebrates the power to survive. It reflects a lifestyle of persons who live on the existential edge where the creative and the destructive, the wise and the foolish, the sacred and the secular, the agony and the ecstasy, the up and the down are impartible contrarieties of human existence in the presence of the divine."[3] (Or at least it has functioned this way traditionally.) And beyond Black church "performance," the Black church still serves as the cornerstone for African-American lives. Priest and religion scholar Kelly Brown Douglas attests: "The [B]lack church's importance to black life is undeniable, if not insurmountable . . . it is the [B]lack church's active commitment to the social, political, emotional, and spiritual needs of [B]lack men and women that makes it [B]lack."[4] Some of this operation faces contest in the twenty-first century, with millennials and Gen Z. However, the framework of Black church continues to operate powerfully psychologically.

During the Passing of the Peace, church attendees connect bodily and verbally through shaking hands, hugging, smiling, and often sharing the words "peace be with you," followed by the response "and also with you." Beyond the opportunity to move, meet, and greet, this scripturally inflected act supports the conditioning of hearts in the ways of relationship and community. I use this part of the service as a framework to demonstrate other nuances, tendencies, suggestions, and recognizable resonances of Black Christian religious experiences and the ways humor acts as an agent for peace-making and affirmation of humanity. In the community of saints, many African-Americans chuckle about somebody's church lady announcements as parodied by Rickey Smiley, Jehovah's Witnesses ministering on early Saturday morning, or late-night outfits seen on Sunday morning. The funny bone gets tickled with familiarity of living in a Black cultural milieu. To effectively reframe the seeming incompatibility of Black church, Black church people, and humor, I briefly explore the history of humor and holiness.

Holy Fun and Formality

Suggesting that people find humor in God and the Word of God is not a recent or new concept. Since the early 1960s, scholars have considered how humor and religion cohere.[5] Either expressly, in covert/insider conversations, or within the Bible itself, ideas related to a God that appreciates humor abound. Some trace historic resonances of (or at least a speaking to) humor to the early Christian church.[6] Much of this discourse talks about the workings of the Christian church during the fifteenth and sixteenth centuries. This makes connections to the Christianity of Africans and Africans in the New World difficult given the transformations occurring at that time in people, ideas, and ways of implementing and using the gospel.[7]

English scholar Samuel Joeckel talks about contemporary theories surrounding the compatibility of humor and the church: theories of superiority, incongruity, paradox, and preconditionalism. First, he believes people's foolery is funny. "When people behave ridiculously—acting foolishly or immorally—we laugh; and as [superiority] theory implies, our laughter seems to proceed from an implicit sense that we are superior to those at whom we laugh."[8] Second, Joeckel believes the confluence of humor and church highlights ideas aimed around incongruity and paradox. Many of the teachings within Christianity suggest paradox in both word and deed. Like comedy, as noted by religion historian Conrad Hyers, "In the world of the Bible . . . everything seems turned upside down. The whole hierarchy of human values, and the ladders of human greatness and self-importance, are inverted and collapsed."[9] Third, Joeckel argues through the idea of preconditionalism, "laughter can serve an epistemological purpose by beneficially preparing the mind for the discernment of truth."[10] Employing philosophers across time, he claims, "Laughter familiarizes and removes distances (Bakhtin); laughter can dissolve hatred (Quintilian); laughter can promote humility (Niebuhr); and laughter can offer a transcendental perspective (Berger)."[11]

These theoretical framings, along with the ideals of Passing of the Peace, help in thinking about humor and religion broadly construed. They set the stage for understanding the complexity of the purported collapse of the sacred and the secular as interrogated in the Processional. In honing the focus on humor in religion, however, I recognize that additional factors contribute to how humor functions within Black church and among Black church people.

One central concern in not playing with God comes from the possibility of God's wrath and shame. Serious Black church traditions rely on conditions of decency and order. Operating outside of this paradigm could land you in the depths of disgrace or, more seriously, burning in hell. The use of shaming and the threat of hell often shape attitudes, behaviors, and life choices for Black church congregants. Yet within these conflicted paradigms, a deep-seated appreciation for and understanding of the necessity of laughter exists. In talking about play, gaming, and BIPOC, informatics and visual arts scholar Aaron Trammell argues for the need to "recognize the ways that the affective and the aesthetic work together to produce evocative experiences."[12] Black leaders of the church, ministers, preachers, and/or priests, make humor a part of their larger preaching enterprise. These men (and some women) of God tell jokes about their own pasts, jokes about their present circumstances, and jokes about their families. It is, as I addressed in Tithes and Offering, a part of the great talent of Black preaching. And beyond the titular head, humor emerges in the work of the ushers, in the parishioners' negotiation of the choir (and the performances that inhere within it), in the ways in which young people (at least those left) take up church and often, if allowed to, make it their own.

As mentioned earlier, the church in general, and the Black church in particular, has a history of decrying entertainment, especially all manner of secular entertainment. For example, in a 1922 article, journalist Jean Voltaire Smith reminded readers of the Black church's antipathy to cinema and other entertainment forms that, as paraphrased by film scholar Anna Everett, "threatened to usurp its influence and income."[13] Poignantly, consciousness and contentiousness around respectability play a large part in the apprehension around humor in the Black church. Respectability (the rigorously debated term that constrains behavior, insists on a uniform aesthetic cultural code, and shifts righteous anger from structural racism to the need for personal responsibility)[14] structures much of the angst surrounding Black Christian life. From the perspective of the first "recognized" religious practices for Blacks in the U.S., slave religion helped Black people be seen as human, both the visible and invisible aspects of it. This acceptance enabled the enslaved to replicate roles occupied by slave owners. As religion scholar Albert Raboteau writes in *Slave Religion*: "In the role of preacher, exhorter, and minister, slaves experienced status, achieved respect, and exercised power, often circumscribed but nonetheless real."[15]

And certainly, ideas of respectability continue to exist, even if they have morphed. What was respectable and right in the late nineteenth and twentieth centuries has shifted in the 2020s. This shift has been spurred by a few factors, including continued cultural assimilation, the explosive growth and development of technologies, the widening divide across economic class, the move away from the church, and the COVID-19 pandemic. Thus, right now, respectability politics means anything from claiming (or reclaiming) professional corporate appointment of hairstyles, dress, fragrance choice, housing, and food intake to media coverage, how to handle state violence, or academic tenure and promotion. What comedian Wanda Sykes identifies as a central conundrum about and rationale for dignified Black people is that "White people are looking at you!"[16] still resonates. Yet whether churched or unchurched, spiritual or spiritless, Black church operates in the background or in the collective subconscious of Black folks. And as I've argued elsewhere, while scholars argue that capitalism structures everything contemporaneously, the foundational imprint of European ways of being continue to stranglehold many Black (and brown) people's notions of the world and themselves.[17] Despite this continued struggle with respectability, humor remains part and parcel of Black church life as Black church continues to be a central aspect of Black American consciousness. I suggest humor functions in at least three ways in relation to Black church: (1) to expose, (2) to engage, and (3) to express humanity.

Hypocrisy on Notice: Exposing Black Church Folly

Writers, artists, comedians, and cultural critics use humor to expose hypocrisy in the Black church. Comedians and writers Moms Mabley, Richard Pryor, Whoopi Goldberg, Chris Rock, Aaron McGruder, Wanda Sykes, Tiffany Haddish, KevOnStage, and James Finley all understand and comment on the ways Black church operates humorously. For example, in an online video, Goldberg talks about her grandmother's job at her Baptist church as the "fall-outer spotter."[18] Moms Mabley expresses a similar observation when she talks about the backhanded church.[19] Aunt Esther (LaWanda Page) in the 1970s sitcom *Sanford and Son* always decried "Oh glory" in her dealings with Fred (Redd Foxx). Although a religious woman, she knows how to get with Fred in the flesh. Shaming and condemning him to hell are part of her work with him. She argues, criticizes, chastises, and corrects Fred in his wrongdoing, humorously, in the name of the Lord.[20] This role allows audiences to see playfulness with piety, and piety aligned with Black cultural ways of being.

Page's reprisal of that religious type in F. Gary Gray's 1995 *Friday*, however, hilariously illuminates the often thin line between sanctity and impiety. Ringing the doorbell early Saturday morning of a sleepy and grumpy Craig (Ice Cube), she says sweetly: "Good morning. Are you prepared for Jehovah's return? Because if you not, I have a pamphlet here." In mid-sentence, he slams the door in her face. Speaking to the closed door she quips, "Well, fuck you! Half dead motherfucker. Come on, sister." This scene opens the $28 million grossing film *Friday*[21]

LaWanda Page in *Friday* (1995).

and prepares audiences for not only a raucous ride but also nostalgia. Many Black community members remember hiding from Jehovah's Witnesses on Saturday mornings as their saints work for the Lord, door to door in Black communities. In addition to her response, the scene also critiques the witness Page supposedly bears as both a Black middle-class woman and seasoned saint as she curses Craig out in the saltiest way possible just before saying, "Come on, sister." In thirty-eight seconds, this small opening scene demonstrates or exposes ongoing Black communities' conversations around hypocrisy within Black church folks' witness. The most pious woman of God may, underneath it all, not only be uncouth but a hypocrite as well.

Comic personifications of church people exist throughout Black popular culture. As discussed in the Prayer of Confession, Spike Lee humorously relives community religious grappling in his *Do the Right Thing* (1989) and *Red Hook Summer* (2012). Audiences are tickled by characters such as Florence Johnston (Marla Gibbs) in her forthrightness about going to church on *The Jeffersons* (CBS, 1975–1985); preacher/pimp Daddy Rich's style (Richard Pryor) in *Car Wash* (1976); the characters of *Amen* (NBC, 1986–1991); Rev. Brown (Arsenio Hall) presiding over the talent show in *Coming to America* (1988); Boyce Ballantine's call (Cedric the Entertainer) in *The Soul Man* (TVLand, 2012–2016); Key and Peele's skit "Old Ladies and Satan" (Comedy Central, 2012–2015); Aaron McGruder's completely irreverent *Black Jesus* (Comedy Central, 2014–2019); and even Jamie Foxx talking about real church in his stand-up comedy act *Unleashed: Lost, Stolen and Leaked* (2002).[22]

YouTube hosts brothers Emmanuel and Philip Hudson's take on Black religion in their comedy vignette *Church Folks*. Excoriating Black church attendees' behavior, appearance, and hypocritical stances, these two made their way into national consciousness via their 2012 *Ratchet Girl* video. In *Church Folks*, they use call and response, musicality, and the cadence of the Black preacher to situate themselves as critical commentators, nativists in a Black religious milieu with the help of a hip-hop beat.

Sitting in choir robes, they begin the musical skit by stating their intention—to address church attendees who hypocritically attack others. "Yes, Lord, hallelujah. Feel the Holy Spirit, let it move ya." As part of their critique, Phillip flippantly rhymes, "I'm in church every Sunday, so please don't judge me. Yeah, I smoke weed, but Jehovah still loves me. Offerin', I paid it, and yes I'mma little faded. But I still know all the words to 'I Never Would Have Made It.'"[23] The Hudson brothers' ditty suggests that while some of the criticism heaped upon their generation may be valid, they behave no differently than the adults they grew up seeing in church. They simply fail to value secrecy (or discretion) and find comfort in openness about their actions.

Even when not emerging from Black popular culture, the Black digiverse will yoke up folks who get out of pocket, even religiously. Take, for example, evangelist Paula White's prayer for a Donald Trump victory during the 2020 election season. In prayer, White not only claimed to speak in tongues but also called for dispatches of angels from Africa and South America to bring him victory. Black Twitter and the larger social media world lit her up with memes, TikTok videos, and critical and comedic condemnation.[24]

Writer, producer, and actor Issa Rae's YouTube series *Mis-Adventures of Awkward Black Girl* brings an extended treatise on religious hypocrisy. Usurping the character name Whoopi Goldberg dons in both *Sister Act* (Ardolino, 1992) and *Sister Act II* (Duke, 1993), actress Leah A. Williams portrays a new convert to Christianity. She's born again. In *Sister Act*, Goldberg uses the piety of the cloth as a refuge (as the mob hunts for her). As Sister Mary Clarence, she pretends to be a nun until she can reconfigure her situation. In the process, she transforms the lives of the children in the nun-run school as well as reinvigorates the convent itself. Although pretending, using humor allows audiences to reimagine Catholic evangelism and to reinscribe a Baptist Blackness cultural potency through Goldberg's characterization.

In *Awkward Black Girl*, on the other hand, Delores Clarence as Sister Mary exhibits piousness to a fault. She evangelizes in the workplace, evangelizes on the phone (she works phone sales), and rebukes sinners for their fornication. She consistently refers to their boss Jesus (Spanish pronunciation) as "Jesus, our Lord and savior," reminds people of their holiness (or lack thereof), and finds every opportunity to insert the name of Jesus (God et al.) into work conversations. Her character offers constant hypocritical tension in this narrative—a narrative ostensibly about the diversity and unknown awkwardness of people within Blackness. Rae's direction suggests a preferred reading of Delores/Sister Mary as a hypocrite. Moreover, unlike Goldberg's character, one rendered colorless and

Sister Mary, *Awkward Black Girl* (YouTube, 2012).

asexual in *Sister Act*,[25] this Sister Mary's inability to let go of her sex-positive background and former life provides a source of both tension and hilarity.

In this Delores, we find a "hood rat." The Pleasure Chest adult store personnel know she and her man Tariq by name. She flaunts her body and often offers speech that runs afoul of any sense of religious holiness. Her demand for attention and leadership leaves no question as to which Mary you address at any moment.

In one such example, Sister Mary critiques the intimate relationships of series lead J (Issa Rae). J comes into their morning office meeting smiling, greeting, and in a great mood (ready to tell her best friend CeCe (Sujata Day) about her first sexual encounter with her new boyfriend). Delores, retooled in her Sister Mary piousness, begins to hyperventilate and fan her face. She pants: "Oh my God, oh, oh my God. I smell . . . I smell, SEX! Oh, I can't take all of these hoe activities. It's arresting my spirit. Oh, Jesus, help me."

This overt shaming of J for having sex outside of marriage comes from the most "promiscuous" person in the office. J's thoughts narrate: "This holy hoe-bitch ain't about to play me today." She responds: "Hey, Sister Mary, how's that robo-cock you ordered?"[26] And while Sister Mary feigns shock and unfamiliarity with the term, another coworker chimes in and says, "She's talking about a robo-COCK"—clicking his tongue for emphasis. J's retort resonates with audiences wanting to call religious people out for hypocritical stances. The exchange between the two speaks to both the perceived realness and authenticity of Black religious representations in visual culture and humorously deals with the sanctimony of some Black church people.

Yet Sister Mary, at least partially, also illustrates differing faces of evangelism. In a tangential video, "Sister Mary's Video Diary" on the series website, Sister

Mary testifies in her bathroom. Confessing to those watching, she effuses about winning a jingle competition at the job. In this monologue she wrestles with spiritual mindedness and her fleshly pleasures. Evangelism, as articulated in a U.S. context, connotes a certain sincerity that may or may not be at its core. Black Christians are shown frequently as essentially, culturally, and biologically evangelical in general.[27] Evangelical Christians, on the other hand, appear as white, rabid, and likely hypocritical. However, Sister Mary's commentary addresses the more than real-lived sanctimonious stances of many religious folks across racial and ethnic differences.

Popular and traditional cultures continue to polarize and binarize Black women by putting them into the corners of frigidity and freak, virginal and pure. Whether in her position on sex, listening to secular music, or talking up the name of God, Sister Mary's walk and talk find themselves at odds or at least stretched in many of the web series scenarios. Another example comes from Issa Rae's 2013 *The Choir*, where the web series opens with a gospel choir rendition of Janet Jackson's 1993 "Anytime, Anyplace"—lyrically and demonstratively. The lead singer Jessie (Yutopia Essex) tells the pissed pastor afterwards: "You wanted contemporary gospel. You wanted to relate to the youth. The youth like sex. I made Jesus sexy."[28] While easy to condemn, between chuckles, the scenario provides an opportunity for productive dialogue on what hypocrisy means. As Joeckel contends: "Paradox artfully applied illustrates in humorously powerful ways how . . . worldly patterns can be reversed so that a new spirit—both comic and Christlike—emerges."[29] Perhaps, instead of shaming and castigating ways of being that appear at odds with certain assertions, thinking of these tensions as another side of humanity—of people exercising one aspect, while still occupying and working through others—might lead to more compassionate and useful relations. This reading of Sister Mary and Jessie complicates Rae's directives for both narratives.

In *The Mis-Adventures of Awkward Black Girl*, pretense and play provide a liberating space for Black women. Holes get poked into holy tropes. Black women's grappling with piety gets pushed throughout the series, where the mantle of respectability leaves no room for anything but supreme confidence and striving. When J calls Sister Mary out, she claims a space for different types of Black women to operate in this world and for play within the religious performative. In all these examples, exposing the foibles and hypocritical tensions of church people through humor allows for what can be both introspective and receptive assessments. It also encourages the religious and nonreligious to rethink fixed positions around matters of identity, sexuality, gender, and Blackness.

Taking it further, Pastor Donald L. Robinson Jr. of Marine and Mt. Moriah Baptist Church in Jefferson, Louisiana, suggests hypocrites don't even exist in the church. He says, rather, church people are real folks—with real failings, real issues, and real setbacks. He asserts that no one goes to church regularly and works in the church regularly with the mindset of hypocrisy. But they are real people who struggle every day to do better, to be better—even though they often fail.[30] Taking up real people proves valuable in thinking about hypocrisy and religion conceptually, especially regarding Black popular culture—and a way to better understand the role humor plays in these spaces.[31] Engagement of the larger Black church delivers another path for humor to manifest.

Bringing Funny to the People

Tickling the funny bone at church requires an intimate knowledge of how Black church works. It also suggests that if you are going to examine it reverently, you must participate in church, at least on some level. Comedians and others in Black popular culture can use Black church and church folks as a source of comedy because their audiences recognize the references. To be sure, Black church humor operates fully in the realm of parody as opposed to pastiche, as it resonates poorly otherwise, if at all. For example, amid the COVID-19 pandemic, comedian Will Johnson blessed users with the Facebook video "Wash Your Hands." With the requisite Black church choir and hand clap (both of which he emulates in triplicate squared and with piano accompaniment), he tells folks to go wash your hands "if you don't want corona." Shout-outs come from various choir members admonishing the water "better be hot" while they tap the Ajax tambourine and take the chorus up after every iteration.[32] This video hit over a million views in forty-eight hours in March 2020. This Black church humor reinforces Joeckel's ideas around incongruity and paradox.

Stand-up comedian, radio host, television actor, reality star, and gospel musician Rickey Smiley understands many of the hip-hop generation's connections to Black religious experiences even with their frequent disregard for religious things. Admittedly old-school Christian but unabashedly secular in many ways, Smiley uniquely blends his traditional church background with cutting-edge, right-now knowledge that feeds Black comedy and larger Black popular culture enterprises. Said another way, Smiley as a brand, just as Mary Mary shows in the Processional, operates necessarily in between the religious and the secular simultaneously. His radio program features Black musical artists, actors, and political figures who synthesize their respective worlds and lives, Black lives, openly. So, in many instances, a blend of their hearts and minds gets articulated in all the spaces Smiley operates. His syndicated radio show broadcasts on Black old-school stations nationally, with easy access to Black up-and-coming as well as bona fide stars. Yet when listeners hear his morning drive program,[33] a discombobulating confluence of musical genres and sensibilities emerges.

Interviewing Smiley on TBN, comedian Steve Harvey talked about these musical and cultural discordances as Harvey himself hosts a nationally syndicated radio program, a program on TBN, among many other ventures.[34] Talking about their respective radio music lists in 2011:

HARVEY See my audience is a much deeper sinner. . . . I gotta keep mine more
   current. I got Marvin [Sapp], Donnie [McClurkin], Yolanda [Adams], Mary
   Mary. I got to stay right there.
SMILEY But see, I'll play Albertina Walker and then have to play Waka Flocka
   "No Hands" so [Laughter of hosts and audience]. . . .
HARVEY See, Rickey's station require[s] that he play hip-hop. I'm adult con-
   temporary. I don't play it. . . .
SMILEY Shirley Caesar and Lil' Wayne, you know, it's hard. It's hard.
HARVEY Yeah, see you need that. After you play Lil' Wayne, you need "Hold
   My Mule."[35]

Harvey's largely Black TBN audience hollers with laughter, with the crux of
the funny being familiarity with all the artists named. You must know Shirley
Caesar, Mother Church, is the queen of old-school gospel. All gospel artists and
churched audiences recognize her, her stature, and her longevity. She is an old-
time saint (as is Albertina Walker). McClurkin, Adams, and others on Harvey's
list represent contemporary gospel artists (contemporary meaning since the latter part of the twentieth century and the beginning of the twenty-first) whose
music often blends Jesus with R&B and hip-hop.[36]
   Both Harvey and Smiley succeed in the secular world of stand-up comedy
(and other ancillary platforms such as television series, radio, and comedy spe-
cials). However, they consistently privilege their previous and current Black
church experiences as part of their comedy acts and in their other spheres of influence. Their intragroup references, multiple media platforms, and relationships
to God afford them unique perspectives and abilities to cement the viability of
Black church and church people finding fun in praise. Smiley, masterfully and
with great talent, understands and weaves together the connections between
R&B, gospel, and hip-hop within Black popular culture—knowing that gospel
founds the other two genres. Says music scholar Teresa Reed: "By the 1940s, the
[so-called] Devil's music had evolved into rhythm and blues, and between the
late 1940s and the 1960s, virtually all noteworthy Black secular artists hailed
from the pews, quartets, and choirs of the Black church."[37]
   Knowing these connections, Smiley transforms one of singer Al Green's signature songs, "Simply Beautiful" (1972), into Black church during one of his live
comedy shows. As a young local man sings Green's song on stage, Smiley creates
a sanctuary by bringing two chairs up front and announcing, "The doors of the
church are open." Smiley talks/preaches about how hard the young man works,
and further intones, within the beat of the song, "Even if you got on a lace front
weave [background], you simply beautiful."[38] His Black preacher affect and words
of invitation make for a hilarious combination of comedy and Black church
acknowledgment and reverence.[39] The pacing of his movement (including his pretending a sway-back, big ol' belly), his word selection, the rhythm and richness
of the song (which already speaks to church with Al Green as both soul singer

and reverend), and his connection to the audience bring a unique synergy between humor and Black church. Beyond opportunities like this, Smiley's church lady impressions are legendary.

"Good Murnin', Good Murnin', Good Murnin'"

For over thirty years, Rickey Smiley has performed his church lady announcements in different mediated forums. These skits center Ms. Bernice Jenkins, a Mother of the church, who reads the printed bulletin announcements to the congregation. Sister Jenkins adds colorful commentary to her reading of these announcements. Again, familiarity with the rhythm, cadence, and formality of old-school Black church moves audiences to deep-down belly laughs. These announcements feature typical Black church matters (especially Baptist traditional ones) such as church picnics, baptisms, the building fund, funerals, and fundraising dinners. Through these announcements, Smiley signifies the historic centrality of Black church in the lives of Black communities.

Writer Jacquinita A. Rose maintains that reading church announcements served a very important role in the church, linking congregants to what was happening with other churches.[40] I suspect reading church announcements aloud, although printed in the church program, has historic antecedents in societal pre-literacy. In the U.S., this illiteracy typified many immigrants (and especially women) and the enslaved, who were forbidden to read and write. Reading announcements also accords special significance to the person reading them as someone intimately a part of the church's operation and business. Thus, a necessary tradition of reading announcements aloud for the congregation continues in many churches, although its efficacy is now debated. For the young, the

Rickey Smiley as Church Lady, YouTube.

formally educated, and megachurch members, the practice may seem outdated and unnecessary.[41] But the activity provides another layer of cultural competence and understanding when parodied by Smiley. In one instance, for example, Smiley as Ms. Jenkins talks about baptism during announcements: "Parents, please! Please, parents, please! Parents, please! If your child is being baptized on next Sunday; please give 'em a bath before you bring 'em down here. Cuz it was a ring around the pool last time. Bruh Burwell got gout and can't get in that cold water."[42]

The humor of this announcement, beyond the way Smiley delivers it, comes through Smiley as Ms. Jenkins getting with congregants. She addresses parenting skills (or lack thereof) and friendship/community familiarity with people of the church (Brother Burwell's medical condition). This approach to understanding and appreciating Black church, and especially through Black women, works within various narratives written and produced by Tyler Perry (gospel theater on the chitlin' circuit, with the taped projects distributed at Walmart and through his television narratives). And regardless of one's inclination toward Perry's work, the billion-dollar net worth generated from his television series, plays, films, and studio allow for an understanding of how Perry's moves within media, religion, and humor resonate with audiences—audiences he knows and targets exceptionally well.

In another example, singing with gospel innovator Kirk Franklin, Smiley takes the solo part of one of Franklin's most popular songs as a seasoned saint of the church.[43] The 1993 certified platinum song "Silver and Gold" turns old-school church when Smiley not only leads the vocal ensemble but begins to direct the song as well through call and response, long riffs, and extra vocal runs. Reviving the tyranny and performance style of Black choir directors (or ministers of music as they are called now), audiences receive a completely different choice of Jesus with Smiley leading. Through this and his own laughter, the mostly African-American in-studio TBN audience supports him with their clapping and laughter. Black audiences recognize Smiley's play with an extremely sacred and revered song as a special (and sanctioned) connectedness between humor, religion, and the Black church.

Humanity Expressed

Humor allows the complexity and humanity of Black church folks to flourish—the good, the bad, and the ugly. The legacy of a people designated as object significantly impacts what abounds in its cultural practices. Meaning, some of the humor that emerges in a Black religious context draws from the simple (or not so simple) desire to be acknowledged as human. One such example of this desire comes through the television series *Preachers of L.A.* Premiering in October 2013, this Oxygen network series (that became a franchise) brings the reality format to the front, back, and side door of the church house. Featuring five major and semi-major male ministers (and their significant others), audiences experience U.S.-based Black megachurch ministry in a broad way.[44] In interviews outside of the show, the ministers say they are doing God's work from the vantage point of a reality series. Incorporated video evidence seeks to support this assertion through scenes where they hold gang summits, attend to homeless individuals, or minister to those enduring the pain of violence in their families and churches. However, the tenor of the episodes (in typical reality TV fashion) points to the intimacy of their lives as a significant point of contention and interest. The sheets become one of the typical places of fun for this series (or more, the thoughts of ministers in them).

As shown with Mary Mary and Mary J. Blige in the Processional, religion on the celebrity stage comes in many different forms (well, mostly the male form) and by way of many vehicles—network, cable, and satellite television, streaming, web series, CDs and cassette tapes (still), billboards for concerts and commissions, music videos, rallies, concerts, revivals, postcards, newsletters, radio broadcasts, public access (okay, television again), podcasts, and increasingly movie screens. Over sixty years ago, historian Daniel Boorstin described commercial celebrity as a "person who is known for his well-knownness. . . . He is neither good nor bad, great nor petty. He is the human pseudo-event."[45] This characterization well captures twenty-first-century pastorpreneurs (as media scholar Sarah Banet-Weiser calls them).[46]

In *Preachers of L.A.*, producers offer up the often-touted dividing line between the spiritual and the sexual. The series' executive producer, Holly Davis Carter, and the show editors incorporate banter between the spouses that speaks not only to their spiritual connection but also to their sexual one. As is well documented, sex sells in any capacity, and religion proves no exception. Ultimately, humor comes from the titillation of sex talk, a sexual look, and sexual innuendo when bumped against Christianity, especially the Christ of Black women. For example, Pastor Ron Gibson, the rich, rhyming preacher, remarks in a season two episode, "I believe we can be saved, sanctified, and sexual."[47] A part of the humor comes from uncomfortableness, insecurity, and respectability politics surrounding sexuality and the Black church. Yet Christianity and sexuality always run together in Black popular culture. Whether in the sensuality and gospel chords Aretha Franklin sings in "Dr. Feelgood" (1967) or the recommendation in many churches for women to cover their skirted legs with cloth (in order, presumably, not to tantalize the men on the pulpit), Black folks know the two exist centrally (if hidden) as part of the very fabric of Black humanity (and thus, Black church).

Given this context, critical and derisive commentary around *Preachers of L.A.* emerged even before the program aired. Once in progress, critics, especially from the pastoral ranks, said things such as, "There is an unwritten code that we deal with our issues privately so that we can be strong publicly. . . . They are giving the world ammunition to shoot back at the church and not accept the message that it is trying to convey. . . . They've sold out. It will call for pastors all over the

First ladies of *Preachers of L.A.* (Oxygen, 2013).

country to have to defend their integrity because these men have decided to chase their dream of being in the public eye."[48] But really, the sex talk makes this program compelling and humorous (beyond the opening of private spaces for public consumption and the accoutrements of success demonstrated by these men of God). For example, audiences meet First Lady Myesha Chaney as a rather conservative, young Christian woman, but who audiences see, in time alone with Pastor Chaney (and the program's cameras and crew), consistently talks about keeping the bedroom spicy. She muses about getting and giving enough and even twerking for Jesus. She says in an interview outside of the show: "Our marriage has been the best it's ever been when I'm satisfied and he's satisfied.... There's something to two people feeling very confident in life in what they're giving and getting in marriage."[49] Every time this narrative emerges onscreen, the framing plays for peering into something secret and being titillated by the discovery.

The series positions First Lady Chaney against Sister Dominique Haddon (identified as just Dominique in the first season as she and Minister Deitrick Haddon had yet to marry). With one child out of wedlock and apparently pregnant with the second one when they marry at the end of season one—classic cliché reality—she earned the right to a last name once they marry officially (side-eye). The youngest first lady on the program, she serves as the foil to her husband, who offers himself up as a particularly sexual man. In fact, the running refrain for the show's program promotion in early fall 2014 was, "I'm a pastor, but at the end of the day, I'm a man."[50] Moreover, Haddon's dual life as a major gospel music recording artist (and tainted by his first marriage) inserts more potential fodder for humor, sexuality, and religious ways of being.

And finally, the series focuses on Loretta. It presents Loretta (Jones) as the "special friend" of Bishop Noel Jones, pastor of megachurch City of Refuge in Los Angeles. The nature of their relationship becomes a significant point of contention for one of the other ministers and becomes a problem for the couple within the reality narrative. An internationally known purveyor of the gospel, beyond leading a 17,000-member church, Bishop Jones travels extensively and is the brother of singer/actor Grace Jones.[51] In the series, he lives as a divorced bachelor in a relationship with Loretta. An unmarried minister who dates raises church folks' flags of sin—the possibility of fornication and the like. Thus, sexual tension permeates most scenes featuring the two of them. The idea of getting and receiving sex falls under the purview of winks and nods—knowing chuckles that make sexual innuendo the selling point of the series lying quietly under moving Black church fans.

Considering Black people and their sexuality as depraved gets overturned through this series, despite African-American respectability narratives and some expressed disappointment.[52] The dialogue and allusions to these ministers as sexual beings force a recognition of Black people as religious and human. Moreover, many Black community members recognize and call for the Black church (and other Black institutions such as HBCUs) to stop denying that sex exists and suggesting it's bad. They encourage the address of some of the deleterious outcomes of unvoiced and hidden sexual activity.[53]

Shake It for The Lord!

In *Honk for Jesus. Save Your Soul.* (Ebo Twins, 2022), Lee-Curtis Childs (Sterling K. Brown) and his First Lady Trinitie (Regina Hall) strive to get their megachurch members to return after several scandals. One such effort finds them on the curbside of their huge and empty church edifice assailing cars to honk for Jesus. Because Trinitie's simply displaying her sign doesn't get that much acknowledgment, Lee-Curtis tells her to shake it for the Lord. And in obedience (despite the hard head turn of the groundskeeper behind them), she rhythmically shakes her body to get honks for Jesus. While the scene reflects their ridiculous fall from grace and culminates in a painful confrontation, it's also funny as hell.[54]

Many Black ministers maintain that "I wouldn't worship a God who couldn't have fun." That fun translates variably in Black popular culture. The sacralization of the secular occurs routinely through humor, as demonstrated here and in other areas of Black popular culture. Historian C. Eric Lincoln reminds us that the "Black Church has always been the cultural matrix out of which has developed the genius of the Black experience. That genius embraces the whole spectrum of effective responses Black Americans have made to the peculiar circumstances of their existence: their art, their politics, their humanism and their religious understanding"[55]—an understanding Black culture holds of itself regarding faith and fun, even moving beyond Christianity. For example, comedian Damon Wayans parodied Nation of Islam leader Minister Louis Farrakhan in the 1990s sketch comedy series *In Living Color.* In "The Wrath of Farrakhan,"[56]

Wayans as Farrakhan (along with the Fruit of Islam) comes aboard the starship *Enterprise* to liberate people of color from their mental enslavement by Captain Kirk and the future world. Wayans mimics Farrakhan's mannerisms and ministerial flourish to make audiences laugh. In doing so, however, the skit also supports the Nation of Islam's religious beliefs and Black nationalistic visioning. Other examples of having fun in Black church come through everyday Black culture.

For example, Father Tony Ricard, formerly of Our Lady Star of the Sea Catholic Church in New Orleans, celebrated the win of the New Orleans Saints in Super Bowl XLIV in 2010. The saints of the church literally joined him, as shown in a well-circulated 2010 YouTube video.[57] Father Tony shed his robe to display a New Orleans Saints jersey underneath. He reached beneath his pulpit for the requisite umbrella and with rapper K. Gates's "Black and Gold" (Who Dat) playing, begins to second line down the church center aisle along with his deacon. The congregation, dressed in their Saints paraphernalia as well, hoist their umbrellas, dance, and celebrate with him.

Performance studies scholar Dwight Conquergood talks about the ways in which culture and fun coexist. He argues: "Performance privileges threshold-crossing, shape-shifting, and boundary-violating figures, such as shamans, tricksters, and jokers, who value the carnivalesque over the canonical, the transformative over the normative, the mobile over the monumental."[58] The priests' dance in service to joy, gratefulness, culture, and relief demonstrates not only boundary violation of the painfully decorous Catholic Church but also the transformative power of gaiety and fun in Black church. And despite the many posts claiming blasphemy in the behavior, the performance articulates the fullest expression of biblical scripture—particularly as written in the book of Psalms. For New Orleans, the perennially losing Saints team emblematizes a whole cultural and citywide dispossession. Their win, however, symbolized the phoenix.

Black church people form King's "beloved community." The same sort of resonances resound in the collective memories, experiences, and jokes of those either raised in the church or family or friends adjacent. Like other types of Black institutions (HBCUs, the Divine Nine, civil rights organizations), Black church still provides and inhabits spaces and opportunities to draw on a shared or at least resonating cultural consciousness of being. Humor helps audiences alleviate religious anxiety. But more than that, humor within and about Black church and church people taps into a shared consciousness and provides a sort of cathartic release. Rev. Dr. Dominique Robinson remarks: "Millennials use social media to make fun of things in church that we couldn't do in person, 'cuz we clown a lot."[59]

Humor brings joy to believers in God. Humor allows joy to manifest and express itself within sacred spaces and in a popular way. Cultural theorist Stuart Hall calls popular culture a "theater of popular desires" and a "theater of popular fantasies" where we "discover and play with the identifications of ourselves, where we are imagined, where we are represented, not only to the audiences out there who do not get the message, but also to ourselves for the first time."[60] With the many ways that living while Black forces those so identified to struggle, negotiate, code-switch, endure, and try to survive, the wonder and reprieve of Black church comes not only in the bosom of Jesus but also in the belly laugh of its members, outliers, and through its saving grace.

Selection

Offering a musical selection prior to the sermon helps usher in the intent of God's messenger. It takes congregants to a higher place and a different plane of spiritual expression as they prepare their hearts and minds for the message.

Never Losing Its Power

• •

(Re)Visioning the Roots and Routes of Black Spirituality

> Love your flesh; love it hard. Yonder, they don't love your flesh.
> —Baby Suggs Holy in the clearing, *Beloved*[1]

> When the present has given up on the future, we must listen for the relics of the future in the unactivated potentials of the past.
> —Mark Fisher[2]

> God by any name is still God.
> —Bishop Yvette A. Flunder[3]

The Blood Introduction

In returning to our seats from Passing the Peace, the mood becomes still and serious in preparation for the Word; it begins musically. The song of the U.S. South provides a particular context for and closeness of peoples and beliefs from the continent of Africa. Because the slave trade languished longest in the South, returning over and over again to sell humans in the French Quarter, filling the red dirt of Georgia with the blood of enslaved men and women, capturing and keeping Black bodies and souls hanging in Mississippi, Alabama, and Texas, dredging and drowning Black bodies in Haiti and Jamaica, something about that process and the resiliency of the people forced to endure it shapes spiritual practices largely settled there. The Bible belt retains its name because so many people openly claim (and attempt to control with) Christianity as their religious practice. Yet the same dirt and sand, with the blood, sweat, and tears of the past, carry and keep the spiritual practices of Black folks from long ago alive today as well. Through Vodou, Santería, Candomblé, and with healers and conjuring women and men, Black folks live, love, worship, heal, and empower in the South (and elsewhere) as part of a sustaining legacy. Coming to understand how blood never loses its power, many Black creatives (writers, visual artists, musicians, and media makers) attempt to capture the connectedness of disparate religious traditions through stories of practitioners and adherents through and beyond Christianity.

Religion scholar Rachel Elizabeth Harding discusses the function of music from the very beginning of Blacks' encounter with the New World. She writes: "The songs, almost always accompanied by ritual movement and dance, melded biblical language to African religious values and New World experiences of struggle. They provided the foundation for the emergence of a distinctive, African American Christianity marked by many elements common to other traditions of the diaspora such as Santería, Vodou and Candomblé."[4] While how *Black* creatives *envision* the Black spiritual, religious, and sacred has received limited examination, especially practices connecting them to the past, books, scholarly articles, and fiction take up syncretic religious practices and sometimes express their visual articulation from other perspectives, often pejoratively. This happens despite an actual increased exploration of world religions and a rise of African-originated religious practices. Audiences are seeing new ways of understanding Black spiritual engagement. This musical Selection offers a lyrical rendition of Vodou and conjure inside Hollywood. Claiming, explaining, and refashioning Black initiates, Vodou and conjure can provide a prescient way to undermine the continued denigration of indigenous African religious practices in visual culture.

Like African philosophy, Vodou and conjure maintain no written sacred texts but continue to return repeatedly to take up residence in the psyche and souls of Black people. Some may characterize it as a haunting—something returning or persisting from the past, as in the manner of a ghost.[5] But unlike philosopher Jacques Derrida, who proposes the concept or even the ways in which women and gender studies take it up, this haunting, this specter, reveals itself in a widening of culture and spirit—a connectivity of ancestors, land, blood, and body. Through the examination of alternative visionings of Vodou and conjure, I sing anew about the viability of an expanded and syncretic Black spirituality visualized in three different melodies: Toni Morrison's novel *Beloved* (1987) as directed by filmmaker Jonathan Demme (1998), filmmaker Kasi Lemmons's *Eve's Bayou*

(1997), and Natalie Baszile's *Queen Sugar* (2014) reimagined via OWN and creator/writer/director Ava DuVernay (2016–2022).

The Roots of Indigenous African Spiritual Practices

Religion scholar and priest John S. Mbiti has been writing about the centrality of religion or spirituality for Black Africans since the 1960s. He believes religion "is the strongest element in traditional background and exerts probably the greatest influence upon the thinking and living of the people concerned."[6] Moreover, as religion scholar Jacob Olupona expounds, even "the word 'religion' is problematic for many Africans, because it suggests that religion is separate from the other aspects of one's culture, society and environment. But for many Africans, religion can never be separated from all these. It is a way of life, and it can never be separated from the public sphere."[7] In fact, in many African languages, no word exists for God because in these cultures, everything and every place embodies God. Some believe society as a whole is organized around values and traditions drawn from a common origin, created by one supreme being. Others share common tenets such as a belief in a community of deities and the idea of ancestors serving as a way to communicate with these deities. They use ritual and magic to communicate among and between human beings, nature, and gods. Says Mbiti, to "ignore these traditional beliefs, attitudes and practices can only lead to a lack of understanding of African behaviour and problems."[8]

Historical records and journals document how Christian missionaries came from Portugal to proselytize to Africans in the late fifteenth century. However, the colonial powers' fight for the continent encouraged a concerted missionary effort in the late nineteenth century. As of 2020, 62 percent of sub-Saharan Africa claimed Christianity, with another 31 percent embracing Islam.[9] In this moment, a proselytizing push continues on the continent, not so much from external voices but from internal ones. These newer crusades come by way of home-grown disciples—ones, in some respect, predicted well in writer Chinua Achebe's novel *Arrow of God* (1964). In fact, the last two sentences of his novel really tell the story. He writes: "In his extremity many an Umuaro man had sent his son with a yam or two to offer the new religion and to bring back the promised immunity. Thereafter any yam that was harvested in the man's fields was harvested in the name of the *Son*."[10] Contemporarily, Black African missionaries offer a Jesus who retains his Europeanization, as shown on posters for conferences, billboards, church programs, and children's videos. The continued visual whiteness of Jesus rings particularly problematic and strange, especially given the shift, at least in some parts of the African diaspora, from worshipping a white Jesus to one pictured as Black or one not racially identified. After all, no dispute seems to exist that the land Jesus emerged from and traversed lay off the continent of Africa and in the Southern Hemisphere, where people of color dominate.[11]

Jesus in Nigeria. (Author's collection.)

Vodou as known to the West exists as an outgrowth of the religious practices of the Yoruba nations of Nigeria and Benin, West Africa—land historically known as Dahomey. Beyond missionaries, Western knowledge of Vodou comes from the slave trade that ran from the mid-1500s to the mid-1800s, from anthropological expeditions, and from military occupations. Denounced by the West as a religious atrocity, Vodou has followers in Nigeria, Benin, Haiti, the Dominican Republic, and the United States—with similar practices in Cuba, Brazil, Bahia, and Mexico. The religious practices of the Yoruba include worship of various spirits (or *orishas*) under a supreme being. These spirits act as messengers and an embodiment of *ashé*, the sacred power from spirits or the power to make things happen. They present God's own enabling light rendered accessible to women and men. The Yorubas call the supreme deity Olorun (or Olodumare), master of the skies. Olorun is neither male nor female but transcendent and omniscient. Olorun is the creator of all things, the quintessence of *ashé*.

In U.S. news, government, and popular imaginary, Haiti serves as the home of Vodou. Ridiculous narratives by reputed journalists and novelists such as William Seabrook began shortly after Europeans and Americans encountered the island. His 1929 journalistic fiction fueled the flame and fury against a religion of Black demons. Vodou practitioners endured persecution during the 1896, 1913, and 1941 anti-superstition campaigns in Haiti. These hunts destroyed shrines and led to the massacre of hundreds of people who admitted their adherence to Vodou. The period of the American occupation (1915–1934) as well as the post-Duvalier era were also times of severe persecution of Vodouists. Much like the enslaved of the U.S., enslaved Haitians were forced to embrace Christianity—Catholicism in this case. But African traditions strongly persisted in Haiti through song, dance, and music. The practices of Vodou allow Africans in Haiti to covertly maintain their ties to the continent of Africa while covering and syncretizing their religious beliefs with Catholicism.

Haiti stands as the only Black nation to overthrow its enslavers.[12] In independent Haiti, 95 percent of its inhabitants are descendants of enslaved Africans; the remainder carry French ancestry. The economy is predominantly rural and agricultural. The island recognizes Vodou as an official religion and incorporates Creole as an official language.[13] These elements of Blackness, language, and history of will and religious autonomy all work in tandem to demonize Haiti, Haitians, and to banish Vodou from the world's lexicon of religions. And thus, because Haiti came to represent racist manifestations overturned, Vodou as part of the country's religious character connoted evil. It helped further a pejorative insistence of the terms Black, foreign, and strange embodied within a word and even spelling of a sacred religious practice; Vodou became *v-o-o-d-o-o*.

Anthropologist Alfred Métraux characterized the need for problematizing Vodou when he wrote in his 1959 book *Voodoo in Haiti*, "the anxiety which grows in the minds of those who abuse power often take the form of imaginary terrors and demented obsessions. The master maltreated his slave, but feared his hatred. . . . And the greater the subjugation of the Black, the more he inspired fear; that ubiquitous fear which shows in the records of the period."[14] Sixty-plus years later, Hollywood's vision of Vodou and its practices reflect these early perceptions and ostensibly serve to visually titillate. They often bear little resemblance to and have no cultural context for actual rituals. This demonization extends to outside contexts as well. For example, unlike her smart, talented, and favorite other children, 2020 U.S. Supreme Court appointee Amy Coney Barrett can only describe her adopted Haitian children as physically "strong" and "happy go lucky." This fear remains in-house and gets reified on screens.

The Routes of Visualized Black Spiritual Practices

Haitian zombies arrived on U.S. screens in the 1932 film *White Zombie*.[15] This type of racist dominant narrative about Vodou blossomed and then faded, only to be revived across many different screens, over and over. In them, Vodou and Santería always serve as a deadly force perpetuated by Black people on unsuspecting and guileless whites. For example, Wes Craven's 1988 *The Serpent and the Rainbow* contributes to the legacy of Vodou raising people from the dead, even as it attempts to dispel it. This film's particular cult classic status informs the works proceeding it. In Clint Eastwood's *Midnight in the Garden of Good and Evil* (1997), Vodou becomes the backdrop for the mysteries of Savannah, Georgia. Accepted as part of the cultural fabric, the religious practice connects death, evil, and, interestingly, Black mother wit. In the film, Vodou priestess Minerva (Irma P. Hall) attempts to cast a spell against the already dead Billy, killed by Jim (Kevin Spacey). Minerva is the widow of Vodou practitioner Dr. Louis Buzzard. She tells a befuddled John (John Cusack): "Listen boy, to understand the living, you must commune with the dead." Numerous and generically disparate U.S. television episodes enjoin or leave room for some heinous crime or calamity to come through Vodou or Santería across time.[16]

In addition to film and television narratives, Vodou is invoked across multiple areas of popular culture. For example, in 1980, presidential candidate George H. W. Bush derided Ronald Reagan's radical tax cuts as "voodoo economics." The New Orleans Saints called on the resident Voodoo Queen (and pastor) to win the 2010 Superbowl. As part of their Christian and assimilationist practices, Black folks themselves, diegetically and as audience, often embrace deviant aspersions of these religious beliefs and expressions. Mostly due to its pejorative framing, this stance also provides a rare opportunity to side with the majority. Yet, even in the 1990s, writers such as Gloria Wade Gayles tried to disabuse this fascination with demonizing traditional practices, writing that children "need not talk in whispers among themselves about a deranged lady who carries voodoo dust in a brown paper bag. Real voodoo dust is an accessible commodity in our country, targeted for sale in poor Black neighborhoods."[17] Despite the veracity of Gayles's observation, problematic characterizations have dominated discourses on Vodou and conjure. As grotesque as many mainstream visualizations of Black religiosity can be in general, those associated with Vodou and conjure repulse even further. This repulsion expresses itself frequently through Black women.

African-descended women occupy central space in the world of conjure. Unlike Black Christian women, who are mostly shown as middle-aged, overly clothed, and overweight, especially within non-Pentecostal displays, Hollywood's imagination of Vodou and conjure ties Black women's spirituality provocatively to their taut and young bodies. As writer Lina Buffington maintains, the "more foreign or African the spirituality is to that of the White Christian male, the more sexually promiscuous the woman appears. In establishing all that is non-White as other and therefore 'primitive' or 'savage,' the White male is able to maintain the hierarchy that places him at the pinnacle."[18] I suggest a part of the continued demonization and devaluation of African religious practices is to not only challenge the authority and authenticity of Black spiritual practices but also Black women's centrality in them. It helps to, metaphorically, put them in their place.

For example, in 1987, *The Cosby Show* kid Lisa Bonet expanded her acting repertoire in a very different narrative than her clean-cut Denise Huxtable brand. Marketed as "controversial," the film's promotion decries, *Angel Heart* "takes us on a journey of violence and murder that canvasses the desperate streets of Harlem, smoke-filled jazz clubs of New Orleans, and ultimately to voodoo rituals in the sweltering swamps of Louisiana." The text highlights: "in her feature film debut, including the notorious 'unedited' X-rated love scene with Mickey Rourke, *Angel Heart* surfaces as one of the most visually provocative American movies to date."[19] As *Angel Heart*'s Epiphany Proudfoot, Bonet practices Vodou, characterized as demonic, a threat, and deadly.

The practices of Vodou suggest a cycle of life and death, and because of this, Vodou initiates may exhibit extraordinary ability as part of spiritual control. Ceremonies call forth ancestors to be in contact with the departed, and the spirit returns. Writes feminist studies scholar and anthropologist Gina Athena Ulysse: "[S]pecters of divine encounters reveal . . . themselves in the subtlest of movements. Some tentative, others emboldened. A barely lifted foot in motion. Unchoreographed internal and relational dialogues. Another planted firmly. We are balancing. Between the dead and the living. Kinetic flashes of connectivity and reunion. Always with grace. In salutation. Devotion. Sometimes with reverence."[20] The beauty of these rituals, however, is supplanted by demonic notions about Vodou and a connectedness to deviant Black sexuality. This latter idea congregates in one short scene of *Angel Heart* with blood serving as the predominant visual metaphor. Blood becomes the devil incarnate in Louis Cyphre (Robert De Niro) and flows out of chickens and women. Before the advertised "X-rated love scene," director Alan Parker prepares the audience for the conduit of this evil, Proudfoot herself. In this scene, Proudfoot's role as Vodou priestess deteriorates to whore as the iconography suggests profane and aberrant connections between blood, sex, religiosity, and Black bodies.

In Vodou, divine possession exists as a routine way for divinity to communicate with the devotees. Drums serve as a force to attract the deities, and the body becomes central as a medium for carrying messages. Usually in a possession, a significant amount of graceful and elegant twirling occurs, frequently appearing as expertly choreographed. However, Protestant denominations and the Roman Catholic Church often see drumming and dancing as an "affront to the social, as well as the aesthetic, order" and bar it.[21]

In *Angel Heart*, Proudfoot dances while holding a chicken within a circle of Black drummers and dancers. Upon being handed a switchblade, she slits the chicken's throat, allowing the blood to fall upon her sheer, white linen dress. Sacrifice as honor is a part of Vodou practice. Moreover, the Bible's Old Testament offers many examples of sacrifice as sacred, even human sacrifice. Catholicism suggests God supernaturally answers prayers using focal points such as candles, beads, statues, texts, and ornaments on which believers concentrate. Vodou replicates this system in sacrifice. The practice differs from Catholicism by using living focal objects like chickens. This, the Oba of Oyotunji, South Carolina, maintained, activates fire energy (blood). He offered: "You don't have to use animals. You can use plants. But blood is much more active and energetic. . . . The

Lisa Bonet as Epiphany Proudfoot possessed in *Angel Heart* (1987).

reason we smear the blood all over [people] is to activate their fire energies."[22] Fire energies are said to be in tune with the *orishas*.

Literary scholar Kameelah Martin further examines this film with an eye toward how it articulates Black women's construction within a white male gaze. She writes, the "inscription of a Voodoo aesthetic on the black female body is a device used to further relegate Africana women to the realm of Other. It is Epiphany's association with African-based spirituality that shifts her body from desirable pornographic object to the abject disrupting the visual pleasure of a tri-part audience: Angel (in the film), Parker (from behind the camera), and the target white male viewer (viewing the screen)."[23]

With Proudfoot still dancing wide-legged, the blood, the light shining through her sheer dress, and the drumming congeal to make the ceremony less about religious fervor and more about sexual titillation. By the end of the scene (where audiences find her on the ground and seemingly humping another overcome practitioner),[24] Harry Angel (Mickey Rourke) runs off, having served as the audience's eyes during this construed atrocity. The act exemplifies both the sacred and the profane, but as it centers Vodou, profane sexual images sear Western audiences' visual consciousness. Later in the film, Proudfoot "seduces" Angel. But audiences already predict this; the constructed sexual tension of the possession ceremony ensured it.[25] This extremely common visualization of Vodou and conjure gets disrupted, however, within the works of creatives, Black women creatives in particular.

Black women (and some men) make generous use of Africanist spirituality to empower characters. Within Black literature[26] and independent film, they centralize Black syncretic spaces, expanding readings of Black spiritual and religious dimensions. *Their Eyes Were Watching God* (Hurston, 1937), *for colored girls who have considered suicide when the rainbow is enuf* (Shange, 1976), *Cycles* (Davis, 1989), *Daughters of the Dust* (Dash, 1991), *Voodoo Dreams* (Rhodes, 1993), *Sankofa* (Gerima, 1993), *Mother of the River* (Davis, 1995), *Lemonade* (Beyoncé, 2016), and *Sing Unburied Sing* (Ward, 2017)—all exemplify and demonstrate the productive fusion of the religious, spiritual, and sacred beyond and through Christianity. I take up *Beloved*, *Eve's Bayou*, and *Queen Sugar* to uniquely demonstrate these assertions in practice.

It Reaches to the Highest Mountain: *Beloved*

Writer Toni Morrison's *Beloved* explores the trauma, choices, loves, and lives of Black women (and some men) around slavery. The 1987 novel was inspired by an enslaved Black woman named Margaret Garner. In late January 1856, Garner escaped slavery in Kentucky by fleeing to Ohio, a free state. In the novel, the protagonist Sethe, another enslaved woman, escapes her plantation, Sweet Home, and runs to Ohio. After twenty-eight days of freedom, a posse of white men arrives to claim her (and her children) under the Fugitive Slave Act of 1850. This act gives slave owners the right to pursue the enslaved across state borders. Before this claim can be executed, however, Sethe slashes the neck of her two-year-old daughter rather than allow her to be recaptured and taken back to Sweet Home. A young woman, presumed to be her daughter, calling herself Beloved, appears in the flesh years later. The story opens with an introduction to the child's spirit haunting Sethe's home at 124 Bluestone Road: "124 was spiteful. Full of a baby's venom." Morrison's novel won the Pulitzer Prize for fiction in 1988 and became a finalist for the 1987 National Book Award. An adaptation appeared on the big screen in 1998 starring (and executive produced by) Oprah Winfrey.

Morrison's *Beloved* forces audiences to consider the ways spirit, faith, and bodies get reimagined during slavery and after enslavement. Scholar Therese E. Higgins suggests beliefs in *Beloved* reflect African traditional ones, especially of the Mende people. These beliefs come through the veracity of spirits, where spirits stay always already present and can return in the flesh. Central, crucial, and sacred elements of both texts (book and film) include water (birth, cleansing, and purification), memory (and re-remembering), and bonds (of mother and daughter).[27] These elements connect the figures to their spiritual forebears and expose audiences to another way of understanding resilience through spirit. Yet writer Mark Fisher suggests Demme's version of Morrison's book fails because "the words are too raw, the ghosts too real. When you leave the cinema, there is no escape from their specters, their apparitions of a Real which will not go away but which cannot be faced."[28] His trepidation over this film's realness reflects a day-to-day, real-lived experience for African-Americans, who must find ways to face and move through, physically and psychically, even in the presence of a devastating past and a harrowing present.

Beah Richards as Baby Suggs Holy in *Beloved* (1998) (Courtesy Touchstone Pictures.)

Beloved as both narrative and visual text also allows audiences to grapple with the confluence of traditional practices in Christianity. The first example comes through Baby Suggs Holy in the clearing. Baby Suggs (Beah Richards) uses the body, land, and basic humanity to dispel participants' notions of inferiority and owned-ness. "Uncalled, unrobed, unanointed, she let her great heart beat in their presence."[29] In the film, encircled by all in sepia tones of the past, she commands children to laugh, men to dance, and women to cry as an expression of their own humanity. Their performance of these things makes sacred the need for touch, joy, and sorrow—connections made between people and the land, between people and spirit. Beloved's emergence from the water to land and to people reflects that need and craving, even from the grave.

The second demonstration of traditional religious practices merging with Christianity comes from the "thirty women" who exorcise the child come to flesh—one who is "haunting" and whooping the mama. These Black women come in the name of Jesus, but also with what they know and learn before the Son. (They move like the Iya Mi of Yorubaland, who operate on a spiritual level and are comprised of "powerful women who use their innate power to favor their own agenda.")[30] The thirty women walk directedly with tambourines, shakers, and voices, traveling down the road of redemption and righteousness. Some of the singers in this cadre are part of the renowned real-lived choral group Sweet Honey in the Rock. They bring the tonal quality of Black church and Black mothers to bear on this fleshly spirit who lives to indict the mother.

Through wailing, sonorous song, and steadfast resolve, their vibrations call Sethe to the porch alongside her naked, pregnant, and undead two-year-old adult

Thirty women in *Beloved* (1998).

daughter. Shaken but not broken by the sight, the women's sound continues. Sound, as singer Bernice Johnson Reagon reflects, offers "a way to extend the territory you can effect. People can walk into you way before they can get close to your body. . . . And, so anybody who comes into that space, as long as you're singing, they cannot change the air in that space. The song will maintain the air as your territory."[31] The spirituality of song and music traces its way from the continent. It brings forth the rhythms of life connecting God, land, and people to everything. The women claim this space by conflating Christianity with African-derived spirituality and thereby vanquish the woman-child Beloved.

Some argue *Beloved* sits in the seat of magical realism—invoking both a literary device and a way of talking about the appearance of the unknowing (and unknown). However, Morrison's drawing on certain African spiritualities allows for something different. Filmmaker and scholar Montré Aza Missouri sees *Beloved* as an art that reflects Yoruba-Atlantic religious sensibilities.[32] Morrison (and Demme) blend nomenclatures of Black Christianity with Black resiliencies. In this example, audiences witness a successful interaction of traditional African spiritual practices within Christian belief. This same confluence emerges in *Eve's Bayou*.

It Flows to the Lowest Valley: *Eve's Bayou*

Actor Debi Morgan's Mozelle Batiste Delacroix torches the screen in filmmaker Kasi Lemmons's *Eve's Bayou*.[33] In the story, Mozelle buries three husbands while continuing to attract and be attracted to other men. She possesses what she calls "second sight"—the gift of clairvoyance. According to the narrative, this gift runs through the women of their south Louisiana family—a family born of an enslaved Black woman and a white slave owner. In *Eve's Bayou*, Vodou and second sight exist as gifts passed on through generations. The backstory of the Batistes includes two Eves, the first a medicine woman and healer who saves slaver Jean-Paul Batiste (the illustration of which comes through voice-over from Tamara Tunie) and Black and white imaginings of the bayou. Eve the second gets her name and gift from her ancestral grandmother. This story sings compellingly due in part to the ways in which Mozelle's sensuality melds with her Christianity and second sight.

The Batiste women are beautiful, dispelling the dominant notion that "remnants of an African past are monstrous and abject."[34] When Mozelle extends her hands and closes her eyes, nothing magically happens in the room. She sees (and audiences vision), however, her neighbor Hilary's boy shooting up in a room far away. This scene blesses audiences by demonstrating and normalizing culturally centered religious practices. Mozelle has already shown her clairvoyance but further incorporates Vodou as a healing, beneficial, and sometimes necessary tool. Yet even those privy to Vodou's knowledge, veracity, and gift are influenced by media's racist and ignorant claims. For example, later in the film, young Eve asks Mozelle: "How do you kill someone with voodoo?" Mozelle replies, "I guess you put the hair on a quarter and stick pens on it or something. I really don't know." Even though she knows better, this response allows Mozelle to both articulate and dismiss the Vodou perpetuated in media and white literary culture. Besides, as literary scholar Tarshia Stanley argues, Lemmons "does not present the conjure woman as an exoticized Other. She is instead a part of the family, part of the landscape, part of the memory—a part of the whole culture."[35]

For paying customers, Mozelle describes what is happening or will happen to loved ones. She assumes a Christian prayer posture when meeting clients and

Debbi Morgan as Mozelle Batiste helping and communicating in *Eve's Bayou* (1997).

giving readings. By taking their hands, she provides visioned knowledge of down-falls and frailties but also offers ways to heal and restore. Film scholar Kara Keeling argues Mozelle's work is taken up by "many of the residents of Eve's Bayou [who] share a conception of the world in which certain things that official common sense deems irrational—voodoo, magic, communicating with spirits, seeing nonchronological time . . . to make the world appear reasonable and amenable to their survival."[36] Moreover, Mozelle's passions and gifts embody the simultaneous operation of spirituality and sexuality. As she recounts the loss of her third husband Maynard to her youngest niece Eve (who also shares the gift), audiences get to visualize the memory and her actualization of what that day looked like.

Mozelle's own past of betrayal, love lost, and death seems to confine her to solitude and loneliness. She shares with Eve and us: "You too young to understand. But when I was with Hosea, it was like my whole body was burning. I'd come home and have to rub ice on my face and neck to cool down." She illustrates how Hosea came to claim her. In the memory, Mozelle's husband instructs her to tell this lover she wasn't leaving. And realizing the love she had for her husband, Mozelle continues: "I stood next to my husband, and I looked at my lover, this man who had lit this great fire in me, and I said, please leave our house. I never want to see you again." These last words she utters before Hosea shoots her husband dead. Returning from the vision, out of the reflection, we glimpse how her second sight can reify love and loss.

Moreover, writer Audre Lorde's theorization of the erotic as a creative and powerful energy and life force[37] merges aesthetically through Mozelle's body and voice and her ability to heal and see. Even at the end of the film, when Eve takes her sister Cisely's hands (Meagan Good), we discover erotic tension at the heart of the disruptive matter between Cisely and their father Louis (Samuel L. Jackson). Keeling writes of this scene: "*Eve's Bayou* puts the unthought—voodoo, fortune-telling, nonchronological time, a kiss between father and daughter—into thought and obliterates the out-of-field, making its spectators seers without a system of judgment by which to adjudicate what they see, but equipped with a sense that something happened that upset Cisely and made Eve want to kill her father."[38] Grappling with non-Christian belief and belief systems fails to alter the force and connectedness of Christianity, Vodou, conjure, sexuality, and spirituality articulated through the sighted characters of *Eve's Bayou*. In fact, the visualization makes this synergy stronger.

Singer Erykah Badu sings over the film's credits. Badu, as I preach about in The Message next, bookends a certain boundlessness to Black women's spiritual ways of being. This deeply Catholic Black community of *Eve's Bayou* refers to and invokes the Christian God at every turn. Nonetheless, practices of their other ancestry, those Black medicine women and healers as practitioners of Vodou and conjure operate openly and squarely within these same communities as well. The melodies operating in *Eve's Bayou* call for a blend of blues and jazz, vagaries and clarity, the past and present, dancing through the night air as soft as a kiss between a father and a daughter.

Hauntology asks Black folks to remember through their spiritual practices what kept them here—alive and able to survive. The irony being, as Fisher notes, "to wish for the erasure of slavery is to call for the erasure of itself [Black America]. What to do if the precondition for your being is the abduction, murder and rape of your ancestors?"[39] Like Eve Batiste, released from slavery and whose descendants reap the results and Baby Suggs Holy ministering to the masses, perishing is not an option. We see this resolve in twenty-first-century mediated offerings like *Queen Sugar*.

The Blood That Gives Me Strength from Day to Day: Queen Sugar

A figure similar to Mozelle exists with the character Nova Bordelon (played by Rutina Wesley) in Ava DuVernay and Oprah Winfrey's television series *Queen Sugar*. Operating as the elder sibling rabble rouser and Black activist, her striking naked body, beautiful dark brown skin, and flowing locs open the first scene of the first episode of the series. In the narrative, Nova works as a journalist, community activist, family gatherer, medicinal weed seller, and spiritualist. Like *Eve's Bayou*, the setting is once again south Louisiana. While this character does not exist in Natalie Baszile's book (on which the series is based), DuVernay brings her to life in the televisual version. In fact, her character brings a substantial depth and serves as a mighty linchpin for the entire narrative. Film scholar Josslyn Luckett describes her and the pastor in *Shots Fired* as womanist women who "employ their spiritual practices in the service of social justice, family, and community healing in ways that connect them back to the women conjured in [Julie] Dash's and [Kasi] Lemmons's earlier films, now on a radically transformational small screen."[40] While Nova's role as a spiritualist is what concerns us here, it is important to understand it as just one aspect of her character.

Nova's spirituality doesn't come from the Christian domain exclusively but from spirits connected to the past, to the land, to ancestors, and the forgotten. DuVernay describes Nova in part as "a healer in the great tradition of priestesses of New Orleans and Louisiana and the South, yet she's very much in the world as a journalist at a major paper."[41] People come to Nova (as to Mozelle) to receive understanding, peace, and love. And something about Louisiana, and New Orleans in particular, frees minds to foster natural and supernatural connections.

The tone, both in terms of colors and sound, is purposely and carefully set in *Queen Sugar*. For example, Luckett beautifully describes Nova in a cleansing ceremony for her sister Charley (Dawn-Lyen Gardner) where yellow and the flickering of candles make the space sacred as she calls on Oshun for healing and silent prayer.[42] The colors selected throughout the series personify the richness of

African diasporic people and chocolate skin in general. But specifically, the blue-violet used to characterize the season two ending (and what colors almost all of season three) brings audiences into a particularly spiritual and sexual space. Although the beauty of the stories told in *Queen Sugar* allows all the women (and many of the men) to be gloriously sexual in their sacredness, something about positioning Nova as both spiritual and openly sexual, across gender, frees and radicalizes. Writer Bilal Qureshi describes the series direction and cinematography: "The camera lingers on lips, skin, and hair in a manner that feels revolutionary in its heightened sensuality."[43]

In addition to the visual, the series creates a sonic resonance diegetically and for those watching. Black people often rely on music to help soothe pains and release tensions, found in almost every aspect of Black popular culture. *Queen Sugar* retains musician Meshell Ndegeocello as its musical director, an artist who consistently blends and confronts the fallibility of religion and its possibility for a different path.[44] The theme song for the series, "Nova," written and performed by Ndegeocello, feels out of this world with its synthesized and ethereal quality. Ndegeocello vocalizes the few words of the song with a husky and impassioned contralto, singing, "Dreams never die. Take flight. As the world turns, keep the colors in the line." Black cultural studies scholar L. H. Stallings suggests: "Ndegeocello's subtle reference to a spirituality located in Black oral customs and 'pagan' myths is a challenge to Black spiritual traditions that ignore sexual desire in their considerations of blackness and spirituality. While seeking sexual freedom, she constantly expands blackness."[45] This expansion also includes a broadening out of the ways spirituality and religiosity appear, operate, and resonate for spiritual Black folks with, through, and beyond Christianity.

An episode in season three finds Nova blessing the land with the spirit of her father. Directed by DeMane Davis and written by Erika L. Johnson, episode eight, "Come Clad in Peace," focuses on several different subplots of the larger story, but out in the field alone, the vastness, historicity, and significance of the land allows this Black woman to conjure the spirit of her ancestors.[46] The land, as Qureshi asserts, "is the Bordelon's affliction and their healing."[47] In the field of the family's legacy, Nova begins on her knees with a bag. From it, she pulls out a picture of her father and a homemade incense stalk. She lights it and through a series of luxurious dissolves, cleanses, worships, and prays with her whole self. Her body mixes with the green of the crops, her dreams bound up in the composition notebook exposed in the bag.

The materials she brings for her altar serve as a metaphor for the connectedness of everything. The nondiegetic singing of Sara Niemietz wafts over a simple guitar with "Let me be, everything I am. Let me be, wild and free. Let me be, myself again. Oh, oh, oh, oh let me be." Nova, embroiled in controversies regarding her own sexual and romantic choices and her family, operates as the same character through whom the spirit of the ancestors flows. The synthesis of her

Rutina Wesley as Nova Bordelon worshipping on the land in *Queen Sugar* (2016–2022).

heightened sexuality and her spiritualism makes her the most dynamic character in the series. Her clamoring for a certain type of rooted freedom demonstrates a future, an Afro future, where Black folks' liberation exists on its own spiritual terms.

It Will Never Lose Its Power

Black women's sacredness gets exemplified through their ability to procreate, their nurturing of the world, their historic and preservational knowledge, and their iconographic connection to the spiritual.[48] Priestesses serve and direct healing—healing of relationships between people, between people and spirits, and between people and ancestors. Women head a large percentage of Vodou temples worldwide. Strikingly, all possession priests, whether male or female, are considered "wife of the orisha."[49] Traditional religious practices of Africans and their descendants continue to rise in the U.S. and around the globe. Much of the animosity around African indigenous religions harkens back to the colonialist enterprise, slavery, and misogyny. Artists recognize these connections and frequently imagine them as a claiming or possession. This claiming of someone (white men claiming Sethe's milk and Black bodies as property in *Beloved*), a lover like Mozelle in *Eve's Bayou*, and the many claims on the land of the Bordelon family in *Queen Sugar* all point back to historical theft and attempted possession of Black bodies and souls by whites.

Yet nearly 1.5 million people in the U.S. practice some African-based religion, while many others incorporate practices and beliefs as part of their Christian or Islamic faiths. Articles appearing in journals such as *African American Review* and *Journal of Interreligious Studies*, popular magazine *Essence*, and even Quincy Jones's hip-hop magazine *Vibe* document Blacks' search for cultural and spiritual connection to antiquity. In writer Octavia Butler's *Parable of the Sower*, the central character Lauren Olamina constructs an alternate religion to Christianity to help them move through the dystopian (1993, feeling very 2020) world in which they live. Calling her religion Earthseed, the guiding principle involves understanding everything is change. This text still resonates in 2024 through webinars that center her work as religious gospel.[50] Other popular texts resonate as well.

Beyoncé's song "Hold Up," from her visual album *Lemonade* (2016), gives larger audiences an opportunity to ponder the connection Black artists make with spiritualities beyond Christianity. In its music video opening, she describes her embrace of various religious practices to help quell the distrust of her man. She meditates on Christian and Islamic texts and invokes practices of the Yoruba as shown in Louisiana. Religion scholar Yolanda Pierce talks about the multiplicity of religions represented in the visual album, arguing, "It's a powerful reminder that every faith is syncretic; every religion is a blending of traditions and rituals from multiple sources. Christianity as it exists and is practiced in America today owes much of its theology, ritual, and doctrine to the experiences and beliefs of enslaved Africans."[51]

As Beyoncé presumably embodies a different consciousness, some describe the doors opening with water gushing forth as orgasmic, a rebirth, or Oshun coming to bear.[52] Understanding that transition and transformation happen through water, the sexual sounds in the video relate to the Holy Spirit. Beyoncé's singing "They don't love you like I love you" becomes a chant, a new form of prayer. Moreover, as film scholar Jamie Rogers suggests, this syncretism might be looked at as a sort of "diasporic community"—where a "transmission of stories, histories, and cultural codes via inter- and extratextual exchange . . . generate intimate, discursive, relationships across time and space among diasporic subjects."[53] It suggests Black women's sexuality need not be facilitated by another.

Like the narratives discussed, other documentaries and fictional media embrace African indigenous religious practices. Through their (re)remembering and reasserting these sacred practices, the visual garbage that de(con)fines the religiosity of Black folks outside of Christianity receives contest. In her 2019 sermon "Brand New Thing," Bishop Yvette Flunder starts with song and preaches on how oppressive religions castigate other different ones, particularly those practiced by Black and brown peoples—as if they don't know God. Calling it "self-imposed theological ignorance," she reminds those listening that God by any name is still God.[54] Progressive creative work within Black popular culture allows us to think about and reimagine how circulating spiritual blood ties never lose their power. This reconsideration of Black spiritual practices helps set our minds and hearts for The Message.

The Message

Urgent Like a Mofo

● ●

The Sublime Synergy of Spirituality and Sexuality in Black Music Culture

> No matter what, it is with God
> —John Coltrane, *A Love Supreme* liner notes (1965)

> Nina: You always want what you want when you want it. Why is everything so urgent with you?
> Darius: Let me tell you somethin'. This here, right now, at this very moment, is all that matters to me. I love you. That's urgent like a motherfucker.
> —*Love Jones* (1997)

From the moment Darius Lovehall (Lorenz Tate) begins to check for Nina Mosley (Nia Long), audiences hear a soulful beat, feel a slow groove, and appreciate smooth talk. Moreover, his spoken word poem to her invokes the most sensual of sex dreams while couching it within the reflection: "Is your name Yemaya? Oh, hell naw. It's got to be Oshun."[1] Punctuated with the bass, low lighting, and oh-so-beautiful Black people, the reading and the scene cause arousal by just watching. Yet the partnering of a most intimate heterosex allusion with the sacred orishas of traditional Yoruba worship brings to the fore a connection known but limitedly explored.

Better than most, Black folks, Black women and people of color more broadly, capture and articulate the connection between sexuality and spirituality and do so more overtly in popular culture. Many Black diasporic artists suggest that sanctified but sexless spirituality has fallen short, humanity failing to work effectively within this framework. Religiosity, often framed as sacredness within texts, constrained bodies, and consequential souls, gets deployed to rape, steal, and put on the market—making nothing seem sacred, and as for religion, void. Sex, on the other hand, gets paraded as the devil's work—women with a "Jezebel spirit" and whorish men. Because of the history of degraded Black bodies, many religious African-Americans routinely seek to escape the flesh for an overly spiritual presentation—trying, as theology and psychology scholar Lee Butler suggests, to transform the characterization of unholy to holy by separating sexuality from spirituality.[2]

Yet the tenuous and contested connection between sexuality and spirituality finds synergy in the artistic realm. Whether in song lyrics and instrumentation, music videos, narrative television and film, webisodes, or creative writing, a multiplicity of artists envision a world where these two energies congeal. Artists are accorded (and often presumed to have) a position at the forefront of relevant issues and contentious concerns within Black communities and within their own realms of endeavor. They stand against discriminatory and racist thinking, as exampled by *The Spook Who Sat by the Door* by author Sam Greenlee (1969) and film director Ivan Dixon (1973) and *13th* (Ava DuVernay, 2016). Singer Marvin Gaye asks "What's Going On," the Staple Singers demand people to "Respect Yourself," and D'Angelo indicts systemic gaffes in "The Charade"— all addressing inter- (and intra-) cultural contests. Writers Maya Angelou and Chimamanda Ngozi Adichie peep gendered foolishness in their poems "Still I Rise" and "We Should All Be Feminists." And ridiculous music business practices get excoriated by artists Rick James, Prince, Erykah Badu, and Tobe Nwigwe. Through these and many, many others, the artistic realm involves itself in the most prescient aspects of societal injustice and unrest. In their positioning as leaders and visionaries, artists also normalize the confluence of sexuality and spirituality thoughtfully, seamlessly, and historically.

For example, scholars have long discussed the historic ways in which slave songs conveyed myriad messages about sustaining hope and body, escape and freedom, but also allow for an understanding of self to expand beyond the known and the common. Looking at singers such as Ma Rainey and Bessie Smith in the blues music tradition, these artists forge a vital and necessary connection between the body and the soul. The moment they open their mouths, they announce and claim space as "blues maintains a unified perspective on all dimensions of existence."[3] Writes religion scholar and priest Kelly Brown Douglas, the blues docs not "recognize the sacred and secular as different dimensions of living. The reality of life itself is a reflection of both."[4] In what Rainey and Smith sing about (living life fully), how they sing it (strong and unapologetic), and how they live their lives (as successful and queer), they foreground difference as normative.

R&B singers also make the connection between the sexual and the spiritual. Like blues singers, many of them get their start in Black Baptist and Holy Ghost churches and thus embody the religiosity of the organist chords. The connection to sin and the devil, already so vehemently articulated within blues music (trials that R&B performers face as well), lessen with R&B in part because the secular/sacred line continues to shift. So by 1972, when the quintessential R&B crooner Al Green becomes popular, rather than abandon one style of music for the other, he cemented their relationship. While a number of his hits demonstrate a fluidity of the spirit moving between the notes, I argue his song "Simply Beautiful" supremely exemplifies and calls down the blessings of a sexual and spiritual union—one of the reasons it works so well when comedian Rickey Smiley uses it in his stage show, as discussed in the Processional. Through their work (and often their performances and public personae), Black artists call into question the rabid separation between the religious and spiritual practices of Black folks and their sexual selves.

In today's Message, I explore various mediated sites that illustrate the conversation and confluence of Black sexuality and spirituality. As mentioned during Tithes and Offering, the preaching moment represents one of the central components of spiritual revival in Black church worship. Black preachers interpret the Bible from study alongside an equal dose of observation and practical living; thus, allegorical ascriptions abound. As music provides an inherently inclusive space, I lean into it for greater insights.[5] Thus, during this preaching moment, I take up the musicality and visioning of artists who offer a synergistic understanding of sexuality and spirituality. Specifically, I explore D'Angelo's sensual mediations, the meditations of Erykah Badu, the poetic and politicized engagement of Meshell Ndegeocello, and the omniscience of Prince. These artists reflect an intentional depth and breadth of frame, approach, talent, and fame. Each of them pioneers a unique aesthetic and approach to music and music making, and they possess a body of work to examine. The first three emerged in the 1990s—a period ripe with Black musical energy and innovation (hip-hop, hip-hop gospel, New Jack swing, and neo-soul)—while the Godfather (aka Prince) extended his career from the late 1970s through his death in 2016.

This is a serious and urgent matter because right now, sentient Black beings live in a state of consistent assault on their psyches, bodies, and their very lives. As calamities abound all over the nation and world, love and hope disappear—yet to be found in the separate realms of either religion or sexual connection. Some artists' works stand in the gap for these losses and fear and offer a promise of a better way forward. This exploration should help demonstrate the necessary and inherent connectedness of mind-body-spirit while making clear how spirituality can serve as a space of grace. Perhaps, in recognizing and thinking through where we see, hear, and play with their synergy, a different song and a better groove can emerge than the one currently playing.

Bodily Frameworks

Kelly Brown Douglas argues persuasively about the ways in which the Black church maintains a "respectable" separation of body and mind—disdaining Black bodies that feel and emote—locating sex as the farthest from the ideal. In *Black Bodies and the Black Church*, she writes about a historical, Eurocentric manner of worship positioned as optimal, saying, "a part of the inferior out-group . . . were considered people who seemingly allowed the passion of their bodies to overwhelm the reason of their minds as evidenced in the way they worshipped. The way they engaged their bodies in worship determined what kind of people they were, those of the mind or those of the body."[6] This philosophy permeates newly North families in the Midwest and West. The performance of a certain religious body maintains a mythic presence in the minds of Black folks. Yet with these bodies, these same people, common Black folks, know a righteous Christian God, hear whispers of spiritual practices from back home, and praise Allah out loud—vocally and bodily. This God, this recalibrated religion, teaches them some things about surviving through slavery, post-slavery, and up above but also reminds and connects them to the god(s) they left behind on the African continent.

A longer history of this mind-body-spirit separation lies in the ways Christian missionaries conducted their work across lands of people of color, the administration of slavery, and the ways that a part of the reacculturation, colonialist enterprise was to make what Africans did prior to the coming of the white man deviant, strange, and inhuman. Regarding Western Christian traditions, Douglas suggests the separation of body and soul penetrates deeply,[7] writing: "Desires of the body are to be overcome at all cost, especially sexual desires. Sexual desire is considered the ultimate temptations of the devil, since in states of sexual ecstasy all reason is presumed suspended."[8] Much of this divide centers the visible, physical body—making the body itself problematic. Performance studies scholar E. Patrick Johnson talks about the seen body in his theater piece *Strange Fruit*. He connects his physical body to audiences to show the ways in which "various representations of [his] body in history . . . [get] depicted mostly by white people."[9] The meaning and significance of Black bodies and their deployment in the national (and international) imaginary feed the continuing ruptures surrounding mind, body, and spirit.

In fact, innumerable tragic cultural conditions require a reckoning for their impact on Black bodies across global stages. Real-lived lynchings, molestations, beatings, murders, and pandemic-expendable Black bodies resonate as both historical and right now. The body, its intimacy and nakedness, while personal, private, and beautiful, has also been drawn broadly, explicitly, and sometimes horribly on screens and within soundscapes. Violent, diseased, and murdered Black bodies; trafficked, raped, harassed, and forgotten Black bodies; illegal, immoral, and illegitimate Black bodies, all pervade national and local news and video games. The misremembered Black bodies of incredible athletes who protest racist conditions (Tommie Smith, John Carlos, Muhammad Ali, Colin Kaepernick, Serena Williams) wash our screens. The requirement of a mother's nursing body, Sethe's milk providing for her children as shown in Toni Morrison's *Beloved*, operates against the sexual violence that takes that milk (and consequently, her mind, spirit, and babies), seen in a more contemporary form in something like the Starz Network television series *P-Valley* (Katori Hall, 2020–). Filmmaker, poet, and scholar Marlon Riggs lays out Black bodies (including his own dying one) as a place of identity contest and understanding in both of his award-winning and personal documentaries *Tongues Untied* (1989) and *Black Is . . . Black Ain't* (1995), and as inhabited within stories in the FOX narrative series *Pose* (2018–2021). Or the everyday questioned and indicted Black queer body of Chiron (a body shaped by its "surfaces into proper form," a body oriented toward "proper affects," and one that produces "all the limitations that orientation entails") in *Moonlight* (Jenkins, 2016) exists more openly but still endangered in these regressive States.[10] These narrative, narrativized, and visual illustrations force audiences to grapple with the tangibility and precarity of Black and brown bodies over time and through various circumstances.

Mixed with race(ism) and representation, stranged nomenclature for bodies of color continues to live within battling paradigms. Cultural studies scholar Stuart Hall, sociologist Patricia Hill Collins, and Riggs wrestle with the impact of what structured (and structuring) identity means for Black bodies and the souls inhabiting them. They examine the ways in which difference gets melded unto these bodies, how a stigma of promiscuity and excessive or unrestrained heterosexual desire carries onto these bodies,[11] and how Black men loving one another can be a revolutionary act.[12] Moreover, the Black female body endures constant assessment, comment, and attempted containment in Black religious spaces. Many mothers assume the responsibility for policing their girls' bodies in an effort to be, yes, "respectable," but more alarmingly safe, unharmed, and marriageable. Any number of scholars and lay women talk about the ways they get metaphorically (and actually) yoked up around their dress, their hairstyle, their movement, and their bodies in Black church. Religion scholar Tamura Lomax recalls her "marking" when a deacon told her preacher-father that her butt kept him from focusing during altar call.[13] Religion scholar Monique Moultrie writes about a reification of the mammy stereotype where Black women control their unmarried bodies "to the point of asexuality."[14] And for years, I have remembered the smell of my fifty-plus-year-old pastor kissing my nine-year-old self on the lips as I helped with communion. Black bodies are connected to their spirits, and they matter.

English and gender studies scholar Jack Halberstam suggests: "distinctions between normal and abnormal bodies len[ds] support to white supremacist projects that tr[y] to collapse racial otherness into gender variance and sexual perversion."[15] He suggests, however, the scientific classification system of bodies gets upended with acknowledgment of trans and queer bodies. Yet, when artists such as bounce queen Big Freedia perform, rapper Frank Ocean touts his dynamic "sexuality," or rapper Lil Nas X says "just cuz I'm gay don't mean I'm not straight," unnerved Black consumers, audiences, and religious figures struggle with a larger intracultural disdain grounded in biblical and Quranic interpretations (even as gay and trans people exist as an integral and long-standing part of Black religious communities).

Central to negating these bodies' contexts lies the notion of an inherent sacredness. Religion scholar Robert C. Fuller's writings about the history of religion via biology signify here. In terms of African-American early bodies, he talks about the ways in which constrained and enslaved bodies found ways to move and experience pleasure despite the systematic restrictions of slavers. He suggests bodily movement serves as "[p]art and parcel of the musical foundations of African-American worship . . . the body's proclivity toward unrestricted movement facilitate[s] individuals' experience of spiritual liberation . . . [and] . . . provide[s] the harmonious rhythms of a sacred community."[16] Many slave (and post-slavery) narratives identify this community, including the fictional *Beloved* (where Baby Suggs Holy commands women to cry, men to dance, and children to laugh). Filmmaker and scholar Zeinabu irene Davis's short film *Cycles* (1989) thoughtfully forces audiences to consider the menstrual cycle as both a natural and spiritual part of women's bodies.[17] She demonstrates this sacredness by prominently featuring Haitian Vodou symbols throughout the film[18] and suggesting a bodily spiritual connection, as film scholar Gwendolyn Audrey Foster notes: "Rasheeda's [Stephanie Ingram] spirituality and corporality is unmistakably connected with her smile, her clean sheets, her altar, her copy of Toni Morrison's *Beloved*, her vacuum, her menses, her photographs, her Louis Armstrong and Kassav' albums, the voices of Miriam Makeba and the Orisha, and the signifying symbol ground into the sidewalk."[19] And participants admire and engage the sacred Black bodies of adorned Mardi Gras Indians who second line down New Orleans streets in tribute, sorrow, and joy. Black bodies, maligned as they often are, continue to proffer a valuable space and demonstration of both physicality and inner faith.[20] Reinscribing and remembering the many contexts in which Black bodies signify helps to establish and examine the fusion of sexuality and the spirit.

It's a Thin Line . . .

Since I argue spirituality and sexuality exist as essential parts of our humanity, defining these two again and their connectedness helps discern their appearance in Black popular culture. Spirituality serves as an important aspect of African-American belief systems. While it remains a contested term, I previously cited scholar-pastor Carlyle Fielding Stewart III during Praise and Worship, where he says spirituality represents the "full matrix of beliefs, power, values and behaviors that shape people's consciousness, understanding, and capacity of themselves in relation to divine reality. [It is also] a process by which people interpret, disclose, formulate, adapt and innovate reality and their understandings of God within a specific context or culture."[21] Pastor A. R. Bernard of the Christian Cultural Center in Brooklyn suggests spirituality "is our human capacity to know and experience God."[22] Spirituality may look like a random circle of women who help an overwhelmed mother comfort her child, gather her things, and move back into their own lives. It may emerge as an anointed candle lit in church, a home altar, or a Coptic cross hanging from a neck. It might be theology scholar Karen Baker-Fletcher's "hush harbor," "the sacred space from which Black women's sexual-spiritual wisdom emerges."[23]

Ideas about spirituality even come through philosopher Jacques Derrida's notion of mattering. Theorizing what he calls différance in his 1963 paper "Cogito and the History of Madness," he forces scholars to rethink oppositions. I lift up the singing of Mississippi Mass Choir member Venora Brown, soloist, on the 1989 gospel hit "Having You There" as a demonstration of différance as a spiritual matter. When Brown sings "having you there made the difference," speaking about God, she invokes Derrida's deconstructionist assertions through her spirited vocal enunciation. By reimagining the traditional distinctions between space and time, between writing and speech, between defer and differ, an engagement, possibility, and suturing in of spirituality and sexuality materializes through this Black woman's vocalization of the term.[24] Rethinking constructed binaries becomes clearly possible when choosing to understand spirituality and sexuality as harmonious parts of a whole instead of oppositional ones. Looking to the multiple ways in which spirituality appears and moves gives credence to the many interpretations people embrace.

Sexuality, on the other hand, implies our full feeling capacity manifesting bodily. Douglas believes sexuality can be sacred if expressed "in a way that provides for and nurtures harmonious relationships—that is, those that are loving, just, and equal."[25] In other words, sexuality implies a communal and agreeable coming together—a sacred embodying of spirit. Yet Christian ethicist Katie G. Cannon suggests the gift of sexuality often gets wrestled away, hamstrung by Christianity.[26] Many religious folks quip derisively that people "don't wanna live holy, they want to know how to fornicate safely." Religion, Black church in particular, fails frequently to acknowledge that human bodies are sexual, "represented in part by the libido, as well as by the fuller sense of relationship that is properly understood in terms of a broad definition of eros"[27]—an eros that recognizes "the desire for union with the sacred . . . eros satisfies body and *soul*."[28]

As mentioned in connection with Fuller and in the Selection, many traditional religious practices involve body movements, dance, and, more germane to this lesson, suggest sexual connotations. Certain turns of the body meet with disdain and notions of impropriety and a hedonist's interpretation by non-Black and brown outsiders and insiders as well. Religion historian Elizabeth Pérez writes about the historical sanction of perceived sexual bodies, saying booty shaking incurs "particular censure, defying elite attempts to impose bodily stances associated with meekness, modesty, and obedience. The authorities intuited what many scholars now argue: that bodies remember."[29] And while ideas of reason (logic) and spirituality aren't positioned as close friends, yielding to the sexual self is considered worse.

More problematically, the discussion of sexuality in many Black churches focuses almost exclusively on the "sin" of homosexuality, with heterosexual fornication operating largely "unnamed, unchallenged, and often underdeveloped as a concept of both theological and practical concern."[30] Afrocentric brothers frequently invoke a spiritual connection through heterosexual sex. Explanations range from natural connection to ejaculation and essence, to the Kemetic and Black nature (ontology) of sex for Black folks. For example, as an undergraduate at Clark College (now Clark Atlanta University), I recall a male acquaintance regaling the other three of us, in a very long car ride, about an essay or book he'd read. According to him, this text asserted that heaven could be found between a Black woman's legs. He recalled it much more graphically, but that is the gist.[31] Later, I learned the actual reference comes from 1980s work of historian Yosef ben-Jochannan. Ben-Jochannan suggests Black women represent the support, cradle, and origin of man. Delving deeper, perhaps men's fear of Black women's sexuality, (and especially Black Christian women with an often overt love for Jesus), stems from their recognition of an intimate connection women have with Christ, more than men ever connect with them or Him. Some believe an increased spiritual life leads to more engagement sexually—the energy electrifying the two. This supports the idea that sexuality (as both the performance of our sexual selves and sex itself) conjoins with the spiritual to form a mind-body-soul construct. Illustrating some of these assertions in film and television is where I turn to next.

"When You Believe in Things That You Don't Understand and You Suffer"

Mediated Black popular culture provides many examples of conjoined energies of sexuality and spirituality—ones, however, mostly framed as problematic. As discussed extensively in the Invocation, Oscar Micheaux's *Within Our Gates* (1920) and King Vidor's *Hallelujah* (1929) narrativize the confluence of sexuality and spirituality as a recipe for destruction. In 1941, Spencer Williams's film

The Blood of Jesus presented a moral crossroads between desires of the flesh and a life following Jesus Christ. Temptations of the flesh and sex outside of marriage ground the narrative. Williams wrote and directed this presumed paradox as a way to proselytize Christianity. While I discuss this film in depth when talking about filmmaker Spike Lee during the Prayer of Confession, it bears emphasis here. Religion historian Judith Weisenfeld finds a consistent thread in Williams's films, where he "sets the challenge of transformation from a life of sin to one of Christian commitment before the central male characters, [while] the women accomplish much of the religious work of the films, largely through their suffering."[32] Women-centered behavior serves as part of the central conflict in most stories of sex and the spirit.

For example, the backslid, sex-positive, and outcast Shug Avery (Margaret Avery) sings blues in a juke joint in the first *The Color Purple* (Spielberg, 1985), when she hears the choir of her home church singing "God Is Trying to Tell You Something" from far away. As if the spirit comes upon her, she begins moving toward the church (with patrons and band in tow) and takes over the solo. Cutting between the church choir, the incoming sanctified Shug, the band, and outside patrons, audiences witness and embrace a Christian rebirth. Drenched in the sun yellow of her dress, Shug literally bursts into the church singing "maybe God is trying to tell you something." If the scene ended there, an interpretation of how a Judeo-Christian God works alongside sexual desire might have been made—as audiences already know Shug refuses sexual mores. However, embracing her preacher-father, Shug whispers in his ear: "See, Daddy, sinners have a soul too." Whereby he returns her embrace (reluctantly), and audiences see the cut to her elated and redeemed facial expression. Their exchange returns audiences to a preferred interpretation that God can save you from the "sin" of (unmarried and queer) sexuality, but only if you repent of it.[33]

In twenty-first-century film culture, the explicitness of this warped reading finds voice in Dee Rees's independent film *Pariah* (2011), where a part of a young Black woman's coming out as gay and butch requires traversing the world of restrictive Christianity her mother has built. Mom Audrey (Kim Wayans) pairs femininity and Christianity as the cross for her daughter Alike (Adepero Oduye) to bear. Alike's admitted queerness becomes the final spit in the face—a daughter who won't conform—in dress or in whom she chooses to love. Instead of battling (and channeling) the unspoken knowledge of her husband's infidelity, Audrey hangs her child on the cross. In a striking scene (literally), Audrey attempts to choke and beat the gayness out of her child when Alike admits to her parents that she is a lesbian.

Pariah weaves the very personal, intimate, and sexual self with the struggles of living while framed—frames of gender, of race, of sexuality, of socioeconomic positioning, of Christianity, of naming. Rees tells the story gently and suddenly, almost imperceptibly. It whispers in the webs of secrets and pretense, promises and betrayal occurring among all the characters and their relationships. It evokes tears, and not necessarily because of the story's familiarity, but because it resonates with our capacity to betray our basic humanity but also to reclaim it. The telling part of this narrative lies not only with Audrey's juxtaposing her own sexless and dysfunctional "Christian" marriage against her child's sexuality but also making the road map of shame the Black church the central broken promise. Women and gender studies scholar Jennifer DeClue argues a part of what undergirds this contentious familial narrative is the "conception that Black queer sexuality is not authentic to blackness."[34] Moreover, it posits religion, in this case Christianity, as the arbiter and rationale for this separation—queer and straight desire alike.

Riggs tackles the ways in which Black church culture both informs and excoriates gay Black men and women in *Tongues Untied* and *Black Is . . . Black Ain't*. Both aired on PBS; he follows "in the tradition of documentarians such as William Greaves and alongside documentarians like Henry Hampton—both of whom believed in the power and viability of the media to convey important social concerns regarding African-Americans."[35] *Tongues Untied* centers the realties and civilities of Black male gay love and confronts the Black church as being expressly antithetical and judgmental in its stance. Yet, as I write elsewhere, commentators and congressmen position the documentary as "vulgar and amoral" and "the Christian Coalition edit[s] a sensationalized clip of the film and distribute[s] it to every member of Congress."[36] Black church clergy often call same-sex desire an abomination and use the Bible to legitimize their stance. Riggs says these clergy force many to choose between Blackness and gayness—and asks, which side are you on? The documentary highlights the ways in which Black churches exacerbate and condone feelings of unworthiness and anger of Black men (and women) because of their culture's refusal to acknowledge and accept dual identity categories, tying this stance to the Bible. Riggs's work and films such as *Pariah* painfully present accounts of real-lived hypocritical encounters between sexuality and Black spirituality. And they remind us, as writer Lawrence Ware suggests, "Many in the Black church lose sight of the inherent danger of homophobic theological thinking. It can ruin families, throw one into depression and, at times, lead to suicide."[37]

Black television programming addresses this divide across its genres, again almost always pejoratively. Whether in the comedy *Amen* appearing on NBC for five years (1986–1991), TVLand's comedy *The Soul Man* (2012–2016), or television dramas produced on Oprah Winfrey's OWN network such as *Greenleaf* (2016–2020) or Bounce TVs *Saints and Sinners* (2016–2022), fictional narratives elevate the Black Christian church's aversion to sexual matters. These stories mostly situate the confluence of sexuality and spirituality as problematic and at odds. Moreover, Black popular culture contends with writer, director, actor, producer, and studio owner Tyler Perry, who, as the billion-dollar influencer, informs much of what gets nationally screened featuring Black lives. His philosophical and spiritual bent tilts toward a traditional, Black Baptist

Christian experience. Thus, almost all his narrative forays (film, TV, and theater), tread this ground, including all of the Madeas.[38] His works, narratively and visually, entail women-dominated households needing men to take their rightful place as leaders, a lack of Jesus being central to whatever calamity has fallen on individuals (alongside moving away from family and tradition), and a longing for a "simpler place in time,"[39] while positioning accoutrements as success. Shown explicitly in the film *Temptation: Confessions of a Marriage Counselor* (2013) and the television series *The Haves and the Have Nots* (OWN, 2013–2021), Perry continuously draws an incompatibility between sexuality and spirituality, the former of which always leads to participants' downfall.

Even reality television narrative threads such as the ones within the *Preachers* series franchise (*L.A.*, *Detroit*, and *Atlanta*) employ sexual tension, the pulpit, and traditional Black church expectations as part of their sell.[40] These series, while presumably offering a form of ministry, seed discord within and backlash from Black church communities because of their seeming inconsistencies of walk and talk and their trampling of Black church respectability politics.[41] All three iterations allude to sexual practices and controlling women's sex directly through prescriptions of matrimony, children, and virginity. The most scintillating (and bankable) stories of these men and women of God revolve around their sexual lives as cloaked in their public spiritual ones. Religion scholar Jonathan L. Walton believes that within "media-constructed Christian realm[s], American flags drape the cross of Christianity, material wealth is divinely ordained, and hypermasculinity models God's power just as female docility signifies purity and virtue."[42] Despite the series' high profile (and financial success), within two years of the programs' appearance, the entire *Preachers* franchise disappeared without fanfare. Captivating yet mostly deleterious illustrations of sex and spirit in film and television call for locating artistic and cultural spaces where their synergy provides not only exposure and understanding but also exemplify viability. This comes most expressly in music.

Love and Happiness

Whether Aretha Franklin wails about Dr. Feelgood, Rev. Al Green segues into his top-selling R&B hit "Love and Happiness" at his gospel concert, or Beyoncé religiously prostrates for trust in "Hold Up," the confluence of Black spirituality and sexuality manifests and rules within Black music culture. Music traditions resonate around the confluence of work, struggle, and pleasure. Unlike other cultural groups, music for Black folks moves beyond spectatorship, informing and shaping many aspects of Black life. English literary scholar John Lovell Jr. believes "a folk community dictates and sings the entire range of its deep concern. . . . They are always uniquely the original expression of the community at hand, bathed in its tradition, formed in images respectable to the community at the moment, swept along by its contemporary enthusiasm and its desires for making a special point at a particular time."[43] Black people's music makes explicit the connectedness of spirituality and sexuality.

A number of artists envision a world conjoined by the spiritual and the sexual. Singer Jill Scott takes "A Long Walk" and asks listeners to walk with her through community, love, spirituality, and fun while reading different religious texts with a new lover. The music of Maze featuring Frankie Beverly provides a cultural connection between the spiritual and sexual by the ways it moves through New Orleans. As if the group continued to create new music in the twenty-first century, even the youngest Black child there knows the words to the epic tunes "Joy and Pain" (1980) and especially "Before I Let Go" (1981). The "Happy Feelings" everyone effuses just by hearing the opening riff makes them unique. Their artistry opens the possibilities of bringing both physical and spiritual pleasure to bear on bodies and spirits. In their work, they question and attempt to dismantle the false binaries imposed between sexuality and spirit, to "locate silences, expound desire, and continuously reconfigure the way meanings are negotiated on the cultural stage."[44]

Artists D'Angelo, Erykah Badu, Meshell Ndegeocello, and Prince all possess recognized gifts beyond their ability to sing lyrics. Multitalented in their abilities to play instruments, write, rap, and redefine genres, they personify hyphenates as writer-producer-performer because of their artistry, as opposed to (or maybe in addition to) commerce's sake. They all appear shy and often quite reclusive. D'Angelo, Badu, and Ndegeocello note Prince as a major inspiration for the work they do and how they do it. They offer a body of work through which to understand the trajectory, or at least lineage, of their artistic commitments and receive recognition for their work. Of course, many talented Black artists exist and bless the world with their sounds and insights. In addition, many comment on or recognize spirituality or religion in their lyrics. But few others, save the incomparable Aretha Franklin, consistently and thoroughly blend sexuality and spirituality throughout their discography and imaging.

Though maybe not a part of their initial audience, fans across generations know and follow their music. In talking about Black television of the 1990s and Gen Z's knowledge of and use of these shows for their own purposes, media scholar Patrick R. Johnson notes: "Participants use the Internet to perform their fandom"[45]—music fandom mimics television's via digital sources—affording continued scholarly and listener pursuit of these artists right now and meaningfully across generations. The arrangement of these artists and their music falls not so much under generic categorizations as much as synergy of lyrics and impetus, visualization, and their consistent melding of sexuality and spirituality. No true artist appreciates boxing—generic boxing initiated by music labels. In fact, Erykah Badu comments on this frequently, saying such things as "I'm not a r n b/hip hop artist or an urban artist. I'm an Artist. I'm a musician. If you plan to write about me or my music, take us out of those categories. If not... We good."[46] Music theorist Horace Maxile recommends a tropological reading of Black works to "investigate and analyze the commonalities between various—and sometimes disparate—African American musical realizations,"[47] which is in part what I attempt to do next.

"We Should All Aspire to Be a Black Messiah"—D'Angelo

Coming from the Black church as an early and eager participant, musician and choir director Michael Eugene Archer (aka D'Angelo) believes the Pentecostal church informs all his work. His music embodies and effuses the sentiments and rhythms of that space. The son of a Pentecostal minister, he says: "When I go on the stage, I bring that with me."[48] "The stage is my pulpit . . . [and the give and take from the audience]. . . . That's my ministry."[49] He recalls senior saints' admonition to youth members before going up into the choir stand: "Don't go up there for form or fashion."[50] He carries that instruction within him and seeks to exude what the spirit offers, believing you need to "shut yourself down and let whatever is coming, come through you."[51]

D'Angelo released his first recording, *Brown Sugar*, in 1995 on the Virgin label. Writing, producing, and playing largely by himself, his CD covers a range of emotions but focuses on bluesy and then contemporarily tempoed soul and love music. The album produced several singles that performed well, including "Brown Sugar," "Cruisin'" (a remake of Smokey Robinson's 1979 hit), and "Lady." It debuted at number six on the *Billboard Top R&B Albums* chart and spent sixty-five weeks on the *Billboard 200*. The work received critical acclaim and brought him national attention, earning four Grammy nominations. In a generically typical music video for the single "Brown Sugar," audiences visualize love and lovemaking references. (Most say the song is a thinly veiled ode to weed—à la Rick James's 1978 "Mary Jane." But overtly, it centers relationships between humans.) I argue that visually, it also offers more.

The Brett Ratner–directed music video channels attraction across gender and generation while bringing in the Hammond B–sounding chords of Black church, most explicitly during the intro. From the haze of the smoked-filled juke joint (D'Angelo smokes and blows as he sits down to the electric piano, encompassing the room) to the surveyed bathroom scenes, couples appear grooving together. Women and women, men and women, and the possibilities of men and men undulate to "Brown Sugar." Theology scholar Dwight Hopkins observes how spirit operates in general, writing, love "of the Spirit in oneself provides the condition for self body-love and male-male, male-female body love (sexually and non sexually)."[52] In the music video, the want of brown sugar goes undefined. It implies that the desire for weed, women, or men need not have any name or preference. This openness operates in conjunction with the gospel rhythms and lays the groundwork for his other offerings.

In the final track of this CD, "Higher," D'Angelo directly incorporates his Christianity into a love song for a partner. Equating his love for this person to

D'Angelo performing his song "Higher," live at Zénith Paris (YouTube, 2012).

ecstasy and being taken higher (God's high), he connects sexuality to spirituality lyrically. Talking about God, a new day, heaven, and streets of gold references the book of Revelation. In fact, while several Christian tunes invoke
streets of gold, the extremely popular gospel song "Twelve Gates to the City"
most assuredly informs D'Angelo's gospel musical heritage in "Higher." However, the link between spirituality and sexuality reveals itself most in the gospel
chords and the ad libitum he utters. Harmonizing voices, as with any good
Black church choir (even his choir of one), D'Angelo uses the electric piano to
solder the musical rhythms of Black church and a jazz club. When he sings
"that U and your love will 4-ever take me higher," his falsetto and the music
replicate not only an orgasmic release but also the shout of the Holy Spirit.
Written by his big brothers Luther and Rodney Archer and himself, the selection
takes listeners higher, above the binaries imposed between sexual pleasure
and the pleasure God gives through the spirit. A few YouTube comments
strengthen this assessment, remarking: "HE TOOK US STRAIGHT TO
THE CHURCH FROM THE BEDROOM" (Elaine Jackson), "Horny and
blessed at the same time," (NyaRongo Gerrrt), and responding to them, DrPee-
PeePooPoo suggests, "It's all the same energy."[53] "Higher" concludes the ten-
track CD *Brown Sugar* and launched D'Angelo into producer Kedar
Massenburg–trademarked genre of neo-soul.[54]

How Does It Feel?

Several years later, D'Angelo released his sophomore project, *Voodoo*, in 2000. It
combines African diasporic rhythms with religious spirituality, and musicologist Loren Kajikawa believes the album blends "gospel, soul and funk," not only

suggesting similarities among African-American, Caribbean, and African musical cultures, "but also offer[ing] fans the opportunity to participate in a secular,
spiritual experience. . . . [W]hen listeners of funk and hip hop find themselves
lost in a repetitive groove, they may be accessing a sense of the religious informed
by African cultural memory."[55] Others such as writer Touré describe the work
as a unique piece in the tradition of Sly Stone and Marvin Gaye, calling it "raw,
intimate, naked [and] intensely Black."[56] In fact, on the number seven track,
"The Root," some argue D'Angelo invokes conjure, the lyric suggesting a lover
has put a root on him, possessed him. Writer and filmmaker Faith A. Pennick
and Kajikawa argue D'Angelo most expressively blends rhythms of traditional
African religious practices with sexuality in this tune. Specifically, Kajikawa
argues the song "enacts a trajectory of spirit possession that simulates a powerful experience of sensual, religious ecstasy,"[57] probably due to the doubling of
his voice, recalling mediated demonstrations of spirit possession. Apparently,
D'Angelo's partner at the time, Gina Figueroa, followed Santería, which makes
him leery. Pennick expands on D'Angelo's approach: "Continuing in the tradition of worship, he is his *own* call and response, as the listener falls down the
rabbit hole with him."[58] The song prepares listeners—and more, viewers—for
what becomes his international calling card and nemesis, "Untitled (How Does
It Feel?)."

Watching the 1999 Paul Hunter and Dominique Trenier–directed music
video for "Untitled (How Does It Feel?)," audiences unite visually and sonically
to the past and to the present. They become saturated with sex through the
limitedly specific gendered lyrics, D'Angelo's taut and sculpted body with beads
of water (presumed sweat) running over him, moisturized and full lips (and
nothing else), and the camera tilting toward the presumed place of satisfaction.
Cowritten by Raphael Saadiq and himself as an ode to Prince's early work, the
percussion, guitar, and piano sync with a slow downbeat, recalling 1970s R&B
lovemaking music. Comparing this video to Janelle Monáe's "Cold War," musicologist and African-American studies scholar Shana Redmond maintains that
while D'Angelo's naked body stands in for Black women's often fetishized
desire, he still seems more interested in "getting a piece" than disrupting heterosexual male positioning.[59] Literary scholar Aimé Ellis likens D'Angelo's visualized Black male body to violence, writing that the performance of "Untitled"
"stages the violent effects of a long and collective history of Black male life
shaped by the imminent threat of terror. [It demonstrates, in his mind,] how
many contemporary Black male subjects are always already invoking narratives
of deathly subjection."[60]

While I believe these interpretations include valid points,[61] more convincingly, listeners and viewers also encounter the spirit through this song and
video. As the camera tilts slowly down D'Angelo's body, showing nothing but
abdominal muscles moving to the beat, an orgasmic rush of both flesh and spirit
erupts into an ecstatic, Holy-Ghost-spirit shout. Listeners understand this from

D'Angelo in his "Untitled (How Does It Feel)" music video (2006).

the way the music ushers us before the altar of sonic pleasure and praise. And as Touré adds, the video proves a "visual analogy for the music."[62] The slow and low beat of the drums and the electric piano, the pitch and rhythm of the guitars, and the singer's crucifix-wearing naked body, all make a spiritual-sexual connection manifest and present. In fact, D'Angelo says of the song's climax: "I wasn't really thinking about sex at all. I was really thinking about a spiritual experience. I was thinking about the Holy Ghost, and at the end, when I had to bring the emotion through, that's where I went to get it."[63] D'Angelo believes putting your voice on tape facilitates a "capturing [of] the spirit."[64] The cross and his shout bring his performance and lyrics toward a larger and fuller understanding of where these aspects of our being collide.

D'Angelo's public persona locates him as cis-gender.[65] However, the articulation of his gender plays less of a role than his performance of sexuality in relation to the cross. When *Voodoo* debuted at number one on the *Billboard 200* chart and won the Grammy Award for Best R&B Album in 2001, it reacquainted an anxious fan base with his sound and music. Even with his limited numbers of music videos and public performances, D'Angelo's musical openness allows for a melding of sexuality and spirituality to shape audience perception of his being. One fan wrote about *Voodoo* and D'Angelo's performances in *Teen Vogue*:

> Through D, I came to recognize my own sexual desire as an extension of my spiritual self, a means of actualizing fully and honestly. I learned I can present myself as [a] sexual man without having to receive or reciprocate in kind. I need to be desired for my mind above my body. D'Angelo turned me on to this new way of thinking, expanded the possibilities of what I could look, sound and act like. His confident swagger opened up new spaces for countless other men of color to present themselves in less heteronormative ways. He was

flamboyant but discreet, sensitive yet virile, a publicly straight man unafraid to
let another man squeeze and fondle his bulky frame.[66]

D'Angelo's nonbinary aura aligns with a Black male redefinition tenet articulated by artists before him, including Prince. In his *Voodoo* liner notes, he muses,
"if we are to exist as men in this new world many of us must learn to embrace
and nurture that which is feminine with all of our hearts (he-art)." Adding to
this ideal, theology scholar Dwight Hopkins calls for a new Black mode of masculinity where men operate by appreciating knowledge, truth, and wisdom—a
Black masculinity valuing "process and improvisation," collective work, solitude and "dialogue, listening and harmony." This Black masculinity prizes tenderness, strength, feelings, and tears—where freedom and its responsibilities,
justice, and peace are all valued and valuable.[67] This desire seems to describe the
ground D'Angelo treads in his third original release, *Black Messiah*.[68]

"It's Another Reason for the Season"

After *Voodoo*'s release, D'Angelo disappeared for fourteen years. Before then, he
dominated the "neo-soul" genre, which later includes singers Erykah Badu,
Lauryn Hill, Anthony Hamilton, Jill Scott, and others.[69] He fashioned a return
in 2014 with the release of *Black Messiah*, hurriedly, in response to the deluge of
Black men and women being killed (and videoed) by police around the country
and the Black Lives Matter movement. As a whole, *Black Messiah* takes on the
righteous anger of African-Americans about senseless, unconvicted, and con-
tinuous murders. Remaining true to his own brilliance and eccentricities, he
produced a soulful work harboring humor, questioning external forces, but also
going inside. *Time*s writer Will Hodgkinson talks about D'Angelo's revitaliza-
tion of soul music's "testifying spirit";[70] *Mojo*'s Priya Elan calls it a "single-minded
statement of spiritual rebirth and political reckoning";[71] and Ben Roylance of
Tiny Mix Tapes writes: "The Black Messiah is not D'Angelo himself—his
album is not a Westian divine boast. The Black Messiah is a revolutionary spiritual impulse, more like the Holy Ghost than the Son."[72]

The lyrics of *Black Messiah* call for leadership—Black people directing and
demanding a better way forward without forgoing Jesus. In "1000 Deaths," for
example, D'Angelo excerpts a speech from activist Fred Hampton talking about
a Black Jesus of revolution, the same Lord he invokes in the song "The Charade." Poignantly, concerning his 2015 performance of "The Charade" on *Saturday Night Live*, writer Jumi Ekunseitan muses: "Contrary to his videography
over the years, in which he engages the eroticization of his body, D'Angelo makes
no place for such a gaze in this performance."[73] His musical protests over the
elimination of Black beings find resonance with listeners' on-ground efforts.
For example, ethnomusicologist Stephanie Shonekan writes about Black University of Missouri students who cited both D'Angelo's "The Charade" and

Erykah Badu's collaboration with Janelle Monáe's "Q.U.E.E.N." as part of the soundtrack helping them to cope and move forward in their protest against ongoing campus racism.[74] *Black Messiah* moves D'Angelo in a slightly different direction lyrically and musically. However, the articulation of his sexuality and his faith remain fused. In "Another Life," he sings about an additional reason for the season, merging belief and celebration of the birth of Christ with his desire to be romantically and sexually involved with someone. His talent allows audiences to read and understand what he creates as defying boxes. His music and presentation also open audiences up to actualities of being and relatedness, spirit, and sexuality—a necessary creative synergy expressed similarly by fellow musical artist Erykah Badu.

Erykah Badu on stage singing "Tyrone" live (1997).

Feeling Me Divinely—Erykah Badu

Erica Abi Wright (aka Erykah Badu) serves as a second example of an artist whose music and brand exemplify the connection of sexuality and spirituality. Raised in southwest Dallas by an actor mother, she cultivated her singing ability through Dallas community arts venues and attended the prestigious Booker T. Washington High School for the Performing and Visual Arts, focusing on singing and dancing. For the entirety of her public career, Badu has presented herself as spiritual—intimately connected to her body, to nature, and to music permeating her being. She entered public consciousness within the milieu of neo-soul as a client of Kedar Massenburg, opening on stage for D'Angelo.

Despite her resistance to the category neo-soul, as rightly noted by writer and songwriter Dimitri Ehrlich,[75] the term reflects a paradox—neo meaning new, with soul's timelessness. And although refuted by Badu and other artists saddled with the label, historian Sarah Fila-Bakabadio believes the neo-soul generic construction encompasses much more globally and sonically than label sales management suggests—a designation that can be used as a "tool to forge a counter-discourse on blackness."[76] Fila-Bakabadio writes, "neo soul intersects the histories and cultures of African Americans, Africans and other [B]lack communities worldwide to produce a new sound, confirming Erykah Badu's, India Arie's or D'Angelo's reinvention of themselves as diasporan [B]lacks."[77] Additionally, writer Joel McIver believes labeling artists this way upholds classic soul values of "spirituality, sexuality, honesty and political activism."[78] Employing this pan-African framework, Badu's "Kiss Me on My Neck" (on her 2000 third CD, *Mama's Gun*), for example, epitomizes a merging of Black world musical forms—instrumentation laden with djembe drums, wood flute play, and pulsating rhythms. Alongside the beat of the African continent and the Caribbean, the song wraps up Badu's lyrical assertions, calling for tenderness. The song links divinity with natural elements and fleshly desires. Badu croons: "If you want to feel [fill][79] me, better be divine. Bring me water, water for my mind." In addition to the realm of neo-soul, some position Badu as the queen of Dirty South Bohemia. Sociologist and writer Zandria F. Robinson describes Dirty South Bohemia's creative energy as a place for Black folks on the margins, "poor and working class, quare, blues people for who the body is a site of movement and resistance."[80] Though positioned artistically as part of both the neo-soul marketing brand and Dirty South Bohemia, Badu reps hip-hop.

Badu believes hip-hop affects the world positively, with people worshipping it more than anything else. Scholars such as Tanisha C. Ford in women and gender studies place Badu in a legacy of singer-activists such as Nina Simone, Odetta, and Miriam Makeba. She suggests more contemporary singers such as Badu, Lauryn Hill, Janelle Monáe, and Solange challenge "the musical and aesthetic boundaries of soul."[81] Often put in conversation with Hill, Mary J. Blige, and Beyoncé, Badu resonates with those growing up with hip-hop as their primary life soundtrack. Says communication scholar Aisha Durham, these artists "talk about the experiences of [B]lack women and girlhood and they project a hip hop aesthetic through their self-positioning, comportment, and style."[82] Badu takes up hip-hop as part of her spiritual worldview.

While not religious per se, Badu believes in a higher power, saying, "it's the worship of the thing," and further, "music is my religion." In the song "The Healer" on *New Amerykah Part One* (2008), she chants and talks about this in an interview: "Humdi Lila, Allah, Jehovah, Yahweh, Dios, Ma'ad, Jah, Rastafari, fyah, dance, sex, music. Hip-hop. Is bigger than religion."[83] "In no uncertain words," suggests literary scholar Eve Dunbar, "Badu simultaneously raises Hip Hop to religious significance, while claiming it away from [B]lack men."[84] While African-American studies scholar Imani Perry writes persuasively about the masculinist and degraded articulation of Christianity within hip-hop lyrics in the early 2000s, others like journalist and writer Dianne E. Anderson read Janelle Monáe's and Badu's "Q.U.E.E.N." (2013) as a song arguing against the "structural violence" of religion in its offering "a white God unable to accept [a] transitional, liminal state."[85] Moreover, Robinson invokes Black collective creative spaces as sites of religious resistance that prefigure contemporary Dirty South Bohemian ones.[86] As should be evident in this Message, political "shouting out" mixed with religious questioning provide fertile ground for the reconsideration of faithful paths beginning in the latter part of the twenty-teens.

And despite her assertions, Badu's lyrics, interviews, and brand promote tenets of the Five Percent Nation (aka the Nation of Gods and Earths). In her public offerings, she recommends books about their teachings "for everyone who wants to expand in some kind of way their consciousness."[87] The Nation of Gods and Earth's founder, Clarence X, served faithfully as a member of the Nation of Islam (NOI) prior to leaving it in 1963. Starting something new around the same time, much of its direction reflects the Nation's overarching philosophies and ways of being—the name Five Percenters coming from a tenet of NOI. According to journalist Christopher Johnson, Five Percenters' beliefs include centering Black people as the original beings, Black men as God, unity as key, and the vitality of family.[88] Says rapper Lord Jamar, "I know there is no mystery God, you understand? That's the difference between a belief system and a faith-based system. This is not a belief. It's knowledge. Once you have knowledge, it takes away any fear."[89]

Badu's devotions show up in all her music. For example, from her very first release, the Grammy-Award winning *Baduizm* in 1997, the hit "On & On" invokes ciphers, principles, and the belief that Black people are God.[90] Beyond a deeper inflection of Five Percenters' understanding, this articulation resonates between and within Black diaspora believers of many faiths. When Badu croons/chants "How good it is. How good he is. How god he is" in "Orange Moon" on the *Mama's Gun* release, she centers Five Percent understanding of place and person of men and women. The lyrics in "The Other Side of the Game" from *Baduizm* illustrate the Nation of Gods and Earths system of gender roles—the earth remains central for a successful family while dependent on the god's material provisions.[91] Naming her first-born son Seven, Badu incorporates the "culture" (not wanting to call it a religion) of the Nation of Gods and Earths into every aspect of her personal being. The number seven signifies sacredness, invoking seven planes of reality, seven Christian sacraments, seven emotive sefirot of the Kabbala, and seven-year cell generation.[92] However, in contradistinction to Badu's claims around religion and hip-hop especially, Perry argues hip-hop's religious imagery ties directly and problematically to its masculinist impulses and exploration of Black masculinity. In particular, she suggests, "the presence of the Five Percent Nation in hip hop and in hip hop lyrics, a religion in which Black masculinity is regarded as divine and even godly, signals the spiritual fixation on masculine identity."[93] Even so, Five Percenters' engagement by rappers and other artists provides extended evidence of religious and spiritual use value and a grounding for incorporating sexuality into its framework.

I'm an Orange Moon

I contend Badu exists in the place cultural theorist and Chicana poet Gloria Anzaldúa calls nepantla—"the overlapping space between different perceptions and belief systems [where] you are aware of the changeability of racial, gender, sexual, and other categories rendering the conventional labelings obsolete."[94] This space and the knowing what comes with it places Badu in the unique position of not only understanding but also championing a sexual-spiritual connection. Advancing connectivity of all aspects of our living selves—nature, bodies, circumstances, and being—Anzaldúa's theory of conocimiento (consciousness or knowing) helps listeners and audiences understand the significance of Badu's work. Anzaldúa describes conocimiento as a form of spiritual inquiry. She believes creative acts allow for this inquiry to take place and flourish, "opening all your senses, consciously inhabiting your body and decoding its symptoms."[95]

Badu forces listeners and audiences to embrace the separated aspects of being and the natural world (both physical and metaphysical). A consistent thread winds through her music and what she imagines in her music videos, public performances, Twitter and Instagram feeds, and interviews. She asserts reincarnation in "Next Lifetime," juxtaposes seasons with seeds (of ground and babies) in "Other Side of the Game," sings "if you want to go to heaven lay upon my breast" in "Ye Yo," reveals her naked body at the spot of Kennedy's assassination with EVOLUTION written on her back in the music video for "Window Seat," and sings for NPR Music's *Tiny Desk Concert* series with a full jazz complement (including her son on drums), an initial gold grill in her mouth, big messy locs embedded with golden butterflies, and flowing fabrics draped on her body. Some of the NPR staff said they felt almost a spiritual connection even before she began to sing.

The music video for Badu's 2001 Grammy-nominated "Didn't Cha Know" (*Mama's Gun*) opens underneath a cracked and dry ground with a Black beetle moving toward the camera. With sounds of bongos, wind, and women's voices flowing with a lyrical "oh," the video cuts to distant smoke. And in an instant, Badu is walking directedly from a distance and then across the screen. In medium close-up, she proceeds in a white-silver-bluish-tinted and "Egyptian-Kemetic" inspired robotic jumpsuit and an equally impressive (and matching) spatialized headwrap that sports a long, sand-colored gauze train. Despite the confidence

Erykah Badu on NPR's *Tiny Desk Concert* series (2018).

in her strut, the lyrics suggests she's lost among the elements of the Mojave Desert's land, sun, and wind, and has turned wrong "back there somewhere." By the end of the video, audiences see what the object of her search must be as she emerges from a deep hole filled with water—bald, clean, and refreshed, with the lyric "Free your mind. And find your way. There will be a brighter day." This last image of water and etchings in the sand suggests perhaps a connection to water birth (as cleansing and renewal), instinctive resetting (with the black beetle moving forward), and a pathway that might not always be straight but one that must be pursued.

Moreover, Badu's relationship with nature, as expressed through her artistry, places her heart in alignment with a sexual and spiritual connection. She arrives there through space (metaphysics) and the Nation of Gods and Earths. By example, she leads with her care and forwarding of her body. Vegetarian since 1989 (in her teens) and vegan since 1997, Badu talks about and demonstrates eating and food choice to "treat your body like the luxury vehicle it is."[96] She places stock in her body—what goes into it and what goes on top of it. She makes bodily connections out of her spiritual enterprises and sexuality as well—keeping connected with the fathers of her three children. When she sings about "The Other Side of the Game," she describes and meshes the baby growing inside of her body with the planets, the earth, and the moon. In the song "Orange Moon," she anthropomorphizes herself as the moon and her sun/ God as her partner. Badu conceives beauty as both spiritual and physical— claiming Mother Nature as one of her mothers.[97] With sounds of chimes, women's beautiful and windful moaning, and the lyricism of the flute, listeners float with Badu on her journey of space, nature, sexuality, and spirit.

My Eyes Are Green

Badu's interiority manifests externally through her performance, dress, spiritual otherness, and exuberant sexuality. Performing with an old-school interpretation of style, whenever she appears, Badu offers a whole lot of sangin' and very little jumping around type of show. During a concert, Badu performs with her voice. As my aunt Noella (Lettie) Cain often says, "singers need to stand there and sing." Badu does just that as she reimagines the space and sets the tone. Often infusing the spot with incense and a softly calibrated lighting schema, she seeks to create a soothing, dare I say sacred space. She harbors and exudes old soul sensibilities—someone who acknowledges, appreciates, and incorporates the past into her being and music. For example, in her B-side cut "No Love" on *Baduizm* and on "Green Eyes" (*Mama's Gun*), she includes the marvelous crackle of a needle on a record—bringing those songs in alignment with what Generation Xers and boomers remember and love so well.

Over the course of her career, Badu has recognized her positioning and interpretations by larger communities through the framing she herself constructs. In the beginning, she carried talismans and amulets around with her. She not only wore and foregrounded ankhs (an Egyptian symbol for life) but also centered them in many of her songs. In talking about her early accoutrements, she recalls visiting Cuba in 2001 and having a Santería reading. While waiting and during the session, she considered a beer-drinking man with shorts moving through the space as random and unnecessary until she found out he was the actual priest. She says, "That day changed my life. I don't wear a head wrap anymore, and I realized that maybe the people I had been trying to impress weren't looking for a savior, but for someone who just looked like one."[98] Calling her contemporary manner of dress "functional art," she fashions her own clothing, applies her own makeup, and creates her own hairstyles, remarking, "If you're truly practicing what you're about, you become that thing."[99] Beyond her outer trappings, Badu's exuberant sexuality makes the connection of her spirit-filled artistry most conspicuous.

Badu's sexual aura serves as a central narrative device for the way audiences and fans take her up. She exudes a sensuality connected to a spiritual otherness many crave. This Black woman's eyes mesmerize because of their color's perceived beauty but also their uniqueness for highly melanated skin tones. *Spin* magazine suggests "her sex appeal lies within her own private sensuality,"[100] while McIver says, "few female singers can emit as much sensuality as Badu does, with her open, confident stare, her liquid eyes, flawless features and compact, perfectly formed body."[101] Sex-positive and unencumbered by people's perception of her choices, Badu rides hard for Black men. She sings and talks about her children's fathers, the most tangible evidence of her sexual activity, as well as the beauty, strength, and love of Black men. Like Black women who feel empowered to discuss and articulate their own sexual desire as part and parcel of their spiritual humanity, every aspect of Badu's artistry exudes it as a healing and natural force. While some of her negotiations uphold patriarchy and a problematically constructed Black masculinity, other aspects identify feminist and womanist stances.

Communication science scholar Khatija Bibi Khan champions Badu's navigation of feminist articulations within her artistry. Khan believes in the song "One" with Busta Rhymes, for example, audiences recognize not all Black Muslim women or female singers accept subordination as their inherent position. She suggests these women artists use "the discourse of Muslim as a frame of referencing Islam in their works to enable them to sift the patriarchal attitudes, contest them so that the songs become the spaces for cultural resistance to oppression emanating from American racism, Black male chauvinism, and also the oppression that is perpetuated when some women internalize their oppression as natural and God given."[102] Khan rightly positions Badu's lyrical dexterity as pushing back on dominant male and misogynist discourses while advancing women's connections to all things natural, bodily, and spiritual.

Whether talking about Tyrone, schooling women on owning and discarding their emotional baggage, or green-eyed envy, Badu's womanist and spiritual stances resound. She makes room to indict the choices women make in songs such as "Rim Shot" and "Bag Lady." English and Africana studies scholar Kimberly Juanita Brown argues within the music video "Window Seat," a video just mentioned, Badu's slow movement along with her disrobing on Dallas city streets make room for her body to act as a "collective force of will—the vantage point of hypervisible [B]lack subjectivity enacted by public space."[103] Her willingness to operate in these ways allows her artistry to embrace whole beingness.

The Sensational and Sensual Relationship of Music and Producing

Fila-Bakabadio believes sound "creates space, communities and artistic kinship."[104] She unites Badu with artists such as Jill Scott and Meshell Ndegeocello over time and space, believing through their work, "the African American memory are not merely negative and distressing journeys back to a lost past or to an unachievable motherland but they are a celebration of the transnational nature of African Americans' trajectory."[105] The literary and pop cultural assumptions of Afrofuturism—a movement of science fiction and/or the future that centers Black culture and history—come into play when thinking about Badu. Badu's blending of the sexual and spiritual recalls the character Laura Olamina from Octavia Butler's novel *Parable of the Sower* (1993), invoked during the Selection. In this case, Butler specifically endows Olamina with hyperempathy, the ability to physically feel another's pain. However, the converse exists as well, the gift of feeling another's pleasure. Badu's way of exuding her persona exemplifies this gift.

Badu understands and promotes the world she creates around herself—her body, her seeming impact on the men in her life, and her artistry. This way of being involves material aspects as well. Like her mentor Prince, Badu seems to make good business moves. From the very beginning of her career, she claimed a stake in her publishing. Divine Pimp Publishing receives its cut on every recording. She sells perfume and other items through her online store. Expanding her brand (and revenue stream), Badu sells paraphernalia of not only her music but also of her literal self. One venture includes hawking her vagina-scented and infused incense online beginning February 20, 2020, at BaduWorldMarket.com. "Badussy" sold out in nineteen minutes at fifty dollars for a twenty-stick pack. One of the best (and funniest) responses to this sale came via a Twitter post by MR_FULLERSHIT: "They say the erykah badu pussy incense sold out in minutes. U niggas sick bro . . . Mine will b here Monday."[106]

During the 2020 pandemic, as many artists performed for the public in a multiplicity of digital ways, Badu invited fans (and crew) into her home, thrice in April, to perform some of her to-be-released CD. The COVID-19 virus impacted artists directly by cutting off touring revenue. To combat this, Badu hosted an online concert series to help feed the whole "ecosystem" of people her work supports (catering staff, bus drivers, runners, etc.).[107] Moving visually and sonically through her space, audiences, fans, and potential consumers observe where she cultivates creativity. In the process, she also charted a new streaming platform experience and business enterprise. (Prince would be proud.) On May 9, 2020, Badu "battled" singer Jill Scott in the Timbaland and Swiss Beatz produced "Verzuz" battles on Instagram and Facebook Live—a series that also began during the COVID-19 shutdown. The two offer a lovefest of Black women appreciating one another's artistry, exuding mutual stank faces. More than 700,000 viewers showed up for all of it, and they collectively hauled in 6.7 million U.S. streams on Saturday and Sunday from their total song catalogs, according to Nielsen Music/MRC Data. This number compares to the 2.1 million yielded for the Thursday and Friday preceding the showdown.[108] During the set, Badu remarked: "Religion is a real boat that can get us to the next shore. I believe there is only one."

Women's studies scholar Lakesia D. Johnson believes Badu and fellow artist Meshell Ndegeocello theorize a "revolutionary agenda" for the affirmation of Black communities. She believes they enact this agenda "through strategies that focus on self-definition and naming, embracing a [B]lack aesthetic, asserting women's sexual agency, and confronting oppression in all forms."[109] Additionally, I believe their spiritual connection to sexuality also serves as a revolutionary call. Ndegeocello, invoking writer James Baldwin, champions water, women, and openness as most precious resources. Badu embodies this idea through a naturalized binding of spirit and sexuality as Ndegeocello makes it her guiding force.

"You Sell Your Soul Like You Sell a Piece of Ass"—Meshell Ndegeocello

This lyric above from "Dead Nigga Blvd. (Pt. 1)" aptly introduces the monster bassist, songwriter, singer, rapper, and producer Meshell Ndegeocello.[110] Many music aficionados meet her through one of her few "pop" offerings, "If That's Your Boyfriend (He Wasn't Last Night)." The Grammy-nominated 1993 conversation/rap/song she initiated with another woman forces listeners to double take and ask, "What did she just say?" On her inaugural CD, *Plantation Lullabies*, she catapults her artistic and public grappling into the ways of the world through an uncategorizable sound and articulation. Illustrating problematic conditions associated with race, racism, gendering, homophobia, and sexuality, she brings a consistent word about the ways of religion, expressly Christianity, and its relationship to Black folks.

Born in Berlin, Ndegeocello came into the world as Michelle Lynn Johnson and grew up in Washington, D.C. From her own recollections, her home held discipline and dogmatic religion in high regard—replete with regular church attendance. She got interested in music around the age of fifteen, citing Parliament as her earliest musical inspiration, with Prince serving as an aspiration. Outside of the singing and songwriting she introduced in 1993, many

Meshell Ndegeocello in her "If That's Your Boyfriend" music video (1993).

worldwide knew her work as a bassist, playing for artists as diverse as John Mellencamp, Lalah Hathaway, Santana, and Madonna to the Indigo Girls, Chaka Khan, and the Blind Boys of Alabama since the late 1980s. Operating largely outside of popular mainstream venues and Black radio, she performs as a session artist even after being in the music game as a solo artist for over thirty years, with ten Grammy nominations. Many call her a musician's musician due to her keen artistry and insights. Her first five albums appeared on Madonna's Maverick recording label as its first female artist. Beyond her thirteen solo album releases, one EP, and innumerable collaborations on the recordings of others, her work appears on more than a dozen film soundtracks, and she scored the acclaimed OWN television series *Queen Sugar* (2016–2022). She also periodically reprises her 2016 stage musical "Can I Get a Witness? The Gospel of James Baldwin."

As talented as she is ubiquitous, Ndegeocello considers herself open—musically, spiritually, and sexually. Raised Christian, she has explored different religious practices throughout her adulthood, practicing Buddhism and a long stint in Islam—a time that pushed her artistry further, as recognized in her Grammy-nominated sixth studio album, *The Spirit Music Jamia: Dance of the Infidel* (2005). In fact, scholars and writers keep talking about Ndegeocello's wide-ranging, badass address of societal concerns: race and the impact of racism, Black nationalism, gender inequality, homophobia, and Black beauty. She also writes, sings, and plays a lot about love, in all its vagaries. For example, the whole of her 1999 *Bitter* release grapples with the difficulties inherent in love's dealings. From this CD emerged the hit "Fool of Me," a tune so beautiful and apropos to its title, it sonically illustrates many visual heart narratives including the climactic romantic tussle in Gina Prince Bythewood's *Love & Basketball* (2000). In fact, even though *Queen Sugar* uses another tune for the season three–ending episode "Dream Variations" in 2017 (the television series Ndegeocello musically directed), the climax stylistically invokes every bit of "Fool of Me," with its compelling, painful, and discordant sonic energy.[111]

Ndegeocello has, as African-American studies scholar L. H. Stallings discerns, "gravitated toward a spirituality that can express difference without concerns of hierarchical struggles for power."[112] Pseudo-labeled as part of hip-hop and a contributor to the development of neo-soul, she uniquely brings to this message the necessary understanding of sexuality as integral to our spiritual being. Her work directly advocates for an openness in who we choose to love against the religious tenets and interpretations that debase and deny these insistences. English scholar Francesa Royster puts Ndegeocello in the artistic realm of Afrofuturism. Using her 2007 *The World Has Made Me the Man of My Dreams* as the template, she suggests Ndegeocello creates a soundtrack of machines and human beings to enliven her desire for "political and spiritual freedom and transcendence.... [She] seeks to open up [B]lack aesthetics to make connections so that [B]lack sound is also global and even interplanetary.... She examines the problematics of [B]lack embodiment through music to convey the relevance of fluidity and vulnerability as key to the projects of spirit, love, and healing—all important aspects of a free queer future."[113] Moreover, Lakesia Johnson asserts Ndegeocello's self-performance of "masculinity and femininity reflect the revolutionary way that her work negotiates binary oppositions."[114] And while many acknowledge how she also consistently grapples with the constriction of Christianity, few think through what it means for this artist's spirit and the spirits of her audience to address her sexual being. Openly queer, she uses her artistry to question how restrictions, binaries, and labels not only impact our civil and social rights and lives but also limit the ways in which we come to understand God.

Niggas Need to Redefine Freedom: Black Nationalism

In terms of her career and trajectory, Ndegeocello considers herself a seeker and a conduit for music . . . a believer waiting for transmission. She believes her work has changed at different points in her career—in sorrow, catharsis, in preparation for lovemaking, and hyped for war. In her music, she speaks the truth of her experiences and the truth of the ways in which humanity resonates. She croons about systematic racism that impacts notions of beauty and love, economic wherewithal, and Black death. For example, she offers the song "Jabril" (*Cookie: The Anthropological Mixtape*) as a tribute to slain rappers Tupac and Biggie and "all those whose names we will not celebrate." Or, on "Make Me Wanna Holler" (*peace beyond passion*), she describes parental discord wrapped in dream deferment, respectable gender expectations, and Black economic inequities.

Throughout different points in her artistic journey, especially early on, Ndegeocello has unflinchingly taken societal ills to task on both sides of the racial divide. While I orient this Message most around those addressing our spiritual and sexual selves, her other observations must be included to fully grasp her insightful critiques and their connectedness to each part of our everyday lived experiences. For example, she remembers Rev. Jesse Jackson's call for Blacks to know "I am somebody," while also calling attention to many Africans' complicity in the slave trade. Using writer James Baldwin's *The Fire Next Time* as a spirit guide, she castigates Black worship of capital as "Slave to the dead white leaders on paper" ("Dead Nigga Blvd. Pt. 1"), reflects on how "the white man fights wars and enslaves, all in God's name" ("Shoot'n Up and Gett'n High"), and on the powerful "Soul on Ice" (*Plantation Lullabies*), she indicts Black men for allowing social climbing and illusions of white women's "virginal white beauty" to subvert their nationalistic inclinations (as they "let my sisters go by")[115]—always with a groove, beat, and urgency so funky you may wreck your car driving if not careful.

Literary scholar Stefanie Dunning makes a compelling argument for reconsidering a Black nationalism that includes gay and lesbian identity via

Meshell Ndegeocello at Emory University (2019). (Author's collection.)

Ndegeocello. Her reception by Black audiences (or lack thereof) illuminates a perpetual conflict that places Black nationalist discourses and same-sex desire at odds. Yet the bloodied bodies Ndegeocello imagines in "Leviticus: Faggot" (*peace beyond passion*), for example, are among the same Black men and women, gay, straight, and trans murdered by white police officers and other white men over the course of U.S. history. Coming out of the Old Testament text of Leviticus, so often invoked in Black churches' castigation of queerness, this song

directly confronts both Christianity that labels same-sex love as an abomination as well as Black mothers' refusal or inability to step in on their children's
behalf beyond prayer and admonition of "the wages of sin are surely death, chile."
Feminist studies scholar Matt Richardson talks about the complicity of the
song's mother within the "very system of patriarchal domination that oppresses
her."[116] He observes: "Her commitment to the brutalizing patriarchy that aban-
dons her son and leaves him bloody in the street"[117] gets painfully and sarcastically proclaimed with Ndegeocello's dry lyric, "all hail the queen." Raw, powerful,
and direct, Ndegeocello narrates the tragic life of and identifies with the broken
body of the castigated and evicted boy, comforting: "Beautiful angels dance
around my soul as I ride. . . . Swing low my sweet chariot. Let me rise." In the
music video, viewers see this happening after this child's beating and possible
suicide. Lying on the floor, Ndegeocello dissolves into the boy's place, moves
from the floor, and out the door.

Writer Terry Nelson reflects on the release: "Twenty years ago, not many
artists were directly taking aim at the pervasive homophobia in religion like
Ndegeocello does in the song. . . . When I first heard the song, it was admittedly
jarring. . . . While the lyrics are harsh, the strength of this song lies in its brutal
honesty."[118] Directed by Kevin Bray, the music video, one of very few Ndegeocello has offered over the course of her career, closely illustrates the lyrics. Stark,
disjointed, and jolting, black and white mixed with a lurid sepia, the repeated
debasement of a Black boy by his father, mother, and church screen powerfully
as a narrative perpetuated in late 1990s popular and actual culture. As mentioned
earlier, the same myopic thinking and address of Black Christianity about gayness reimagines itself in twenty-first-century film and television narratives such
as Rees's *Pariah*, FX's *Pose*, and STARZ's *P-Valley*, where Black respectability
overrides and denies Black desire and care, despite the recognition of harm to
Black beings and its antithesis to the ways of Christ. The experiences of Black
Christianity often undermine Christ's grace and promise of salvation.[119]

"Who's Your Daddy?" Black Sexual Agency and the Spirit

In addition to her ever-changing sound and lyrical emphasis, Ndegeocello's
sexual fluidity confuses and often repels some Black audiences. Hinting at her
identity in *Plantation Lullabies*, her 1996 sophomore offering *peace beyond passion* makes her position clear. In this second project, she goes all in to address
ridiculous and hypocritical ways of the Christian church and its pejorative stance
on sex outside of both heterosexuality and the confines of marriage. Refusing to
stand silent about her desires and loves, she foregrounds, invokes, and proclaims
without restricted specification. Mixing reggae with space-sounding melodies
on her complicatedly titled fifth release, *Comfort Woman*[120] (2003), she perpetually points listeners to love. Desire and love assume vaulted status and sanction
in their own right. Ndegeocello maintains, love is.

She claims an inescapable and generative "potential and power . . . [for] Black female sexuality."[121] Through her continued religious, spiritual, and musical journeys, she makes sexual fluidity synonymous with humanity and thus the spirit as well. Reflecting self-awareness and owning one's failings, she sings on "Michelle Johnson" (*The World Has Made Me the Man of My Dreams*, 2007) about doing right and wrong, praying, letting God guide, and being "just a soul on this planet. Trying to do good, be good, feel good." Her whispered questioning, "who's your daddy?" in "La Petit Mort" (*Weather*, 2011) calls for an obvious response, "you are, you are"—a well-worn trope of masculinist power, control, and ownership. Yet, as LaKesia Johnson suggests, Ndegeocello's assumption of a Black queer aesthetic "comments on Black masculinity while simultaneously performing a version of Black female sexuality that resists a strictly heteronormative narrative of sexual identity and expression."[122] Furthermore, because Ndegeocello both imagines and embodies our presumed gendered twoness, she articulates and merges religious texts with innate sexual desire.

The idea of individuals joining when they marry, when two become one,[123] fails to reflect the wholeness of self prior to that union. Assuming our sexual-spiritual selves reflect the constructed identity of a Judeo-Christian God, love for other beings blends when we join together. Ndegeocello's works foreground the body as part of her visioning of a conjoined spiritual and sexual force. As rightly surmised by Stallings and discussed earlier, the female body "offers symbolic fluidity that can free those engaged in an exchange of love and desire. The love Ndegeocello espouses a yearning for is not devoid of sexual desire or spirituality. . . . [She] replaces the sentiments of the Negro spiritual, 'take me to the water to be baptized,' with her own: 'take me down to your river, I wanna be free.' The phrase creates a space for spiritual rebirth and sexual freedom."[124] As religion scholar Roger A. Sneed argues, Ndegeocello's *peace beyond passion* demonstrates the experiences "betwixt and between racial, sexual, gendered, and religious identities. . . . [These experiences foster] creative responses that attempt to make sense of this liminality. . . . The creative response birthed out of this tension reflects the state of not being what you were (or were presumed to have been), but not quite being something or someone else."[125] So when Ndegeocello raps about the deployment of Jesus via his perceived whiteness, privilege, and inconsistencies in "The Way," for example, she forces believers to rethink their understanding of both text and context of biblical teachings.

Insisting women's bodies serve as vessels for formation (of babies, sin, and semen) as well as Holy Spirit, religion scholar Judith Casselberry examines singer and actor Grace Jones as an excellent case study. Jones's Pentecostal background and family inform her sexualized now—the knowledge of spirit and sexual energy manifesting together. The same can be said about Ndegeocello. She understands how bodies, rhythms, and spirit move together, and she "practices what she preaches—liminality as the key to freedom."[126] Ndegeocello suggests, for example, "the uterus is very responsive to bass tones. It's the low frequencies."[127]

Meshell Ndegeocello in her "Clear Water" music video (2023).

African-American studies scholar Daphne Brooks theorizes about voices like Ndegeocello's—contralto women where "cultural notions of scale, mass, sound, vision, race, and gender oddly converge, where a woman's voice can be likened to that which is mystically 'veiled.'"[128] Brooks continues: "These women of the lower registers, like their brothers up high, push our imagination, our desires, our quotidian needs to engage with the traces of suffering by challenging us through sound to (other) extremes and border regions, to tarry the boundaries of the elsewhere. By way of their location on these 'lower frequencies,' they 'speak for' us."[129]

Ndegeocello's creativity cultivates and allows for a privileged access to sexuality in ways benefiting everyone. As addressed by religion scholar Tamura Lomax in another context, Ndegeocello demonstrates that "Pleasure is not confined to men and boys. And sexual identity can no longer remain hedged between tropes delineating between promiscuity and virtue or hos and ladies."[130] Pleasure presents itself between queerness and spirit. In a 1996 *Rolling Stone* interview, Ndegeocello muses: "Women are probably closest to God. . . . What I think is lost in so many religions . . . is that the greatest thing the Creator ever did was create. . . . And women constantly have that ability to create, even if you don't have children, you always know."[131] And within her music, she demonstrates how the spirit and love of God flow through and between our bodies universally.

Good Day Bad

Many consider Meshell Ndegeocello the female Prince (although they never collaborated or, apparently, even got along).[132] For the preponderance of her career thus far, she has constructed and played the music she wanted. Prior to her 2023 Blue Note Records release, *The Omnichord Real Book*, her previous four recordings appeared on the French Naïve record label. According to its translated website, the Parisian company (founded in 1998) operates "with one watchword: no watchword. With a fierce desire for independence and eclecticism, Naïve continues to take up the challenge of diversity and originality, in France and abroad, within all repertoires: classical, jazz, pop and world." For Ndegeocello, this translates into her ability to revere singer Nina Simone because she tells "painful truths and [sings] with a singular voice,"[133] and create her tenth CD, the 2012 *pour une ame souveraine a dedication to nina simone*. Through the support of the record company, this offering exemplifies her devotion. Yet her independence means most of her career exists outside of mainstream recognition.

Like the offerings of her idol Prince, much of Ndegeocello's work reflects biblical parables. Side by side, parables offer possibilities. In the liner notes to "Dead Nigga Blvd. (Pt. 2)" (*Cookie*), she writes: "No longer do I search for a Messiah. I believe salvation and truth will come in the form of Spirit, not in flesh, not with melanin, not man or woman, from East or West, neither great nor powerful. Freedom is not given or taken, it is realized." She fills her music with lyrical silences, thoughtful spaces of reverie, and freedom. While many equate silence with the absence, fear, or vacuity of speech and sound, Ndegeocello's silences read as strategy, contemplation, and recovery. For example, in "Make Me Wanna Holler" (*peace beyond passion*), the bass and drums stand in for the unrecognized frustration and pain of a child who knows her parents exist in a way that destroys but is unable to do anything about it. Yet the freedom Ndegeocello craves and articulates manifests through her wide-ranging musical dexterity, unabashed sexuality, and spiritual speech. Considering herself a two-spirit person, she says: "I feel like I have two spirits inside myself. . . . So I try to be kind to both,"[134] trying to not make a good day bad. This desire to listen and adhere to her heart's desires, regardless of how they resonate, resembles the work of our final artist, Prince.

Nothing Compares to You—Prince

Per my 1979 Christmas request, my Aunt Lettie bestowed on me my first Prince album, his second. The artist sits in a medium head shot on the self-titled cover, positioned against a baby blue background with a bare, slightly hairy chest, wonderfully feathered hair, an earring, and a mustache. Too young to know "Lil' Red Corvette" is more than a car in 1982, too naïve to fully understand the implications of "Bambi" in 1979, too enthused with the beat of "Head" to think about what you did with it in 1980, the man and his music ushered in a maturation inundated with talk of sex and sexuality, gender nonconformity, and a spine-tingling string set. For Black audiences whose foundation lies deep in R&B and gospel, the magic of Prince catches teenagers up in a literal purple haze of musical otherness. And while my aunt bought and sent it to me (Tyler to Omaha), she conveyed her in-store thinking to me: "Who in the world is this?" Who in the world indeed!

Prince in his "When Doves Cry" music video (1984).

The artist who inspires all the preceding ones entered the world on June 7, 1958. Born to African-American parents,[135] he came from and represented Minneapolis and the Midwest his entire career. He kept his personal truths very close, valuing and protecting not only his privacy but also his biography. Fans learned about him in whispers and shadows and most certainly, in some fabricated measure, through his music, films, performances, and public persona. The same criteria used to attribute beauty to women describe him. His pitch-perfect falsetto drops down to a growling bass as he raps in between lyrics on hits like "Adore." The strength and apparent athletic skill he possessed flies in the face of his musical and dance dexterity—a joke that comedian Dave Chappelle highlights well in his eponymous Comedy Central series. When the announcement of his death appeared online on April 21, 2016, a cacophony of surrealism swirled. For many in my generation, not quite baby boomers but very early Generation Xers, the man and his music offered the space of possibilities. Prince Rogers Nelson transformed music and cultural worlds with his brilliance, artistry, and confidence to present fully and mostly unencumbered by societal expectations.

Prince registers differently for various audiences. Many know and love him for his musical genius (a person able to play several instruments), for his writing acumen (rumored to keep a vault of compositions as he wrote constantly for himself and sold to others), and for his work ethic (he pursued music making professionally and hungrily). Fans know him as a businessman, expert marketer, and recognizer of the possibilities in the duality of complete exposure (ubiquitous images, videos, music, and performances) and anonymity (slipping into artists' sets and hosting private listening sessions and parties). And most important to this Message, he professed his love of God always and often. In fact, Prince gave special thanks to God as his first acknowledgment on his debut 1978 album *For You* liner notes and on every recording afterward. Seemingly for him, throughout his lyrics of sex and love, is God. More than any other artist examined, Prince explicitly normalizes and melds sexuality (in all its manifestations) with spirituality in his music, performances, and theatrical presentations.

I Feel for You

Theology scholar Lee Butler believes the roots of African-American spirituality lie in African spirituality. This spirituality promotes an understanding of self, wholeness, and holiness connected to sexuality. He suggests not only are they related, but they share "the same purpose as the end goal, that is, to integrate human persons with one another and the Divine through the harmony producing activities of communality."[136] This wholeness understanding of sexuality and spirituality points to the need for and viability of Black joy—Black expressions that often get characterized as overly emotive, performative, loud, and excessive.[137]

Beyond the "holy hug" imposed by Black Christians to minimize bodily touch and sexual desire (one often invoked by Black Muslims with the same rationale), intimate, erotic love and touch blend the tactility of our bodies with the sacredness of our beings. In the mediated reality series *Preachers of L.A.*, for example, the couples, particularly the young ones—the Chaneys and the Haddons—connect joy and sex to salvation. Although completely bound by hetero and religious marital dogma, they consistently link their godliness with sexual satisfaction (wedded and sometimes nonwedded). Even the seasoned saint, First Lady LaVette Gibson, forthrightly proclaims an anointed man knows how to "carry it [his holiness] on into the bedroom."[138]

In thinking about Prince's impact, some scholars turn to affect theory and phenomenology to frame it. However, their concentration on feelings, emotions, and the structure of experience not only ignore the spiritual resonance of his reach but also read (feel) almost like cannibalization—capturing Black and brown folks' feelings and what Black and brown scholars have addressed for many years, all wrapped in updated language. The affective turn in cultural studies seems to sometimes exclude the weight, essence, and omnipresence of Blackness—placing Black emotions and bodies as a point beyond civility and humanity—as excess and excessive as I mentioned above. Yet, as philosopher

Fred Moten argues, "light and sound *are* the materiality of our living, the basis of our revolutionary pedagogy, the ground of our insurgent, autoexcessive feel."[139] The work of Prince demonstrates this well.

While some suggest Prince likens himself to Jesus or even as the second coming,[140] a more apt assertion might be that he takes up the ways and mindset of Jesus as a structuring for his aestheticized beliefs. Prince too embodies cultural theorist Gloria Anzaldúa's ideas of conocimiento in his lyrics, body, performance, and aura. Associated with Badu earlier, Anzaldúa characterizes conocimiento as an "aspect of consciousness urging you to act on the knowledge gained."[141] She describes it as a "form of spiritual inquiry . . . reached via creative acts— writing, art-making, dancing, healing, teaching, meditation, and spiritual activism—both mental and somatic (the body, too, is a form as well as site of creativity)."[142] Anzaldúa suggests and Prince incarnates "binaries of colored/ white, female/male, mind/body . . . collapsing." Thus, beyond centering and exemplifying ways in which sexuality and spirituality fuse, Prince forces listeners and audiences to reflect upon and imbibe his ways of seeing the world and its people. He uses his platform to relate to audiences and for them to relate to themselves—to see themselves with fresh and open eyes via his music and light. Because Prince's music touches and reaches out to the worldwide spirit, his lyrical thinking proves especially useful in broadening out U.S. Blackness to recognize Black peoples across the African diaspora.

Let's Work

When Prince died, fans became sort of holy in their recollections—remembering not when he died, but where they encountered him first. His peers loved and revered him as well. D'Angelo says his "main musical love was Prince";[143] Erykah Badu writes: "You will live F O R E V E R in my cells"; and even Meshell Ndegeocello, who acknowledges she did not have the most positive interaction with him, says he is "the reason I play music."[144] In her longer social media tribute, Badu reflects on Prince's lengthy influence on her maturation, posting: "The time you sang 'I wanna be your lover' on the 3rd grade talent show wearing a swim top and the teachers cut you short because it was 'inappropriate.' . . . The moment you remember how much he means to you. . . . You've been here all my life."[145]

As much as he always appears supremely chill, Prince grinds constantly, creating music always. Those close to him, like musician Sheila E., talk about him knowing "what he wants and that's the way he wants it."[146] Prince centers lyrics heavy with explicit sex, sexuality, and concerns of the world, especially early on, but also beauty and tenderness—pregnant with the possibilities of redemption and salvation—on your own terms, as long as they connect with God. Writer Touré suggests as lead and background, Prince reminds you of church with "six people around you. Some can sing better than others and they all have obvious personalities to them."[147]

Erykah Badu added 2 new photos.
April 21 at 8:11pm · ✍

▶ That time Prince was your rhythm guitarist
then sent you the picture.
The time Prince was so gracious to come to your club in the hood of South Dallas and
play for 4 hours into the night...
The time you recorded "Today -the earth song"
at Paisley Park.
All the times y'all shot pool and argued over religion.
The time Prince got in your Lemo to tell you that 'World Wide Underground ' wasn't
finished yet and you 'felt a way'. Lol
The time Prince "evolved " and wouldn't sign yo mama's 'Dirty Mind' album cover cause
he said he wasn't into that no mo and yo mama told him
"well you shouldn't have made it then" and you were embarrassed.
The time Prince had a "swear jar" and you just put a 20 dollar bill in it when you walk in.
The time Prince and Larry Grahm had you cornered in a Jehova's Witness...well, witness
session.
The time you presented Prince with the ICON Billboard AWARD with 20 (Janell Monáe).
The time you sang "I wanna be your lover" on the 3rd grade talent show wearing a swim
top and the teachers cut you short because it was "inappropriate".
The moment you remember how much he means to you...
You've been here all my life .
And You will live F O R E V E R in my cells.

Sometimes it snows in April?

Badu

Erykah Badu's social media tribute to Prince.

Like few multitalented artists before him, Prince defined, controlled, and owned the period in which he operated. When Prince's "Let's Go Crazy" aired on Black radio in 1984, I'd lived already in a purple haze as a new graduate of Omaha Central High—Eagles with purple and white as our school's colors. Starting at the HBCU Clark College that August, we lost our collective minds with the opening scene of his "When Doves Cry" music video. The purple one wore only a solid gold cross as he luxuriated in a bathtub surrounded by purple lilies strewn about an empty room (set), coming to our viewing pleasure courtesy of both BET and MTV. Scenes from the film *Purple Rain* (1984) are intercut within the official music video soundtrack with the same title and released the same year. This album opens with the single "Let's Go Crazy," a song where Preacher Prince begins his sermon by addressing the dearly beloved congregation, enveloped in gospel Hammond B organ chords and invocational lyrics. He talks about how we manage life and what we get to after death, the after world. He calls it: "A world of never-ending happiness, you can always see the sun, day or night."

This message, his preaching moment, received widespread radio airplay, albeit in a redacted form that minimizes the sermonette. Moreover, Prince kept making biblical references throughout his music that in large measure seem to emanate from his faith as both a Seventh-day Adventist and Jehovah's Witness—two Christian denominations promoting rather restrictive beliefs. For example, "Sign o' the Times" remarks: "Some say a man ain't truly happy, till a man truly

Aliesh Pierce
15 hrs · Southampton, PA ·

I have 3 memories of Prince. The first was probably the same as everyone else my age. It was that now legendary performance I watched with Beretta Smith-Shomade on American Bandstand and the almost wordless interview that followed with Dick Clark. (What was that? 1979?)
The second was his concert in Milan in which he rose to the stage in a purple Cadillac and blew my mind. That memory is a blur. However I still feel joy when I think about it. (Circa 1989)
The third was standing next to him in the green room backstage at the NAACP Awards. He was so small yet still so dynamic. (Around 2003 maybe)
Prince, I will always be grateful for your presence on the planet and the pure joy I feel every time I hear you share your gifts. You will be missed.
#gonetoosoon

👍 Like   💬 Comment   ➤ Share

 You, Aliesh Pierce and 38 others

Celebrity makeup artist Aliesh Pierce's social media post about Prince.

dies. Oh why? Oh why? Sign of the times." The number seven evokes many things (as alluded to with Badu), including the biblical seven deadly sins (or cardinal sins), the seven signs of Jesus's return, and the number of Prince's birth. Plus, he offers the song "7" on *LoveSexy*. In the latter part of his career, his music turned more to race and equity with a little bit of God thrown in.

Over his career, he scored his films *Purple Rain* (1984) and *Under the Cherry Moon* (1986) while his music painted the sonic picture for other films such as *Batman* (1989), *Graffiti Bridge* (1990), and *Girl 6* (1996). He won seven Grammy Awards and a total of thirty-two music awards. He won Golden Globe and Academy Awards for *Purple Rain*. BET and the American Music Awards honored him with Lifetime Achievement Awards, and he won the Icon award from *Billboard*. He was inducted into the Grammy, R&B, and Rock and Roll Halls of Fame. At his death, Prince had an estimated net worth between $100 and $300 million. His global acclaim provided the platform for the incursions he made at forwarding a synergy of sexuality and spirituality.

LoveSexy

No one would ever accuse Prince of not promoting a certain type of traditional heterosex and Westernized romanticism alongside his overt sexual energy. Yet, whether he sings about his coming home and sleeping on the couch or a deep love, his sexual lyrics and music connect directly and explicitly with the spiritual. In his 1987 "Adore" (*Sign o' the Times*), for example, he croons about being there for a lover and being controlled by them heart and mind while hearing and feeling the tears of joy-filled angels crying for their sexual union. So much

BET clapback at the Grammys' lackluster tribute to Prince (2016).

adoration, he suggests: "If God one day struck me blind, your beauty I'd still see. Love is too weak to define, just what you mean to me."

For those attracted to him and his music, he embodies the beautiful blend of constructed opposites. His masculinist low vocal register against his falsetto high, womanish range. The flawless skin and underlined eye against his James Brown strength, taut body, and performance agility make audiences know (and love) him over and over again. His small stature heightens his highly sexual and suggestive body movements—conjuring penile/pleasures in his motion. Influenced in style by singer James Brown, "This Is a Man's World," and contemporary Michael Jackson, he matches their talent, but ups the game with his artistry and overt spiritual connectedness. He expresses a deep appreciation for the feminine form (both within and exterior to himself) but also induces audiences to feel as if he can bring every bit of his phallic-having sex to bear on women's (and men's) bodies. While women's studies scholar Sara Ahmed theorizes the ways in which emotions get associated with women—their closeness to nature, appetite rule, and lessened ability to "transcend the body through thought, will and judgement,"[148] Prince takes fans to these very same places with an ambiguous masculinity. His album covers signify duality or ambiguity of man/woman, beautiful and mischievous, inviting others to join, especially on the cover of *LoveSexy* (1988)—his most spiritual-sexual release, according to pop culture scholar Joseph Vogel. He offers something for everyone open to the humanity of others. That Prince, that bad mofo, is the same one that in all his musical genius infuses a certain consistent allusion to God. In fact, while he seems to ask for someone to "save us" at the end of his salacious and sexually juicy "Darling Nikki" in 1984, playing the lyrics forward, he actually intones he's fine "'cause the Lord is coming soon."

Prince represented a sort of gender fluidity before the term existed. From album covers of a shirtless, womanish man (*Prince* and *LoveSexy*) to his Chantilly lace collars, sleeves, and ruffles (*Purple Rain* and *Prince: The Hits*) to his furs, eyeliner, and four-inch heels, he always sits as the prettiest in the room—male, female, or nonbinary. From the late 1970s, he made sex fun and free, sensual and loving. Prince created palpable sexual energy in his performances. When I saw him in Omaha during his 1982 Controversy tour, audiences delighted in the bed floating down to the stage and the imaginative and performative play he added to it. In a live performance clip shown in writer Nelson George's documentary *Finding the Funk* (2013), the camera captures a shirtless Prince moving to the ground, gyrating, and talking about his plans for the invisible girl/stage, with a black cross swinging from his neck. He isn't about f-**ing a woman raw but always with strength and heightened intimacy. His innuendo and explicitness made him a favorite across generations and eventually across race, class, and sexuality. Prince captured but also disassembled duality—binaries constructed to divide and separate.

In fact, on his third release, the 1981 *Controversy* album, Prince explores myriad dichotomies occupying the cultural stratosphere. In particular, the cut "Sexuality" asks "mama, are you listening?"[149] as he invites hearers to the second coming, where anything goes. He insists weapons and clothes are unnecessary. Sexuality is all that is needed. "Sexuality let the body be free." In a *Los Angeles Times* interview, Prince talks about what sexuality means to him considering his 2001 conversion to the Jehovah's Witness faith. He answers: "I've studied Solomon and David now. . . . [In biblical times] sex was always beautiful. You come to understand that, and then you try to find a woman who can experience that with you."[150] Fans (and most surely industry personnel) express concern about what his publicly taken up religion means to his music. However, this uneasiness reveals that many must fail to listen closely and discern his music prior.

While scholars draw attention to Prince's consistent insertion of religiosity in his music, very few seem to connect the synergy of Prince's sexuality and spirituality in the same ways the artist himself does. Spirituality (and religiosity) emanated through every lick of the guitar or tickle of the keyboard throughout his career. Prince innately understood, and more importantly, demonstrated a genius and intent in placing together sexuality and spirituality—whether it comes through musical chords, lyrics, voices, or bodies melding on stage or digitally, the synergy betwixt and between always manifests as one. He consistently links the spiritual to life, sex, and beauty and shares an understanding of the erotic in ways described by poet and cultural critic Audre Lorde when she asserts the power of the erotic to share joy: "whether physical, emotional, psychic, or intellectual, [the erotic] forms a bridge between the sharers which can be the basis for understanding much of what is not shared between them and lessens the threat of their difference."[151] This knowing manifests across his works and, as Vogel believes about *LoveSexy*, demonstrates Prince's marriage of sex and spirit. He writes: "Spiritual ecstasy is not only *like* sexual ecstasy; they represent the same concept of union, intimacy, and love."[152]

Sexy MF

Prince's influence extends to many musicians, genres, and other artists. Beyond the ones already mentioned, African-American studies scholar Marc Anthony Neal argues rapper Jay-Z, for example, incorporates Prince's aesthetic and sound as part of his post-masculinist success.[153] Percussionist Questlove writes: "Much of my motivation for waking up at 5 A.M. to work—and sometimes going to bed at 5 A.M. after work—came from him. Whenever it seemed like too steep a climb, I reminded myself that Prince did it, so I had to also. It was the only way to achieve that level of greatness."[154] And filmmaker Spike Lee, a longtime fan of Prince, commissioned him to score the music for his film *Girl 6* (1996), and in both seasons of his Netflix series *She's Gotta Have It* (2017–2018) used Prince's work liberally.[155] In true Lee fashion, the Nation Time Retreat (on Martha's

Vineyard) scene melds perceived dichotomies of Black life (well, Black upper-middle-class life anyway). Dance, music, sex, romance (reminiscent of Prince's "DMSR," 1982) beautifully coalesce with Black bodies and a little bit of religious discourse. Lee even ends his Oscar-winning *BlacKkKlansman* (2018) with Prince's unreleased 1983 version of "Mary Don't You Weep," an undeniable connection Lee makes to Prince's music, sexuality, and spirituality.

Throughout his career, Prince performed on the biggest stages in the biggest cities in the world but called home a small community, outside a very Midwestern and white city. Reconciling binaries, Prince allowed multiple communities to make him the quintessential example of a synergized spirituality and sexuality. Fans embrace him because they identity with his fluidity; LGBQT fans love how he unboxes through his dress, makeup, and voice (although he starts homophobically with his song "Bambi"). Christian fans love his God shout-outs (although he characterized his own *Black Album* as evil). African-American fans claim his membership (though he denies this connectedness in *Purple Rain*). The complexity (or is it simplicity?) of his purple persona, performativity, and purpose confront the dogma of Christianity.[156] The God Prince adores calls adherents to love unconditionally, freely, constantly, emphatically, and passionately through bodies, minds, and spirit. Maybe like the Bible's Peter, Prince reimagines the power and porousness of Christianity by sometimes betraying it, queering it, and coming back home to it.

A Love Supreme

As I bring this Message to a close, I recall hearing jazz saxophonist John Coltrane's "Love Supreme" for the first time as the climactic soundtrack to Spike Lee's *Mo' Better Blues* (1990). In the film, Lee attempts to bring life full circle for jazz trumpeter Bleek Gilliam (Denzel Washington) by showing what becomes of him once a Black woman he's wronged agrees to save him. Scholars and enthusiasts frame Coltrane's well-regarded work as a spiritual tribute. In it, he connects his artistry to God, saying as the last line of the recording: "One thought can produce millions of vibrations and they all go back to God . . . everything does." Certain artists manifest these ideas. Anzaldúa believes, "Reflexive awareness and other aspects of conocimiento if practiced daily overrule external instructions transmitted by your ethnic and dominant cultures, override the internal mandates or your genes and personal ego. Knowing the beliefs and directives your spiritual self generates empowers you to shift perceptions . . . and use these new narratives to intervene in the cultures' existing dehumanizing stories."[157] When Ndegeocello asks us to "free [our] mind[s] so [our] soul[s] may fly," we begin to connect freedom of spirit to praise with abandon the sacredness and power of religious texts (texts that previously held power to transform, produce miracles, and impact people's lives directly).

Prince's New Orleans second line celebrant (2016). (Author's collection.)

On August 16, 2018, the Queen of Soul, Aretha Franklin, transitioned. Known for her sixty-year womanist, gospel-inflected R&B singing and activist ways, Franklin's work and presence transcend time and space. Her Christian background always shapes the way listeners hear "Respect," "Think," and "Chain of Fools." Music producer Jerry Wexler suggests that from the beginning, Franklin's voice reflected "not that of a child but rather of an ecstatic hierophant."[158] But as New Orleans NPR contributor Gwen Thompkins remarks in a radio special reminiscing about her life and impact, Franklin always sang as a grown-ass woman—singing about things that grown folks discuss, often with a "church-ified" air.[159] While this Message centers more contemporary artists, longtime singers such as Aretha Franklin make audiences very clear about the confluence of spirituality and sexuality—in everythaaang. The way she holds her notes and her breath, her musicianship on the piano and her arrangements, how the keys she plays might as easily run a gospel scale as an R&B song, and her own biography invoke an undeniable synergy. "Natural Woman" and "Something He Can Feel" reflect the "real" joy of both sexual and spiritual satisfaction. Theology scholar Dwight Hopkins reminds us: "For the flesh to endure the pleasures of a healthy eroticism, it must first embrace the spirit. This is the ultimate life force already present in the erotic Black body."[160]

In a 1971 performance of the Franklin-penned "Dr. Feelgood" at San Francisco's Fillmore West, she ecstatically, sexually, erotically talked about a man she calls Dr. Feelgood but also about how people move through the vagaries and crises of life. Writer Emily Lordi describes the scene:

> Seated at the piano, where she was always most at home, Franklin starts the song's slow build. "I don't want nobody," she sings, and draws out the next word to painful effect: "sssssssssssssssssittin' around me and my man." . . . Her brilliant sense of the erotics of performance meant knowing just how to generate tension, and when to release it. . . . The crowd, singing along with the chorus, becomes a congregation. . . . The band draws the song to a close, but Franklin isn't ready to stop, so she ad-libs a call and response . . . which amount to perhaps the most beautiful and unexpected sermonic passages in American popular music. . . . The passage . . . extravagantly justifies Franklin's claim that, although she recorded secular music, she never left the Church; she took it with her. But the very structure of this performance, from blues to prayer, makes an additional case: that a woman's sexual authority need not compromise her spiritual leadership but might actually fuel it.[161]

During this performance, through the chords of the Hammond B and her singers, Franklin catches the Holy Ghost. And what may appear as calculated, may in fact be the confluence of those two ways of being, sexual and spiritual, operating through the music and her voice. While she sings about sexual ecstasy, the piano, organ, conocimiento, and spirit usher her right into a praise break. Watching New Orleans's Treme black community celebrate her life in a second line via Facebook Live and Nola.com (as well as Black Harlemites at the Apollo), feelings of hopefulness emerge. These same sorts of feelings permeate the second line for Prince upon his death. Hopeful, our humanity gets expressed through every aspect of our being. Nothing is gratuitous, left out, or for only private and solitary purpose. As human beings, we embody both the spiritual and the sexual together. Artists who recognize, invite, and harmonize this union transform world possibilities, and hope- (whole-) fully those who listen to and review their work. And that is the good news. Let the church say Amen.

New Orleans second line tribute to Prince. (Author's collection.)

The Invitation

If you confess with your mouth that Jesus
is Lord and believe in your heart that
God raised him from the dead, you will
be saved.
—Romans 10:9 (ESV)

I Shall Wear a Crown

• •

Black Oprah the Savificent

In the twenty-plus years since the publication of my 2002 book *Shaded Lives: African-American Women and Television*, the media landscape has shifted dramatically. The ubiquity of cell technology, the dominance of the internet and streaming services, the blending of media content, and the prominence and centrality of a banal, entertainment-driven media-(e)scape, propel platforms and content for lulling difference. The penultimate chapter of that book focuses on Oprah Winfrey, and I return today to think about what brand Winfrey means in this moment. In *Shaded Lives*, I argue Winfrey operates essentially as both an authoritative and knowledgeable voice of women, all women, while simultaneously being castigated and objectified as a Black mammy and conduit for white women. As an object of credible (implied atheistic) voice, Oprah Winfrey inserts herself into U.S. consciousness as both an American and a model minority. Her body served as a playground for reconciled binaries existing in opposition to white American male culture and as a balm for Americans' religious thirst. To this day, few other singular names garner comparable worldwide recognition.[1]

The Oprah Winfrey Show (*OWS*) aired for twenty-five years, from 1986 to 2011. During that period, the church's waning relevance in many lives pushed some to embrace salvation outside the bounds of organized, Protestant religion. This embrace displaced itself onto different figures; intriguingly, Winfrey is one of them. Standing on the foundation of excellence, Black respectability, and capitalism, she moved into both her promise and billions on that ground. In addition, she presented herself as a moral and spiritual beacon for a nation steadily moving away from its religious underpinnings—one still clinging tightly to a Christian framing for political purposes and power. I argued previously that during the broadcast of her talk show, the splitting of binaries across Winfrey's body enabled her to move beyond the iconic to some semblance of subjecthood; while the producer, Winfrey herself, suffered, becoming absent in her presence. Yet contemporary Winfrey moves quite differently than the host of *The Oprah Winfrey Show*.

Some might wonder what more is there to say about Ms. Oprah Winfrey, interviewer extraordinaire, mogul, content provider, and whisperer of all good things? I suggest first, as should be evident throughout this service and within larger popular culture, Black women make things happen—politics reflects this, the economy indicates it, and Winfrey's audience research confirms it. This may be one reason why in this first quarter of the twenty-first century, she now seems to support Black women more actively and more visibly. Her shift may come from recognizing humanity—from seeing the God in Black women and God as Black women. Perhaps she serves as an apostle for Her, Him/Her, and Them. Maybe she identifies Black women as the chosen people or synthesizes a bricolage of Christian-based, religious ideas that always-already capture the spiritual and religious enterprise of Black women. Or, maybe, the change is good business. In rethinking the significance of Oprah Winfrey for Black women, and especially through religion, I begin to discern what her industrial and representational strategies mean for audiences in this moment and for the legacy of Winfrey herself. Specifically, I imagine brand Winfrey as Black Oprah, the Savificent.

When It's All Over: *The Oprah Winfrey Show* Recap

Before it ended, *The Oprah Winfrey Show* appeared in 144 countries, with approximately 42 million U.S. viewers watching weekly. From its inception, participants (audience and guests) always called and referred to Winfrey by her first name, like Jesus.[2] This gesture indicated a certain familiarity not accorded or taken up by participants of the *Donahue* show, an early competitor, nor is it common in the culture of Black folks. *Vanity Fair* writer Yohana Desta calls her the "audience whisperer," someone "capable of cultivating a dedicated viewership by evolving with her fame and paying special attention to what they like most."[3] With the elevation of Donald Trump to president of the United States in 2016, some wanted to call her President Oprah.[4] Because the name and actuality of Oprah Winfrey resonated then and now with people, its enunciation still conjures ideas of self-help, the expelling of secrets, and authority. But now, I argue, it also even suggests salvation.

To that end, Winfrey always considered her talk show as more than a program, saying: "It's a platform; it's a ministry; it's a way to stay connected with people."[5] Through her race and gender, Winfrey maintains ties to spirituality in the folklore of Black representation, and in *The Oprah Winfrey Show*, she offered a salvational grace as a listener and conciliator. She brought warring parties together, initiated and directed the touch of flesh and mind, and asked appropriate questions to elicit redeemed responses.[6] In her presence on national and world stages, Winfrey connotes and claims a self-actualized, spiritualized, and balanced agency.

People read Winfrey (then and now) as success. Like the *OWS* audience, white women make up most of the show's staff. Winfrey justifies and likens this racialized privileged labor to the dominant viewership of her program. After the show's ending, the rationale of continued employment of mostly white women suggests, perhaps, business savvy, connection, longevity, and/or loyalty. Despite her encasement in whiteness, Winfrey has never denied her "Black card" per se. Meaning, she allows circulating discourses of Black women's ways of being as keepers of culture not only to define how she works, but also to curate a Black cultural milieu around her. For example, she remains a proud alumna of Tennessee State University,[7] an HBCU, and in 2005, she hosted her first "Legends Ball," honoring twenty-five Black women living legends in the arts. Black communities recognize and revere these honored artists, whereas outside audiences may or may not be familiar with all of them. A three-day affair, the weekend includes twenty-five "young'uns" (younger Black women artists and entertainers) who greet and welcome the legends across a luncheon, white-tie ball, and gospel brunch. She monetized the event, as ABC featured parts of the affair as an hour-long special the following year (2006), with behind-the-scenes looks and interviews with guests. YouTube continues to host the special and clips from various aspects of it for audience's ongoing pleasure and admiration of both the recognized and the convener.[8]

Viewing *OWS* over time, many African-Americans suggested Winfrey hugged more whites than Blacks and befriended them more readily. For example, in a 1989 segment addressing gun control and featuring parents whose children had been fatally shot accidentally, Winfrey, in tears, sat between a Latina woman and a white couple, mediating and negotiating the ideological position of gun control and their personal feelings of loss.[9] Her Black body effectively stood in for the nonrepresented Black women who have lost their children through gunfire—even when the overwhelming narrative of guns and violence centers Black people. But employing a white articulation and framing of the problem, she decolorizes or rather universalizes it.[10]

In addition to language used and the quantity of guests featured, the charge of attending to white women more often emerged also from the amount of touch Winfrey bestowed upon her guests. Christianity interprets the laying of hands as the transference of the Holy Spirit or Holy Ghost from one person(s) to another to heal, curse out, or relieve. It symbolizes the outpouring of God's spirit through those present to those facing a time of crisis or need.[11] Ministers perform this act often, not so much anyone else. However, an apropos and well-circulated example of nonclergy laying hands comes when Tyler Perry laid hands on Bishop T. D. Jakes during a 2013 church service in which Perry donated $1 million dollars toward the church's youth building.[12] The importance of this hands laying comes from the privileging and sanctioning of touch given to Black folks not necessarily authorized to do it. It extends holiness beyond the ordained—suggesting certain laypeople can be holy too. Within her show, Winfrey embodied the position of both victim and savior. Moreover, she spent most of her early career operating in the little b of Blackness as opposed to the big B that she later occupies. This was the Winfrey of *The Oprah Winfrey Show*. Her way seems and feels different now.

I Shall See Her Face: The Now

In her 2009 announcement about ending her show in 2011, Winfrey operated from the vantage point of being recognized worldwide, and she continued to accrue wealth. For the announcement, she began with the reflection, "after much prayer and careful thought." Sociologist Shane Sharp suggests that with this invocation of prayer, "Winfrey attempts to deflect criticism and avoid being negatively characterized. . . . [As] many Americans view prayer as a legitimate decision-making activity, Winfrey's prayer utterance may deter her viewers from questioning her motives and believing that she made the decision for reasons that might disappoint them."[13] Once *The Oprah Winfrey Show* ended in May 2011, Winfrey turned immediately to addressing her in the red Oprah Winfrey Network.

The January 1, 2011, launch of the Oprah Winfrey Network (OWN) came with much fanfare.[14] But as beloved as she had been among white women throughout her career, they failed to follow her to OWN. Hemorrhaging viewers (aka money), OWN executives identified the one show performing well on the network, the Black reality series *Welcome to Sweetie Pie's*. Debuting in October of that year, it brought African-American women viewers in droves. OWN President Erik Logan said to *Adweek*, "we saw that the African-American audience really had a connection with that show. . . . We're going to look at ways to nurture and grow that."[15]

By the fall of 2012, taking the helm as CEO, Winfrey pivoted further by partnering with Tyler Perry in an exclusive deal for programming on OWN. With Perry's content as an anchor, the OWN network became a more viable destination for twenty-five- to fifty-four-year-old Black women and Black people more broadly—across class markers of distinction, taste, and buying power. Media scholar Samantha Sheppard suggests that with these moguls' collaboration, "Black viewers get a version of racial empowerment and enlightenment characteristic of Winfrey that, while at times 'cartoonish,' fills a huge hole in Black representation on US television."[16] Of the twenty-six series appearing on the network in early 2019 (original scripted, reality, and syndicated), twenty-five of them featured Black casts or participants and narratives. Further, on the 2019 inaugural episode of *The OG Chronicles*, Oprah and Gayle's advice-giving web series on OprahMag.com (and YouTube), users/audiences see Oprah 3.0 in all her glorious, salvific Blackness. Winfrey's comfort with best friend Gayle King really belies the point. The two communicate deeply in cultural references from the heart of Black America. Satisfaction for Stedman comes through soul food—the distribution of cornbread and black eye peas; "Boy bye"; and "It's hard out here for a pimp," according to King, adding, "why buy the milk if you can get the cow for free?"—a Black grandmother aphorism if there ever was one;[17] the two traffic in seemingly genuine, Black-cultured, girlfriend talk.

During this episode, Winfrey revealed that interviewing 37,584 people over the years made her "pretty good at advice." This advice references "the brother" (in the universal sense, as she is pushed by King to clarify why he had to be Black) who isn't getting up to go to work. *This* Winfrey need not so much worry about how respectable she sounds—billions of dollars and followers do that for you. She can simultaneously chop it up with Gayle and laud Jesus—both of which audiences know she does. In addition to the monetary boon of the Winfrey–Tyler partnership[18] and the switched target demographic that comes with it, a central underexamined aspect of this shift lies with Winfrey's pronounced Black spirituality.

A Black spiritual and religious foundation transforms and reimagines OWN's televisual and digital landscape. Winfrey's confession of faith, much like the confessions she elicited as host of her talk show, relies on various technologies and strategies, but for the same effect and for a different demographic. Along with Perry's series,[19] the network added OWN-originated fictional narratives *Greenleaf* (2016–2020), *Queen Sugar* (2016–2022), and the short-lived *Love Is* (2018). These fictional narratives directly, in the case of *Greenleaf*, or as part of the narrative thread within the other two, center tales of Black spirituality and Black church religiosity. OWN has also hosted reality programs *Iyanla: Fix My Life* (2012–2021), *Black Love* (2017–2022), and the canceled *The Book of John Gray* (2017–2019) that have similar tendencies.[20] To this schedule, Winfrey contributes her own hosted programs, *Super Soul Sunday* (2011–) and *Oprah's Super Soul Sessions* (2015–). In the marketing for *Super Soul Sunday*, audiences learn the very explicit goals for her talk now: "Fans of 'Super Soul Sunday' have likened it to their in-home church as it explores thought-provoking and life-changing issues. True to Oprah's mission of striving for the best in herself and her viewers, Super Soul Sunday is focused on awakening the highest self and deepening relationships and connections to the world."[21] These series bring her into conversation with both outwardly secular (but spiritual) entertainers and the overtly godly. They come to talk about the role of spirit in their lives with Winfrey pastoring the conversation.

I'm Going to Put on My Robe: Black Women and the Word

Quiet as it's kept, Black women have always inhabited and brought the word of God. Historically, Black Christian women have ministered through word and song, including Sojourner Truth, Jarena Lee, Maria Stewart, and Florence Spearing Randolph. More contemporary women of God fill these roles, such as Renita Weems, Kelly Brown Douglas, Juanita Bynum, Vashti Murphy McKenzie, Cynthia Hale, Yolanda Adams, and Iyanla Vanzant, along with many others.[22] These women and scholars have shaped womanist scholarship and utilized various media platforms (television series, books, organized conferences, distributed and performed music, and larger mediated stages) to perform their work. The calling and authority of these women belie the past (and often present) role they are supposed to occupy in most major religions. But, using their feet, their voices, and their vision, they strike a path using whatever tools are available to proclaim God as she/he/they come to them. They can do nothing else.

Like some of these Black preaching women, Winfrey walks in preacher purpose. As early as fourth grade, Winfrey tells of classmates saying, "Here comes that preacher." Particularly mindful of the multiplicity of platforms at her disposal, she uniquely ushers in a Jesus that people fail to acknowledge. Doctrinally, hers is not a straight-talking, Bible-based Christianity. In fact, many vehemently contest her witness as a Christian. According to them, her twenty-first-century speeches, interviews, and events find her proclaiming a more pantheistic view of God rather than a traditional, Christian (and white) vision.[23] Yet Winfrey claims Christianity and operates in the narratives of it. Focusing on a universal spirituality, she stated matter-of-factly in her 2012 master class in New York City's Radio City Music Hall, "I am not talking about religion. . . . I am a Christian. That is my faith. I'm not asking you to be a Christian. If you want to be one, I can show you how. But it is not required. I have respect for all faiths."[24]

According to Rev. Dr. Nicholas C. Cooper-Lewter and religion scholar Henry H. Mitchell, everyone possesses a belief system enunciating certain value judgments. Whether expressed or internalized, "an assumption inescapably involving some sort of faith determines all conscious choices and influences all unthinking response."[25] In the biblical text of Mark, the demon-possessed, the leper, the paralytic, the dying child, the hemorrhaging woman, and the blind man all, in the face of apparent hopelessness, receive God's blessings and mercy, freeing them of their pains and problems.[26] These transformations come through faith, and while artist Meshell Ndegeocello sarcastically sings about how Jesus cured the blind man so he could see the evils of the world, many Black Christians count miracles as gospel and hope.[27]

In this same vein, audiences and users believe in Oprah Winfrey. They cite her net worth, access, breath, and breadth of endorsements and her own confessional and surrendering practices, especially during the early days of her talk show, as proof of God's grace.[28] In fact, spiritual leanings pervade all discourses and visual manifestations creating her figure. For example, when asked who the "Which Witch" character is for her in A Wrinkle in Time (DuVernay, 2018), the character she plays in the film, Winfrey imagines a combination of Glenda the Good Witch from The Wizard of Oz and Maya Angelou.[29] The confluence of

Oprah Winfrey in *A Wrinkle in Time* (2018). (Courtesy of Photofest.)

these two women suggests she strategically understands salvation comes not only to those represented as good and white but also to those women whose sweat, work, and voices only get to be known as phenomenal when called out loud.

Using the framework of biblical scripture, Romans 10:9 exemplifies Winfrey's salvific possibilities—for OWN, her network's new Black audience, and herself. With this network and new digital reach and as before, Winfrey bridges long-elided gaps. On her platforms, she continues to encourage victims, debates institutional problems (racism, sexism, homophobia), addresses relational problems (marriage, adultery, dysfunction), and uncovers unspoken pain (rape, incest, molestation)—all of which touch nerves and eat at American consciousness, physical beings, and souls. But at this moment, she does it *through* rather than *with* her Black body. In the twenty-first century, she exhibits a bit of religion scholar and minister James Cone's liberation theological thinking. In *The Cross and the Lynching Tree*, he writes: "The real scandal of the gospel is this: humanity's salvation is revealed in the cross of the condemned criminal Jesus, and humanity's salvation is available *only* through our solidarity with the crucified people in our midst."[30]

In 2020, Winfrey faced ire on Twitter when she called out white supremacy in response to the murder of George Floyd, saying: "Will people recognize systemic racism for the problem and evil that it is? Where do we go from here? So I'm gathering critical thinkers (like @ava) that match their words with actions because that's what we need: ACTION."[31] She goes further by putting Breonna Taylor on the September 2020 cover of *O: The Oprah Magazine*. Taylor was the young Black woman murdered by Kentucky police who burst into her home with a no-knock warrant and shot her dead. On the cover, a quote from Winfrey states: "If you turn a blind eye to racism, you become an accomplice to it." This cover's significance lies not only in Winfrey's taking a very direct stance, but more, in it being the only image of someone other than Winfrey herself appearing there in the twenty-year existence of the magazine.

Despite successes and confirmations of their call, women's ability to stand before God's people still receives condemnation and often outright refusal and rebuke in many Black churches. Harkening back to Tithes and Offering that talks about the lack of women ministers addressed or recognized in big Black religious organizations, fascinating fictionalized illustrations of this sustained problematic appear as critical narrative threads in both OWN's *Greenleaf* and Starz's *P-Valley* series (2020–). While *Greenleaf* positions one daughter as The Way, the other daughter continually gets denied access to the pulpit. Ostensibly, Charity (Deborah Joy Winans) gets told to just go "sat down and sang!"[32] Winfrey performs as Mavis, the righteous (but wrong-acting) sister to the Greenleaf first lady. In the case of *P-Valley*, wannabe minister Patrice Woodbine (Harriet D. Foy) tries everything to stand in the pulpit as God's servant voice, only to be told (and physically moved) by the male pastor to stay in her place.[33] Despite these blockades, religion anthropologist Marla Fredrick argues women are drawn to women ministers (and in particular, televangelists) because their stories are "real." Women want to create "an authentic self"[34] through following women in the pulpit, and Winfrey, too, uniquely serves this purpose.

Tell the Story: Salvation through Celebrity, Philanthropy, and the Political Pulpit

Religion scholar and practitioner Pete Ward places Winfrey under the heading of celebrities who operate and/or appear as saviors. Suggesting Winfrey's spirituality emerges from her experiences, he believes she "transforms what religions call 'transcendence' into something that is secular and inspiring."[35] Moreover, he argues, her importance lies in her representation of a "new kind of religious authority that comes from media visibility."[36] Over Winfrey's career, Black women have maintained a love/loveless relationship with her. While clearly someone in the number, both in form and fashion, her walk served as a particular reminder to whom she consistently addressed—white women (or at least so it seemed). For example, Black academics such as literary scholar Kim Hester Williams believe Winfrey's brand of "mind over matter spiritualism" reifies the neoliberalist enterprise, forwarding capitalism and the advancement of self-help, "despite any and all circumstances and regardless of the material realities of race and poverty."[37] Invoking Winfrey's executive-produced film *Precious* (2009), Williams maintains Winfrey's focus elides certain "womanist ethics of care and communalism"[38] present in Sapphire's book *Push*, which the film adapts.

232 • The Invitation

Others such as women and literary studies scholar Rebecca Wanzo believe Winfrey focuses on "ethical education" as opposed to "God's grace,"[39] while religion scholar Kathryn Lofton calls Winfrey an icon. Lofton suggests Winfrey collects elements of spirituality that she likes and offers them as commodities in her empire. She writes: "These decisions are not just product plugs but also proposals for a mass spiritual revolution, supplying forms of religious practice that fuse consumer behavior, celebrity ambition, and religious idiom. Through multiple media, Oprah sells us a story about ourselves."[40] Or as I postulate, Winfrey walks in a promise of faith. And beyond the world of self-help and talk, she balloons her celebrity and anointed platforms through acting.

Although not trained as an actor, she has appeared in several roles over her career—most of which are situated as meaningful to both her and Black America's reflecting itself. When she talks about her very first acting role as Sofia in Alice Walker's *The Color Purple*, she focuses on its life-changing impact, saying:

> I heard they were going to do a movie. People were saying, "Somebody's going to make a movie about that." And I say, "God, you've got to get me in that movie." Now, I had never been in a movie. I didn't know anything about movies. But, I started praying to be in the movie.... [After she didn't think she got a part in the film, she went to a "fat farm."] So, I start running around the track, and there was this song, "I Surrender All." I start singing that song to help me let it go. I was singing and praying and crying to let it go.... [She got the role of Sophia.] *The Color Purple* changed my life. It changed everything about my life because, in that moment of praying and letting go, I really understood the principle of surrender. The principle of surrender is that, after you have done all that you can do, and you've done your best and given it your all, you then have to release it to whatever you call God, or don't call God. It doesn't matter because God doesn't care about a name. You just release it to that which is greater than yourself, and whatever is supposed to happen, happens. And I have used that principle about a million times now. You release it to Grace.[41]

In this remembering and testimony, Winfrey expresses her fears and hopes in a way that implicates a particular spirituality connected to Black women, especially with the song "I Surrender All."[42] The last part of her testimony when she talks about God, "in whatever way you call him," can be couched as a certain openness about how God and spirit work. Notwithstanding, it speaks to her belief in a higher power while providing a powerful branding opportunity for a less-restrictive Christian god simultaneously.

Of the eleven films Winfrey has acted in since the end of her talk show, four are historical Black fictions: *The Butler* (2013), *Selma* (2014), *The Immortal Life of Henrietta Lacks* (2017), and *Six Triple Eight* (Netflix, 2024). She has voiced two shorts trafficking in Christian tropes, *The Star* (2017) and *Crow the Legend*

(2018). And beyond sundry roles playing herself on television sitcoms over the years, she plays the irreverent, formerly abused sister of a Black church family dynasty in OWN's *Greenleaf*. This series, while traversing the formulaic night-time serial genre, connects the perceived (and often real) hypocrisy of the Black church with notions of humanity and grace.[43] Narrative threads like these tease out Black church tensions in sometimes unflattering but important ways. For example, the underlying narrative enigma in the series drives the return of a daughter—one positioned as the prodigal child—who returns home for the funeral after a sibling's suicide. However, the story moves into familial sexual molestation, affairs, Christian homophobia, and sibling rivalry while grappling with the monetary imperatives (and sometimes unscrupulous practices) of big business church. These examples demonstrate the sacralization of the Black popular secular and situate Winfrey in the center of them—diegetically in the narrative but outside the diegesis as the executive producer. Both Ward and Lofton grapple with Winfrey's objectification, commodification, and consumptive encouragement and what they mean for religion.[44] What they fail to take into consideration are the ways in which her operation and celebrity impact, shape, and resonate for Black women and their spiritual sense of self.

Winfrey's OWN recognizes the power to produce and distribute content that centers a particular spiritual life through a secular space. The network's website controls and limits its paratextual materials—lessening the possibilities of conflicting messages appearing there. As part of its target market Black, OWN airs documentaries as well.[45] Two significant ones are directed by filmmaker and actor Bill Duke: *Dark Girls* (2011) and a sequel/response to it, *Light Girls* (2015). They explore the impact of colorism on Black communities in general and Black women in particular. In *Light Girls*, inspirational speaker Iyanla Vanzant characterizes colorism as "cell-ular" trauma, which is also recalled in a different medical way by psychologist Gabriel Crenshaw. And in 2022, the network began *The Hair Tales*, a miniseries that grapples with Black women's and girls' negotiations with hair, beauty, and self-worth. These documentaries engage a level of Black specificity undeniable to those who question what the target demographic has become and its significance in centering the intimate lives of Black women.

Yet communication scholar Raven Maragh-Lloyd talks about the affective labor Black women provide in the discourse of programming these series. She argues users and audiences responding to and through the documentary *Light Girls*, for example, allows for a rewriting and recentering of the narrative, "privileging *their* experiences over the representation of them on television."[46] Like other such institutions, Maragh-Lloyd suggests television and social media, namely OWN and Twitter in this case, seek out "Black women online, as primary audience targets only to be *always already* relied upon as the source of labor. The fact of Oprah Winfrey's race and gender does little to belie this critique, as we know that networks, and race, operate at a structural level rather than an individual one."[47] But while I don't disagree with the critique, here's the conundrum. Black voices and visions cannot be heard and seen unless they are invited to the table and, what . . . heard and seen. We may not like or agree with the telling or the underlying capital imperatives that shape it, but as cultural theorist Stuart Hall so eloquently expresses, the meaning of an event, idea, or subject "does not exist until it has been represented. . . . We're talking about the fact that it has no fixed meaning, no real meaning in the obvious sense, until it has been represented . . . representation will change, so the meaning of the event will change . . . representation doesn't occur after the event; representation is constitutive of the event."[48]

The voices contribute to the opening of a larger understanding of Black women's (and men's) interior lives, even when unpaid, or more, especially so. Using Hall and this frame allows us to reconsider the dismissiveness of Winfrey's efforts. If indeed we seek to not actually overthrow the system but to modify or transform its flawed operation, Black women need to eat from, serve at, and exist on the table. Winfrey's OWN attempts to do that and bring other Black women (and men) with her. She recalibrates whose stories live at the center. Moreover, she also directly employs the language of the system to offer salvation—cash.

Through her continued philanthropy, Winfrey offers a financial balm in Gilead. As early as September 1994, she announced her "Families for a Better Life" program that literally attempts to rescue, to save people from the life of poverty they occupy as members and residents of Chicago's "inner city" (aka the area where poor Black and brown people live).[49] Although Winfrey gave a considerable amount of money to initiate the program, it suspended services after helping only five families. According to some, over the years, Winfrey has not only curtailed her support to Chicagoans more broadly with a construed narrative of disappointment, but also helped hamper other middle-class volunteerism. Switching continents, however, the Oprah Winfrey Leadership Academy for Girls in South Africa dominates her current philanthropic and salvific discourses.

Opening in 2007, the boarding school educates girls from eighth through twelfth grades and on through college—attending universities in the U.S. and elsewhere. The idea for the school emerged from a conversation Winfrey had with then South African President Nelson Mandela. At the school's opening, Mandela remarked: "The school is important because it will change the trajectory of these girls' lives and it will brighten the future of all women in South Africa. Oprah understands that in Africa, women and girls have often been doubly disadvantaged. They have had the curse of low expectations and unequal opportunities."[50] To date, over 500 girls have graduated from this boarding school and gone on to "prestigious" colleges around the world.[51] Winfrey maintains ongoing mentorship and relationship with these girls, "saving" Black girls worldwide.

The difference between her works in Chicago versus South Africa are stark. Certainly, differences in scope and levels of destitution exist between these two places. Poverty surrounds much of South Africa and not U.S. poverty, exactly. Thus, Winfrey was critiqued resoundingly for the choice to start a school there

Oprah Winfrey's Leadership Academy for Girls. (Photo by Ossewa, licensed under CC BY-SA 3.0.)

and for the "lavishness" of its facilities. When asked about it, Winfrey responded: "I became so frustrated with visiting inner-city schools [in America] that I just stopped going. The sense that you need to learn just isn't there," she said. "If you ask the kids what they want or need, they will say an iPod or some sneakers. In South Africa, they don't ask for money or toys. They ask for uniforms so they can go to school."[52] I can imagine what some of the disconnect could be for her. Though she grew up with limited means, Winfrey hasn't known poverty, or anything like it, for nearly forty years. U.S. Black girls and women (and boys and men for that matter) are not always (and don't necessarily aspire to) middle-class polite or middle-class aware—even when people extend support in one way or another. Pain, shame, notions of unworthiness, and recognition that this help might just be temporary often impede expected gratefulness. Caught in an impasse of common ground, sometimes a benefactor's efforts become untenable on both sides. Winfrey's success sometimes traps her empathy and seemingly alters her memory.

Yet donating monies to educational institutions and nonprofit children's organizations, Winfrey continues to seek making a difference with cash. Interestingly, even when the results of her efforts fail, like Families for a Better Life, the failure inconsequentially impacts the perception of Winfrey's salvation ability. She gives of herself actually and financially, especially multiple gifts to Morehouse College, the HBCU for Black men in Atlanta where her Oprah Winfrey Scholars program has funded over 600 students. And in 2021, she

Oprah Winfrey stumps for Barack Obama with Michelle Obama. (Photo by vargas2040, licensed under CC BY-SA 2.0.)

introduced the Oprah Winfrey Leaders Scholarship, awarding fifteen students four-year scholarships to their schools of choice. Moreover, the post-*OWS* Winfrey hasn't stopped with just philanthropy; Black leadership aspirations have also beckoned her impulse and power to serve and save.

Over the course of her career, Winfrey has stumped for only two political candidates: former President Barack Obama and Georgia gubernatorial candidate Stacey Abrams. Winfrey reigns as one of the world's most influential and powerful people. This status comes from media outlets that declare her so, with listings on *Time*'s "100 Most Influential People in the World," to CNN, and in *Forbes* magazine. She endorsed Obama for president even before he declared. For Abrams, she volunteered her endorsement and time, saying, "I'm here today because of the men and because of the women who were lynched, who were humiliated, who were discriminated against, who were suppressed, who were repressed and oppressed, for the right for the equality at the polls. . . . And I want you to know that their blood has seeped into my DNA, and I refuse to let their sacrifices be in vain. I refuse."[53]

Staying in this political vein during the 2020 U.S. election process, Winfrey hosted a series of get-out-the-vote webinars in partnership with twenty-one mostly Black women organizations, including Delta Sigma Theta Sorority Inc., the NAACP, and Stacey Abrams's Fair Fight. #OWNYourVote webinars featured voices—Black women on the street (in their homes during COVID times) and those working for voter turnout. Focusing on the states of Wisconsin, North Carolina, Pennsylvania, Michigan, Minnesota, Ohio, and South Carolina over

Screenshot of the Own Your Vote logo during Winfrey's webinar.

four days, she, along with these partners, called for Black women to show up and show out at the polls. In the North Carolina session, over 38,000 households participated.

On this panel focused on galvanizing the state, NAACP legal adviser Sherrilyn Ifill, organizer Tamika Mallory, and Charlotte Mayor Vi Lyles talked with Winfrey about the necessity of turning out the vote.[54] Mallory, an establishment outsider, says at one point, people need to understand that "if you don't vote, they will kill us." Ifill adds: "We've been leaving power on the table."

Establishing people's need to connect the dots between protest, poverty, and media, Winfrey hopes to help close gaps. Despite her stated intent, *The Atlantic* writer Hannah Giorgis believes Winfrey (and other celebrities) traffic in Black shame in their appeal to Black voters.[55] For example, Winfrey questions the (seeming lack of) organizational leadership of the Black Lives Matter movement, calling for a leader-headed articulation for change. Of course, she is swiftly taken to task by these groups, as expressed on Black Twitter.[56] For this Winfrey brand, she leverages her celebrity for salvation, championing those who believe and follow her example while still inhabiting certain blind spots of generation and class. Ultimately, she thrives, but in her comfort zone, the world of talk and tactility.

How I Made It Over: The Invitation for Transformation with Oprah's 20/20 Vision Tour

In January 2020, Winfrey began a nine-city wellness tour sponsored by WW (the new brand name for Weight Watchers) with lesser cosponsors Degree (deodorant), Love Beauty and Planet (shampoo), and Panera Bread (at least in Atlanta). Not the first of its kind, the daylong worship service/workshop/transformational love fest called for women to commit to their best life.[57] Women from all ethnic spectrums and generations attended. When asking limitedly why some of them came, responses ranged from jump-starting the year with positivity to helping find their life's purpose. Black women spoke convincingly about their desire to be in the number, many not even knowing exactly what the event entailed. Most of the women were Winfrey fans (or friends of fans). Some had followed her from the *OWS* beginning, others pay attention to her now either online or through Instagram. Television scholar Patrick Johnson believes fandom, "like religion, can be understood as aspirational, providing the guidelines for the kind of person one hopes to become."[58] In Atlanta, they referenced the 12,000 mostly women who attended that day.

New Testament–based, Winfrey's approach to this confab lies in Jesus's promise of salvation as opposed to the Old Testament's threat of punishment for not doing things God's way. We see this in the multimedia workshop that addresses mind (with provided booklets to read through and write in), body (with intermittent high-energy guided dance and music to make you want to move and perform before the circulating cameras), and given "healing" lunch, and soul (silent meditation and celebrity sharing—in this case, Dwayne Johnson, aka The Rock). Additions of yoga, deep breathing, well-choreographed lighting, and a beautiful LCD screen with images of nature moving cultivate these aspects as well.

Winfrey provided an aspirational, be-like-me day. When questioned as to whether attendees felt like the event was religious, about half the women I asked said yes, the others, not at all. One commented: "The experience came from a holistic perspective and Oprah referenced hymns and Oprah's reflections felt

Attendees at Oprah Winfrey's 20/20 workshop.

Oprah 20/20 Lunch Ticket.

rooted in spirituality." And while one stated, "it did not feel religious at all," she went on to reflect that when gospel singer Tamela Mann sang and Julian Huff led mediation, "both sessions left me in the same space I've felt when I am in a place of worship." Throughout the day, we heard Mahalia Jackson's "Precious Lord," Tamela Mann's "Take Me to the King," and a lot of amens from the audience/participants. Different people addressed the crowd, including Winfrey, who elicited spontaneous responses such as "Take your time," "Teach, Oprah," or more, "Preach!"

Of course, the service included typical selling tactics—bringing out Eric who has had his leg amputated but used WW to lose weight and help him adjust to his prothesis. A slimmed-down Tamela Mann sang beautifully and extolled the virtues of WW. Panera Bread provided the lunch. Winfrey even talked about seeing a boy, now a dancer with one of her partner companies on the tour, who benefited from her gift to Morehouse. She "discovered" this during the Atlanta 2020 service. These business aspects of the spirituality she purports are part and parcel of her walk. While the entire day presented as largely pantheistic, the undergirding was Black Christian—both from Winfrey and the larger crowd. Even when I talked with someone who wasn't Christian but religious, she felt: "During a number of moments, it felt very spiritual to me, but at times perhaps also religious. As a Jewish woman, raised in a reform home vs. orthodox or conservative, much of my upbringing has to do with Jewish tradition, history and being productive in your community both local and Jewish. Instead of thinking or feeling 'oooh I can't relate to Sunday Church services,' I viewed those moments as relatable since the purpose, in my opinion, not the method is the same."[59]

While the 20/20 Vision Tour occurred before the onset of the COVID-19 pandemic, Winfrey continued her visioning for Black (and other) women, as evidenced by her 2021 *New York Times* bestselling book with psychiatrist Bruce Perry on trauma, resilience, and healing, the development of additional programming on OWN's Spotlight series such as *Speak Sis* (which focused on Black women's mental health), and her 2021 *Oprah Daily*, a newsletter attached to a website. The "offering" of *Oprah Daily* comes to paid subscribers via email, promoting more of her relationship with Gayle and all things Oprah. It encourages the recipient to make time "to give something back to yourself every single day. To connect, to listen, to celebrate yourself and what matters most to you."[60] This Oprah, this Ms. Winfrey, is why I call her the Black savificent.

Soon as I Get Home

When the woman with an issue of blood learns Jesus is coming through the square, the biblical books of Matthew, Mark, and Luke record her believing, "if I can just touch the hem of his garment, I will be healed." This story parallels how Black Oprah the savificent operates currently. Some believe, like writer Jessicah Pierre, "America has a history of looking to Black women to save Americans from themselves—while not providing the proper recognition for their labor or even respect."[61] Thus, as the title of her article suggests, Oprah is not your savior. Or, stated differently, Winfrey cannot save you. But she does provide a mediated and directed window for Black women that few have the platform or financial heft to do.

Winfrey always already offers a salvational aura and content. Her behind-the-scenes work in boardrooms and in performance revolve around life transformation *and* doing unto others, not either/or but also while simultaneously reifying systems that make this transformation extremely difficult for similarly ethnic and gendered travelers. Winfrey moves forward professionally while still being tied to, defined by, and indebted to the past. This past offers struggle and pursuit of excellence as a way of life and deliverance, but not framed extensively by bootstraps. Like cyber theorists who use the term collective intelligence to describe the pooling of responses and skills to obtain knowledge, the AI of it all, I believe collective intelligence applies to the ways Winfrey marshals her background, experiences, conversations, interviews, platforms, and spirit/God-centeredness to strive for heaven on earth—salvation. Unapologetically capitalist and respectability-centered, Winfrey's difference and change since 2011 come from her decision to be in it for Black women—directing how she moves for audiences of color and operating with a mediated power that benefits or at least illuminates Black women.[62]

People with media power can help shift entire paradigms. The platform to voice and vision Black women's possibilities tangibly, digitally, and through inspired examples offers a possible different way of moving through the world. Some suggest that the goal of being a Christian is not to be saved but to be liberated.[63] Twenty-first-century Oprah Winfrey still offers salvific possibilities through confession, as exampled by the nationally broadcast (and worldwide streamed) interview she conducted with Meghan and Harry.[64] But expecting the *OWS* Winfrey to now show up is out of line with the liberated industrial and representational choices she embraces now. Leaning into the word layperson Denise Hill brings at University Church Chicago on Facebook Live, she calls for sistahs to stand in their is-ness. Knowing our gardens are not our own; they are always communal spaces. You don't have to wait for a seat at the table. You need to speak, and speak in the fullness of your humanity. Hill asks women to speak what is, more than what's right. "It is, what is . . . [the sisters in Numbers] is-ness shifted paradigms."[65] I believe Winfrey strives to earnestly embody and include traditional Black Christian ways of being and articulations (though not exclusively) to walk pragmatically with Black women, but she also calls for a certain is-ness as well—for profit, for posterity, and for safe passage to life beyond.

Benediction

The Benediction gives the blessing, Amen, Ashé, and "let it be so" to the service.

But God

● ●

(Reflection)

> So, the mother in me asks, what if this darkness is not the darkness of the tomb, but the darkness of the womb? What if our America is not dead but a country that is waiting to be born? . . . What does the midwife tell us to do? Breathe and then push. . . . Tonight we will breathe, tomorrow we will labor, and through love, our revolutionary love, we will show our children.
> —Valerie Kaur[1]

> They seemed to be staring in the dark, but their eyes were watching God.
> —Zora Neale Hurston[2]

My child saved me from a premature death. When my mother, Evelyn Inell Cain-Smith, died unexpectedly, I was three months pregnant with our first child, my son Salmoncain. She knew he was coming, but we had just begun telling our family and friends. As my mother's only biological child, she and I were very close. I'd always told her, even as a young child, that when she died, they might as well put me in the casket with her. Oh, but God.

I'm not someone who takes this gift called life lightly, but my mother was my light. When she left me, after a last night in the hospital of her being more

Beyoncé's social media pregnancy announcement.

herself than I remembered in a long time, I felt this constant swirling, this feeling of being in a vortex with nowhere to go but down or out or inward. Oh, but God.

What saved me, quite literally, was not the love of my husband, my family, or my wonderful sistah-friends. It was the child growing inside me who needed me to eat and eat good food. This child needed me to try and get rest. My child needed me to walk around and play music and summon some joy for him. This beginning motherhood, this miraculous and transformative presence, kept me from myself and moved me toward God.

On February 1, 2017, Beyoncé announced her second sustained pregnancy via social media. She posted a picture on Instagram of her in utero twins taken by Awol Erizku. With a stylized image and text, #blessed, she offered fans a glimpse into her personal space—the intimate workings of her (deemed sanctioned) married body and the results of that union. In some ways, the display offered the quintessential example of both sexuality (the evidence of both sex and the body itself) and sacredness—the growth and miracle of children growing in one's body. In other ways, it gave evidence as to how media, Black folks, and religiosity continue to be part and parcel of how Black popular culture synergizes and exists.

This service has taken us along the paths, the rhythms, and contours of Black life religiously and spiritually via Black popular culture. And as DMX declared for us in 2009, many times "they" don't know who we be. In this case, outsiders don't always know who Black folks are, and especially how integrally spirituality and religiosity continue to undergird Black life. In the Call to Worship, I assert that religion and spirituality are the sine qua non of Black popular culture. It is my prayer that through the duration of this service, you believe this too.

#Blessed, They Ain't Ready for Me

Scholars across disciplines make a case for practicing scholarship outside of the Ivory Tower. Religion scholar Arthur Buehler encourages academics to move beyond armchair theorizations to radical participation to honor those who participate in the practice as fellow collaborators.[3] Educator and scholar-activist Paulo Freire makes a similar plea in his landmark treatise *Pedagogy of the Oppressed*, where he calls for educators to hang back, arguing for the oppressed to lead the struggle. Like others, he centers the necessity of praxis (reflection and action).[4] And my own mentor, film scholar Teshome Gabriel, often encouraged us to use our own experiences as a theoretical lens. I hope these calls resonate through my discernment and elevation of Black folks, religion, and media's convergence contemporarily.

Finding God in All the Black Places: Sacred Imaginings in Black Popular Culture not only changes up the telling of the gospel but also who gets to tell it. It gives evidence to how others outside of the church take up Black church worship and fill their lives. In this moment, hip-hop operates as the rhythm and blues of Black millennial life—the lens by which many now do and understand religion and church, and twenty-first-century examples of Black millennials doing worship differently appear across all mediated platforms. Talking about her 2015 hit song "I Luhh God" on the *Tom Joyner Morning Show*—a radio show and format directed at old-school R&B audiences—gospel singer Erica Campbell quipped, "God don't live in a box, why should I?"[5] In San Francisco (and touring other places around the country and world), Rev. Yolanda Norton curates Beyoncé Mass—a "womanist worship service" where the gospel of Jesus Christ gets filtered through the "music and personal life of Beyoncé as a tool to foster an empowering conversation about Black women—their lives, their bodies, and their voices."[6] And in yet another example, from the beginning of his career, rapper Kanye West offered extended dalliances with Christianity. Calling himself "Yeezus" on his very first release in 2004, his third selection from *The College Dropout* is "Jesus Walks"—a song that won a Grammy for best rap song, a BET Best Video award, and an MTV Best Male Video award. In 2019, he declared himself a "born-again" Christian, which translated into the release of his 2019 *Jesus Is King* recording and the beginning of his Sunday Service.

Yeezy's Sunday Service offered gospel music and a message to believers, fans, and/or the curious outside on his lawn, in a borrowed church space, or in coliseums. The goal was, according to his cousin and collaborator Tony Williams, to "administer and communicate the message of love effectively."[7] He partnered with prominent ministries and spaces around the U.S., including Black mega-church New Birth Missionary Baptist Church in Decatur, Georgia (with Rev. Dr. Jamal Bryant), Coachella, and on Chicago's Northerly Island. He announced the biggest collaboration of them all in his mega partnership with Minister Joel Osteen that was to be held at Yankee Stadium in May of 2020 during Lakewood Church's "Night of Hope," but then COVID happened.[8] These three examples coming through music give credence to the assertion some make of music being the only way to your soul without asking permission.[9]

Reflecting the larger target demographic shift and quest for young listeners and viewers, the thirty-fifth anniversary Stellar Awards program aired on Sunday, August 30, 2020, on FOX-owned WATL in Atlanta and in other markets, as well as streamed. Although gospel veteran Kirk Franklin served as the main virtual host, newcomers Jonathan McReynolds and Koryn Hawthorne served as co-hosts. And while many of the award winners ended up being gospel music veterans, the performers on this virtual COVID-19 platform skewed toward those under thirty-five. By the 2023 iteration, millennials McReynolds and Tasha Cobbs-Leonard were in the second year of co-hosting. These examples signal what the new kids already know and take up—God but different.

Often when I'm talking with my perpetually young students about their media-industry choices and their paths, I tell them to think about what they want their headstone or their funeral program to say. And once they imagine what the end will be, I encourage them to forge paths that get them there. Millennial gospel singer Yolanda (Yoli) DeBerry magnificently expressed this same sentiment with her rendition of "I Shall Wear a Crown," sung at an Ohio Black church funeral in January 2019, but magnified on YouTube.[10] With over 9.2 million views by April 2024, this digital, soul-stirring Thomas Whitfield–composed homegoing song exemplifies what my *Finding God in All the Black Places* service has tried to offer—a vibrant connectivity between the what was, using ideas and tools from the what is. In the same ways Le'Andria Johnson and Kelly Price move the in-person and televised live and recorded audiences during Praise and Worship, DeBerry extends this ability through Facebook, Instagram, and You-Tube. Millennials following her on the Gram sing her praises from the clip she posts and hunt down the original on the First Church Ohio website. YouTube and Instagram users comment on the anointing of her voice and the musicians as they all come together to send the young woman home. Whether they be churchified young Black people or experiencing the faith of their mothers, the camera captures the enraptured choir and pulpit ministers, the musicians' dexterity, and DeBerry's vocal abilities, stylings, and attentiveness to her friend—putting the affective turn into practice via digital media. Thus, beyond who gets to share the gospel, *Finding God in All the Black Places* highlights various ways mediation embodies and *continuously* transforms all aspects of Black religious and spiritual life through Black popular culture and vice versa.

Refusing Sense

Serious flaws remain despite the progressive spiritual work in Black popular culture even in 2024. Black Entertainment Television (BET), the network I write about in *Pimpin' Ain't Easy: Selling Black Entertainment Television* (Routledge, 2007), continues to provide and allow its platform to peddle healing and financial gain (or turnaround) in its Sunday morning programing. Tuning in to the Universal Church's *Showdown of Faith*, audiences can listen to and watch Bishop Bira Fonseca instruct on how to sow a seed of $113 in line with Psalm 113 to be one of the 7,000 blessed by God. Packaged around on-site recorded interviews, LCD screens, videos, and a call center (along with a host), the program directs viewers on how to stay connected through YouTube and its Facebook page. Every Saturday and Sunday we can watch. The usage and imperatives of media to address souls, both earnestly and for profit, especially Black ones, remains strong. This *Finding God* service does not dispute this ongoing capitalist and problematic enterprise.

More, the hypermediated contemporary moment encourages anyone and everyone to pick a problem, a platform, and amplify it. Yet by cultivating every hurt, relishing every flaw, and lashing out with a viciousness and breadth never before possible, we fail to recognize how we diminish humanity with each post. Long-standing animosities and suspicions get exacerbated in this climate. As should be evident during the singing of the Selection, Africans, West Indians, and other Blacks of the diaspora who negate their connection with African-Americans find that stance untenable in the U.S. The reality of living while Black means nationality takes a back seat to the color of race. The undergirding of spirituality and religion has not eliminated this cultivated tension.

Many Black ministers pit intellectual pursuits and success against attributing all things to God. It emerges through something like, "I have four degrees and can teach three different types of homiletics, but through it all, if I can't say 'ain't God good.' . . ." Always rubbing me wrong, this line of preaching literally constructs a false dichotomy—academic success and inquiry set in opposition to faith in God and spirituality. Often, marginalized audiences stake a position of opposition—you're either with us or against us. If businesses, performances, and products are not FUBU, they become suspect, as well they frequently should be. And in this post–George Floyd moment, many jumping-on-the-Black-bandwagon businesses and educational institutions are receiving a rightful, hard side-eye. However, audiences and users often fail to recognize (or ignore) their own complicity in allowing for—and more, supporting—structural injustices, racist constructions, and gendered biases. Black lives mattering in 2020 vehemently demonstrate this.

And even within loving, we haven't quite found peace. Religion scholar Monique Moultrie argues the Black church has never been silent on sexuality,

often making gays feel as if they are doomed. Yet while "Black gays are perse-
cuted [in a great deal of Black churches, many] . . . feel most at home in [these]
punishing [spaces]."[11] Paradoxically (or strategically), celibacy movements have
become billion-dollar businesses. But Moultrie maintains the Bible does have a
good word for sexual matters. For example, its Song of Songs talks about oral
pleasure (or even 69 as KevOnStage jokes about on the Gram).[12] And in popular
culture, as writer Lawrence Ware suggests about a previously discussed television
narrative: *Greenleaf* is "unapologetic in its examination of the real costs of
homophobia clothed in biblical misinterpretation. The showrunners do not theo-
logically defend the right of people to love whom they were born to love;
instead, audiences merely watch what this way of thinking does to the lives of
people who love God but are not taught to fully love themselves."[13] The Black
paratextual through line of connective spirit, sexuality, and identity returns over
and again to a real-lived God who centers love.

Celebrity sometimes creates an opening and carves a path for difference.
Assessing the viability of Tyler Perry's work for those open to his message,
approach, and target demographic, media scholar Brandy Monk-Payton argues:
"In his tactic of cinematic ministering, [Perry] makes available another type of
filmic literacy, rendering visible a form of spectatorial worship"—one associated
with Black and faith-based practices.[14] The same sort of consideration applies to
African-American studies scholar Judith Casselberry's thinking about singer and
actor Grace Jones and speaking in tongues. In her presentation "Solving the Mystery of Grace Jones: It's the Holy Ghost," Casselberry says coming from a family
of preachers, Jones, like her famous megachurch peaching brother Noel Jones,
knows the mutability of the Pentecostal church and understands how to heat
up and cool down a space.[15] Further, Casselberry argues, Jones operates not from
the place of the recovery of nonsense but of the refusal of sense having its way.
Refusing sense allows mediated Black popular culture to be grounded by a religious and spiritual agency that may be unacknowledged, undercover, and sometimes contradictory, but in its imperative and entirety, recognizes the humanity
of Black people.

Love God, Herself

Finding God in All the Black Places recognizes the many ways Black folks come
to understand and worship God using mediated tools as both continuity and
change agent. It may not look like your grandma's Jesus, but it's still God. In this
U.S. moment, we battle a certain inquietude, the deluge of everything new and
shiny (streaming services, flying to the moon [and under the sea] at will, AI, and
shopping/choosing on demand) bumped up against, rather rubbed against, the
old and traditional and scary (murders by those who swear to protect us, viruses
and anti-vaxxers, mass shootings, insurrections). The ways and means of Black
popular culture are often one of the few things helping to keep our sanity.

Laughing and crying with fictional stories, marveling at web series, listening to podcasts, tweeting the tea (and reviews), media gets deployed in similar ways, but more—now as a central platform for the expression of spirituality and religion. And particularly for Black folks, we can now take up and express ourselves with more of ourselves as both recognition of a problem and a prelude to an answer.

Devotional Guide

Call to Worship

1 Karl Marx, "A Contribution to the Critique of Hegel's Philosophy of Right," 1843, accessed 10 June 2023, https://www.marxists.org/archive/marx/works/1843/critique -hpr/intro.htm.

2 Sigmund Freud, *Civilization and Its Discontents*, *New Introductory Lectures on Psychoanalysis* (1933), and *The Future of an Illusion*, accessed 10 June 2023, https:// www.verywellmind.com/freud-religion-2795858.

3 H. L. Mencken, *The Ascent of Man*, in *H. L. Mencken on Religion*, edited by S. T. Joshi (Amherst, NY: Prometheus Books, 2002).

4 Fredrich Nietzsche, *The Gay Science*, translated by Walter Kaufman (New York: Knopf: 1974 [1882]).

5 Clifford Geertz, *The Interpretation of Cultures* (New York: Basic Books, 1973), 97.

6 For example, Western research on African traditional spiritual practices is often quite shameful. See the Selection for a bit of redress.

7 bell hooks in the documentary *Black Is . . . Black Ain't* (Marlon Riggs, California Newsreel, 1995).

8 Clearly, Christianity is not monolithic. How adherents take it up and practice varies. However, resonances and familiarities exist in the practices of Black Christians, enough to talk about them broadly but with an acknowledgment of differences.

9 Kiana Cox and Jeff Diamant, "Black Men Are Less Religious Than Black women, but More Religious Than White Women and Men," *Pew Research Center*, 26 September 2018, accessed 10 June 2023, https://www.pewresearch.org/fact-tank /2018/09/26/Black-men-are-less-religious-than-Black-women-but-more-religious -than-white-women-and-men/.

10 Stuart Hall, ed., *Representation: Cultural Representations and Signifying Practices* (London: Sage Publications, 1997), 270.

11 Howard Thurman, *The Creative Encounter: An Interpretation of Religion and the Social Witness* (Richmond, IN: Friends United Press, 1954), 45.

12 I thank anthropologist Ana Ortiz for stating this forthrightly in her Anthropology of Religion course, University of Arizona, January 10, 2002.

13 Although, as psychiatrist and theorist Frantz Fanon argues, Blackness often gets positioned in relation to whiteness. However, the pursuit of disentangling that ground not only often falls flat but also gets executed hierarchically. See Frantz Fanon, *Black Skin, White Masks* (New York: Grove Press, 1967), 110.

14 See Catherine R. Squires, *The Post-Racial Mystique: Media and Race in the Twenty-First Century* (New York: NYU Press, 2014), Kristen J. Warner, *The Cultural Politics of Colorblind TV Casting* (New York: Routledge, 2015), and Ralina L. Joseph, *Postracial Resistance: Black Women, Media, and the Uses of Strategic Ambiguity* (New York: NYU Press, 2018).

15 George M. Johnson (@IamGMJohnson), *Twitter*, 17 April 2019, accessed 18 April 2019.

16 Bambi L. Haggins, "There's No Place Like Home: The American Dream, African-American Identity, and the Situation Comedy," *The Velvet Light Trap* 43 (Spring 1999): 23–36.

17 Cultural studies scholar bell hooks writes about home in several of her works as well.

18 Science categorizes gradations of melanin—Negroid (Black) being one of them. The law considers a person racially Black with any known African ancestry—a law originating during slavery and adopted officially in Tennessee in 1910. For the purposes of Southern appeasement and capital accumulation, the Missouri Compromise of 1820 sanctioned and admitted Missouri as a slave state and Maine as a free one.

19 Singer Jill Scott tweeted tremendous praise for Beyoncé and Jay-Z's concert on 24 August 2018. Or recall singer James Brown's 1968 hit "I'm Black and I'm Proud" as a rallying point of collective consciousness and Black pride.

20 Calvin L. Warren, *Ontological Terror: Blackness, Nihilism, and Emancipation* (Durham, NC: Duke University Press, 2018), 39. Look too at Frantz Fanon's *Black Skin, White Masks*.

21 Katie Acosta, guest lecture, Sexuality and Media Narratives course, Emory University, Atlanta, GA, 2 October 2017.

22 Hundreds of books, dissertations, and articles exist on the teleministries of Billy Graham, Oral Roberts, Pat Robertson, Robert Schuller, Jerry Falwell, and Jim and Tammy Faye Bakker, to name a few.

23 Jonathan L. Walton, *Watch This! The Ethics and Aesthetics of Black Televangelism* (New York: NYU Press, 2009), 232.

24 Carolyn Moxley Rouse, John L. Jackson Jr., and Marla F. Frederick, *Televised Redemption: Black Religious Media and Racial Empowerment* (New York: NYU Press, 2016), book cover abstract.

25 Marla F. Frederick, *Colored Television: American Religion Gone Global* (Stanford, CA: Stanford University Press, 2016), 4.

26 LeRhonda S. Manigault-Bryant, Tamura A. Lomax, and Carol B. Duncan, eds., *Womanist and Black Feminist Responses to Tyler Perry's Productions* (New York: Palgrave MacMillan, 2014), 5.

27 TreaAndrea M. Russworm, "Introduction: Media Studies Has Ninety-Nine Problems . . . But Tyler Perry Ain't One of Them?" in *From Madea to Media Mogul: Theorizing Tyler Perry*, edited by TreaAndrea M. Russworm, Samantha N. Sheppard, and Karen M. Bowdre (Jackson: University Press of Mississippi, 2016), xxvi.

28 Market.US, "Global Black Haircare Market by Type (Fake Hair, Shampoo, Conditioner, Hair Dye, and Other), by Application (Household, and Commercial

Use), by Region, and Key Companies—Industry Segment Outlook, Market Assessment, Competition Scenario, Trends and Forecast 2023–2032," accessed 8 June 2023, https://market.us/report/black-haircare-market/.

29 Monica A. Coleman, "'The Work of Your Own Hands': Doing Black Women's Hair as Religious Language in Gloria Naylor's *Mama Day*," *Soundings* 85, nos. 1–2 (Spring/Summer 2002): 121.

30 Nigel Barber, "Sports as Religion," *Huffington Post*, 12 August 2011, accessed 10 June 2023, https://www.huffpost.com/entry/sport-as-religion_b_924601.

31 Aaron Baker and Todd Boyd, eds., *Out of Bounds: Sports, Media, and the Politics of Identity* (Bloomington: Indiana University Press, 1997).

32 Joseph L. Price, ed., *From Season to Season: Sports as American Religion* (Macon, GA: Mercer University Press, 2001).

33 Jualynne E. Dodson and Cheryl G. Townsend, "'There's Nothing Like Church Food': Food and the U.S. Afro-Christian Tradition: Re-Membering Community and Feeding the Embodied S/spirit(s)," *Journal of the American Academy of Religion* 63, no. 3 (August 1995): 520.

34 See Harvey Cox, "The Market as God: Living in the New Dispensation," *Atlantic Monthly*, March 1999, 18–23.

35 Cox, "The Market as God," 20.

36 Tricia Rose, *Black Noise: Rap Music and Black Culture in Contemporary America* (Middletown, CT: Wesleyan University Press, 1994), 100.

37 James C. Scott, *Domination and the Arts of Resistance: Hidden Transcripts* (New Haven, CT: Yale University Press, 1990), xii.

38 I thank Nina Bradley for this encouragement of me during the 2018 SCMS conference.

39 He refers to Frantz Fanon's *Wretched of the Earth* (New York: Grove Press, 1961).

40 I expound on this further during the Invocation.

41 According to its own statement of impact, 2017–2018 found 52 percent of Inter-Varsity members are "ethnic minorities or international students." Specifically, 4,981 Black students, 5,985 Asian American students, 2,412 Latino students, and 174 Native American students participated in focus ministries; accessed 10 June 2023, https://intervarsity.org/about-us.

42 Carmen Cunningham, "ReStorying Blackness and Freedom: Black Popular Culture and Youth Ministry," final paper for Imagining the Sacred in Black Popular Culture fall course, 19 December 2018, 4.

43 E. Patrick Johnson, *Appropriating Blackness: Performance and the Politics of Authenticity* (Durham, NC: Duke University Press, 2003), 40.

44 Carole Boyce Davies, *Black Women, Writing and Identity: Migrations of the Subject* (New York: Routledge, 1994), 4.

45 Be clear, I say this not to dismiss the very excellent scholarship on social media and its usage including Sarah Florini, *Beyond Hashtags: Racial Politics and Black Digital Networks* (New York: NYU Press, 2019); Andre Brock, *Distributed Blackness: African American Cybercultures* (New York: NYU Press, 2020); Francesca Sobande, *The Digital Lives of Black Women in Britain* (Cardiff, UK: Palgrave, 2020); Raven Maragh-Lloyd, *Black Networked Resistance: Strategic Rearticulations in the Digital Age* (Oakland: University of California Press, 2024); and work media studies scholars Meredith Clark and Dayna Chatman are producing.

46 In fact, the name of this project for most of its life was *Aw, the Devil with Hem Untied: The Black Mediated Sacred*. The title came from the book of *Mom-isms*—my mother that is. Evelyn Inell Cain-Smith uttered this phrase periodically throughout

my childhood (and teen and young adult years as well). For as long as I can remember, she frequently exclaimed: "Aw the devil, with hem untied!" (I later found out my great-grandmother, Fredonia Bell Jackson McCormick, invoked it before her). I know what they meant. Something had gone wrong, and of course, the devil had a hand in it. The hem refers to sewing and its coming undone, being not quite finished, or not quite right.

47 Charles E. Lewis, *Reconciliation of Worship in the Black Church: Spontaneous Worship* (Bloomington, IN: iUniverse, Inc., 2011), 65.

48 Donna Jones, "What Is a Confession Prayer and How Do You Pray It?" *Crosswalk Devotional Podcast*, 26 April 2019, accessed 10 June 2023, https://www.crosswalk.com/faith/prayer/what-is-a-confession-prayer.html.

Invocation

1 Anna Everett, *Returning the Gaze: A Genealogy of Black Film Criticism, 1909–1949* (Durham, NC: Duke University Press, 2001), 111.

2 Judith Weisenfeld, *Hollywood Be Thy Name: African American Religion in American Film, 1929–1949* (Berkeley: University of California Press, 2007), 5.

3 Quote from *Half-Century* as found in Everett, *Returning the Gaze*, 159.

4 As quoted in Bijan C. Bayne, "Magical Negro in Chief," *The Root*, 12 November 2008, accessed 9 June 2023, https://www.theroot.com/magical-negro-in-chief-1790900357.

5 Other films include *The Green Mile* (Darabont, 1999), *The Legend of Bagger Vance* (Redford, 2000), *Bruce Almighty* (Shadyac, 2003), and *The Secret Life of Bees* (Prince-Bythewood, 2008).

6 Intriguingly, the actor for Old Ned is not specifically recognized in the film's credits. Although scholars talk about the significance of this character as a crucial way Micheaux may have been commenting on Blacks' complicity with whites, the actor's name is not disclosed—even after scouring numerous sources on the film. Film scholar Miriam Petty speculates that E. G. Tatum, who appears as Efram, the other racialized traitor, may indeed portray Old Ned as well.

7 The character internally recognizes his complicity in a system benefiting whites. This scene of introspection, argues film historian Gerald Butters, provocatively and unusually demonstrates a "director attempt[ing] to explain the psychology of such a human being"—though not discounting Micheaux's derogatory impulse. See Gerald R. Butters Jr., "From Homestead to Lynch Mob: Portrayals of Black Masculinity in Oscar Micheaux's *Within Our Gates*," *Journal for MultiMedia History* 3 (2000), accessed 9 June 2023, https://www.albany.edu/jmmh/vol3/micheaux/micheaux.html.

8 As found in Daniel J. Leab, *From Sambo to Superspade: The Black Experience in Motion Pictures* (Boston: Houghton Mifflin, 1975), 75.

9 See chapter on Micheaux in Jacqueline Stewart, *Migrating to the Movies: Cinema and Black Urban Modernity* (Berkeley: University of California Press, 2005).

10 Leab, *From Sambo to Superspade*, 81.

11 Micheaux's efforts seem to provide a blueprint for several Black male media entrepreneurs including Robert Johnson, founder of Black Entertainment Television, and filmmakers Spike Lee and Tyler Perry. Film and drama scholar Monica White Ndounou asserts that even the UCLA Black Film collective took up his energy—the creative rather than the entrepreneurial part. See her *Shaping the Future of African American Film: Color-Coded Economics and the Story Behind the Numbers* (New Brunswick, NJ: Rutgers University Press, 2014).

12 King Vidor, *A Tree Is a Tree* (New York: Harcourt, Brace and Company, 1952), 175.

13 For reviews in the white press, see Mordaunt Hall, "A Negro Talking Picture," *New York Times*, 21 August 1929, 33; *Variety*, 28 August 1929; and Harry Gray, "Primitive Emotions Aflame in a Negro Film," *Literary Digest*, 5 October 1929, 42–44. For a pulse of the Black press, see Donald Bogle, *Toms, Coons, Mulattoes, Mammies & Bucks*, new expanded edition (New York: Continuum Press, 1989), 30.

14 Weisenfeld, *Hollywood Be Thy Name*, 39.

15 I address the fallacy of this viewpoint in The Message.

16 Armond White, as quoted in "From the Archive: The Blood of Jesus," Texas Film Commission, 17 February 2022, accessed 9 June 2023, https://gov.texas.gov/film /post/from-the-archives-the-blood-of-jesus.

17 For example, see G. William Jones, *Black Cinema Treasures: Lost and Found* (Denton: University of North Texas Press, 1991); Walid Khaldi's documentary *Spencer Williams: Remembrances of an Early Black Film Pioneer* (1996); and the documentary *Pioneers of African American Cinema* (Kino Classics, 2016).

18 Film historian Thomas Cripps writes about the ways in which Black West Coast actors angrily complain about Hollywood's distortion of Black identity in films such as *The Ten Commandments*. See Thomas Cripps, *Slow Fade to Black: The Negro in American Film, 1900–1942* (New York: Oxford University Press, 1993), 100.

19 *The Ten Commandments* and *Quo Vadis* both received best picture nominations, with *Ben-Hur* sweeping the 1960 Academy Awards.

20 Highlighting this ignorance of her "friend" is not particularly common in cinema of the period and applies as well to the lack of (or skewed) knowledge of Black religiosity by whites. Despite their years-long relationship, Lora knows nothing about the personal life of her beloved worker and companion. It is reminiscent of a throwaway line Florida Evans (Esther Rolle) makes in *Maude*. She suggests white characters (and de facto white writers and audiences) know and learn very little about the personal and interior lives of their Black friends, colleagues, and/or employees (CBS, 1972–1978).

21 Livia Gershon, "When Televangelism Got Big," *JSTOR Daily*, 14 September 2015, accessed 9 June 2023, https://daily.jstor.org/televangelism-got-big/.

22 Frank Newport, "This Christmas, 78% of Americans Identify as Christian," *Gallup*, 24 December 2009, accessed 9 June 2023, https://news.gallup.com/poll/124793/this -christmas-78-americans-identify-christian.aspx.

23 Hattie McDaniel was the first African-American to win an Oscar. She received the 1940 best supporting actress award for her role as Mammy in *Gone with the Wind* (Fleming, 1939).

24 Thomas Cripps, *Making Movies Black: The Hollywood Message Movie from World War II to the Civil Rights Era* (New York: Oxford University Press, 1993), 68.

25 Michele Hilmes, *Only Connect: A Cultural History of Broadcasting in the United States*, 4th ed. (Boston: Wadsworth, 2014), 294.

26 See Devorah Heitner, *Black Power TV* (Durham, NC: Duke University Press, 2013), and Gayle Wald, *It's Been Beautiful: Soul! and Black Power Television* (Durham, NC: Duke University Press, 2015). Also see *Report of the National Advisory Commission on Civil Disorders*, 1968, accessed 9 June 2023, https://babel.hathitrust .org/cgi/pt?id=mdp.39015000225410&view=1up&seq=15.

27 See Ellen C. Scott, *Cinema Civil Rights: Regulation, Repression, and Race in the Classical Hollywood Era* (New Brunswick, NJ: Rutgers University Press, 2015), and Steve Classen, *Watching Jim Crow: The Struggles over Mississippi TV, 1955–1969* (Durham, NC: Duke University Press, 2004).

28 Gerald R. Butters Jr., *From Sweetback to Superfly: Race and Film Audiences in Chicago's Loop* (Columbia: University of Missouri Press, 2015).

29 Amanda Howell, *Popular Film Music and Masculinity in Action: A Different Tune* (New York: Routledge, 2015), 88.

30 See Huey Newton, "He Won't Bleed Me: A Revolutionary Analysis of Sweet Sweetback's Baadasssss Song," *The Black Panther* 6, no. 21 (June 19, 1971), and Jon Hartmann, "The Trope of Blaxploitation in Critical Responses to Sweetback," *Film History* 6 (1994): 382–404.

31 Lerone Bennett Jr., "The Emancipation Orgasm: Sweetback in Wonderland," *Ebony* 27, no. 1 (September 1971): 112, 118.

32 As found in Tre'vell Anderson, "A Look Back at the Blaxploitation Era through 2018 Eyes," *Los Angeles Times*, 8 June 2018, accessed 9 June 2023, https://www .latimes.com/entertainment/movies/la-ca-mn-blaxploitation-superfly-20180608 -story.html.

33 Also during this period, Universal Pictures released *Jesus Christ Superstar* (Jewison, 1973), prominently featuring Carl Anderson as Judas Iscariot, a Black betrayer of a very white Jesus. This racialized casting choice persists in most versions of this production—theater, film, and television.

34 The series is based on the 1967 film of the same name.

35 Music educator Samuel A. Floyd surveys the chariot trope in Black music, where he finds the chariot functions to "pick up and carry the slave home." It allows the enslaved to travel home and hails King Jesus to stop for the righteous, which is good news. Moreover, the chariot runs by faith or the grace of God. See Samuel A. Floyd Jr., "Troping the Blues: From Spirituals to the Concert Hall," *Black Music Research Journal* 13 (1993): 32–33.

36 Floyd furthers the trope of the chariot in *The Power of Black Music: Interpreting Its History from Africa to the United States* (New York: Oxford University Press, 1995), and musicologist Horace J. Maxile Jr. builds on this work in his article "Extensions on a Black Musical Tropology: From Trains to the Mothership (and Beyond)," *Journal of Black Studies* 42, no. 4 (May 2011): 593–608. Artist Meshell Ndegeocello calls for the chariot to swing low and let her ride above her fears, sadness, and tears in "Leviticus: Faggot" on her *peace beyond passion* release (1996), which I address in The Message.

37 The HBO special aired on April 23, 2016, the same night she dropped her visual album on Tidal, the company jointly owned by her and husband Shawn Carter (Jay-Z). The various music videos are presumed directed by seven different artists: Jonas Åkerlund, Beyoncé Knowles Carter, Khalil Joseph, Melina Matsoukas, Dikayl Rimmasch, Mark Romanek, and Todd Tourso. Listed as an executive producer on the film, Beyoncé likely exercised considerable directorial authority on each video as well.

38 Beyoncé took up the visual style and spiritual and religious underpinnings of *Daughters of the Dust* in *Lemonade*.

39 Other relevant narratives of the period include *The Preacher's Wife* (Marshall, 1996), starring Whitney Houston, Denzel Washington, and Courtney Vance, remixing its predecessor and reminding Black believers of miracles in the Black church. And even the women of *Waiting to Exhale* (Whitaker, 1995) attend church (not once but twice, though without much explicit narrative rationale). In this Black blockbuster film (and novel), nothing particularly godly materializes in their stories or trajectory. Yet they burst from church service beautifully—colorfully adorned and seemingly refreshed—perhaps as a testament to God's goodness, because nothing

else in the narrative ties their attendance beyond the notion that Black women go to church and believe in God. Terry McMillian's book *Waiting to Exhale*, published in 1992, was a *New York Times* bestseller, and the Twentieth Century Fox film version grossed over $81 million.

40 Well, that and other syndicated programming from a myriad of questionable men and women of God. For more on BET and its modes of religious address, see my *Pimpin' Ain't Easy: Selling Black Entertainment Television* (New York: Routledge, 2007).

41 For example, *Touched by an Angel* (CBS, 1994–2003) and *Nothing Sacred* (ABC, 1997–1998) aired, galvanized by the then flourishing religious right and buttressed by conversations generated from 1980s culture wars that caught fire in the 1990s with the explosion of hip-hop. Moreover, the long-running, highly successful animated program *South Park* (Comedy Central, 1997–) uses humor to tease and critique religion and religiosity from all sides—laying substantial groundwork for the development, content, and explosion of the internet.

42 These series include *Joan of Arcadia* (CBS/CW, 2003–2005), *Big Love* (HBO, 2006–2011), *Saving Grace* (TNT, 2007–2010), *Little Mosque on the Prairie* (CBC, 2007–2012), *Father Brown* (BBC One, 2013–), *The Leftovers* (HBO, 2014–2017), *The Good Place* (NBC, 2016–2020), *Preacher* (AMC, 2016–2019), *The Handmaid's Tale* (Hulu, 2017–2025), *God Friended Me* (CBS, 2018–2020), *Evil* (CBS/Paramount+, 2019–2024), and *The Righteous Gemstones* (HBO, 2019–).

43 See *Six Feet Under*'s season two especially in this regard. In fact, several non-religious-focused "quality" television series incorporate religion as a central narrative thread or subtext. *Oz* (HBO, 1997–2003) fosters tension by the mashup of male religiosity, violence, and race; *The Wire* (HBO, 2002–2008) finds Black ministers who hold (and wield) considerable political power; and *Treme* (HBO, 2010–2013) brings the spirituality of Mardi Gras Indians and Black Catholics to bear on post-Katrina New Orleans. Clearly, premium cable enables much more explicitness and expressivity in its narrative frames due, in part, to its lessened FCC restrictions and because of the perceived sensibilities and expectations of its largely white and affluent audiences. For more on the development and operation of premium cable and cable in general, see Marc Leverette, Brian Ott, and Cara Louise Buckley, *It's Not TV, It's HBO* (New York: Routledge, 2008); Derek Johnson, *From Networks to Netflix* (New York: Routledge, 2018); and Amanda D. Lotz, *We Now Disrupt This Broadcast* (Cambridge, MA: MIT Press, 2018).

44 Past mini-series such as *Roots* (ABC, 1977), *Roots* remake (History Channel, 2016), and the short-lived series *Underground* (WGN America, 2016–2017) provide audiences with a limited look at the ways in which Christianity gets used to justify slavery.

45 For example, a popular *Girlfriends* episode features gospel singer Donnie McClurkin singing his hit "Stand" (season two, episode seven, "Trick or Truth," airdate 29 October 2001). Another example centers a storyline in *Noah's Arc* (Logo TV, 2005–2006) featuring Eddie (Jonathan Julien) and Chance's (Doug Spearman) desire to marry but continued rebuke from an ascribed pathologically homophobic Black church. Of course, the religion episode also gets played for fun, as demonstrated in the season two episode "Churched" of *black-ish* (ABC, 2014–2022) or in the irreverent comedy sketches of *Key & Peele* with their church ladies and Satan (Comedy Central, 2012–2015).

46 I thank my undergraduate student Leila Yavari for making me consider television in this way; Emory University, 17 April 2017.

47 Mara Einstein, Katherine Madden, and Diane Winston, eds., *Religion and Reality TV: Faith in Late Capitalism* (New York: Routledge, 2018), xviii.

48 Mediated, or tele-evangelism has a long history and comes through virtually every mass communicative outlet. While white evangelists once dominated the scene, staunch journeymen and women with U.S.-based Black, Nigerian, and Korean ministers now hold sway. Substantial scholarship explores the history, content, and impact of these ministries, which I address during Tithes & Offering.

49 Einstein, Madden, and Winston, *Religion and Reality TV*, xx.

50 Specifically, Meyers says: "With all spiritual and actual thanks to Kendrick . . . sometimes I think about it and I'm like, 'Well, I am that guy in music videos.' There's a lot of other directors that showboat and do what they do and are fly. And I'm very grounded, always have been grounded. But was I chosen cosmically, because I put out that energy and maybe Kendrick absorbed it? These are the things I think about at night." Catherine Green, "The Director behind Some of the Most Iconic Music Videos of the 2000s," *The Atlantic*, 11 August 2017, accessed 26 June 2023, https://www.theatlantic.com/entertainment/archive/2017/08/the-art-and-business-of-making-music-videos/535254/.

Processional

1 Adrienne Lanier Seward, "A Film Portrait of Black Ritual Expression: *The Blood of Jesus*," in *Expressively Black: The Cultural Basis of Ethnic Identity*, edited by Geneva Gay and Willie L. Baber (New York: Praeger Publishers, 1987), 200.

2 Judith Casselberry, *The Labor of Faith: Gender and Power in Black Apostolic Pentecostalism* (Durham, NC: Duke University Press, 2017), 169.

3 Alice Walker as found in Arisika Razak, "Sacred Women of Africa and the African Diaspora: A Womanist Vision of Black Women's Bodies and the African Sacred Feminine," *International Journal of Transpersonal Studies* 35, no. 1 (2016): 131. Walker's quote comes from Alice Walker, *In Search of Our Mothers' Gardens: Womanist Prose* (San Diego: Harvest Harcourt Brace Jovanovich, 1983), xii.

4 Razak, "Sacred Women of Africa and the African Diaspora," 131.

5 Razak, "Sacred Women of Africa and the African Diaspora," 133.

6 See, for example, Pete Ward, *Gods Behaving Badly: Media, Religion, and Celebrity Culture* (Waco, TX: Baylor University Press, 2011); Kathryn Lofton, "Religion and the American Celebrity," *Social Compass* 58, no. 3 (September 2011): 346–352; or the chapter on "Celebrity" in Gary Laderman, *Sacred Matters: Celebrity Worship, Sexual Ecstasies, the Living Dead, and Other Signs of Religious Life in the United States* (New York: New Press, 2009).

7 Too many mass shootings, deportations, racialized COVID-19 deaths, recorded police murders, and even disrespect of congresswomen by the forty-fifth president of the United States continue at the time of this writing to even provide a coherent, finite, or even anecdotal list.

8 Similar festivals exist in Los Angeles, Atlanta, Morocco, and other locales.

9 John Hartley, "Text," in *Communication, Cultural and Media Studies: The Key Concepts*, 4th ed. (London: Routledge, 2011), 246.

10 Jason Miccolo Johnson, *Soul Sanctuary: Images of the African American Experience* (New York: Bulfinch, 2006), preface.

11 Frank J. Lechner, "Secularization," accessed June 9, 2023, https://www.scribd.com/document/480834714/Lechner-Secularization#.

12 Conrad Ostwalt, *Secular Steeples: Popular Culture and the Religious Imagination* (Harrisburg, PA: Trinity Press International, 2003), 97.

13 Russell W. Belk, Melanie Wallendorf, and John F. Sherry Jr., "The Sacred and the Profane in Consumer Behavior: Theodicy on the Odyssey," *Journal of Consumer Research* 16, no. 1 (June 1989): 8–9.

14 Panel presentation at the National Communication Association annual conference, "Hip Hop's Spiritual Side: A Discussion of Urban God Talk: Towards Construction of a Hip Hop Spirituality," New Orleans, Louisiana, 17 November 2011. Tim Huffman's quote comes directly from his published essay with Amira de la Garza, "Rap with Soul and Pray with Flow: Youth on Hip Hop Musicality and Catholic Spirituality," in *Urban God Talk: Constructing a Hip Hop Spirituality*, edited by Andre E. Johnson (Lanham, MD: Lexington Books, 2013), 133.

15 Casselberry, *The Labor of Faith*, 165.

16 Patricia Hill Collins, "Black Public Intellectuals: From Du Bois to the Present," *Contexts* 4, no. 4 (2005).

17 Emilie M. Townes, "Washed in Grace," *Christian Century*, 29 June 2010, 30–34.

18 Luke 10:38–42.

19 Melanie Clark, "Interview with Mary Mary: Being Who They Are," *Gospelflava .com*, 2000, accessed 9 June 2023, http://www.gospelflava.com/articles/marymary2 .html.

20 Clark, "Interview with Mary Mary."

21 Erica Campbell won an additional Best Gospel Album Grammy as a solo artist for her CD *Help* in 2014.

22 Tammy L. Kernodle, "Work the Works: The Role of African-American Women in the Development of Contemporary Gospel," *Black Music Research Journal* 26, no. 1 (Spring 2006): 106.

23 Clearly, as exampled in how they judge, they believe God works powerfully. See Praise and Worship for more.

24 As a solo artist and with her producer husband, Erica and Warryn Campbell appeared as *We're the Campbells* on TV One beginning June 2018. Tara Long, Mark Herwick, Kim McCoy, and the Campbells executive-produced this series. She began hosting a morning-drive syndicated radio show *Get Up! Mornings with Erica Campbell* in 2016. Beyond winning a Grammy for *Help* in 2014, she also released her book *More Than Pretty: Doing the Soul Work That Uncovers Your True Beauty* in 2019. Tina also released a book in 2015, *I Need a Day to Pray*, recorded new music on betrayal and forgiveness with her husband Teddy, won a 2016 NAACP Image Award for her solo project *It's Personal*, and dropped a new single, "Pray for Me," in March 2024.

25 Performance studies work also helps in thinking through the connectedness of the seemingly antithetical spirituality and sexuality—examined more fully in The Message.

26 Dwight Conquergood, *Cultural Struggles: Performance, Ethnography, Praxis* (Ann Arbor: University of Michigan Press, 2013); see especially "Performance Studies: Interventions and Radical Research."

27 It reached the top ten of the chart in its forty-second week, the longest climb to the top tier in the survey's sixty-seven-year history, as cited on *Songfacts*, accessed June 9, 2023, http://www.songfacts.com/detail.php?id=13438.

28 Peter Lunt, "Liveness in Reality Television and Factual Broadcasting," *Communication Review* 7 (2004): 333.

29 See Racquel J. Gates, *Double Negative: The Black Image and Popular Culture* (Durham, NC: Duke University Press, 2018), as well as Kristen J. Warner, "They Gon' Think You Loud Regardless: Ratchetness, Reality Television, and Black Womanhood," *Camera Obscura* 30, no. 1 (2015).

30 Clark, "Interview with Mary Mary."

31 Warner, "They Gon' Think You Loud Regardless," 129–153.

32 Townes, "Washed in Grace."

33 For a thorough exploration of the ideas of ratchetness and their applicability to Black women in reality TV, again, see Warner's "They Gon' Think You Loud Regardless," and Gates, *Double Negative*, as cited above.

34 John Consoli, "WE tv, TLC and Investigation Discovery Targeting Women's Upfront Advertisers," *B&C*, 26 February 2013, accessed 26 June 2023, https://www.broadcastingcable.com/news/we-tv-tlc-and-investigation-discovery-targeting-womens-upfront-advertisers-114183.

35 Consoli, "WE tv."

36 This phrase is from the song "Whatever Makes You Happy," appearing on Fox's *Empire* television season 1 soundtrack. Singer Jennifer Hudson remarks at the end of the song, "Yaw'll done made me lose my celebrity religion." Jennifer Hudson and Juicy J, *Empire*, original soundtrack, season one (Columbia, 2015).

37 Actually, African-Americans have lived in California for much longer than this period. See Kelly Simpson, "The Great Migration: Creating a New Black Identity in Los Angeles," *PBS SoCal*, 15 February 2012, accessed 9 June 2023, https://www.pbssocal.org/history-society/the-great-migration-creating-a-new-black-identity-in-los-angeles.

38 Mentioned in the book of John, many scholars believe Magdala is the name of a town in the region of Galilee where Jesus is from and probably from where Mary's name emerges. Other scholars debate this claim. For example, religion scholar Joan E. Taylor suggests Mary's titling of Magdalene may have in fact been a nickname connected with not only general physical location but more significantly, with position in relation to Jesus. While believers know Peter as Jesus's rock, the naming of Mary may suggest her serving as his Tower. See Joan E. Taylor, "Missing Magdala and the Name of Mary 'Magdalene,'" *Palestine Exploration Quarterly* 146, no. 3 (2014): 205–223.

39 Luke 8:3 (NIV).

40 Beyond this assertion, some scholars, and apparently early priests, also believe Mary Magdalene and Mary of Bethany are the same person. I thank art historian Walter Melion for this insight.

41 Renita J. Weems, *Just a Sister Away: A Womanist Vision of Women's Relationships in the Bible* (San Diego: LuraMedia, 1988), 89–90.

42 Sojourner Truth, "Ain't I a Woman?" speech, delivered 1851, Women's Rights Convention, Old Stone Church, Akron, Ohio.

43 As noted by psychology professor Michael Cunningham during a personal conversation.

44 Blige starred in the *Power* sequel *Power Book 2: Ghost* for Starz in 2020 and was tapped to executive produce *Philly Reign* on drug queenpin Thelma Wright for USA Network as well, although the project died in development as of 2022.

45 Mary J. Blige, *A Mary Christmas*, 2013, Verve Music Group/Interscope Records.

46 Andre Harrell, "Interview: Andre Harrell Talks 'A Mary Christmas' Special with Mary J. Blige and More," interview by Max Weinstein, *Vibe*, 28 November 2013, accessed 9 June 2023, http://www.vibe.com/article/interview-andre-harrell-talks

-mary-christmas-special-mary-j-blige-and-more-o. Diddy sold his share of Revolt in 2024 amid legal allegations of abuse against him spanning thirty years.

47 Tammie M. Kennedy, "Mary Magdalene and the Politics of Public Memory: Interrogating 'The DaVinci Code,'" *Feminist Formations* 24, no. 2 (Summer 2012): 123. Kennedy writes also about the ways this notion works cinematically in other films. For example, see her "(Re)Presenting Mary Magdalene: A Feminist Reading of *The Last Temptation of Christ*," *Journal of Religion and Popular Culture* 9 (Spring 2005).

48 Treva B. Lindsey, "If You Look in My Life: Love, Hip-Hop Soul, and Contemporary African American Womanhood," *African American Review* 46, no.1 (Spring 2013): 6–7.

49 Lindsey, "If You Look in My Life," 6–7. Industry, entertainment, and popular presses have widely documented Blige's relationship issues, drug abuse, and financial woes. In addition to Lindsey's critique, see Ebony A. Utley, "'I Used to Love Him': Exploring the Miseducation about Black Love and Sex," *Critical Studies in Media Communication* 27, no. 3 (August 2010), and Daphne A. Brooks, "'All That You Can Leave Behind': Black Female Soul Singing and the Politics of Surrogation in the Age of Catastrophe," *Meridians: feminism, race, transformationalism* 8, no. 1 (2008).

50 La Marr Jurelle Bruce, "'The People Inside My Head, Too': Madness, Black Womanhood, and the Radical Performance of Lauryn Hill," *African American Review* 45, no. 3 (2012): 373.

51 Weems, *Just a Sister Away*, 94–95.

52 Lindsey, "If You Look in My Life," 7.

53 Lindsey, "If You Look in My Life," 8. Lindsey further says: "Her explicit references to the Judeo-Christian God contribute to a tradition of African American artists using religious narratives and masculine God-language in secular music."

54 Beyond success in music, Blige works as an actress, appearing in *Prison Song* (2001), *I Can Do Bad All by Myself* (2009), *Rock of Ages* (2012), *Black Nativity* (2013), as the voice of Irene in the animated *Sherlock Gnomes* (2018), *Rob Peace* (2024), and in television episodes playing herself and others. As mentioned prior, she earned an Oscar nomination for best supporting actor in *Mudbound* in 2017, as well as a nomination for best original song for the same film.

55 Blige posed in a bikini on the December 2013 cover of *Shape* magazine in recognition of her being forty-two and "sexier than ever."

56 Upper-class associations refer to the distinct and privileged European and European American sensibility around culture, education, and the arts that get paraded as normative (and aspirational) for all.

57 Brooks, "'All That You Can Leave Behind,'" 190.

58 As expressed by poet Essex Hemphill in the Marlon Riggs documentary *Black Is . . . Black Ain't* (California Newsreel, 1995).

59 Vaughn Schmutz and Alison Faupel, "Gender and Cultural Consecration in Popular Music," *Social Forces* 89, no. 2 (December 2010): 685.

60 Schmutz and Faupel, "Gender and Cultural Consecration," 704.

61 E. Patrick Johnson, "Feeling the Spirit in the Dark: Expanding Notions of the Sacred in the African-American Gay Community," *Callaloo* 21, no. 2 (Spring 1998): 415.

62 Mary J. Blige, "The Gospel According to Mary J Blige," interview by Ludovic Hunter-Tilney, *Financial Times*, 21 November 2014, accessed 9 June 2023, http://www.ft.com/cms/s/2/ffe4fddc-6f4f-11e4-8d86-00144feabdco.html.

63 For example, even though reports appeared around her 2016 separation and subsequent divorce from husband Kendu Isaacs and the financial aspects of it, the

scenario mediates differently. Blige cites "irreconcilable differences" in her divorce filing form. Apparently, he committed infidelity, but as the sole provider, the court ordered Blige to pay him spousal support of $30,000/month in 2017. The divorce finalized in June 2018. See Annie Martin, "Mary J. Blige Finalizes Divorce from Kendu Isaacs," *UPI*, accessed 26 June 2023, https://www.upi.com/Entertainment _News/Music/2018/06/21/Mary-J-Blige-finalizes-divorce-from-Kendu-Isaacs /1011529585835/.

64 Psalm 34:1.

65 Prior to that, he changed his name briefly to Snoop Lion as part of his exploration of Rastafari spiritual and religious practices.

66 Rapper Kurtis Blow (Walker) is now also a licensed minister and cofounder of Hip-Hop Church at the Greater Hood Memorial AME Zion Church in Harlem. See "Rapper Turned Minister Kurtis Blow is 50," *All Things Considered*, 9 August 2009, accessed 26 June 2023, https://www.npr.org/templates/story/story.php ?storyId=111696969809.

67 See Christian Schneider, "Kendrick Lamar and Chance the Rapper Are Right about God," *USA Today*, 30 May 2017, accessed June 9, 2023, https://www.usatoday .com/story/opinion/2017/05/30/kendrick-lamar-chance-the-rapper-right-about-god -christian-schneider-column/102160680/. This list sometimes includes Kanye West. However, West navigates many imperatives that cloud what he believes and reps.

68 The words and reading of Somali poet Warsan Shire live within Beyoncé's visual album during the interstitials of the longer version of *Lemonade*. Intimate and taut, the poems suggest a familiarity with the vagaries and cruelties of various religions' mix with hierarchical and gendered positioning.

69 Taryn Finley, "Childish Gambino Takes Home Multiple Grammy for 'This Is America' Song, Video," *Huffington Post*, 10 February 2019, accessed 9 June 2023, https://www.huffpost.com/entry/childish-gambino-wins-grammy-for-this-is -america-video_n_5c60adc7e4b0f9e1b17e8c67.

70 Childish Gambino, "This Is America," choreographed by Rwandan-British dancer Sherrie Silver, May 2018. More than 909 million YouTube users had screened the video as of March 2024. The song and music video won four Grammy Awards in 2019

71 As seen on YouTube, "#ChoirsBeLikeLIVE Dora," accessed 26 June 2023, https:// www.youtube.com/watch?v=CerBNnnlIhE.

72 See Charlie Wilson, *Tiny Desk Concert*, NPR, 5 June 2023, accessed 26 June 2023, https://www.youtube.com/watch?v=J3jUEB7qmt8.

73 For the full story, see *Billboard*'s reporting: Adelle Platon, "Watch Birdman Ask the Breakfast Club to 'Respect My Name' in Swift Sit-Down," *Billboard*, 22 April 2018, accessed 9 June 2023, https://www.billboard.com/articles/columns/hip-hop /7341706/birdman-breakfast-club-short-interview. See the clip of the actual event, https://www.youtube.com/watch?v=4jLT7GQYNhI, 22 April 2016, accessed 9 June 2023.

74 Shawnee H. reviews song. The Hamiltones, "Put Some Respeck on It," *YouTube*, 25 April 2016, accessed 9 June 2023, https://www.youtube.com/watch?v =rzTaRK9ntFE.

75 The Hamiltones with Anthony Hamilton, October 2016, accessed 9 June 2023, https://www.youtube.com/watch?v=7yU7UqXF68M.

76 These include Black religious luminaries such as Kirk Franklin with pornography, Le'Andria Johnson with children born out of wedlock, alcoholism, and questioned public behavior, and anti-gay Bishop Eddie Long being accused of sexual relations with boys.

77 Shawn M. Anglim, "Mary in Her Own Voice," sermon, 22 December 2013, from the scripture Luke 1:47–55, First Grace United Methodist Church, New Orleans, LA.

78 I thank sociology scholar Katie Acosta for sharing these insights during our Academic Learning Community at Emory University in the spring of 2018. I also thank film scholar Tess Takahashi and an anonymous reader who provided suggestions on my rehearsal of this processional.

79 Mitzi J. Smith, "A Tale of Two Sisters: Am I My Sister's Keeper?" *Journal of Religious Thought* 52, no. 2 and 53, no. 1 (Winter 1995–Spring 1996): 75.

Prayer of Confession

I thank Miriam Petty, Noliwe Rooks, VaNatta Ford, Kristen Warner, Robin Means Coleman, and two anonymous reviewers for their insights and comments along the way of writing this prayer.

1 In addition to Lubiano and hooks (cited below), see Paula Massood, *Black City Cinema: African American Urban Experiences in Film* (Philadelphia: Temple University Press, 2003); Beretta E. Smith-Shomade, "I Be Smackin' My Hoes," in *The Spike Lee Reader*, edited by Paula Massood (Philadelphia: Temple University Press, 2008); Jasmine Nichole Cobb and John L. Jackson, "Spike Lee, Documentary Filmmaking and Hollywood's Savage Slot," in *Fight the Power! The Spike Lee Reader*, edited by Janice D. Hamlet and Robin R. Means Coleman (New York: Peter Lang, 2009); and Karen M. Bowdre, "Spike and Tyler Beef: Blackness, Authenticity, and Discourse of Black Exceptionalism," in *From Madea to Media Mogul: Theorizing Tyler Perry*, edited by TreaAndrea M. Russworm, Samantha M. Sheppard, and Karen M. Bowdre (Jackson: University Press of Mississippi, 2016).

2 Wahneema Lubiano, "But Compared to What? Reading Realism, Representation, and Essentialism in *School Daze*, *Do the Right Thing*, and the Spike Lee Discourse," *Black American Literature Forum* 25, no. 2 (1991): 274.

3 bell hooks, "Whose Pussy Is This? A Feminist Comment," in *Reel to Real: Race, Sex, and Class at the Movies* (New York: Routledge, 1996), 227–235.

4 Hazel V. Carby, *Race Men* (Cambridge, MA: Harvard University Press, 2009), 4.

5 Carby, *Race Men*, 6.

6 Other examples include Smooth Blak (Charli Baltimore) of the Mau Mau decrying "Later for that ole' slave-owner Webster" in *Bamboozled* (2000), *Jungle Fever*'s 1991 film dedication to the murdered Black youth Yusef Hawkins, and actual footage from the Million Man March as part of the narrative of *Get on the Bus* (1996).

7 In a more contemporary example, his approach resembles the credence and deference given to the musings of comedians John Stewart, Stephen Colbert, and Trevor Noah in their respective television programs, even though audiences should know that as comedians, they construct fictional and comedic narratives of real-lived stories.

8 The idea of staying woke emerges in the 2010s lexicon of African-American conscious terminology. Attributed to the Black Lives Matter movement, Erykah Badu's recording "Master Teacher" (2008), Laurence Fishburne as Morpheus in *The Matrix* (1999), and experimental novelist and filmmaker William Melvin Kelley's 1962 *New York Times* article "If You're Woke You Dig It," being aware of history, consequences, and optics has become central to living Black life consciously and righteously. Cultural theorist Gloria Anzaldúa reminds us further: "Staying despierta becomes a survival tool" in "now let us shift . . . the path of conocimiento . . . inner work, public acts" in *This Bridge We Call Home: Radical*

Visions for Transformation, edited by Gloria E. Anzaldúa and Analouise Keating (New York: Routledge, 2002), 549.

9 A couple of other songs include Stevie Wonder's "Living for the City" in *Jungle Fever* and the Staple Singers' "Respect Yourself" in *Crooklyn* (1994).

10 Zeba Blay, "Interview: Investigating 'Da Sweet Blood of Jesus' w/Spike Lee + Lead Actors Zaraah Abrahams and Stephen Tyrone Williams," *Shadow and Act*, 26 June 2014, accessed 10 June 2023, https://shadowandact.com/interview -investigating-da-sweet-blood-of-jesus-w-spike-lee-lead-actors-zaraah-abrahams-and -stephen-tyrone-williams.

11 Ellen C. Scott, "Sounding Black: Cultural Identification, Sound, and the Films of Spike Lee," in *Fight the Power! The Spike Lee Reader*, edited by Janice D. Hamlet and Robin R. Means Coleman (New York: Peter Lang, 2009), 226–227.

12 Ron Neal, "Spike Lee Can Go Straight to Hell! The Cinematic and Religious Masculinity of Tyler Perry," *Black Theology: An International Journal* 14, no. 2 (September 2016): 144.

13 Mychal Denzel Smith, "'Chi-Raq' Reveals Spike Lee's Outdated Race Politics," *The Nation*, 14 December 2015, accessed 10 June 2023, https://www.thenation.com /article/archive/chi-raq-reveals-spike-lees-outdated-race-politics/.

14 Neal, "Spike Lee Can Go Straight to Hell!" 147.

15 Patricia Hill Collins, "Black Public Intellectuals: From Du Bois to the Present," *Contexts* 4, no. 4 (2005): 24.

16 Lee makes this point clear from his very first film, *Joe's Bed-Stuy Barbershop: We Cut Heads* (1983). Zechariah imagines stability and loyalty for their life in Brooklyn, while his wife Ruth envisions their lives away from Brooklyn. In trying to honor her wishes, he steals and gets caught because she reports him.

17 Lee's narrative reflects the actual shooting of singer Marvin Gaye by his father in 1984. Other examples include *He Got Game* (1998), where an argument ensues between Jake Shuttlesworth (Denzel Washington) and his wife Martha (Lonette McKee) over his treatment of their son Jesus (Ray Allen). He kills her accidentally by pushing her into a kitchen cabinet. These violent episodes consistently center a Christian subtext in Lee's work.

18 Actor Tracy Camilla Johns plays the bit role of Mother Darling in *Red Hook Summer* (2012). She is the same lead actress in Lee's breakout film *She's Gotta Have It* (1986). Lee says he wanted to show what happens to the character. Apparently after her "feminist" sex positivity, she turns to a very restrictive God.

19 As a point of clarification and pride, while Lee graduated from Morehouse, his undergraduate film training came from Clark College (Clark Atlanta University), my alma mater. In addition, Morehouse grad Rev. Dr. Raphael Warnock became the first Black senator from the state of Georgia in 2021.

20 Billie Holiday (1939) and Nina Simone (1954), artists, "Strange Fruit," written by Abel Meeropol.

21 Spike Lee, *Spike Lee: That's My Story and I'm Sticking to It, as Told to Kaleem Aftab* (New York: Norton, 2006), 233.

22 This little ditty resurfaces as Troy recalls it back home in Brooklyn. Clearly the song enters her subconscious as she sings it following her mother's funeral. Nola (DeWanda Wise) also sings it with the character Skylar (Indigo Hubbard-Salk) in the Netflix series *She's Gotta Have It* (2019).

23 bell hooks, "*Crooklyn* the Denial of Death," in *Reel to Real: Race, Sex, and Class at the Movies* (New York: Routledge, 1996), 34–46.

24 As found in *Red Hook Summer*.

25 Like Teapot in *Joe's Bed-Stuy* and X (Xavier) in *Get on the Bus*, Flik characterizes Lee's POV and uses visual media to tell stories.

26 Edward J. Blum and Paul Harvey, *The Color of Christ: The Son of God and the Saga of Race in America* (Chapel Hill: University of North Carolina Press, 2012), 22.

27 As chronicled in the biblical scriptures, Mark 15:16–20.

28 Andrew Lapin, "Spike Lee Wants You to Hate Him: In Defense of 'Red Hook Summer,'" *The Atlantic*, 29 August 2012, accessed 10 June 2023, http://www .theatlantic.com/entertainment/archive/2012/08/spike-lee-wants-you-to-hate-him -in-defense-of-red-hook-summer/261702/.

29 Manthia Diawara and Phyllis Klotman, "*Ganja and Hess*: Vampires, Sex, and Addictions," *Jump Cut: A Review of Contemporary Media* 35 (April 1990): 30–36 (originally published 1983); as found online, accessed 10 June 2023, https://www .ejumpcut.org/archive/onlinessays/JC35folder/ganja-Hess.html.

30 See Ellen C. Scott, *Cinema Civil Rights: Regulation, Repression, and Race in the Classical Hollywood Era* (New Brunswick, NJ: Rutgers University Press, 2015), 85.

31 Judith Weisenfeld, *Hollywood Be Thy Name: African American Religion in American Film, 1929–1949* (Berkeley: University of California Press, 2007), 90. Theater and media scholar Monica White Ndounou also notes it as probably the most financially successful of the so-called "race films" of the period in *Shaping the Future of African American Film: Color-Coded Economics and the Story Behind the Numbers* (New Brunswick, NJ: Rutgers University Press, 2014), 59. The figurative crossroads Lee offers in *Da Sweet Blood of Jesus* appears as a literal one in Spencer Williams's *The Blood of Jesus*. Williams positions his central protagonist at a visual and moral crossroads—her choice between hell or Zion. At the climax of *The Blood of Jesus*, Williams shows actual blood dripping from the crucifixion picture of Jesus's pierced side. The literal blood of Jesus falls onto Martha Ann Jackson (Cathryn Caviness) as she awakens from her near-death shooting. From this, she decides to follow the path to Zion. Williams's filmic evangelism points to Christ as the best way to leading a fulfilling life.

32 Filmmaker Oscar Micheaux and writer Richard Wright narratively question the Christian enterprise for Black people, and both harbor problems with preachers. See J. Ronald Green, *With a Crooked Stick: The Films of Oscar Micheaux* (Bloomington: Indiana University Press, 2004), and Christine Thomas Wells, "Attitudes toward Religion in the Fiction of Richard Wright" (master's thesis, Atlanta University, August 1971), accessed 10 June 2023, http://digitalcommons.auctr.edu /cgi/viewcontent.cgi?article=2538&context=dissertations.

33 According to the Bible, a savior comes by way of the blood (1 John 5:6). The blood of Jesus atones (Leviticus 17:11), purifies (Hebrews 9:22), sanctifies (Hebrews 13:13), and cleanses (1 John 1:7). Without the shedding of blood, there is no forgiveness (Hebrews 9:12–14). I return to the way blood moves in the Selection.

34 Blay, "Interview." Out of the 800 songs received, he selected twelve.

35 Further on this ambiguity, like the original, Lee refuses to make the film a horrific, "supernatural monstrosity." To read more on the original film, see Robin R. Means Coleman, *Horror Noire: Blacks in American Horror Films from the 1890s to Present* (New York: Routledge, 2011), and Maisha Wester, "Re-Scripting Blaxploitation Horror: Ganja and Hess and the Gothic Mode," in *B-Movie Gothic: International Perspectives*, edited by Justin D. Edwards and Johan Hoglund (Edinburgh: Edinburgh University Press, 2018), 32–49.

36 For example, both protagonists' names in *Joe's Bed-Stuy* are biblical: Ruth—the Moabite who stays with her mother-in-law when her husband dies, and

Zechariah—a priest who prophesizes about the coming of the Lord. Interestingly, when Lee appears as a character (or has a character that represents Lee the film-maker), he always gives himself a nickname: Mars, Half-Pint, Giant, Mookie, Shorty, Snuffy, Smiley, Teapot, Flik, and X.

37 Amos 5:24 (NIV): "But let justice roll on like a river, righteousness like a never-failing stream!"

38 Lee appreciates the work of Ossie Davis and wrote a letter to him in graduate school introducing himself. Spike Lee, "Spike Lee Remembers Ossie Davis, 18 December 1917–4 February 2005," *Entertainment Weekly*, 23 December 2005, accessed 10 June 2023, https://ew.com/article/2005/12/23/spike-lee-remembers-ossie-davis/.

39 Ossie Davis, "Eulogy for Malcolm X," 27 February 1965, accessed 10 June 2023, http://malcolmx.com/eulogy/.

40 Ossie Davis in Spike Lee, *Uplift the Race: The Construction of School Daze* (New York: Fireside Book, 1988), 16.

41 See TreaAndrea Russworm, Samantha Sheppard, and Karen M. Bowdre, eds., *From Madea to Media Mogul: Theorizing Tyler Perry* (Jackson: University Press of Mississippi, 2016), and forthcoming work by film scholar Miriam Petty, *How Do You Solve a Problem Like Madea?* (University of Illinois Press), on the significant impact Tyler Perry's work makes on Black communities and the Hollywood box office.

42 According to *Box Office Mojo*, *The War Room* has grossed over $73 million world-wide, accessed 26 June 2023, http://www.boxofficemojo.com/movies/?id=warroom2015.htm.

43 Interestingly, since Perry named one of his sound stages on his film lot after Lee in 2019, the beef is essentially dead.

44 "I'm Building Me a Home: The Sacred and Spatial in Black Multi-Media Texts" panel at the American Studies Association annual conference, 17 November 2016. The panel included scholars VaNatta Ford, Miriam Petty, Noliwe Rooks as chair, and me.

45 Facebook Live Stream by Pastor Sean Weaver, Charlotte, North Carolina, 23 September 2016.

46 Quote from Spike Lee in Jen Yamato, "Spike Lee Talks *Red Hook Summer*, Religion, Michael Jackson, and *Oldboy*," *Movieline*, 21 August 2012, accessed 26 June 2023, http://movieline.com/2012/08/21/spike-lee-red-hook-summer-religion-michael-jackson-oldboy/.

47 Some scholars suggest Lee approaches cinema as Bertolt Brecht approached theater. In Brecht's "epic theater," flattened characters are imbued with self-referentiality and alienation. This construction allows for the rejection of audiences' emotional identification and investment with "characters and situations, but instead draws attention to its own constructed theatricality in order to force viewers into self-reflection and critical engagement with the piece." Shelley Farmer, "In 'Chi-Raq,' What Is the Influence of Brecht and Epic Theater?" *TheTake.com*, accessed 10 June 2023, https://the-take.com/read/in-chi-raq-what-is-the-influence-of-brecht-and-epic-theater. This argument, this theoretical framing, however, belies and negates both Lee's own articulations about how he likes his work to function for audiences and the ways he incorporates African-American culture as legitimacy within his narratives. In fact, Donald Glover's FX television series *Atlanta* (2016–2022) received this same critique and mainstream enjoyment suggestion of a Brechtian narrative construction existing for the characters or audiences who watch them. Again, however, it seems to me, this interpretation of Glover's (and Lee's) work belies the realities of living while Black.

48 Dialogue from the Netflix version of *She's Gotta Have It*.
49 However, writer Jagger Blaec suggests about this version: "The Nola Darling of 2017 is a self-described 'sex-positive, polyamorous pansexual' woman. It's progressive, but still feels restrictive of a fluid sexual experience. There always seems to be a need to categorize what [B]lack femmes are doing in their sex lives instead of allowing us our own agency." Jagger Blaec, "There's Nothing Wrong with Being a 'Hoe': How Some Black Women Are Reclaiming Their Sexuality," *thelily.com*, 4 December 2017, accessed 10 June 2023, https://www.thelily.com/theres-nothing-wrong-with-being-a -hoe-how-some-black-women-are-reclaiming-their-sexuality/.

Testimony

1 Neil Gross and Solon Simons, "How Religious Are America's College and University Professors?" *Social Science Research Center*, 6 February 2007, accessed 13 June 2023, http://religion.ssrc.org/reforum/Gross_Simmons.pdf.
2 Erykah Badu and Jaborn Jamal, "On and On," producers Madukwu Chinwah and Erykah Badu, 1996, Kedar/Universal/MCA Records.
3 Kirsten T. Edwards and Denise Taliaferro Baszile, "Scholarly Rearing in Three Acts: Black Women's Testimonial Scholarship and the Cultivation of Radical Black Female Inter-Subjectivity," *Knowledge Cultures* 4, no. 1 (2016): 86.
4 Steven Halliday, "Bakhtin and Foucault Go Pentecostal: How the Rhetoric of Prophetic Utterances Redistributes Power Dialogically," paper presented at the National Communication Association 96th Annual Convention, San Francisco, CA, 16 November 2010.
5 As found in Brian Hiatt, "The Second Coming of D'Angelo," *Rolling Stone*, July 2015. See The Message for more on him.
6 Miriam Petty, "Testifying in the Dark: Tyler Perry and the Problem of Genre," paper presented at the Society of Cinema and Media Studies Annual Conference, Boston, MA, 25 March 2012.
7 Edwards and Baszile, "Scholarly Rearing in Three Acts," 88.
8 Mitzi J. Smith, "A Tale of Two Sisters: Am I My Sister's Keeper?" *Journal of Religious Thought* 2, no. 1 (Winter 1995–Spring 1996): 75.
9 For example, Yeezus's (Kanye West) Sunday Service started in 2019, offering an opportunity to conflate popular culture with religious and spirituality with no strings attached. It provided limited shared understanding of meaning beyond the visceral musical and celebrity feel good of it all. For more on this, see Marta Djordjevic, "The Untold Truth of Kanye West's Sunday Church Service," *Nicki-Swift.com*, 21 February 2023, accessed 13 June 2023, https://www.nickiswift.com /160173/the-untold-truth-of-kanye-wests-sunday-church-services/, https://www .foxnews.com/entertainment/kanye-west-jesus-christian-kardashian-sunday -service, or "Kim Kardashian West on Kanye Sunday Service, Health, Grief," *The View*, 13 September 2019, accessed 13 June 2023, https://www.youtube.com/watch?v =2orVaJWtooM.
10 KevOnStage, "This Is Why We Don't Do Testimony Service No More," 2 January 2018, accessed 13 June 2023, https://www.youtube.com/watch?v =BEWiWiSiAkM.
11 *Bobby Jones Gospel*, 4 November 2015, accessed 13 June 2023, https://www.youtube .com/watch?v=y1L3k9_q1S8.
12 bell hooks, *Teaching to Transgress: Education as the Practice of Freedom* (New York: Routledge, 1994), 174.

13 Trinh T. Minh-ha with Fukuko Kobayashi, "Is Feminism Dead?" in *The Digital Film Event* (New York: Routledge, 2005), 168.
14 Petty, "Testifying in the Dark."
15 Lecrae, "Church Clothes," 10 May 2012, accessed 13 June 2023, https://www.youtube.com/watch?v=tlWvxowdySk.
16 Kirsten T. Edwards, "College Teaching on Sacred Ground: Judeo-Christian Influences on Black Women Faculty Pedagogy," *Race Ethnicity and Education* 20, no. 1 (2015).
17 Edwards and Baszile, "Scholarly Rearing in Three Acts," 95.
18 Ruth Forman, "I Will Speak Genius to Myself," in *We Are the Young Magicians* (New York: Beacon, 1993), 48.
19 Edwards and Baszile, "Scholarly Rearings in Three Acts," 85.
20 Prajna Parasher, "Specters and Images: *When the Levees Broke—A Requiem in Four Acts*," *International Journal of Applied Psychoanalytic Studies* 8, no. 2 (2011): 169.
21 Edwards and Baszile, "Scholarly Rearings in Three Acts," 87.
22 Thomas Hoyt Jr., "Testimony," in *Practicing Our Faith: A Way of Life for a Searching People*, edited by Dorothy C. Bass (Minneapolis: Fortress Press, 2019), 100.

Praise and Worship

I give thanks to scholars Nghana Lewis, Katie Acosta, Rebecca Chaisson, Kristen Warner, and Miriam Petty for their valuable critiques and insights in thinking through this praise and worship. As well, I thank Elana Levine and two anonymous reviewers for their help in sharpening my insights and making them more accessible to those unfamiliar with the terrain in an earlier published version, as found in *Cupcakes, Pinterest, and Lady Porn: Feminized Popular Culture in the Early Twenty-First Century* (Champaign: University of Illinois Press, 2015), 157–174.

1 Pentecostalism forms a part of several Christian denominations that, among many things, calls for an expressive recognition of God's work in the lives of its believers and their relationship with Him. This relationship is evidenced through speaking in tongues, baptism by the Holy Spirit, prophecy, and healing. The term Bapticostal suggests the blending of Black Baptist and Black Pentecostal traditions. These expressions are what the Black women scholars discuss more fully during the Testimony.
2 For example, Psalm 150:1–6 says: "Praise the Lord! Praise God in his sanctuary; praise him in his mighty heavens! Praise him for his mighty deeds; praise him according to his excellent greatness! Praise him with trumpet sound; praise him with lute and harp! Praise him with tambourine and dance; praise him with strings and pipe! Praise him with sounding symbols; praise him with loud clashing symbols! Let everything that has breath praise the Lord! Praise the Lord!" (English Standard Version). In the New Testament, Luke writes in Acts 4:31–32: "And they were all filled with the Holy Spirit and spoke the word of God boldly. All the believers were one in heart and mind" (New International Version).
3 Louis Hoffman, "An Existential-Phenomenological Approach to the Psychology of Religion," *Pastoral Psychology* 61 (2012): 791.
4 "739 The Nicene Creed," in *The Methodist Hymnal: Official Hymnal of the Methodist Church* (Nashville: Methodist Publishing House, 1966).
5 "740 A Modern Affirmation," in *The Methodist Hymnal: Official Hymnal of the Methodist Church* (Nashville: Methodist Publishing House, 1966).

6 Glenn Hinson, *Fire in My Bones: Transcendence and the Holy Spirit in African American Gospel* (Philadelphia: University of Pennsylvania Press, 2000), 2.
7 Giuseppina Addo, "Join the Holy Spirit on Zoom: African Pentecostal Churches and Their Liturgical Practices During COVID-19," *Approaching Religion* 11, no. 2 (2021): 45–61.
8 "Wayne Francis—Praise Break Medley," *YouTube*, 2008, accessed 15 June 2023, https://www.youtube.com/watch?v=mU6ICsj7SSQ.
9 For example, when the 2013 Full Gospel's Generals of Faith called for "movers and shakers of the kingdom" to revitalize the Black church, this call excluded women. See Hazel Cherry, "Black Church Leadership Gathering Excludes Women," 12 December 2013, accessed 14 June 2023, https://religiondispatches.org/black-church-leadership-gathering-excludes-women/. And in another religious body, ten years later, the Southern Baptists ratified their expulsion of several churches with female pastors at their annual convention, June 2023.
10 See DeBerry's rendition of "I Shall Wear a Crown" on YouTube for the First Church of God, Columbus, Ohio, with 9.2 million views, 10 January 2019, accessed 24 March 2024, https://www.youtube.com/watch?v=liASWXrjKt4&list=FLzyVZwDi8ISUXYU2U3FNpFA&index=15.
11 See Teshome Gabriel, "The Gift of Poetics: By Way of a Preface beyond Axum," *Emergences* 10, no. 1 (2000): 5–7; "The Intolerable Gift," in *Home, Exile, Homeland: Film, Media and the Politics of Place*, edited by Hamid Naficy (New York: Routledge, 1998), 75–84; and "Ruin and the Other: Towards a Language of Memory," in *Otherness and the Media: The Ethnography of the Imagined and the Imaged*, edited by Hamid Naficy and Teshome H. Gabriel (Langhorne, PA: Harwood Academic Publishers, 1993), 211–220. Gabriel forces readers to embody their work, to consciously place themselves at the center of their critical interests, and to move out from that space. He asks readers/writers/thinkers to take up elements and institutions of their own lives to discover what a theoretical application may be within or outside of the subject.
12 Hoffman, "An Existential-Phenomenological, 785.
13 Vivian Sobchack, *The Address of the Eye: A Phenomenology of Film Experience* (Princeton, NJ: Princeton University Press, 1992), 4–5.
14 Elizabeth Stephens, "Sensation Machine: Film, Phenomenology and the Training of the Senses," *Continuum: Journal of Media and Cultural Studies* 26, no. 4 (August 2012): 529.
15 Michele White, "Networked Bodies and Extended Corporealities: Theorizing the Relationship between the Body, Embodiment, and Contemporary New Media," *Feminist Studies* 35, no. 3 (Fall 2009): 619–620.
16 Phillip J. Hutchison, "Mister Rogers' Holy Ground: Exploring the Media Phenomenology of the Neighborhood and Its Rituals," *Journal of Media and Religion* 20, no. 2 (2021): 67.
17 As found in the *Stanford Encyclopedia of Philosophy*. The entry cited Mircea Eliade, *Patterns in Comparative Religion* (London: Sheed and Ward, 1958).
18 Christian Smith, "Why Christianity Works: An Emotions-Focused Phenomenological Account," *Sociology of Religion* 68, no 2 (2007): 174.
19 Harald Stadler, "Film as Experience: Phenomenological Concepts in Cinema and Television Studies," *Quarterly Review of Film and Video* 12, no 3 (1990): 44. Don Ihde, *Experimental Phenomenology: An Introduction* (Albany: State University of New York Press, 1986), 29–54, offers a similar outline of steps.

20 *Sunday Best* consistently ranks number one for its day and time in African-American households. The series ran initially from 2007 to 2015 and returned in 2019. For more on BET and its pantheon of programs targeting Black audiences, including religious ones, see my *Pimpin' Ain't Easy: Selling Black Entertainment Television* (New York: Routledge, 2007).

21 To learn more about Mary Mary in particular, return to the Processional. In this example and there, you get a fuller of picture of why Tina Campbell is so well considered.

22 To view Johnson's performance, go to Daily Motion, accessed 14 June 2023, https://www.dailymotion.com/video/x2m1on5.

23 Joshua Lawrence Lazard, "This Is Why Folks Don't Take Church Seriously Pt. II: The Shout or Praise Breaks," *Uppity Negro Network* blog, 25 May 2009, accessed 14 June 2023, https://uppitynegronetwork.com/2009/05/25/this-is-why-folks-dont-take-church-seriously-pt-ii-the-shout-or-praise-breaks/.

24 Gregory Currie, "Visual Fictions," *Philosophical Quarterly* 41 (April 1991): 143.

25 This happens, in some measure, in the same way supporters and audiences take up Mary J. Blige, as discussed in the Processional, though not necessarily in the Holy Ghost sense.

26 The Brooklyn Tabernacle Choir won a Grammy Award for the 2000 CD *Live—God Is Working*, which includes this song.

27 Quote from Kelly Price, *Celebration of Gospel*, BET, 28 January 2007.

28 Several recognizable audience members appear on screen, including actor Loretta Devine, singer Aretha Franklin, and producer/actor/writer Tyler Perry. This matters to the telecast because it not only demonstrates and exploits other artists in attendance but, more importantly to this work, it validates the connection of potential Holy Ghost spirit moving as a part of these celebrities' brands as Christians.

29 To view Price's performance, go to YouTube, https://www.youtube.com/watch?v=UUlPVtBFo8I&list=RDNQhpcoXdzlo&index=3, accessed 15 June 2023.

30 This comes from Matthew 18:20. Scholars argue this verse actually references ideas of accountability and belief. However, it is commonplace in many Christian communities to invoke it as a testament to corporate prayer.

31 Hinson, *Fire in My Bones*, 15.

32 Tina Campbell, as taken from *Sunday Best*, season three, original airdate June 2010, viewed on YouTube, 1 November 2012. It can be screened now on Daily Motion, accessed 14 June 2023, https://www.dailymotion.com/video/x2m1on5.

33 "Phenomenology of Religion," in *Stanford Encyclopedia of Philosophy*, edited by Edward N. Zalta, 1 October 2008, revised 2 November 2022, accessed June 14, 2023, http://plato.stanford.edu/entries/phenomenology-religion/

34 Carol J. Clover, *Men, Women, and Chainsaws* (Princeton, NJ: Princeton University Press, 1992), 74.

35 Babatunde Lawal, "The Use of Visual Metaphors for Mass Communication," public talk, University of Arizona, 26 January 2002.

36 Hinson, *Fire in My Bones*, 19–20.

37 Rebecca Chaisson, personal correspondence, 25 October 2012.

38 Facebook dialogue, 6 September 2012.

39 These are figures as of 21 December 2013. They continue to rise.

40 As found on YouTube comments of the video, posted in 2012, accessed 21 December 2013, https://www.youtube.com/all_comments?v=eZoZ90GqBXM&page=1. Viacom removed this content sometime before 1 October 2019. However, the

content can be found at https://www.dailymotion.com/video/x2m1on5 as of
14 June 2023.
41 As found on YouTube comments of the video, posted March 2013, accessed
21 December 2013, https://www.youtube.com/watch?v=jVKarYVYoIM&lc
=vKHSg4Ixm8GpMmUZneEAb6NVAiaWS4JbYKhV6rtiUx4. This video is no
longer available here as of 20 May 2021. However, the performance can be found at
https://www.youtube.com/watch?v=NQhpcoXdzlo, accessed 14 June 2023.
42 Rebecca Chaisson offers this assessment so beautifully.
43 "Phenomenology of Religion."
44 Anonymous reviewer comments from the original version of this writing.
45 Nghana Lewis, personal conversation, 26 October 2012.
46 Carlyle Fielding Stewart III, *Black Spirituality and Black Consciousness: Soul Force,
Culture and Freedom in the African-American Experience* (Trenton, NJ: Africa
World Press, 1998), 1.
47 Clearly, warped mediated conceptions of these experiences can come through
spiritualized bodies, especially as demonstrated by white, Western eyes. I address
this within the Selection.

Tithes and Offering

Thanksgiving to my former Emory University research assistants Jumonke (Jumi)
Ekunseitan and Caitlin Sweet for their help with research, transcription, and coordi-
nation of this offering. I thank the many ministers and minster-scholars who talked
church with me and about Black church specifically in the digital (and pandemic) age,
including Rev. Dr. Anthony Bennett (Mt. Aery Baptist Church, Bridgeport, CT),
Pastor Shawn Anglim (First Grace UMC, New Orleans), Rev. Dr. Dominique
Robinson, Pastor Olu Brown (founder, Impact Church, Atlanta), Rev. Dr. De'Edra
Lewis Johnson (Nashville, TN), music minister/scholar/novelist Dr. Daniel Black
(Atlanta), and Rev. Dr. Khalia Williams (assistant dean, Candler School of Theology,
Atlanta). I also appreciate the participants of the Faculty Forum roundtable
convened by the Fox Center for Humanistic Inquiry in January 2020, for their
insights, including Drs. Dianne Stewart, Deboleena Roy, Courtney Baker, Todd
Cronan, Rev. Dr. HyeMin Na, Prof. Dehanza Rogers, Ms. Allyson Smith, and
Mr. Ricks Carson.

1. Bishop William Murphy, senior pastor, dreamCenter Church of Atlanta, Decatur,
GA, 12 March 2017, https://www.facebook.com/dReamcenteratl/videos
/1339006996157785/.
2 White People Time, as James Evans (John Amos) shouts in the episode "Florida's
Problem" on *Maude*, CBS, season 1, episode 18, 13 February 1973.
3 Geometry defines an affine transformation as a function between affine spaces that
preserves points, straight lines, and planes. Sets of parallel lines remain parallel after
an affine transformation.
4 Marlin D. Harris, "Meet Me at the Corner," sermon, New Life Church, Decatur,
GA, 16 September 2018.
5 And as scholar/elder Erika D. Gault argues in her *Networking the Black Church:
Digital Black Christians and Hip Hop* (New York: NYU Press, 2022), for Black
millennials, with so little research done on them, identifying "persons of African
descent with common experiences with regard to religion and digital media
technology" might be the best way to consider the generation (51).

6 See Denis J. Bekkering, "From 'Televangelist' to 'Intervangelist': The Emergence of the Streaming Video Preacher," *Journal of Religion and Popular Culture* 23, no. 2 (July 2011).

7 Erika D. Gault, *Networking the Black Church: Digital Black Christians and Hip Hop* (New York: NYU Press, 2022), 68.

8 Benjamin Barber, "Jihad vs. McWorld," *Atlantic Monthly*, March 1992, 53–65, as found in *Religion and Foreign Affairs: Essential Readings*, edited by Dennis R. Hoover and Douglas M. Johnston (Waco, TX: Baylor University Press, 2012), 311.

9 Givelify, "About," accessed 16 June 2023, https://www.givelify.com/about/.

10 This is similar to colleges and universities' limited thought and problematic employment of business models for education.

11 Warren Bird, "World's First Megachurch?" *Leadership Network*, 4 May 2012, accessed 16 June 2023, http://leadnet.org/worlds_first_megachurch/.

12 Tilton lays claim as the first television preacher to follow up "saturation television exposure, (as he aired in all 235 American TV markets) with a massive and sophisticated direct-mail operation." Stephen Bender, "Oh God, You Devil," *salon.com*, 22 November 2000, accessed 16 June 2023, https://www.salon.com/2000/11/21/tilton/.

13 See Jessica Johnson, *Biblical Porn: Affect, Labor, and Pastor Mark Driscoll's Evangelical Empire* (Durham, NC: Duke University Press, 2018).

14 Shayne Lee, *America's New Preacher: T. D. Jakes* (New York: NYU Press, 2005), 182. International megachurches actually have the highest-paid ministers of God and largest congregations. They exist in Nigeria and South Korea.

15 See her digital footprint at Instagram, @sarahjakesroberts, accessed 25 March 2024.

16 Marlin Harris, "1 Corinthians 13: A Portrait of Biblical Love," sermon, New Life Church, Decatur, GA, 7 October 2018.

17 Mara Einstein, "The Evolution of Religious Branding," *Social Compass* 58, no. 3 (2011): 332.

18 Einstein, "The Evolution of Religious Branding," 334.

19 Sheron C. Patterson, "Fishing with Flavor: Untraditional Evangelism in the African American Church," in *Growing the African American Church*, edited by Carlyle Fielding Stewart III (Nashville: Abingdon Press, 2006), 28.

20 Harvey Cox, "The Market as God: Living in the New Dispensation," *Atlantic Monthly*, March 1999, 20.

21 Abundant Life Cathedral, Houston, TX, 2 September 2001.

22 Carlyle Fielding Stewart III, "Introduction," in *Growing the African American Church* (Nashville: Abingdon Press, 2006), xii.

23 Bruce Wrenn, "Religious Marketing Is Different," *Services Marketing Quarterly* 32, no. 1 (2010): 46–47.

24 Bolashade Olaoluwa Hanson, "Branding Faith: Do Christian Ministries Reach Millennials with Branding?" (master's thesis, Liberty University School of Communication and Creative Arts, April 2016), 14.

25 For more on ways AI might be taken up, see Mark Harris, "Inside the First Church of Artificial Intelligence," *Wired*, 15 November 2017, accessed 17 June 2023, https://www.wired.com/story/anthony-levandowski-artificial-intelligence-religion/.

26 "Something New Under the Sun," *Off Our Backs* 24, no. 4 (April 1994): 15.

27 HyeMin Na, workshop, "The Church in a Digital Age," Bandy Preaching Conference, Emory University, 24 March 2017.

28 Olu Brown, the Impact Lead Team, and Christine Shinn Latona, *Zero to 80: Innovative Ideas for Planting and Accelerating Church Growth* (Atlanta: Impact Press, 2010), 153–154.

29 Rev. Dr. Anthony Bennett, conversation with author, 21 May 2021.

30 Aaron Earls, "Churches Are Open but Still Recovering from Pandemic Attendance Losses," *Lifeway Research*, 8 November 2022, accessed 17 June 2023, https://research .lifeway.com/2022/11/08/churches-are-open-but-still-recovering-from-pandemic -attendance-losses/.

31 Michelle Faverio, Justin Nortey, Jeff Diamant, and Gregory A. Smith, "Online Religious Services Appeal to Many Americans, but Going in Person Remains More Popular," *Pew Research Center*, 2 June 2023, accessed 17 June 2023, https://www .pewresearch.org/religion/2023/06/02/online-religious-services-appeal-to-many -americans-but-going-in-person-remains-more-popular/?utm_source =Pew+Research+Center&utm_campaign=54b3fd90d4-Weekly_6-3-23&utm _medium=email&utm_term=0_-54b3fd90d4-%5BLIST_EMAIL_ID%5D.

32 Yeon-soo Kwak, "Yoido Full Gospel Church to Celebrate 65th Anniversary," *Korea Times*, 19 May 2023, accessed 17 June 2023, https://www.koreatimes.co.kr/www /culture/2023/05/135_351219.html?fbclid=IwAR2lwVtuHGTvBwLsj0Y8zynaqKA emgmegoGq81MRMOVz717bGbtFAqz51LI.

33 See report by Lucky Severson, "World's Largest Congregation," *Religion & Ethics Newsweekly*, 10 August 2012, accessed 16 June 2023, http://www.pbs.org/wnet /religionandethics/2012/08/10/august-10-2012-worlds-biggest-congregation/10162/.

34 Rev. Dr. Anthony Bennett, conversation with author, 21 May 2021.

35 David P. King, "Millennials, Faith and Philanthropy: Who Will Be Transformed?" *Bride/Work* 1, no. 2 (2016).

36 Joy K. Challenger, "Infused: Millennials and the Future of the Black Church" (doctoral dissertation, Divinity School of Duke University, 2016), 83.

37 Daniel Cox, "College Professors Aren't Killing Religion: But College Degrees Certainly Aren't Helping," *FiveThirtyEight*, 10 October 2017, accessed 16 June 2023, https://fivethirtyeight.com/features/college-professors-arent-killing-religion/.

38 "In U.S., Decline of Christianity Continues at Rapid Pace: An Update on America's Changing Religious Landscape," *Pew Research Center*, 17 October 2019.

39 "An Epidemic? Why Millennials Are Abandoning the Church," 15 January 2019, accessed 26 June 2023, https://www1.cbn.com/cbnnews/us/2019/january/an -epidemic-why-millennials-are-abandoning-the-church; "Religion Declining in Importance for Many Americans, Especially for Millennials," *Religion News*, 10 December 2018, accessed 26 June 2023, https://religionnews.com/2018/12/10 /religion-declining-in-importance-for-many-americans-especially-for-millennials/; "Why Millennials Are Really Leaving Religion (It's Not Just Politics, Folks)," *Religion & Ethics Newsweekly*, 16 July 2018, accessed 26 June 2023, https://www.pbs .org/wnet/religionandethics/2018/07/16/millennials-really-leaving-religion-not-just -politics-folks/34880/; "Religion among the Millennials," *Pew Research Center*, 17 February 2010, accessed 26 June 2023, https://www.pewforum.org/2010/02/17 /religion-among-the-millennials/.

40 See Erin Griffith, "Why Are Young People Pretending to Love Work?" *New York Times*, 26 January 2019, accessed 26 June 2023, https://www.nytimes.com/2019/01 /26/business/against-hustle-culture-rise-and-grind-tgim.html.

41 Tyree Boyd-Pates, "Why Black Millennials Are Hopping from Church-to-Church," *Huffington Post*, 12 April 2016, accessed 16 June 2023, https://www.huffpost.com /entry/this-is-why-black-millenn_b_9640358.

42 Boyd-Pates, "Why Black Millennials Are Hopping from Church-to-Church."

43 See Emmett G. Price III, ed., *The Black Church and Hip Hop Culture: Toward Bridging the Generational Divide* (Lanham, MD: Scarecrow Press, 2012).

44 Price, *The Black Church and Hip Hop Culture*, xvi.

45 Hanson, "Branding Faith," 10.

46 Hanson, "Branding Faith," 61–62.

47 Challenger, "Infused," 124.

48 Eric Thomas, "How to Make Millennials Hate You, the Pepsi Way," *LinkedIn*, 5 April 2017, accessed 16 June 2023, https://www.linkedin.com/pulse/how-make -millennials-hate-you-pepsi-way-eric-thomas. In my 2020 roundtable discussion, art historian Todd Cronan remembered not wanting to be pandered to during service as well, and he's a Generation Xer.

49 Jeaney Yip and Susan Ainsworth, "'Whatever Works': The Marketplace Mission of Singapore's City Harvest Church," *Journal of Macromarketing* 36, no. 4 (2016): 447.

50 Challenger, "Infused," 69.

51 Rev. Dr. Anthony Bennett, senior pastor, Mt. Ary Baptist Church, Bridgeport, CT, conversation with author, 14 March 2017.

52 Challenger, "Infused," 3.

53 Challenger, "Infused," italics mine.

54 Melva Wilson Costen, *African American Christian Worship*, updated ed. (Nashville: Abingdon Press, 2007), 79.

55 Costen, *African American Christian Worship*, 1.

56 Nicholas Buxton, "Seeing the Self as Other: Televising Religious Experience," in *Exploring Religion and the Sacred in a Media Age*, edited by Christopher Deacy and Elisabeth Arweek (London: Ashgate, 2009), 165. See also Paul Heelas and Linda Woodhead, *The Spirituality Revolution: Why Religion Is Giving Way to Spirituality* (London: SCM Press, 2005), 13–14.

57 Howard Thurman, *The Creative Encounter* (Richmond, IN: Friends United Press, 1972).

58 As found in *BU Today*, accessed 16 June 2023, http://www.bu.edu/articles/2011 /who-was-howard-thurman/.

59 This insight is given sharp relief through my attending the Maximizing Your Ministry Conference at Atlanta's House of Hope, Atlanta, GA, October 2019.

60 Cornerstone Knowledge Network is a company that "develops and disseminates meaningful knowledge that radically improves how facilities impact ministry." As of March 2024, their business seems to have closed.

61 Barna Research Group, "Designing Worship Spaces with Millennials in Mind," *Barna Group*, 5 November 2014, accessed 16 June 2023, https://www.barna.com /research/designing-worship-spaces-with-millennials-in-mind/.

62 *Outreach Magazine* tracks the one hundred fastest-growing Protestant churches with more than 1,000 people in average attendance yearly. Impact Church appears on their 2016 list. But by 2022, the church is no longer climbing there (or at least, not participating in the survey).

63 Olu Brown, pastor, Impact Church, conversation with author, Atlanta, GA, 10 May 2017.

64 Brown, conversation with author.

65 As I stated earlier, I've had the pleasure to worship in many, many churches around the country of different size, denomination, and orientation. Thus, the questions I pose are not necessarily only for millennials.

66 Khalia Williams, Emory University, conversation with author, 23 January 2020.

67 Audre Lorde, "The Master's Tools Will Never Dismantle the Master's House," in *Sister Outsider: Essays and Speeches* (Berkeley, CA: Crossing Press, 1984), 110–114.

68 Jeremiah A. Wright Jr., "Growing the African American Church through Worship and Preaching," in *Growing the African American Church*, edited by Carlyle Fielding Stewart III (Nashville: Abingdon Press, 2006), 63–81.

69 Wright, "Growing the African American Church," 73.

70 Challenger, "Infused," 168.

71 If, for example, I take my own first ten YouTube favorites list in 2020, two are gospel songs—one old school, "I Won't Complain," and one new school, Erica Campbell's "Help"; three are R&B oldies, Natalie Cole's "This Will Be," Aretha Franklin's "Dr. Feelgood," and Teddy Pendergrass's "Only You"; one old-school hip-hop, DJ Kool, "Let Me Clear My Throat"; and two newer hip-hop tunes, Ciara's "Gimme That" and Jaguar Wright's "The What Ifs." They are rounded out with Sweet Honey in the Rock's "Dream Variations" and a speech against racism given by Valarie Kaur. This music, this talking, and this healing exist for me as Black soul music.

72 Jerma A. Jackson, *Singing in My Soul: Black Gospel Music in a Secular Age* (Chapel Hill: University of North Carolina Press, 2004), 64.

73 Tammy L. Kernodle, "Work the Works: The Role of African-American Women in the Development of Contemporary Gospel," *Black Music Research Journal* 26, no. 1 (Spring 2006): 98.

74 Religiosity has always been a part of hip-hop, rocking most brazenly with followers of Islam in its various branches, but also with African traditional spiritualities and Christianity. For a brief introduction to the genre, see Josef Sorett, "Beats, Rhymes and Bibles: An Introduction to Gospel Hip Hop," in *The Black Church and Hip Hop Culture: Toward Bridging the Generational Divide*, edited by Emmett G. Price III (Lanham, MD: Scarecrow Press, 2012), 107–113.

75 Patricia Hill Collins, "Black Public Intellectuals: From Du Bois to the Present," *Contexts* 4, no. 4 (2005): 24.

76 Daniel Black (music minister and author), in conversation with the author, 11 December 2019.

77 Even though the Black artist Mandisa flourishes in this area of Christian music, not many others have as of this writing. She was found dead in her Tennessee home in April 2024.

78 Omotayo O. Banjo and Kesha Morant Williams, "A House Divided? Christian Music in Black and White," *Journal of Media and Religion* 10, no. 3 (2011): 115–137.

79 This phenomenon is not confined to the United States. For example, the sanitized, emotionless worship and songs sung and arranged away from gospel to a very Europeanized rhythm in Nigerian churches point to a place far beyond the continent—places connected with modernity and promise. The music is accompanied by the persistent image of a white Jesus in churches and on church promotions. Beyond the pictures and sound, the whole ambience of Anglo-styled praise—perpetuated by many denominations—dominates the style of praise in many African church services, with a bit of talking drum thrown in for good measure.

80 This corporate inclination gets expressed clearly during new children's church. The booming business of children's church instruction comes through the supply of prepackaged children's curriculum (content that includes music and lyrics, video, and sometimes printed literature). Forefronted by white megachurches, the corporate model for conducting Christian services for K–12 children is a million-dollar industry.

81 See it on YouTube or DailyMotion for the example: https://www.youtube.com /watch?v=mU6ICsj7SSQ, https://www.dailymotion.com/video/x32b96e, both accessed 16 June 2023.

82 Costen, *African American Christian Worship*, 6.
83 This references Beyoncé's hit "Church Girl," *Renaissance* (2022), which samples the Clark Sisters song "Center Thy Will," *You Brought the Sunshine* (1981).
84 Quentin Schultze, *Televangelism and American Culture: The Business of Popular Religion* (Eugene, OR: Wipf and Stock, 2003), 220.
85 Dominique Robinson, conversation with the author, Atlanta, GA, April 21, 2017.
86 Robinson, conversation with the author.
87 Challenger, "Infused," 180.
88 Stewart, "Introduction," xiii.
89 Brown et al., *Zero to 80*, 169.
90 Workshop, "The Church in a Digital Age," Bandy Preaching Conference, Emory University, 24 March 2017. I thank the sistah-youth minister for making this critical point.
91 Steven Halliday, abstract for paper presented at the annual meeting of the National Communication Association, San Francisco, CA, 16 November 2010.
92 See "Abandoning the Church," *CBN News*, 16 June 2023, https://www1.cbn.com /cbnnews/us/2019/january/an-epidemic-why-millennials-are-abandoning-the -church.
93 Kimberli Lira, "Why the Church Doesn't Need Any More Coffee Bars," *For Every Mom*, 13 March 2017, accessed 16 June 2023, https://foreverymom.com/faith/why -the-church-doesnt-need-any-more-coffee-bars-kimberli-lira/.
94 Monique Moultrie, Q&A from her Zoom talk, "Leading from the Margins: Authenticity, Authority, and Black Women's Sexual Agency," Emory University, 5 October 2020.
95 As found in Kristal Brent Zook, "Can the Black Church Return After Covid?" *The Root*, 7 February 2023, accessed 18 July 2023, https://www.theroot.com/soul -survivors-covid-19-and-the-black-church-1849678515.
96 Ponce Turner, YouTube comments, 17 October 2016, accessed 16 June 2023, https://www.youtube.com/watch?v=AQPNUiWp3rE.
97 I thank public health scholar Rebecca Atkinson for giving me this good insight.
98 Shawn Anglim, pastor, First Grace United Methodist Church, conversation with the author, New Orleans, LA, 28 March 2017.
99 Rev. Julian DeShazier, sermon, 17 January 2021, Facebook Live online.

Passing of the Peace

An earlier version of this section appeared as "Don't Play with God! Black Church, Play, and Possibilities," *Souls: A Critical Journal of Black Politics, Culture, and Society* 18, nos. 2–4 (2016): 321–337.

1 See Marlon Riggs's film *Black Is . . . Black Ain't* (California Newsreel, 1995).
2 Evelyn Brooks Higginbotham, *Righteous Discontent: The Women's Movement in the Black Baptist Church 1880–1920* (Cambridge, MA: Harvard University Press, 1994), 5.
3 William B. McClain, "The Genius of Black Church," *Christianity and Crisis* 2, no. 16 (November 1970): 251.
4 Kelly Brown Douglas, *Black Bodies and the Black Church: A Blues Slant* (New York: Palgrave Macmillan, 2012), 64.
5 See, for example, Peter Berger and Harvey Cox, *The Feast of Fools: A Theological Essay on Festivity and Fantasy* (Cambridge, MA: Harvard University Press, 1969),

and M. Conrad Hyers, *Holy Laughter: Essays on Religion in the Comic Perspective* (New York: Seabury Press, 1969).

6 See, for example, Mikhal Bakhtin, *The Dialogic Imagination* (Austin: University of Texas Press, 1994 [1981]), and Samuel Joeckel, "Funny as Hell: Christianity and Humor Reconsidered," *Humor* 21, no. 4 (2008): 415–433.

7 In fact, in a somewhat unrelated way but germane to this point, the usage of Christianity and the insanity of the slaver/raper/owner who also takes on the role of pastor presents one of the most fascinating and painful aspects of the film *12 Years a Slave* (McQueen, 2013). Or in a nonfictionalized example, U.S. Attorney General Jeff Sessions used the Bible's Romans 13 as justification for separating immigrant children from their parents in June 2018. See Kyle Swenson, "Sessions Says the Bible Justifies Separating Immigrant Families. The Verses He Cited Are Infamous," *Washington Post*, 15 June 2018, accessed 19 June 2023, https://www.washingtonpost .com/news/morning-mix/wp/2018/06/15/sessions-says-the-bible-justifies-separating -immigrant-families-the-verses-he-cited-are-infamous/?utm_term=.e5f137db9935.

8 Joeckel, "Funny as Hell."

9 Conrad Hyers, *The Comic Vision and The Christian Faith: A Celebration of Life* (New York: Pilgrims Press, 1981), 150.

10 Joeckel, "Funny as Hell," 424.

11 Joeckel, "Funny as Hell," 425.

12 Aaron Trammell, *Repairing Play: A Black Phenomenology* (Cambridge, MA: MIT Press, 2023): 53.

13 As found in Anna Everett, *Returning the Gaze: A Genealogy of Black Film Criticism, 1909–1949* (Durham, NC: Duke University Press, 2001), 155.

14 Anthea Butler talks about the Black church and this shift in "The Black Church: From Prophecy to Prosperity," *Dissent* 61, no. 1 (Winter 2014): 38–41.

15 Albert J. Raboteau, *Slave Religion: The "Invisible Institution" in the Antebellum South* (Oxford: Oxford University Press, 1978), 318.

16 See Wanda Sykes, "Dignified Black People," *YouTube*, 6 November 2009, accessed 20 June 2023, https://www.youtube.com/watch?v=a1XvvmTjuA8&t=22s.

17 See, for example, my *Pimpin' Ain't Easy: Selling Black Entertainment Television* (New York: Routledge, 2007) for a discussion of the ways Blackness and capital operate uneasily together in visual culture.

18 Goldberg learned about Black church while attending her grandmother's Baptist one. See "Spotting Faller-Outers at the Church of Whoop," *Rollin' with Whoopi*, 11 November 2014, accessed 19 June 2023, https://www.youtube.com/watch?v =huSEhrr-JFU.

19 Moms Mabley, "Comedy Ain't Pretty," *YouTube*, 13 January 2004, accessed 19 June 2023, https://www.youtube.com/watch?v=qUvgEPakVaM. This was likely recorded in the 1960s but has no liner notes.

20 For more on LaWanda Page and her role in *Sanford and Son*, see Adrien Sebro, *Scratchin' and Survivin': Hustle Economics and the Black Sitcoms of Tandem Productions* (New Brunswick, NJ: Rutgers University Press, 2023).

21 According to Box Office Mojo, *Friday* earned nearly $28 million worldwide with a budget of $3.5 million. See http://www.boxofficemojo.com/movies/?id=friday.htm, accessed 26 June 2023.

22 While writer Aaron McGruder's series *Black Jesus* (Adult Swim, 2014–2019) should fit into this Passing of the Peace, and I think it is supposed to do so, the series has a diminished sense of humor. It traffics in surface humor for an Adult Swim audience

rather than taking any political-social (or unfortunately even really comedic) address of Christianity and Black Comptonites.

23 Emmanuel and Phillip Hudson, "Church Folks," *YouTube*, 25 September 2012, accessed 19 June 2023, https://www.youtube.com/watch?v=nuyRdgi7VWg. This link directs you to the initial version. In an updated version, instead of the two brothers sitting in front of their computer acting and rapping the text, they offer a music video.

24 For example, see KevOnStage, https://www.youtube.com/watch?v=iiLicFOoFtg, accessed 19 June 2023, and *Roland Martin, #Unfiltered*, 7 November 2020, accessed 19 June 2023, https://www.youtube.com/watch?v=ak_aRYroZZU.

25 For more on this point, see Bambi L. Haggins, *Laughing Mad: The Black Comic Persona in Post-Soul America* (New Brunswick, NJ: Rutgers University Press, 2007), 154–157.

26 *The Mis-Adventures of Awkward Black Girl*, season two, episode seven, "The Group," Issa Rae, *YouTube*, 13 December 2012, accessed 19 June 2023, http://www .awkwardblackgirl.com/season-2/episode-7.

27 This take on evangelism connects to but differs from the actual learning and dissemination of religious information. Blacks have been significant in this latter effort despite history's erasure of their presence. For more on this, see Cain Hope Felder, *Troubling Biblical Waters: Race, Class and Family* (Maryknoll, NY: Orbis Books, 1989).

28 *The Choir*, season one, episode one, "Genesis," *YouTube*, 29 August 2013, accessed 19 June 2023, https://www.youtube.com/watch?v=K-JNViRetbI.

29 Joeckel, "Funny as Hell," 423.

30 Donald L. Robinson Jr., Marine & Mt. Moriah Community Church, http://www .marineandmtmoriah.org/.

31 Anthropologist John L. Jackson theorizes a distinction between authenticity and racial sincerity that resonates here as well. See John L. Jackson Jr., *Real Black: Adventures in Racial Sincerity* (Chicago: University of Chicago Press, 2005).

32 Will Johnson, "Wash Your Hands," *YouTube*, March 9, 2020, accessed 19 June 2023, https://www.youtube.com/watch?v=P-Mwcnelr4w, on Facebook, https://www .facebook.com/story.php?story_fbid=10212621362328123&id=1806818305&paipv =0&eav=AfYHlLkoR8m3rifSw9QXNgdOAngD2Ndg3WglGHN31 _uGxOTJYNkyH29PCroozxl-bzw&_rdr, accessed 26 March 2024.

33 In radio, morning drive is generally the period from 6:00 A.M. to 10:00 A.M.

34 In 2018, Steve Harvey hosted six shows: a nationally syndicated morning drive radio program, the game show *Family Feud*, a daily television talk show on NBC, and others in addition to an occasional program on TBN and a few award programs. *The Hollywood Reporter* dubbed him 2018's "Unscripted TV Player of the Year." In 2024, he was still going strong.

35 Rickey Smiley on TBN, posted 4 April 2011, accessed 19 June 2023, https://www .youtube.com/watch?v=9wtbYvB9h_U.

36 Interestingly, the efforts of Smiley and Harvey reverberate across nonreligious spaces. In radio, for example, 2021 found longtime radio DJ Frank Ski (Frank Rodriguez) on R&B station 104.1 in Atlanta daily, offering his "Inspirational Vitamin." This pill takes the form of biblical verses, gospel music, and a whole lot of repping for God on one of the city's most popular nonreligious stations of which he left in early 2024 to pursue other opportunities.

37 Teresa L. Reed, *The Holy Profane: Religion in Black Popular Music* (Lexington: University of Kentucky Press, 2003), 92.

38 Rickey Smiley, "Rickey Smiley Simply Beautiful Remix," *YouTube*, 13 December 2011, accessed 19 June 2023, https://www.youtube.com/watch?v=yFyQmoCFxDo.

39 I've seen Rev. Al Green perform a gospel song live and segue clean into "Love and Happiness," one of his most popular secular hits. The character Boyce Ballentine (Cedric the Entertainer) in *The Soul Man* is based on singers Al Green and Mase.

40 Jacquinita A. Rose, *Shhh, Grown Folks Is Talking: The Stuff I Learned from the Kitchen Door* (Port Hueneme, CA: Grown Folks' Publishing, 2010), 93.

41 Hence, as discussed in Tithes and Offering, reading announcements aloud no longer happens much in new Black church—transferred instead to giant church screens, prerecorded video, or minimized with a millennial giving church event highlights.

42 "Rickey Smiley Church Announcements," *YouTube*, 13 April 2009, accessed 20 June 2023, https://www.youtube.com/watch?v=yhE_KzwlKf8.

43 Rickey Smiley and Kirk Franklin on TBN, accessed 19 January 2016, https://www.youtube.com/watch?v=YnfJ84tiu4M.

44 The series actually hosted one white pastor and his family. But the tone, focus, and expectation of the narrative remains with Black church.

45 Daniel J. Boorstin, *The Image: Or What Happened to the American Dream* (New York: Atheneum, 1961).

46 Sarah Banet-Weiser coined this term in her book *Authentic™: The Politics of Ambivalence in a Brand Culture* (New York: NYU Press, 2012).

47 *Preachers of L.A.*, season two, episode nine, "Meet the Godparents," aired 15 October 2012.

48 Rev. Michael J. T. Fisher of the Greater Zion Church Family of Compton, California, as found in Jonathan P. Hicks, "Black Pastors Denounce the Reality Show *The Preachers of L.A.*," *bet.com*, 18 October 2013.

49 Christine Thomasos, "'Preachers of L.A.' Pastor Wayne Cheney Wants to Provide Alternative to 'Love and Hip-Hop' Relationships," *Christian Post*, 2 October 2014, accessed 19 June 2023, http://www.christianpost.com/news/preachers-of-l-a-pastor-wayne-cheney-wants-to-provide-alternative-to-love-and-hip-hop-relationships-127397/.

50 *Preachers of L.A.*, promotional segue, Deitrick Haddon, aired 1 October 2014, Oxygen network.

51 Grace Jones's career as a singer and actor pushes all sorts of boundaries. Understanding her background as a child and sibling of Pentecostal preachers, makes her trajectory even more fascinating. African-American studies scholar Judith Casselberry is working on these aspects of Jones's life, music, and performance. See her talk "Solving the Mystery of Grace Jones: It's the Holy Ghost," https://www.youtube.com/watch?v=vYZUoIG1iPo, accessed 28 March 2024.

52 See commentary by Bishop T. D. Jakes, gospel singer Kirk Franklin, minister Rev. James C. Perkins, and comedian D. L. Hughley in Jonathan P. Hicks, "Black Pastors Denounce the Reality Show Preachers of LA," *bet.com*, 18 October 2013, accessed 19 June 2023, http://www.bet.com/news/national/2013/10/17/black-pastors-denounce-the-reality-show-the-preachers-of-la.html; Nicola Menzie, "Kirk Franklin Expresses Disappointment in 'Preachers of LA' Amid Suggestion Reality Show Turned People Away from God," *Christian Post*, 31 May 2014, accessed 19 June 2023, http://www.christianpost.com/news/kirk-franklin-expresses-disappointment-in-preachers-of-la-amid-suggestion-reality-show-turned-people-away-from-god-120678/.

53 See, for example, Walter M. Kimbrough, "Time for HBCUs and the Black Church to Talk about Sex," *NewsOne*, 8 February 2011, accessed 19 June 2023, http://newsone.com/1021165/time-for-hbcus-and-the-black-church-to-talk-about-sex/.

54 Ebo Twins, *Honk for Jesus. Save Your Soul.* (2022).

55 C. Eric Lincoln, *Christianity & Crisis*, November 2–16, 1970, 225.

56 *In Living Color*, season one, episode two, aired 21 April 1990, Fox, accessed 20 June 2023, https://www.youtube.com/watch?v=slqtjqDHQqY.

57 Father Tony Ricard, posted 12 February 2010, accessed 19 June 2023, https://www.youtube.com/watch?v=BY4wx27vC2E.

58 Dwight Conquergood, "Of Caravans and Carnivals: Performance Studies in Motion," *Drama Review* 39, no. 4 (1995): 137–138.

59 Dominique Robinson, conversation with the author, Atlanta, GA, 21 April 2017.

60 Stuart Hall, "What Is This Black in Black Popular Culture," *Social Justice* 20, nos. 1–2 (1993): 113.

Selection

1 Toni Morrison, *Beloved* (New York: Vintage Books, 1987), 88; Jonathan Demme, 1998.

2 Mark Fisher, "The Metaphysics of Crackle: Afrofuturism and Hauntology," *Dancecult: Journal of Electronic Dance Music Culture* 5, no. 2 (2013): 53.

3 Yvette Flunder, "Brand New Spirit," sermon, January 27, 2019, Cathedral of Hope United Church of Christ, Dallas, TX, accessed 21 June 2023, https://www.youtube.com/watch?v=F5RMBcALFjE.

4 Rachel Elizabeth Harding, "You Got a Right to the Tree of Life: African American Spirituals and Religions of the Diaspora," *CrossCurrents* 57, no. 2 (2007): 269.

5 I thank Michael Patrick Vaughn for introducing me to this concept.

6 John S. Mbiti, *African Religions and Philosophy*, 2nd ed. (Oxford: Heinemann, 1989), 1.

7 As found in an interview with religion professor Jacob Olupona, "The Spirit of Africa," *Harvard Gazette*, by Anthony Chiorazzi, 6 October 2015, accessed 26 June 2023, https://news.harvard.edu/gazette/story/2015/10/the-spirituality-of-africa/.

8 Mbiti, *African Religions and Philosophy*, 1.

9 Saifaddin Galal, "Distribution of the Population of Sub-Saharan Africa as of 2020, by Religious Affiliation," *Statistica*, 28 April 2023, accessed 21 June 2023, https://www.statista.com/statistics/1282636/distribution-of-religions-in-sub-saharan-africa/

10 Italics and capitalization are mine.

11 Perversely, as African-Americans try to better understand their African origins through sites such as ancestry.com, *Finding Your Roots*, and group trips to Ghana and South Africa, people on the continent strive for closer identification with white Americans and Europeans.

12 In 1804, enslaved Haitians revolted and took their independence from France. It was the first successful slave uprising, and for the colonial powers (including the U.S.), a threat. The U.S. and the larger colonial world believed a "recognition of a Black Empire founded upon insurrection and the massacre of the white population would have a most pernicious moral effect" (per the French prime minister in 1825). Thus, the U.S. did not recognize Haiti as a sovereign state until 1862—fifty-eight years after Haitian independence. And history further fails to record Vodou as a religion that provides a "spiritual force" and "forms of communication and organization" that are an "integral part of resistance and rebellion." Ulrike Sulikowski, "Hollywoodzombie: Vodou and the Caribbean in Mainstream Cinema," in *Ay BoBo: African-Caribbean Religions/Part 2: Voodoo*, edited by Manfred Kremser (Vienna: WUV-Universitätsverlag, 1996), 79.

13 As found on the website of the embassy of the Republic of Haiti, accessed 21 June 2023, https://www.haiti.org/haiti-at-a-glance/.

14 Alfred Métraux, *Voodoo in Haiti* (New York: Oxford University Press, 1959), 15.

15 Sulikowski, "Hollywoodzombie," 77.

16 Films such as *I Walked with a Zombie* (1943), *Sugar Hill* (1974), *The Believers* (1987), *The Devil's Advocate* (1997), *Blues Brother 2000* (1998), *The Skeleton Key* (2005), and *Princess and the Frog* (2009), among scores of others, offer Vodou as evil personified. Even the 1970s Black horror/thriller *J. D.'s Revenge* (Marks, 1976) explores the idea of Black possession, redemption through Christianity, and the unspoken but implied connection to Vodou as the story takes place in New Orleans. Not confined to film, television boasts a Santería or Vodou episode almost anywhere Black characters exist (or anywhere white characters want to go with a majority Black population). Series examples include everything from procedurals to sitcoms to documentaries such as *Miami Vice* ("Tell of the Goat" and "Whatever Works," 1985), *Golden Girls* ("The Housekeeper," 1987), *In the Heat of the Night* ("Don't Look Back I–II," 1988), *Murder, She Wrote* ("Night of the Tarantula," 1989, and "Big Easy Murder," 1995), *New York Undercover* ("Old Tyme Religion," 1995), *Autopsy 6: Secrets of the Dead* (1999) *Poltergeist—The Legacy* ("Spirit Thief," 1997), *Law & Order—Criminal Intent* ("The Gift," 2003, and "The Healer," 2006), *Law & Order—SVU* ("Ritual," 2004), *CSI Miami* ("Curse of the Coffin," 2006), *Monk* ("Mr. Monk and the Voodoo Curse," 2009), *Orange Is the New Black* (2013–2015), and *NCIS* ("Pound of Flesh," 2018). These Vodou and Santería episodes provide a mishmash of white fear and Black heathens.

17 Gloria Wade-Gayles, *Pushed Back to Strength: A Black Woman's Journey Home* (New York: Avon Books, 1993), 27.

18 Lina Buffington, "Body and Soul: Crossing Borders," unpublished manuscript, Spelman College, Images of Women and Gender in Media course, 5 May 1998, 2.

19 As found on the videotape box cover of *Angel Heart*.

20 Gina Athena Ulysse, "One Priestess's Salutation: A Study in Movement," *Frontiers* 43, no. 3 (2022): 242.

21 Elizabeth Pérez, "The Ontology of Twerk: From 'Sexy' Black Movement Style to Afro-Diasporic Sacred Dance," *African and Black Diaspora: An International Journal* 9, no. 1 (2015): 8.

22 The Oba of Oyotunji African Village, South Carolina, as quoted in Rod Davis, *American Voudou: Journey into a Hidden World* (Denton: University of North Texas Press, 1998), 234.

23 Kameelah L. Martin, *Envisioning Black Feminist Voodoo Aesthetics: African Spirituality in American Cinema* (New York: Lexington Books, 2016), 70.

24 Art historian Robert Farris Thompson writes, "deities . . . [manifest] themselves by possessing ('mounting') the bodies of their devotees. This aspect of [Vodou is] reinforced by contact with French services for Roman Catholic saints who were said to work miracles." Robert Farris Thompson, *Flash of the Spirit: African and Afro-American Art and Philosophy* (New York: Random House, 1983), 164.

25 At the box office, *Angel Heart* flopped. Made for $17 million, its domestic gross earned just a little over that. With mixed reviews, Parker's direction was cited as a central point of contention.

26 For more on the literary aspect, see Thrity N. Umrigar, "Tools of Empowerment: The Use of Magic, Voodoo, and the Supernatural in the Novels of African-American Women Writers" (doctoral dissertation, Kent State University, 1997).

27 Therese E. Higgins, "The Influence of African Cosmological Beliefs in *Beloved*," in *Religiosity, Cosmology and Folklore: The African Influence in the Novels of Toni Morrison* (London: Taylor and Francis, 2014).

28 Fisher, "The Metaphysics of Crackle," 51.

29 Toni Morrison, *Beloved* (New York: Plume, 1988), 87.

30 Oyeronke Olajubu, "Seeing through a Woman's Eye: Yoruba Religious Tradition and Gender Relations," *Journal of Feminist Studies in Religion* 20, no. 1 (Spring 2004): 56.

31 Bernice Johnson Reagon, *The Songs Are Free: Bernice Johnson Reagon with Bill Moyers*, Public Affairs Television (South Burlington, VT: Mystic Fire Video, 1991).

32 Montré Aza Missouri, *Black Magic Woman and Narrative Film: Race, Sex and Afro-Religiosity* (New York: Palgrave Macmillan, 2015), 18.

33 The film earned a 1988 Film Independent Spirit Award for best first feature.

34 Martin, *Envisioning Black Feminist Voodoo Aesthetics,* 80.

35 Tarshia L. Stanley, "The Three Faces in *Eve's Bayou*: Recalling the Conjure Woman in Contemporary Black Cinema," in *Folklore/Cinema: Popular Film as Vernacular Culture*, edited by Sharon Sherman and Mikel J. Koven (Logan: Utah State University Press, 2007), 154.

36 Kara Keeling, *The Witch's Flight: The Cinematic, the Black Femme, and the Image of Common Sense* (Durham, NC: Duke University Press, 2007), 153.

37 Audre Lorde, "Uses of the Erotic: The Erotic as Power," in *Sister Outsider: Essays and Speeches by Audre Lorde* (Freedom, CA: The Crossing Press, 1984), 53–59.

38 Keeling, *The Witch's Flight*, 155.

39 Fisher, "The Metaphysics of Crackle," 51.

40 Josslyn Luckett, "The *Daughters* Debt: How Black Spirituality and Politics Are Transforming the Televisual Landscape," *Film Quarterly* 72, no. 4 (2019): 11.

41 Ava DuVernay, *Queen Sugar*, season one promo, accessed 21 June 2023, http://www.oprah.com/own-queensugar/nova-bordelon-journalist-herbalist-activist-video.

42 Luckett, "The *Daughters* Debt," 12.

43 Bilal Qureshi, "The Cultural Consolation of Ava Duvernay's *Queen Sugar*," in *Film Quarterly* 70, no. 3 (Spring 2017): 65.

44 I take up Ndegeocello as a central figure in The Message as well as address this series further in my chapter, "I'm Digging You: Television's Turn to Dirty South Blackness," in *Watching While Black Rebooted! The Television and Digitality of Black Audiences*, edited by Beretta E. Smith-Shomade (New Brunswick, NJ: Rutgers University Press, 2023), 185–200.

45 L. H. Stallings, *Mutha Is Half a Word: Intersections of Folklore, Vernacular, Myth, and Queerness in Black Female Culture* (Columbus: Ohio State University Press, 2007), 235.

46 *Queen Sugar*, "Come, Clad in Peace," season three, episode eight, 8 July 2018.

47 Qureshi, "The Cultural Consolation," 67.

48 In Catholicism, for example, one of the most sacred religious icons remains the Black Madonna housed in protective glass and gold on a mountain in Spain.

49 Marc Schlitz, quoting anthropologist J. Lorand Matory in his review of Matory's *Sex and the Empire That Is No More and the Politics of Metaphor in Oyo Yoruba Religion, Journal of the Royal Anthropological Institute* 3, no. 2 (June 1997): 390.

50 For example, Afrofuturist writer Tananarive Due and womanist process theologian Monica Coleman hosted the webinar series "Octavia Tried to Tell Us XIII: Parable for Today's Pandemic," 2020–2022.

51 Yolanda Pierce, "Black Women and the Sacred: With 'Lemonade,' Beyoncé Takes Us to Church," *Religion Dispatches*, 3 May 2016, accessed 25 June 2023, https://religiondispatches.org/Black-women-and-the-sacred-beyonce-takes-us-to-church/.

52 I thank my Emory spring 2018 Academic Learning Community for this observation.
53 Jamie Rogers, "Intertextuality and Diasporic Communication in Julie Dash's *Daughters of the Dust* and Beyoncé's *Lemonade*," Society for Cinema and Media Studies Annual Conference, 2018, Toronto, Canada. See her publication on the subject, "Diasporic Communion and Intertextual Exchange in Beyoncé's *Lemonade* and Julie Dash's *Daughters of the Dust*," *Black Camera* 11, no. 2 (Spring 2020).
54 Flunder, "Brand New Spirit."

The Message

1 From the 1997 film *Love Jones*, Regie Gibson contributed the poem "Brother to the Night (A Blues for Nina)." The words speak to the richness of sexual tension and Black urban '90s soul.
2 Lee Butler, "The Spirit Is Willing and the Flesh Is Too: Living Whole and Holy Lives through Integrating Spirituality and Sexuality," in *Loving the Body: Black Religious Studies and the Erotic*, edited by Anthony B. Pinn and Dwight N. Hopkins (New York: Palgrave Macmillan, 2004), 116.
3 Kelly Brown Douglas, *Black Bodies and the Black Church: A Blues Slant* (New York: Palgrave Macmillan, 2012), 110.
4 Douglas, *Black Bodies and the Black Church*.
5 I thank my colleague Dan Reynolds for making me think through this notion.
6 Douglas, *Black Bodies and the Black Church*, 72.
7 For example, René Descartes, considered the founder of Western philosophy, forwarded the notion of a separation of mind and body in the early and mid-1600s. His ideas continue to be taught and debated.
8 Douglas, *Black Bodies and the Black Church*, 78.
9 E. Patrick Johnson, "Passing Strange: E. Patrick Johnson's *Strange Fruit*," interview by Jennifer DeVere Brody in *Blacktino Queer Performance*, edited by E. Patrick Johnson and Ramón H. Riversa-Servera (Durham, NC: Duke University Press, 2016), 230–231.
10 Daren Fowler, "To Erotically Know: The Ethics and Pedagogy of *Moonlight*," *liquid blackness* 4, no.7 (October 2017): 50.
11 Patricia Hill Collins, *Black Sexual Politics: African Americans, Gender, and the New Realism* (New York: Routledge, 2005).
12 See Marlon Riggs, *Tongues Untied* (PBS, 1989).
13 Tamura Lomax, *Jezebel Unhinged: Loosing the Black Female Body in Religion and Culture* (Durham, NC: Duke University Press, 2018), x.
14 Monique Moultrie, *Passionate and Pious: Religious Media and Black Women's Sexuality* (Durham, NC: Duke University Press, 2017), 10.
15 Jack Halberstam, *Trans*: A Quick and Quirky Account of Gender Variability* (Berkeley: University of California Press, 2018), 6.
16 Robert C. Fuller, *The Body of Faith: A Biological History of Religion in America* (Chicago: University of Chicago Press, 2013), 26.
17 The menstrual cycle can cause considerable consternation depending on the circumstances of its flow (or lack thereof).
18 Davis draws a Vèvè symbol in the film to invoke Erzuli Freda, the goddess of fertility and creativity.
19 Gwendolyn Audrey Foster, *Women Filmmakers of the African and Asian Diaspora: Decolonizing the Gaze* (Carbondale: Southern Illinois University Press, 1997), 12.
20 Clearly, we view the Black body in myriad other contexts—often violent ones. For example, see African-American studies scholar Mark Anthony Neale's interview

with minister and religion scholar Eboni Marshall Turman on *Left of Black*, season six, episode twenty-six, "Religion + Policing + The Fear of the Black Body," 23 April 2016, accessed 25 June 2023, http://leftofblack.tumblr.com/search/religion.

21 Carlyle Fielding Stewart III, *Black Spirituality and Black Consciousness: Soul Force, Culture and Freedom in the African-American Experience* (Trenton, NJ: Africa World Press, 1998), 1.

22 As shown on *Oprah's Super Soul Conversations*, OWN, season eight, episode 802, 10 September 2017, accessed 25 June 2023, https://www.oprah.com/own-super-soul -sunday/pastor-ar-bernard.

23 Karen Baker-Fletcher, "The Erotic in Contemporary Black Women's Writings," in *Loving the Body: Black Religious Studies and the Erotic*, edited by Anthony B. Pinn and Dwight N. Hopkins (New York: Palgrave MacMillan, 2004), 200.

24 Vocal instructor Jaron M. Legrair analyzes this song and her voice in particular online in early 2024, as the video of it experienced a viral moment. See his analysis of it at https://www.youtube.com/watch?v=CKDn9pQxcBg.

25 Kelly Brown Douglas, *What's Faith Got to Do with It? Black Bodies/Christian Souls* (Maryknoll, NY: Orbis Books, 2005), 214–215.

26 Katie G. Cannon, "Sexing Black Women: Liberation from the Prisonhouse of Anatomical Authority," in *Loving the Body: Black Religious Studies and the Erotic*, edited by Anthony B. Pinn and Dwight N. Hopkins (New York: Palgrave MacMillan, 2004), 13.

27 Anthony B. Pinn, "Introduction," in *Loving the Body: Black Religious Studies and the Erotic*, edited by Anthony B. Pinn and Dwight N. Hopkins (New York: Palgrave MacMillan, 2004), 4.

28 Baker-Fletcher, "The Erotic in Contemporary Black Women's Writings," 202.

29 Elizabeth Pérez, "The Ontology of Twerk: From 'Sexy' Black Movement Style to Afro-Diasporic Sacred Dance," *African and Black Diaspora: An International Journal* 9 (2015): 8.

30 Moultrie, *Passionate and Pious*, 5.

31 Just to be clear, he is not referencing Maya Angelou's diamonds from "And Still I Rise."

32 Judith Weisenfeld *Hollywood Be Thy Name: African American Religion in American Film, 1929–1949* (Berkeley: University of California Press, 2007), 95–96.

33 Writer Alice Walker indeed wants to problematize Christianity for African-American women and especially regarding sexuality (the act and with whom). However, it seems film director Steven Spielberg harbors other ideas about this notion. In Walker's book *The Color Purple*, Celie and Shug engage in an intimate and passionate lesbian relationship. In addition, she incorporates a strong anti-Christian sentiment. The film, however, not only limitedly alludes to their coupling but also revises the anti-Christian plot. Seemingly, Spielberg seeks to heal the divide of restrictive Christian belief and sexuality through the body of Shug Avery (Margaret Avery). This religious and sexual twist, particularly as it impacts Shug's behavior and sexuality, illuminates sexual power simultaneously accorded and denied to African-American women and the impact this constant denial makes on Black women and men's culture. The denial of sexual freedom alongside moral condemnation critically disempowers these women. For more insight into this film and book's interpretive distance, see Jacqueline Bobo, *Black Women as Cultural Readers* (New York: Columbia University Press, 1995), and Kristen Proehl, "*Fried Green Tomatoes* and *The Color Purple*: A Case Study in Lesbian Friendship and Cultural Controversy," *Journal of Lesbian Studies* 22, no. 1 (2017). And hallelujah,

the revised film version of *The Color Purple* in 2023, reframed the redemptive scene and at least, got the preacher loving his daughter first.

34 Jennifer DeClue, "The Circuitous Route of Presenting the Black Butch: The Travels of Dee Rees' *Pariah*," in *Sisters in the Life: A History of Out African American Lesbian Media-Making*, edited by Yvonne Welbon and Alexandra Jahasz (Durham, NC: Duke University Press, 2018), 230.

35 Beretta E. Smith-Shomade, "Marlon Riggs," in *The Concise Routledge Encyclopedia of the Documentary Film*, edited by Ian Aitken (New York: Routledge, 2013), 1125.

36 Smith-Shomade, "Marlon Riggs," 1126.

37 Lawrence Ware, "4 Reasons Why Greenleaf Is the Show the Black Church Needs," *theroot.com*, 1 September 2016, accessed 13 July 2018, https://www.theroot.com/4 -reasons-why-greenleaf-is-the-show-the-black-church-ne-1790856577,

38 Some of this work includes *Diary of a Mad Black Woman* (2005), *Daddy's Little Girls* (2007), *Why Did I Get Married* (2007), *The Family That Preys* (2008), *Meet the Browns* (2008), *I Can Do Bad by Myself* (2009), *The Haves and Have Nots* (2013–2018, OWN), and *If Loving You Is Wrong* (2014–2017, OWN).

39 This phrasing (beyond Gladys Knight's "Midnight Train to Georgia") comes from a discussion of Perry and the home space during film scholar Miriam Petty's presentation at the 2016 American Studies Association annual conference. Petty is completing a book project on Perry for the University of Michigan Press with the working title *How Do You Solve a Problem Like Madea? Tyler Perry's Black Aesthetics*.

40 *Preachers of L.A.* (2013–2014), *Preachers of Detroit* (2015), and *Preachers of Atlanta* (2016) are all reality series created by Holly Carter and Lemuel Plummer for the Oxygen Network. While *L.A.* posted a production start and end date, the other two did not. Each of the series caused considerable contentiousness in Black church communities.

41 Beyond reality television, check out news stories on former megapastor Eddie Long's overt and political protestations of homosexuality from the pulpit and the streets—only to be accused by several young men of sexual relations with them. See a fictionalized visioning of this situation with the Ebo Twins film *Honk for Jesus. Save Your Soul.* (2022). Long is not the first for this to happen to nor will he be the last. But fictionalized or not, battles between loving, bodies, and believing continue to be waged.

42 Jonathan L. Walton, *Watch This! The Ethics and Aesthetics of Black Televangelism* (New York: NYU Press, 2009), xii.

43 John Lovell Jr., *Black Song: The Forge and the Flame* (New York: MacMillan, 1972), 138.

44 This assertion comes via a description of work published on artistic performance and Blackness. However, I think it well frames the work of Black artisans in addressing sexuality and sacredness. See Jean-Paul Rocchi, Anne Crémieux, and Xavier Lemoine, "Introduction: Black Beings, Black Embodyings: Notes on Contemporary Artistic Performances and Their Cultural Interpretations," in *Understanding Blackness through Performance: Contemporary Arts and the Represen-tation of Identity*, edited by Anne Crémieux, Xavier Lemoine, and Jean-Paul Rocchi (New York: Palgrave Macmillan, 2013), 2.

45 Patrick R. Johnson, "Where Did Tommy Work?" Presentation at the Society for Cinema and Media Studies conference, Atlanta, GA, 1 April 2016.

46 @erykahbadu, Instagram post, 2 April 2020, https://www.instagram.com/p/B -f2RiiFRfn/?utm_source=ig_web_copy_link.

47 Horace T. Maxile, "Extensions on a Black Musical Tropology: From Trains to the Mothership (and Beyond)," *Journal of Black Studies* 42 no. 4 (May 2011): 605.

48 As found in Evan Minsker, "D'Angelo Discusses *Black Messiah*, Black Lives Matter Religion on 'Tavis Smiley,'" *Pitchfork*, 4 September 2015, accessed 25 June 2023, https://pitchfork.com/news/61051-dangelo-discusses-black-messiah-black-lives -matter-religion-on-tavis-smiley/

49 "A Conversation with D'Angelo," hosted by Nelson George, Red Bull Music Academy, May 2014, Brooklyn Museum, Brooklyn, NY, posted 23 May 2014, accessed 25 June 2023, https://www.youtube.com/watch?v=WD10aBCmZWA.

50 "A Conversation with D'Angelo."

51 "A Conversation with D'Angelo."

52 Dwight N. Hopkins, "The Construction of the Black Male Body: Eroticism and Religion," in *Loving the Body: Black Religious Studies and the Erotic*, edited by Anthony B. Pinn and Dwight N. Hopkins (New York: Palgrave Macmillan, 2004), 191.

53 YouTube comments on the music video, accessed 9 March 2020.

54 A categorization that D'Angelo later rejected as too restrictive.

55 Loren Kajikawa, "D'Angelo's 'Voodoo' Technology: African Cultural Memory and the Ritual of Popular Music Consumption," *Black Music Research Journal* 31, no. 1 (Spring 2012): 137–159.

56 Touré, "D'Angelo Is Holding Your Hand," *Rolling Stone*, 11 May 2000, accessed 25 June 2023, https://www.rollingstone.com/music/music-news/dangelo-is-holding -your-hand-181009/.

57 Kajikawa, "D'Angelo's 'Voodoo' Technology," 148.

58 Faith A. Pennick, *33⅓ Voodoo* (New York: Bloomsbury Academic, 2020), 62.

59 See Shana L. Redmond, "This Safer Space: Janelle Monáe's 'Cold War,'" *Journal of Popular Music Studies* 23, no. 4 (2011): 393–411.

60 Aimé J. Ellis, "'Singing Love Songs to Mr. Death': Racial Terror and the State of Erection in D'Angelo's '(Untitled) How Does It Feel,'" *African American Review* 43, no. 2 (Summer 2009): 297.

61 Well, at least Redmond's.

62 Touré, "D'Angelo Is Holding Your Hand."

63 Steve Jones, "D'Angelo's Timeless Magic: R&B Revivalist Conjures Spirit of Hendrix to Craft *Voodoo*," *USA Today*, 25 January 2000, 1D.

64 "A Conversation with D'Angelo."

65 His relationship with singer Angie Stone and their son forms an essential part of his public background.

66 Angel E. Fraden, "D'Angelo Taught Me How to Own My Queerness," *Teen Vogue*, 23 June 2017, accessed 25 June 2023, https://www.teenvogue.com/story/dangelo -queerness-masculinity-sexuality.

67 Hopkins, "The Construction of the Black Male Body," 190.

68 D'Angelo and Vanguard released several live recordings and a couple of compilation CDs over his career. They include music from each of the recordings of the period and covers of other artists he admires.

69 Record producer and manager William "Kedar" Massenburg coined the term neo-soul.

70 Will Hodgkinson, "Black Messiah D'Angelo and the Vanguard," *The Times*, 27 December 2014, accessed 25 June 2023, https://www.thetimes.co.uk/article /black-messiah-dangelo-and-the-vanguard-qs56h8lh9zs.

71 Priya Elan, "D'Angelo and the Vanguard—Black Messiah," *Mojo*, 16 December 2014, accessed 24 July 2018, https://web.archive.org/web/20141219201111 /http://www.mojo4music.com/18113/dangelo-vanguard-black-messiah/.

72 Ben Roylance, "D'Angelo and the Vanguard—Black Messiah," *Tiny Mix Tapes*, 5 January 2015, accessed 25 June 2023, https://www.tinymixtapes.com/music-review /dangelo-and-the-vanguard-black-messiah.

73 Jumi Ekunseitan, "Meet Me at the Margins: Performing Resistance to Police Brutality" (master's thesis, Emory University, May 2018). While VH-1 named it one of the "50 Sexiest Videos," D'Angelo struggled with the ways in which audiences took it up and demanded a sexual image after its release. His struggle included drug use, arrests, and accidents.

74 Stephanie Shonekan, "Black Mizzou: Music and Stories One Year Later," in *Black Lives Matter and Music: Protest, Intervention, Reflection*, edited by Fernando Orejuela and Stephanie Shonekan (Bloomington: Indiana University Press, 2018), 14–33.

75 Dimitri Ehrlich, "Young Soul Rebels: Neo-Soul Isn't Just a Subgenre Tailored to the Dread Set. It's a Sublime Paradox, Too," *Vibe*, February 2002, 72–73.

76 Sarah Fila-Bakabadio, "'Pick Your Afro Daddy': Neo Soul and the Making of Diasporan Identities," *Cahiers d'Études africaines* 54, no. 4 (2014): 920.

77 Fila-Bakabadio, "'Pick Your Afro Daddy,'" 919.

78 Joel McIver, *Erykah Badu: The First Lady of Neo Soul* (London: Sanctuary Publishing, 2002), 266.

79 I add the fill as it works as well with what Badu proclaims.

80 Zandria F. Robinson, "Space, Time, and Race in Dirty South Bohemia," in *The Bohemian South: Creating Countercultures, from Poe to Punk*, edited by Shawn Chandler Bingham and Lindsey A. Freeman (Chapel Hill: University of North Carolina Press, 2017), 234.

81 As found in "Author Q&A" in Tanisha C. Ford, *Liberated Threads: Black Women, Style, and the Global Politics of Soul* (Chapel Hill: University of North Carolina Press, 2017), accessed 25 June 2023, https://uncpress.org/author-qa/9781469636139/. Ndegeocello fits in this listing as well. Her tenth recording is a tribute to Nina Simone titled *Pour une Âme Souveraine: A Dedication to Nina Simone* (2012).

82 Aisha S. Durham, *Home with Hip Hop Feminism: Performances in Communication and Culture* (New York: Peter Lang, 2014), 12.

83 Lyrics from the song "The Healer." She adds in an interview: "All those things [names for God] are the same to me." Interview with Erykah Badu on Chronyx.BE, 2008, Recontre Avec Anissa et Jon Hess Montana au Festival Couleur Café, accessed 25 June 2023, https://www.youtube.com/watch?v=HZi1nfEcUy8.

84 Eve Dunbar, "Hip Hop (Feat. Women Writers): Reimagining Black Women and Agency through Hip Hop Fiction," in *Contemporary African American Literature: The Living Canon*, edited by Lovalerie King and Shirley Moody-Turner (Bloomington: Indiana University Press, 2013), 91.

85 Dianne E. Anderson, *Problematic: How Toxic Callout Culture Is Destroying Feminism* (Lincoln: University of Nebraska Press, 2018), 61.

86 Robinson, "Space, Time, and Race in Dirty South Bohemia," 233.

87 Meg Butler, "Did You Know These Celebrities Were Five Percenters?" *madamenoire .com*, 13 August 2014, accessed 25 June 2023, http://madamenoire.com/456949 /know-celebrities-five-percenters/2/.

88 Christopher Johnson, "God, the Black Man and the Five Percenters," *NPR*, 4 August 2006, accessed 25 June 2023, http://www.npr.org/templates/transcript

/transcript.php?storyId=5614846. The nine tenets specifically include: "1.) That [B]lack people are the original people of the planet Earth. 2.) That [B]lack people are the fathers and mothers of civilization. 3.) That the science of Supreme Mathematics is the key to understanding man's relationship to the universe. 4.) Islam is a natural way of life, not a religion. 5.) That education should be fashioned to enable us to be self-sufficient as a people. 6.) That each one should teach one according to their knowledge. 7.) That the [B]lack man is God and his proper name is ALLAH—Arm, Leg, Leg, Arm, Head. 8.) That our children are our link to the future and they must be nurtured, respected, loved, protected, and educated. 9.) That the unified [B]lack family is the vital building block of the nation."

89 Johnson, "God, the Black Man and the Five Percenters."

90 Badu's "On and On" gets treated to several interpretations. For example, see Maxile, "Extensions on a Black Musical Tropology," and Thor Christensen, "Old School, New Lessons—Erykah Badu Bonds '70s Influenced Soul, Philosophical Lyrics," *Dallas Morning News*, January 30, 1997.

91 Khatija Bibi Khan, "Erykah Badu and the Teachings of the Nation of Gods and Earths," *Muziki: Journal of Music Research in Africa* 9, no. 2 (2012): 81.

92 On this, see Gloria E. Anzaldúa, "now let us shift . . . the path of conocimiento . . . inner work, public acts," in *This Bridge We Call Home: Radical Visions for Transformations*, edited by Gloria E. Anzaldúa and Analouise Keating (New York: Routledge, 2002).

93 Imani Perry, *Prophets of the Hood: Politics and Poetics in Hip Hop* (Durham, NC: Duke University Press, 2004), 148.

94 Anzaldúa, *This Bridge We Call Home*, 541.

95 Anzaldúa, *This Bridge We Call Home*, 542.

96 Ashley Weatherford, "Everything You Need to Know about Wellness According to Erykah Badu," *New York*, 23 August 2017, accessed 25 June 2023, https://www.thecut.com/2017/08/erykah-badu-health-fitness-wellness-advice.html.

97 Badu privileges women in her life who have shaped her. She includes Mother Nature in this list.

98 Britni Danielle, "We See You, Erykah Badu," *Essence*, May 2014.

99 Beyond her own construction, the larger public tends to place Badu's outward spiritual ways of presenting into a myriad of pots. Her film, television, and digital media forays often position her way of being as humorous. For example, in *Blues Brothers 2000* (Landis, 1998) she becomes Queen Mousette, a voodoo priestess in the swamps of Louisiana. In 2016, she seems to amuse herself by offering Twitter palm readings to fans. Trade palm reader Tony Leggett suggests she has potential psychic hands, locating her "long fingers and long palms" in the realm of spiritual connection. The film *What Men Want* (Shankman, 2019) frames Badu as a tarot card reader and weed seller who conjures hearing men's thoughts for the protagonist Ali (Taraji P. Henson).

100 McIver, *Erykah Badu*, 208.

101 McIver, *Erykah Badu*, 208.

102 Khan, "Erykah Badu and the Teachings of the Nation of Gods and Earths," 88–89. However, a minor problem surfaces with her further analysis of the early part of the song's lyrics as proof that "natural fun" and sexual empowerment tie to Islam. As the song samples the consistently replicated 1981 Tom Tom Club hit "Genius of Love" lyrics and hook, it can be read just as easily as an inventive way to bring in ideas about the enjoyment of sex.

103 Kimberly Juanita Brown, "Erykah Badu's Ambulatory Acts," *TDR: The Drama Review* 62, no. 1 (Spring 2018): 163.

104 Fila-Bakabadio, "'Pick Your Afro Daddy,'" 934.

105 Fila-Bakabadio, "'Pick Your Afro Daddy,'" 928.

106 MR_FULLERSHIT, Twitter post, 22 February 2020, https://twitter.com/MR _FULLERSHIT/status/1231220046485127168?s=20.

107 Press conference with Erykah Badu, April 2020, https://baduworldmarket.com /pages/stream.

108 Trevor Anderson, "Erykah Badu and Jill Scott Streams Triple after 'Verzuz' Battle," *Billboard.com*, 13 May 2020, accessed 25 June 2023, https://www.billboard.com /articles/news/9377588/erykah-badu-jill-scott-streams-triple-verzuz-battle.

109 Lakesia D. Johnson, *Iconic: Decoding Images of the Revolutionary Black Woman* (Waco, TX: Baylor University Press, 2012), 106.

110 Ndegeocello revisions and revises the spelling of her name over the course of her career. I use the 2023 articulation of it for this Message.

111 So much so, I misremembered it as the nondiegetic music to the powerful ending scene.

112 L. H. Stallings, *Mutha Is Half a Word: Intersections of Folklore, Vernacular, Myth, and Queerness in Black Female Culture* (Columbus: Ohio State University Press, 2007), 236.

113 Francesca T. Royster, *Sounds Like a No-No: Queer Sounds and Eccentric Acts in the Post-Soul Era* (Ann Arbor: University of Michigan Press, 2013), 175, 185.

114 Johnson, *Iconic*, 105.

115 In this tune, she directly addresses writer and Black Panther Elridge Cleaver's 1968 memoir, *Soul on Ice*.

116 Matt Richardson, "Make Me Wanna Holler: Meshell Ndegeocello, Black Queer Aesthetics, and Feminist Critiques," *Journal of Lesbian Studies* 18, no. 3 (2014): 245.

117 Richardson, "Make Me Wanna Holler."

118 Terry Nelson, "Meshell Ndegeocello's 'Peace beyond Passion' Turns 20," *Albumism*, 24 June 2016, accessed 2 June 2020, https://www.albumism.com/features/tribute -celebrating-20-years-of-meshell-ndegeocello-peace-beyond-passion.

119 I thank my colleague Javier Villa-Flores for this insight to grapple with and chew.

120 The title references Korean women forced to work as sex laborers by the Japanese military during World War II.

121 Nghana Lewis, "'You Sell Your Soul Like You Sell a Piece of Ass': Rhythms of Black Female Sexuality and Subjectivity in MeShell Ndegeocello's 'Cookie: The Anthropological Mixtape,'" *Black Music Research Journal* 26, no. 1 (Spring 2006): 126.

122 Johnson, *Iconic*, 103.

123 As found in Genesis 2:24.

124 Stallings, *Mutha Is Half a Word*, 235.

125 Roger A. Sneed, "Dark Matter: Liminality and Black Queer Bodies," in *Ain't I a Womanist, Too? Third Wave Womanist Religious Thought*, edited by Monica A. Coleman (Minneapolis: Fortress Press, 2013), 145.

126 Stallings, *Mutha Is Half a Word*, 255.

127 Quote in Alison Powell, "Sybil of Soul," *Interview*, July 1996.

128 Daphne A. Brooks, "Afro-Sonic Feminist Praxis: Nina Simone and Adrienne Kennedy in High Fidelity," in *Black Performance Theory*, edited by Thomas F. DeFrantz and Anita Gonzalez (Durham, NC: Duke University Press, 2014), 219.

129 Brooks, "Afro-Sonic Feminist Praxis," 220.

130 Tamura Lomax, *Jezebel Unhinged: Loosing the Black Female Body in Religion and Culture* (Durham, NC: Duke University Press, 2018), 106.

131 As found in Ann Powers, "Me'Shell Ndegeocello: Black and Blue: The Singer Fights for Your Rights on 'Peace beyond Passion,'" *Rolling Stone*, 5 September 1996.

132 She mentions this in her Emory talk. Emory Provost Lecture Series, 3 October 2019, Atlanta, GA.

133 Quote as found in Meredith Ramsey, "Ten Questions with Meshell Ndegeocello," *www.offbeat.com*, 1 October 2014, accessed 25 June 2023, https://www.offbeat.com /articles/ten-questions-meshell-ndegeocello/.

134 Meshell Ndegeocello, lecture, Emory Provost Lecture Series, 3 October 2019, Atlanta, GA.

135 A fact that he clouds with his first film, *Purple Rain* (1984).

136 Butler, "The Spirit Is Willing and the Flesh Is Too," 116–117.

137 In 2018, for example, graduating Black students crossing university stages got rushed off for their expressions of joy—described as too loud, undignified, and disruptive. Yet in his keynote address to the 2018 Black graduating students at the Modupe Dayo (Black graduation) ceremony at Emory University, political scientist Michael Owens talked about the need for expressed and recognized Black joy. In addition, "hoe theologies," proffered by media makers such as Tyler Perry and even T. D. Jakes, stand in often for any sort of reasoned or reflected-upon address of sexuality and sacredness.

138 LaVette Gibson in *Preachers of L.A. Special*, in between seasons one and two (2014). Religion scholar Monique Moultrie examines white Christian sexual purity against racialized holy sex and how the couples of *Preachers of L.A.* negotiate it all. See Monique Moultrie, "Black Female Sexual Agency and Racialized Holy Sex in Black Christian Reality TV Shows," in *Religion and Reality TV: Faith in Late Capitalism*, edited by Mara Einstein, Katherine Madden, and Diane Winston (New York: Routledge, 2018), 31–45.

139 Fred Moten, *Black and Blur* (Durham, NC: Duke University Press, 2017), 218.

140 Touré, *I Would Die 4 U: Why Prince Became an Icon* (New York: Atria Books, 2013), 114–116.

141 Anzaldúa, *This Bridge We Call Home*, 577, n2.

142 Anzaldúa, *This Bridge We Call Home*, 542.

143 "A Conversation with D'Angelo."

144 Ndegeocello, Emory Provost Lecture.

145 Erykah Badu, Twitter message, 21 April 2016.

146 Sheila E., quoted in Duane Tudahl, *Prince and the Purple Rain Era Studio Sessions 1983 and 1984* (Lanham, MD: Rowman & Littlefield, 2018), 381.

147 Touré, *I Would Die 4 U*, 8. In the social media world, oodles of videos and memes reify the diversity of Black church singing styles as expressed by entertainers such as James Finley and notkarltonbanks.

148 Sara Ahmed, *The Cultural Politics of Emotion* (Edinburgh: Edinburgh University Press, 2004), 3.

149 In the song, Prince intones: "Mothers make sure your children don't watch television until they know how to read. Or else all they'll know how to do is cuss, fight and breed. No child is bad from the beginning. They only imitate their atmosphere." This narrative loops back to Ndegeocello's "Dead Niggas (Pt. 1)" and her philosophy of not watching television much. It links them as well to their admittedly sometimes difficult relationships with their mothers.

150 Ann Powers, "Where Music Meets Religion: What an L.A. Times Writer Learned Spending a Night with Prince in 2009," *LA Times*, 11 January 2009, accessed 25 June 2023, http://www.latimes.com/entertainment/music/posts/la-et-archives-my-night-with-prince-20160421-story.html.

151 Audre Lorde, "Uses of the Erotic: The Erotic as Power," in *Sister Outsider* (Freedom, CA: The Crossing Press, 1984), 56.

152 Joseph Vogel, *This Thing Called Life: Prince, Race, Sex, Religion, and Music* (New York: Bloomsbury Academic, 2018), 154.

153 See Mark Anthony Neal, *Looking for Leroy: Illegible Black Masculinities* (New York: NYU Press, 2013), 50–53.

154 Questlove, "Questlove Remembers Prince: In This Life, You're on Your Own," *Rolling Stone*, 25 April 2016, accessed 25 June 2023, https://www.rollingstone.com/music/music-news/questlove-remembers-prince-in-this-life-youre-on-your-own-162611/.

155 Particularly in 2018, season two, episode five, the narrative of protagonist Nola enmeshes with the annual Purple Power block party and what true Black artistry means. A different Prince tune bookends almost every scene. Lee has hosted this party in Brooklyn since 2016.

156 His later works take up his other passions around Black worth and Black musical equity. On the music video for "The Holy River" from his *Emancipation* release, for example, Prince nods to his fight with Warner Bros. Records and the release from his contractual (slave) obligations to them. The song suggests God and Jesus will provide salvation.

157 Anzaldúa, *This Bridge We Call Home*, 559.

158 As found in Thomas McMahon, *Creative and Performing Artists for Teens* (New York: Gale Group, 2000).

159 Paul Ingalls, "Some Respect for Aretha," *NPR*, 16 August 2018.

160 Hopkins, "The Construction of the Black Male Body," 191.

161 Emily Lordi, "Aretha Franklin's Astonishing 'Dr. FeelGood,'" *New Yorker.com*, 16 August 2018, accessed 25 June 2023, https://www.newyorker.com/culture/culture-desk/aretha-franklins-astonishing-dr-feelgood?mbid=nl_Daily%20081618&CNDID=39492525&utm_source=Silverpop&utm_medium=email&utm_campaign=Daily%20081618&utm_content=&spMailingID=14075899&spUserID=MjYxMjAwOTYiMzcySo&spJobID=1461484072&spReportId=MTQ2MTQ4NDA3MgS2.

The Invitation

1 Others include musical artists Elvis, Prince, Madonna, Beyoncé, and Rihanna.

2 However, following her lead, many celebrities try to rock a mononym.

3 Yohana Desta, "Oprah Re-Invented TV Once. Can She Do It Again with a Revamped OWN?" *Vanity Fair*, 8 November 2017, accessed 27 June 2023, https://www.vanityfair.com/hollywood/2017/11/oprah-own-network-revamped.

4 Interestingly, on a 7 October 1999, interview on *Larry King Live* (CNN), Donald Trump stated that if he ever ran for president, Oprah Winfrey would be his ideal running mate.

5 "Most Famous People in the World," *Oprah Winfrey Show*, ABC, 28 September 2009.

6 "Coming Out Day for Abusive Parents," *Oprah Winfrey Show*, ABC, 13 January 1992.

7 And, they are equally proud of her as evidenced by a large, indoor electronic TSU billboard greeting arrivals to the Nashville International Airport with her image and words (ala 2024).

8 Clip of Oprah's Legends Ball, posted 26 September 2017, accessed 27 June 2023, https://www.youtube.com/watch?v=W-VCiH2ifOg.

9 "Gun Control," *Oprah Winfrey Show*, ABC, 27 June 1989.

10 We can also think of how, potentially, Winfrey's standing in for actual Black women and the recording of their tragic losses, lessens its function as a continuing trauma.

11 "Christian Leaders Consult with Clinton," *Christian Century*, 6 December 1995, 1169.

12 You can see this on YouTube, https://www.youtube.com/watch?v=xevVk_aIMGA, accessed 1 April 2024.

13 Shane Sharp, "Prayer Utterances as Aligning Actions," *Journal for the Scientific Study of Religion* 51 no. 2 (2012): 261.

14 Winfrey partnered with Discovery Communication to take over its Discovery Health Channel for her own. This was not her first network-ownership move. Winfrey previously partnered with Geraldine Laybourne, Marcy Carsey, Tom Werner, Lisa Gersh, and Caryn Mandabach in founding Oxygen Television Network in 1998.

15 Mia K. Kanatisse, "Oprah Wants Black Audiences to Back OWN," *The Grio*, 12 December 2011, accessed 27 June 2023, https://thegrio.com/2011/12/12/oprah-wants-her-black-audience-back-for-own/.

16 Samantha N. Sheppard, "'Tyler Perry Presents . . .': The Cultural Projects, Partnerships, and Politics of Perry's Media Platforms," in *From Medea to Media Mogul: Theorizing Tyler Perry* edited by TreaAndrea M. Russworm, Samantha N. Sheppard, and Karen M. Bowdre (Jackson: University of Mississippi Press, 2016), 15.

17 *The OG Chronicles*, as screened 24 January 2019.

18 This partnership is addressed by media scholars Aymar Jean Christian, Khadijah Costley White, and Paul Reinsch in *From Medea to Media Mogul*, referenced above. See also the "Introduction" to *Womanist and Black Feminist Responses to Tyler Perry's Productions*, edited by LeRhonda S. Manigault-Bryant, Tamura A. Lomax, and Carol B. Duncan (New York: Palgrave Macmillan, 2014), and *Tyler Perry: Interviews*, edited by Janice C. Hamlet (Jackson: University of Mississippi Press, 2019).

19 *The Haves and the Have Nots* (2013–2021), *Love Thy Neighbor* (2013–2017), *Tyler Perry's For Better or Worse* (revived after being on TBS for two seasons, 2011–2017), and *If Loving You Is Wrong* (2014–2020) were series created by Tyler Perry for OWN.

20 Both *Love Is . . .* and *The Book of John Gray* performed for OWN. For example, for its 28 April 2018 airing, *The Book of John Gray* was listed as 109 of the top 150 original cable telecasts. And according to tvseriefinale.com, over its entire season run, *Love Is . . .* ranked as the #1 cable series in its time period with women twenty-five to fifty-four. These two series were both canceled, however, in part due to claimed sexual improprieties of co-creator Salim Akil in the case of *Love Is . . .* and for similar circumstances with the series namesake in *The Book of John Gray*.

21 Description of the series as found in Lanee Neil, "Super Soul Sunday Features Oprah Interview with Seat of the Soul Author Gary Zulav on OWN Network," *LAs the Place*, accessed 27 June 2023, https://lastheplace.com/2012/03/09/super-soul-sunday-features-oprah-interview-with-seat-of-the-soul-author-gary-zulav-on-own-network/.

22 See Jasmine Grant, "10 Notable Black Female Preachers You Should Know," *Newsone*, 2 April 2021, accessed 27 June 2023 https://newsone.com/4065565/famous -black-female-preachers/, and Kenyatta R. Gilbert, "Hidden Figures: How Black Women Preachers Spoke Truth to Power," *The Conversation*, accessed 27 June 2023, https://theconversation.com/hidden-figures-how-black-women-preachers-spoke -truth-to-power-73185.

23 For example, see Trysh Travis, *The Language of the Heart* (Durham: University of North Carolina Press, 2010), especially chapter 6, where she talks about "New Thought Religion" and Winfrey.

24 Oprah Winfrey, master class, 2012, accessed 27 June 2023, https://www.youtube .com/watch?v=RAQHADpZDfY.

25 Nicholas C. Cooper-Lewter and Henry H. Mitchell, *Soul Theology: The Heart of American Black Culture*, 3rd ed. (Nashville: Abingdon Press, 1992): 1.

26 James Ayer, "Mark 3:20–35: Between Text and Sermon," *Interpretation* 51, no. 2 (April 1997).

27 These lyrics appear as part of Ndegeocello's song "The Way."

28 As I wrote previously, according to *Forbes*, *The Oprah Winfrey Show* earned $115 million in revenue during its first season. Winfrey credits the acquisition of a new agent in 1985 for promoting her from "employee" to mogul, quoted as saying, "I had to get rid of that slave mentality. . . . He took the ceiling off my brain." Established in August 1986, Winfrey produced several television works under the auspices of Harpo Productions (Oprah spelled backwards, and coincidentally, the name of her husband in *The Color Purple*). Working with respectable and highbrow programming, the company produced *Women of Brewster Place* (March 1989), *Brewster Place* (May–June 1990), *Scared Silent* (September 1992), and *There Are No Children Here* (November 1993). The first two programs showcased Black women in a dramatic fiction. The latter two examined traumas that Winfrey herself endured. These productions received endorsements from nonprofit organizations.

29 "Oprah Winfrey on Who She Channeled for 'A Wrinkle in Time' Character," *CBS News This Morning*, 6 March 2018, accessed 27 June 2023, https://www.cbsnews .com/video/oprah-winfrey-on-who-she-channeled-for-her-a-wrinkle-in-time -character/.

30 James Cone, *The Cross and the Lynching Tree* (Maryknoll, NY: Orbis Books, 2011), 160.

31 Oprah Winfrey, Twitter, 9 June 2020.

32 The color dynamics of the Greenleaf family members around who gets access to the pulpit are also in play in the series, but that is for another discussion.

33 She then goes on to steal her daughter's dance money to start her own storefront church and later, become mayor and pastor.

34 Marla F. Frederick, "The Gospel of Sexual Redemption: White Evangelicals, Black Suffering, and Televised Faith," talk, Emory University, 3 October 2018.

35 Pete Ward, *Gods Behaving Badly: Media, Religion, and Celebrity Culture* (Waco, TX: Baylor University Press, 2011), 128.

36 Pete Ward, *Celebrity Worship* (New York: Routledge, 2019), 143.

37 Kim D. Hester Williams, "'Fix My Life': Oprah, Post-Racial Economic Dispossession, and the Precious Transfiguration of PUSH," *Cultural Dynamics* 26, no. 1 (2014): 67.

38 Williams, "'Fix My Life,'" 63.

39 Rebecca Wanzo, *The Suffering Will Not Be Televised: African American Women and Sentimental Political Storytelling* (Albany: SUNY Press, 2009), 79.

40 Kathryn Lofton, *Oprah: The Gospel of an Icon* (Berkeley: University of California Press, 2011), 2.

41 Christine Radish, "Oprah Winfrey Talks Her Career, How The Color Purple Changed Her Life, The Butler, Refusing to Do Prisoners, and More at SBIFF," *Collider*, 7 February 2014, accessed 27 June 2023, http://collider.com/oprah-winfrey-the-butler-color-purple-interview/.

42 The hymn "I Surrender All" was published in 1896 and taken up by evangelist Billy Graham, Black R&B singers such as Deniece Williams, and Black church choirs. Williams won a Grammy for her rendition of the song in 1987.

43 *Greenleaf* premiered as the highest-rated opening series for the OWN network. According to *Wired*, it sat as one of the top five original scripted series for ad-supported cable for women twenty-five to thirty-four. Jason Parham, "How Oprah's Network Finally Found Its Voice," *Wired*, 19 June 2018, accessed 27 June 2023, https://www.wired.com/story/how-oprahs-network-finally-found-its-voice/.

44 See chapter 5 in my *Shaded Lives: African-American Women and Television* (New Brunswick, NJ: Rutgers University Press, 2002) or its reprint in *Feminist Television Criticism: A Reader*, 2nd ed., edited by Charlotte Brunsdon and Lynn Spigel (New York: Open University Press, 2008), 111–138.

45 For more on the targeting of Black audiences, see my "Target Market Black: BET and the Branding of African America" in *Cable Visions: Television Beyond Broadcasting*, edited by Sarah Banet-Weiser, Cynthia Chris, and Anthony Freitas (New York: New York University Press, 2007), 177–193 and my *Pimpin' Ain't Easy: Selling Black Entertainment Television* (New York: Routledge, 2007).

46 Raven S. Maragh, "'Our Struggles Are Unequal': Black Women's Affective Labor between Television and Twitter," *Journal of Communication Inquiry* 40, no. 4 (2016): 360.

47 Maragh, "'Our Struggles Are Unequal,'" 365.

48 Stuart Hall, *Representation and the Media*, Media Education Foundation, 1997.

49 Louise Kiernan, "Oprah's Poverty Program Stalls: Despite High Hopes, Only 5 Families Graduate in 2 Years," *Chicago Tribune*, 27 August 1996, N1.

50 Nelson Mandela, quoted in "Oprah Winfrey—The TIME 100," *Time*, 3 May 2007, accessed 27 June 2023, http://content.time.com/time/specials/2007/time100/article/0,28804,1595326_1615754_1616833,00.html.

51 "Oprah Winfrey Leadership Academy for Girls Celebrates New Graduates," accessed 27 June 2023, http://www.oprah.com/own/oprah-winfrey-leadership-academy-for-girls-celebrates-new-graduates.

52 As found in an editorial by columnist Clarence Page, "Oprah's Truth Shouldn't Hurt," *Chicago Tribune*, 7 January 2007, accessed 27 June 2023, https://www.chicagotribune.com/news/ct-xpm-2007-01-07-0701070457-story.html.

53 Quote found in Caroline Simon, "'I Don't Plan to Run': Oprah Winfrey Campaigns for Stacey Abrams. Here's What She Said," *USA Today*, 2 November 2018, accessed 27 June 2023, https://www.usatoday.com/story/news/politics/elections/2018/11/02/oprah-winfrey-campaigns-democrat-stacey-abrams-georgia/1856224002/. In a campaign PSA for voting, she talks about a racist robo-call implemented in her name during the 2018 Georgia election cycle. She tells the perpetuators, "Jesus don't like ugly."

54 #OWNYOURVOTE, Zoom with oprah.com, 27 October 2020.

55 Hannah Giorgis, "Oprah, Cousin Pookie, and the Long Tradition of Shaming Black Voters," *The Atlantic*, 8 November 2018, accessed 27 June 2023, https://www

.theatlantic.com/entertainment/archive/2018/11/oprah-beyonce-and-obamas-harsh
-appeals-to-black-voters/575242/.

56 Sandhya Somashekhar, "Protestors Slam Oprah over Comments That They Lack
'Leadership,'" *Washington Post*, 2 January 2015, accessed 27 June 2023, https://www
.washingtonpost.com/news/post-nation/wp/2015/01/02/protesters-slam-oprah-over
-comments-that-they-lack-leadership/.

57 In Atlanta, with an estimated 12,000 attendees on 25 January 2020, I estimated
maybe fifty to seventy-five men in the audience. Winfrey told them they would get
eight weeks of whatever they want from the person who dragged them there.

58 Patrick Johnson, "Popular Religion and Participatory Culture Conversation
(Round 6): Brandy Monk-Payton and Patrick Johnson (Part 2)," *Confessions of an
Aca-Fan*, 5 October 2018, accessed 27 June 2023.
http://henryjenkins.org/blog/2018/9/30/popular-religion-and-participatory-culture
-conversation-round-6-brandy-monk-payton-and-patrick-johnson-part-2.

59 Personal communication with friend, February 2020.

60 "Oprah Welcomes You to the New Oprah Daily!," 25 March 2021, accessed
27 June 2023, https://www.oprahdaily.com/life/a35906098/oprah-daily-welcome/.

61 Jessicah Pierre, "America, Oprah Is Not Your Savior," *Institute for Policy Studies*, 17
January 2018, accessed 27 June 2023, https://ips-dc.org/america-oprah-not-savior/.

62 She engages respectability politics and has accrued wealth like fellow entertainer
Bill Cosby. However, she doesn't employ his frame (and white folks' notion) of
bootstraps.

63 Pastor Shawn Anglim preached this on Facebook Live at First Grace United
Methodist Church, New Orleans, LA, 14 June 2020.

64 On 7 March 2021, CBS aired a two-hour special interview with Winfrey, Meghan
Markle, and former Prince Harry about their lives as royals. The powerful interview
shines a light on the ways in which race and wealth penetrate the British aristocracy.
The interview became the highest-rated special since the previous year's Academy
Awards and renewed Winfrey's position as the best at what she does and who she
is—a safe harbor in a storm.

65 Denise Hill, "Sistah! I'm Keeping My Eyes on You," sermon, University Church
Chicago, Facebook Live, 7 March 2021. She comes from the book of Numbers
27:1–7.

Benediction

1 Valerie Kaur, "Watch Night Speech: Breathe and Push," 31 December 2016, accessed
27 June 2023, https://valariekaur.com/2017/01/watch-night-speech-breathe-push/.

2 Zora Neale Hurston, *Their Eyes Were Watching God* (Champaign: University of
Illinois Press, 1937), 236.

3 Arthur Buehler, "The Twenty-First-Century Study of Collective Effervescence:
Expanding the Context of Fieldwork," *Fieldwork in Religion* 7, no. 1 (2012): 70–97.

4 Paulo Freire, *Pedagogy of the Oppressed* (New York: Herder and Herder, 1970).

5 As found in "Kirk Franklin on 'Trap Gospel' and Taking Heat from the Church,"
NPR, 26 April 2015, accessed 27 June 2023, https://www.npr.org/2015/04/26
/401978156/kirk-franklin-on-trap-gospel-and-taking-heat-from-the-church. Return
also to Erica Campbell with her sister Tina as Mary Mary in the Processional.

6 As found on the Beyoncé Mass site, https://www.beyoncemass.com/home/#faqs,
accessed 27 June 2023.

7 Ben Roazen, "Kanye West's Sunday Service—a Religious Experience or a Celebrity Cult?" *okayplayer.com*, 19 April 2019, accessed 27 June 2023, https://www.okayplayer.com/music/kanye-west-sunday-service-coachella-what-is-it.html.
8 All this happened pre-Kanye's 2020 presidential run, divorce, and further move from humanity.
9 Pastor Shawn Anglim, First Grace United Methodist Church, 15 August 2021, Facebook Live.
10 Yolanda DeBerry, "I Shall Wear a Crown," First Church "The City," 2 February 2019, accessed 27 June 2023, https://www.youtube.com/watch?v=liASWXrjKt4.
11 Monique Moultrie, "Leading from the Margins: Authenticity, Authority, and Black Women's Sexual Agency," presentation, Emory University, 5 October 2020.
12 KevOnStage, "69," Instagram, 24 June 2023.
13 Lawrence Ware, "4 Reasons Why Greenleaf Is the Show the Black Church Needs," *theroot.com*, 1 September 2016, accessed 27 June 2023, https://www.theroot.com/4-reasons-why-greenleaf-is-the-show-the-black-church-ne-1790856577.
14 Brandeise Monk-Payton, "Worship at the Altar of Perry: Spectatorship and the Aesthetics of Testimony," in *From Madea to Media Mogul: Theorizing Tyler Perry*, edited by TreaAndrea M. Russworm, Samantha N. Sheppard, Karen M. Bowdre (Jackson: University Press of Mississippi, 2016), 90.
15 Judith Casselberry, "Solving the Mystery of Grace Jones: It's the Holy Ghost," presentation, 17 September 2018, Emory University, Atlanta, GA.

Concordance

academia, 5, 38, 80, 94–96, 144, 246, 248; Black women in, 15, 78–100
acculturation. *See* assimilation
Acosta, Katie, 7, 21, 263n78
activism, 26, 90, 126, 173, 219, 246; music as, 194–196, 212. *See also* BLM (Black Lives Matter); protest
Adams, Yolanda, 41, 106–107, 150, 229
advertising, 21, 31, 26–27, 44, 51, 110, 122, 166. *See also* marketing
affect, 9, 103, 143, 150, 182, 212, 247
affective labor, 226, 233–234, 240
African traditional spiritualities, 160–176; Christian and other religious syncretism with, 161–162, 164, 167–168, 175–176. *See also* Candomblé; Caribbean spiritual practices; Santería; Vodou; Yoruba traditional religion
Afrocentrism, 88, 185
Afrofuturism, 201, 204, 282n50
Amen (NBC series), 27, 35, 145, 187
American South, 81, 86, 93, 103, 195–197, 252n18; and African religious traditions, 160–161, 166–167; in film and television, 22–23, 58, 63–65, 170–176
Angel Heart, 35, 165–168, 281n19, 281n25
Angelou, Maya, 179, 229–230, 284n31
Anglim, Shawn, 54–55, 136–137, 295n63
anointing, 35–36, 111, 113–114, 212, 247. *See also* praise break
Anzaldúa, Gloria, 198, 213, 219–222, 263n8, 288n92

assimilation, 21, 64, 132, 144, 165, 181
Atlanta, 37, 90, 237–238, 240, 247, 258n8, 278n36, 295n57; churches in, 116, 124, 128–129, 136, 274n59; colleges and universities in, 63, 88, 185, 235, 264n19; reality tv set in, 30, 44–45, 188, 285n40
authenticity, 39, 44, 93, 147, 165, 231; and Black identity, 58, 68, 88, 187, 278n31; of church experiences, 126, 129, 133–134

baby boomer generation, 118, 125, 200, 211
Badu, Erykah, 16, 31, 179–180, 189–190, 194–202, 213–216, 263n8, 288n90; beliefs and spirituality, 52–53, 79, 172, 216, 288n99, 288n102
Bakhtin, Mikhail, 79–80, 142, 277n6
Bamboozled, 11, 72–73, 263n6. *See also* Lee, Spike
barbershops, 42, 60, 62
Baszile, Denise Taliaferro, 79–80, 99
Baszile, Natalie, 162, 173. See also *Queen Sugar*
beauty, 9, 199–200, 204–205, 217, 233
Beloved (film), 16, 75, 104, 160–161, 168–170, 175, 182–183. *See also* Morrison, Toni
Bennett, Anthony, 125, 127
BET (Black Entertainment Television), 11, 29–30, 48, 103, 216, 248; BET Awards, 48, 216, 246. *See also titles of programming*
Beyoncé, 132, 188, 196, 245, 246, 252n19, 276n83, 291n11; *Lemonade*, 28, 53, 168, 176, 256n37, 262n68

About the Author

BERETTA E. SMITH-SHOMADE is a professor in film and media at Emory University in Atlanta. She is the author of *Shaded Lives: African-American Women and Television* and *Pimpin' Ain't Easy: Selling Black Entertainment Television*. She has also edited two anthologies: *Watching While Black: Centering the Television of Black Audiences* (a Choice Outstanding Academic Title), and its remix *Watching While Black Rebooted! The Television and Digitality of Black Audiences*.